Milledoler 010 – 1:10

THE LOCKE READER

Stay, wayfarer,
Near here lies John Locke. If you ask what sort of man
he was, his answer is that he lived content with his modest
lot. Educated in letters, he accomplished as much as satisfied
the demands solely of truth. This you may learn from his
writings; which will also tell you whatever else there is
to be said of him, more truly than the doubtful praises
of an epitaph. Any virtues he had were more slight than
should encourage you, in praise of him, to follow his
example; may his faults be interred with him. If a model
of conduct you seek, you have it in the Gospels; if only
of vices, look for it in no place: if of mortality (of what
benefit it may be) assuredly you have it here
and everywhere.
That he was born in the year of Our Lord 1632 August 29th,
Died in the year of Our Lord 1704 October 28th,
This tablet, that may itself soon perish, is a record.

Sifte Viator.

Hic juxta, fitus eft,

JOHANNES LOCKE

Si qualis fuerit rogas, mediocritate fuâ contentum fe vixiffe refponder: Literis innutritus eoufq3 tantum profecit; ut veritati unice litaret hoc ex fcriptis illius difce; quæ quod de eo reliquum eft, majori fide tibi exhibebunt; quam epitaphii fufpecta elogia, virtutes fi quas habuit, minores fane quam quas fibi laudi tibi in exemplum proponeret Vitia una fepeliantur. Morum exemplum fi quæras, in Evangelio habes, vitiorum utinam nufquam, mortalitatis certe (quod profit) hic et ubiq3.

Natum Anno Dom. 1632. Aug. 29.°
Mortuum Anno Dom. 1704. Oct. 28.°
memorat hæc tabula brevi et
ipfa interitura.

THE LOCKE READER

Selections from the works of John Locke
with a general introduction
and commentary

JOHN W. YOLTON

CAMBRIDGE UNIVERSITY PRESS

Cambridge

London : New York : Melbourne

Published by the Syndics of the Cambridge University Press
The Pitt Building, Trumpington Street, Cambridge CB2 1RP
Bentley House, 200 Euston Road, London NW1 2DB
32 East 57th Street, New York, NY 10022, USA
260 Beaconsfield Parade, Middle Park, Melbourne 3206, Australia

First published 1977

Printed in the United States of America
Type set by the Fuller Organization, Inc., Philadelphia, Pa.
Printed and bound by R. R. Donnelly & Sons Company,
Crawfordsville, Ind.

Library of Congress Cataloging in Publication Data
Locke, John, 1632–1704.
The Locke reader.
Bibliography: p.
Includes index.
1. Philosophy – Collected works. I. Yolton, John W.
II. Title.
B1255.Y64   192   76-9181
ISBN 0 521 21282 0 hard covers
ISBN 0 521 29084 8 paperback

CONTENTS

Contents

PREFACE

Readers of Locke tend to approach his thought through single books, not from a knowledge of the range of his writing. Those who know the *Two Treatises* may have some general acquaintance with the *Essay* but hardly a detailed understanding of the doctrines of that work. Those with a specialist knowledge of the *Essay* may never have looked at the *Reasonableness of Christianity* or *A Letter concerning Toleration*. The *Education* is, I suspect, read by a very restricted audience and then with only a cursory glance at the other works. The *Conduct* may be read by some as a supplement to the *Essay*; but do the readers of the *Education* consult those passages in the *Conduct* relevant to teaching and learning? I think it is probably true that the time given to the study of Locke by these different groups of readers does not allow for more than a selection from one or two of his writings. This *Locke Reader* seeks to allow readers of Locke to have accessible, in one volume, selections from a wide range of Locke's books, structured in such a fashion that some of the interconnections of his thought can be seen and traced.

There are, for example, passages in the *Essay* that talk of the acquisition of ideas by children. Those passages are relevant to what Locke has to say in the *Education* about learning. Similarly, Locke's views on morality and virtue expressed in the *Essay* are echoed and assumed in what he has to say about the family and civil government in *Two Treatises*. One of the major aims and purposes of education for Locke is the formation of a virtuous character. To appreciate the fundamental importance of virtue is to understand the fabric of Locke's views on toleration and education, as well as one of the guiding threads in the formation of civil society. Reading those passages in the *Essay* that identify the true ground and measure of morality as God's law leads us to see the basic role of religious beliefs in his thought.

These are just some examples of the way in which concepts and doctrines Locke elaborated in one work reappear or are supported in other areas of his writing. One needs some organizing principle for reading in such a range of themes. Chance, or simply picking out a few common themes, does not give us any systematic guidance. Locke did not write from a *system* of philosophy, but he did have in mind an overall division of human knowledge, presented at the end of the *Essay*. By following this simple division, we can provide ourselves with a structure that enables us to see systematic connections in his thought.

The selections in this *Locke Reader* are grouped around his classification of knowledge into the science of nature (natural science); ethics, or the science of human conduct; and semiotics, or the science of signs. Within these divisions, topics have been chosen that present the basic doctrines and concepts used or discussed by Locke in that division. The selections are taken from a wide range of his writings. A major portion of the selections are from the *Essay*, the basic conceptual foundation for Locke's thought in all three divisions of knowledge. A glance at the Contents will reveal that works used also include *Two Treatises, Some Thoughts concerning Education, The Reasonableness of Christianity*, the *Conduct of the Understanding, A Letter concerning Toleration, An Examination of Malebranche*, some of his replies to Stillingfleet, a letter to William Molyneux, and an important but usually overlooked preface to his *Paraphrase on St. Paul's Epistles*. The selections are numbered in the order of their appearance: the reference to the work from which they are taken is given at the beginning of each selection. My commentary provides continuity throughout the selections and, it is hoped, some explication and guidance for understanding.

John W. Yolton
York University, Toronto
September 1976

REFERENCES TO LOCKE'S BOOKS

The text used in this reader is that of the Works of 1823, checked against more recent editions of some of the individual titles. References to individual books are given by the following abbreviated code words:

The Conduct of the Understanding, as *Conduct*, followed by section numbers.

Some Thoughts concerning Education, as *Education*, followed by section numbers.

An Essay concerning Human Understanding, as *Essay*, followed by book, chapter, and section number (e.g., 2.21.3).

An Examination of P. Malebranche's Opinion of Seeing All Things in God, as *Examination*, followed by section numbers.

The Reasonableness of Christianity, as Reasonableness, followed by page references to the *Works*.

A Letter concerning Toleration, as *Toleration*, followed by page references to the *Works*.

Two Treatises of Government, as *Two Treatises*, followed by number indicating first or second treatise and section numbers.

Selections from other writings of Locke are indicated by the proper title.

SIGNIFICANT DATES

Born in Wrington, Somerset, 1632
Attended Westminster School, 1647–52
Charles I beheaded, 1649
Cromwell and Parliament ruled, 1649–60
Entered Christ Church, Oxford, 1652
Awarded B.A. degree, 1655
Received degree of M.A., 1658
Met Robert Boyle, 1660 — CHEMIST
Charles II restored to the throne, 1660
Wrote essays on the Civil Magistrate, 1660–1
Lecturer in Greek, 1660
Lecturer in Rhetoric, 1662
Wrote *Essays on the Law of Nature*, 1663–4
Censor of Moral Philosophy, 1664
Secretary to the Mission to Brandenburg, 1665
Physician and Secretary to Anthony Ashley Cooper (later,
    Earl of Shaftesbury), 1667–81
Elected Fellow of the Royal Society, 1668
Secretary to the Lords Proprietors of Carolina, 1668–75
Secretary to the Council of Trade and Plantations, 1673–75
Started writing *Essay concerning Human Understanding*,
    1671
Received degree of Bachelor of Medicine, 1674
Appointed to Medical Studentship at Oxford, 1674
Traveled in France, 1675–9
Deprived of appointment to Christ Church by Royal Decree,
    1684
Voluntary exile in Holland, 1683–9   C+8 + J R
Returned to England in entourage of William and Mary,
    1689   BILL OF RTS.

Published *Essay concerning Human Understanding,* 1690
Published anonymously *Two Treatises,* 1690
Commissioner on the Board of Trade, 1696–1700
Died at Oates, High Laver, Essex, 1704

Introduction

To study the writings of John Locke is to expose oneself to a whole range of issues and concepts typical of seventeenth-century thought. Both in his actions and in his thought, Locke touched most aspects of his century. Born in 1632, during the reign of Charles I, Locke was at Westminster School (1647–52) when Charles was tried and executed in 1649. During the civil wars that preceded this dramatic event (1642–6), Locke's father, a modest landowner and attorney in Somerset, fought for a while in the Royalist army. From 1649 to 1660, Oliver Cromwell and Parliament ruled England in place of a monarch. Cromwell was given the title of Protector in 1653, one year after Locke entered Christ Church at Oxford. When the country returned to a monarchy – of a modified sort – in 1660, Locke was still at Oxford, as a tutor.

These social and political events gave Locke an early exposure to issues that were reflected in his writings. The constitutional struggles between Charles I and Parliament raised, in a striking way, questions about the nature of government, the relations between government and the people, the limits of responsibility and sovereignty. The bold experiment in rule by Parliament tested an alternative to monarchy. These and later conflicts turned Locke's thoughts toward the topics in his *Two Treatises*. The Civil War also raised issues of religious toleration, issues that came more to a head later in the century and about which Locke also wrote.

Locke's education at Westminster School was a standard classical one. The curriculum at Oxford was very traditional, but Locke and other students at Oxford – even some of the faculty – were questioning aspects of the subjects taught and the books read. Locke's discontent with the curriculum at Oxford is reflected in remarks he makes in some of his writings. We know too that he made contacts while at Oxford with some of the important figures in the developing new sciences – Robert Boyle, Robert Hooke, John Wallis, John Wilkins, Thomas Sydenham – who helped to form the Royal Soci-

1

ety. A friendship with Newton came later. Locke also studied medicine while at Oxford, taking a bachelor's degree in that subject in 1674. He became something of a practitioner in medicine. His friendship with Dr. Sydenham was stimulated by their common interests in breaking free from the confines of traditional diagnostics based on theories instead of observation.

Locke did not just think and write about issues raised in politics, religion, science, and philosophy; he was a man of action also. He went as secretary to the diplomatic mission of Sir Walter Vane to Brandenburg (1665). Later he held the posts of Secretary to the Lords Proprietors of Carolina (1668–75), Secretary to the Council of Trade and Plantations (1673–5), and Commissioner in the Board of Trade (1696–1700). Perhaps the most important post held by Locke was that of secretary and family doctor to Anthony Ashley Cooper (later, Lord Shaftesbury) from 1667 to 1683. Shaftesbury played a prominent role in Charles II's reign, engaging in actions after 1672, that were interpreted as treasonable. Shaftesbury fled to Holland, where he died in 1683. Locke believed himself possibly to be in jeopardy, because of his close association with Shaftesbury. There were in fact government spies at Christ Church keeping watch on Locke. Locke followed Shaftesbury to Holland in 1682. He was formally expelled from Christ Church by royal decree shortly thereafter.

All of Locke's writings (published and unpublished) came as reactions and responses to events around him. *Two Treatises* and some early essays on the civil magistrate (1660–1) were clearly responding to social and political events. These two works were also and more directly responses to specific publications with which Locke took exception: for *Two Treatises* it was Robert Filmer's *Patriarcha*, for the civil magistrate essays it was Edward Bagshawe's *The Great Question concerning Things Indifferent in Religious Worship*.[1] His *A Letter concerning Toleration* articulated his thoughts on religious toleration, activated by events and by discussions with a Dutch theologian, Philip Limborch. The *Essay concerning Human Understanding* was begun when, in 1671, Locke and a few friends were discussing certain problems in religion and morality. Correspondence with a close friend concerning a son's education, resulted in extensive advice from the bachelor Locke, which eventually became his *Some Thoughts concerning Education*. When economic problems arose during the reign of William

1 Locke's replies to Bagshawe have recently been published by Philip Abrams as *John Locke: Two Tracts on Government* (Cambridge University Press, 1967).

and Mary, Locke wrote several tracts on coinage, which he meant as advice to the government.

Locke's reactions to events and issues were usually preceded by careful reading in books and pamphlets relevant to each topic. His library provides a handy guide to the publications of his time, as well as to Locke's own interests and knowledge.[2] His holdings are extensive in religion and theology; in the sciences, politics, philosophy; and in travel books. He used his books to make extensive notes in his journals. Often these journal entries were quotations from his readings; sometimes they took the form of jottings of his own ideas. He frequently wrote drafts of his later books; the *Essay* alone had four drafts.[3] With the careful catalogue that Locke made of his library, and from his notebooks, drafts, and occasional jottings, we can reconstruct a fairly trustworthy account of the source and nature of many of his ideas. We are thus able to avoid the error of pushing Locke's thought into molds for which it was not designed. Nor do we have merely to assume that he had some author in mind when he wrote on a particular issue; in very many cases, we can discover whom he had in mind, even when Locke does not always name his target.

It is evident that in philosophy he wrote from an intimate acquaintance with Descartes and the debates among the Cartesians; he followed Arnauld and the Port Royal *Logic* rather than Malebranche.[4] Gassendi's combination of Aristotle and scholastic doctrines is also much in evidence in Locke's writing. That he had a good knowledge of Bacon and had read widely in the many reformulations and modifications of Bacon to be found in writers on the new sciences is also plain from his *Essay* and his library holdings.[5] In religion, it was the Deist and Unitarian notions that

2 Locke's catalogue of his library has been published by John Harrison and Peter Laslett, *The Library of John Locke* (Oxford, 1965; second edition, 1971).

3 Draft A is available as, *An Early Draft of Locke's Essay*, ed. Aaron and Gibb (1936). All drafts will be printed in the collected edition of Locke's works now under way by the Oxford University Press.

4 See Antoine Arnauld and P. Nicole, *La Logique ou l'Art de penser* (Paris, third edition, 1668). Arnauld also had an extended debate with Malebranche over the nature and role of ideas in knowledge, a debate that Locke followed closely: see Arnauld's *Des vraies et des fausses idées* (Cologne, 1683) and Malebranche's *De la recherche de la vérité* (Paris, 1674).

5 Gassendi's works were published in Latin. They were available to Locke but all that was in his library was an abridgment by Bernier, *Abrégé de la philosophie de Gassendi* (Lyon, 1678). For a detailed study of Gassendi, see O. R. Bloch, *La philosophie de Gassendi* (The Hague, 1971). For Locke's knowledge of Bacon, see the important article by Neal Wood, "The Baconian Character of Locke's Essay," in *Studies in History and Philosophy of Science* (1975).

WAS A MODERN IN DEBATE ⅾ⁄ₒ ANCIENTS & MODERNS

he found attractive.[6] In general, it was the newer ideas in all areas of thought to which Locke was attracted and gave support. In the disputes between ancients and moderns, Locke was on the side of the latter. Hobbes was of course well known, although the references to him by Locke are few. His reading among the contemporary theologians, as among the writers on politics and the law of natu.e, was also extensive.

Locke's association with and sympathies for the new and the modern, against tradition, meant that during his life he was never very far from controversy and radical change. A member of the Royal Society, he was associated with those who were the object of attack against the new science. His association with Thomas Sydenham, the doctor, led him into challenges against the medical practices of his day: Sydenham and Locke insisted upon careful observation of symptoms and on cures based upon those observations. Diagnostics in medicine thus broke free of the more traditional indifference to experimentation and observation. Locke's close association with Shaftesbury undoubtedly contributed to his expulsion by royal order from Christ Church, Oxford, and forced him to retreat to Holland. He returned to England as William of Orange came to assume the throne. *Two Treatises*, whether designed to nudge the revolution of 1688 or to justify it, aligned itself with these changing political developments. Holding office in the Board of Trade, he had interests in and business with the new world of America. His sympathies with some of the newer currents in religion placed him again on the side of those who were challenging orthodoxy: the reasonableness and simplicity of doctrine that he insisted upon were seen as threats to religious beliefs.

Many of the doctrines of his *Essay* were quickly seized upon as undermining traditional religion. His rejection of innate ideas and principles, his account of substance and of our limited knowledge of nature, his general skepticism about the extent of human knowledge, his suggestion that matter might be given the power of thought, that immateriality of the soul was not necessary for immortality, that sameness of body was not needed for resurrection after death; all these and more were direct and disturbing challenges to the accepted practices, doctrines, and beliefs of his day. The study of the reception of Locke's works reveals the extent of the reactions against most of his views. The reactions came from learned divines and philosophers, as well as more general readers. But the *Essay*, the *Reasonableness*, the *Education*, his *Toleration*,

6 See my *John Locke and the Way of Ideas* (Oxford, 1956, reprinted 1968), Chapters IV and V.

and his *Two Treatises* spoke for most of the forward-looking movements of the seventeenth century. He himself kept in touch with new developments in all these areas, as his library and reading notes indicate. He became the spokesman for most of the newer views, absorbing ideas, changing and clarifying them, questioning some, articulating doctrines in a more systematic and felicitous way than most other writers. Although some writers anticipated many of the epistemological views of Locke's *Essay*, they tended to stay with more traditional attitudes in religion, or to show little awareness of the developments in science and medicine. Locke, of course, borrowed much from his close friend Robert Boyle, but even there Locke located Boyle's account of original or absolute qualities (in contrast with relative ones), or Boyle's recognition of the conventional nature of our classifications, in a more extensive account of knowledge and meaning. The Cartesian influence on Locke is marked (that of Arnauld in particular), the way of ideas of the *Essay* is Locke's translation of and transmission to Britain of many of the Cartesian concepts and doctrines, but Locke adapts these doctrines to philosophy of science in a way that differs markedly from Descartes' account of science or of scientific knowledge. The recognition of the importance of language for knowledge and communication also finds its defenders in his predecessors (in Wilkins, for example),[7] but here again, Locke gives greater attention to language as a system of signs, relating it more directly to human knowledge and to ideas. There were also many treatises of psychology, works on the soul (Digby, Charleton, Burthogge),[8] that anticipated the more extended developments in Locke's writings, but no one before Locke gave such a systematic account of the operations of the mind.

Developments in logic, an area that Locke is usually thought to have despised, especially those represented by the Port Royal *Logic*, were also picked up and extended by Locke. These logics, and those that followed and for the most part copied Locke in eighteenth-century Britain (Watts, Duncan, Edward Bentham),[9]

---

7 John Wilkins, *As Essay Towards a Real Character and a Philosophical Language* (London, 1668).
8 Walter Charleton, *The Immortality of the Human Soul* (London, 1657) and *Physiologia Epicuro-Gassendo-Charletoniana* (London, 1654); Sir Kenelm Digby, *Two Treatises* (Paris, 1644); Richard Burthogge, *An Essay upon Reason, and the Nature of Spirits* (London, 1694) and *Organum Vetus et Novum* (London, 1678).
9 Edward Bentham, *Reflections upon Logick* (London, 1740; second edition, 1755), *Introduction to Logic* (Oxford, 1773); William Duncan, *The Elements of Logic* (London, 1748); and Isaac Watts, *Logick: Or, the Right Use of Reason in the Enquiry After Truth* (London, 1726).

were epistemic logics concerned with the natural history of the understanding. They, like Locke's *Essay*, followed the classifications of the operations of the mind used by the older logics: simple apprehension, perception, judgment, and reasoning. One of the most popular logics in the eighteenth century was *The Elements of Logic* (1748), by William Duncan. Duncan even calls logic "the History of the human Mind, inasmuch as it traces the Progress of our Knowledge, from our first and simple Perceptions." Duncan's language, examples, and order of presentation are very close copies (sometimes verbatim) of passages in Locke's *Essay*. This fact may seem to tell us more about Duncan than it does about logic, but the truth is that it tells us a very great deal about the nature of eighteenth-century British logics. It also helps us appreciate how Locke was viewed as an important logician, at least as a contributor to logic. Edward Bentham (*Reflections upon Logick,* 2nd edition, 1755) even compared "The Logical Theory contained in *Mr. Locke's Essay*" with "that of the Schools," although Bentham thought Locke went too much into the details of the operations of the mind for a proper logic. Bentham tried to separate the natural history of man from logic, but even he, in his later *Introduction to Logic* (1773), starts off with a chapter on the soul, its powers and operations.

Locke was classed among the logicians by several historians of logic in the early nineteenth century. *Lectures on Locke; or, The Principles of Logic* (1840) was in large part an outline of Locke's *Essay*. The anonymous author divides logic into practical and speculative, the latter being mental philosophy. Before Locke, the author says, this latter kind of logic was never carried very far. Similarly, in his *Historical Sketch of Logic* (1851), Robert Blakey says that Locke's *Essay* "has given birth to a more diversified series of logical systems and speculations, as well as modes of teaching, than any other work since the days of Aristotle." Another late eighteenth-century logic followed Locke closely, *Lectures on Belles Lettres and Logic* (1806), lectures given by William Baron for many years at the University of Saint Andrews.

I stress the developments in eighteenth-century British logics, and Locke's role in them, because it is one way to appreciate how Locke's *Essay* and his *Conduct* set the issues and the language for the eighteenth century. But it is important to be aware of these epistemic logics for another reason: for the way in which they helped to develop the foundations of psychology. They were, as was Locke, in the same tradition with Hume, in seeking bases for the science of man, to match those supplied by Newton for the science of nature. Locke considered theory of knowledge to be the foundation for all three of the divisions of knowledge cited at the end of the *Essay*. Theory of knowledge was for him primarily descriptive. The distinction between it and psychology was hardly drawn. Just as Locke and many of his friends in the Royal Society thought advances in science at that time required much more information, so Locke saw the advance of the sciences of man to be dependent upon a careful account of the various operations, faculties, and capacities of the human mind. Philosophy of mind merged imperceptibly with psychology. The extensive vocabulary of mental-operation words in the *Essay*, together with the fact that the main divisions of the *Essay* were based upon the basic kinds of mental activity recognized in old and new logics, is a clear indication of the extent to which Locke contributed to the emerging science of psychology. That psychological-epistemological doctrines were recognized by Locke's contemporaries as essential to religious and moral doctrines as well is what the many and often violent reactions of divines to Locke's writings indicate. Thus, to read Locke's works in religion, on education, and on political theory with his psychological-epistemological concepts in hand is to arm ourselves with some of the conceptual tools for the science of man that he and some of his followers were supplying.

It was not only the epistemology of the *Essay* that embroiled Locke in heated controversy (in which he seldom took any part). His account of the person and of human action also raised various protests, but it also had several defenders. The concept of the person is especially important for education and politics. Locke's distinction between man and person puzzled many of his readers, especially since he discounted sameness of substance for person identity. The denial of substance as relevant to sameness of person was, in the late seventeenth century, somewhat novel. *Person* for Locke was, as he said, a forensic term, referring to the subject of praise and blame, obligation and duty. Locke did not mean that the person was divorced or separated from the body, only that person and body make up the man, the *moral* man. The person is the agent of action, but actions take place in the world: they require the body for their execution. It is the moral man – the person – on whom we direct our training, for whom civil government is formed. The person is also the basis for Locke's account of property in *Two Treatises,* for my person (an odd phrase but one Locke needs to make his point) is my property; it is also the means whereby I can legitimately acquire more property. The person is the source of privacy, but the person is also a public figure, a social being. It was most important for Locke's view of society that we understand the proper nature of the person: not a metaphysical substance whose nature is unavailable to us, but a living, responsible, responsive being, aware of his intentions and actions, expressing them by means of his organic body.

Another feature of the *Essay* that excited Locke's contemporaries was his offhand suggestion that God might be able to superadd to matter the power of thinking. The controversy surrounding this suggestion extended to the end of the eighteenth century. Around it there focused many important debates over the nature of matter and spirit, debates that involved the Newtonians as well as more general readers. These debates, conducted for the most part after Locke's death, began to modify Locke's concept of the person. They were concerned to understand how it is that the person acts in his body. As long as the body, as matter, was thought of as passive and inert, the defenders of the view that the person or soul is aloof from its body even while attached to it had room for argument. But as the concept of matter moved more toward power and force, many writers were able to make a case for a close integration of self and body. In fact, a new materialism emerged toward the end of the eighteenth century that stressed the complexity of the brain and that sought for some way of expressing the integration of intention and action in one organized piece of matter.

I have given these brief hints of the fate of Locke's doctrines in eighteenth-century British thought – hints that have not yet been fully explored or documented – because it may help us appreciate the centrality of most of Locke's doctrines for those that followed him. Locke's influence on eighteenth-century thought in Britain is extensive. Often that influence goes along with that of the Cartesians, especially Malebranche. The nature of human action (e.g., how I am able to move my arm), the physiological basis for thought and action, the connection or lack of connection between thought and matter: these were eighteenth-century issues that are repeatedly traced to Locke's formulation of them in the seventeenth century. One can find, in the tracts and pamphlets of the eighteenth century, frequent usage of Lockean terminology and concepts. That usage is found not only in the logics, but in works on science, in the sermons and books of theologians, in more general publications such as *The Annual Register, The Monthly*

Review, The Spectator. This absorption of Lockean language and concepts occurred earlier as well, almost as soon as the *Essay* appeared. Many of the divines who attacked Locke were the first to accept or to use his doctrines. Although a writer might attack Locke on his definition of knowledge, that same writer would often accept Locke's account of our ignorance of the real essence of matter. Another writer objects to the many new words Locke introduced into the language, while himself employing some of those words elsewhere in his writing. The quick absorption of Locke's language and concepts by his contemporaries is another indication of the impact his ideas had on his own and the following centuries.

Thus, not only is Locke an important figure in the seventeenth century, but to read eighteenth-century philosophy (certainly in Britain, but also in France, where certain aspects of his theory of knowledge in particular were influential) is to find oneself pursuing problems and issues raised by Locke. Hume's influence did not really get under way much before the nineteenth century. The combination of Hume and Kant has dominated English-speaking philosophy down to our own time. But there were of course a number of philosophical movements in the twentieth century that hark back to Locke, sometimes filtered through Reid and Stewart (even, perhaps, distorted). It is probably fair to say that even the tradition stemming from Kant and Hume has been working with the problems articulated by Locke and other seventeenth- and eighteenth-century philosophers influenced by him in one way or other.

We should not conclude from the sentiments expressed by Locke in the epitaph he wrote for his gravestone (see the Frontispiece) that, like the stone itself, he expected his doctrines to perish. He would not think truth would perish, though he would hope what errors there may be in his works would. What is true is that neither the tablet near his grave nor his doctrines have dissolved with time. The tablet at All Saints Church, High Laver in Essex, has been aided in its survival by being moved inside the Church by persons concerned that this memorial should survive. Locke's doctrines have survived even under the eroding climate of adverse opinion and repeated attacks. Locke is a good place to look for anyone interested in the basic problems of philosophy.

Preliminary: Locke on Hermeneutics — *study of methodological principles of interpretn*

In approaching the work of any author, we need to be
aware of his context, of the assumption he may have taken
for granted, meanings of words that may be indigenous to
his time and place. Texts in languages other than our own,
ancient texts distant from our own time pose even greater
obligations for us to discover the author's meaning and intention. Locke is not so distant from us that we cannot with
care and attention understand him without importing interpretations not intended by Locke. Being not so distant is in
fact a hazard, for we are tempted to think Locke's speech
and thought are more like our own than they may in fact be.
Philosophers have not helped by using labels for linking
doctrines in various periods. *Empiricism* applied to Locke
and to philosophers in each succeeding century has done
much damage in this way. The interpreters of Locke have
subjected him to a host of such labels, all of which should be
put aside if we want to discover what Locke was saying.
Knowledge of the art of reading a text is necessary if we
want to understand Locke, not just use him for our own
devices.

   We know a good deal about Locke's reading; we have his
own catalogue of his library. We can acquaint ourselves
with the scientific, theological, and philosophical world in
which Locke lived. We can discover what doctrines he was
writing against, trace out ideas and concepts borrowed
from others. By reading Robert Boyle or Robert Hooke,
for example, we can find in more detail the general attitudes toward science and some specific doctrines of science
reflected in Locke's *Essay*. By reading in the Cartesian
literature (e.g., Malebranche, Arnauld, and of course Descartes) we can appreciate better the notion of ideas em-

10

ployed by Locke (or perhaps, the duality of that notion). By reading people such as Cumberland, Puffendorf, Hooker, and Cudworth we reach a clearer understanding of the issues confronting Locke in morality, religion, and politics. In short, we must read Locke in context.

Even without reading the many authors surrounding Locke, we can help ourselves toward an understanding of his texts by paying close attention to the way he uses particular words and phrases. An inventory or tracking of *demonstration, coexistence, observation,* and of course *idea* can help us divorce from our minds our own contemporary use of such terms. Locke was especially self-conscious about the use of words in communicating our thoughts to each other; Book 3 of his *Essay* is occupied in large part with the functions of language. His distinction between the *civil* and the *philosophical* use of words recognizes the need for greater precision in specialized discourses than in ordinary life.

1. *Essay*, 3.9.3

First, by their civil use, I mean such a communication of thoughts and ideas by words, as may serve for the upholding common conversation and commerce, about the ordinary affairs and conveniences of civil life, in the societies of men one amongst another.

Secondly, by the philosophical use of words, I mean such an use of them, as may serve to convey the precise notions of things, and to express, in general propositions, certain and undoubted truths, which the mind may rest upon, and be satisfied with, in its search after true knowledge. These two uses are very distinct; and a great deal less exactness will serve in the one than in the other, as we shall see in what follows.

2. *Essay*, 3.9.8

Common use regulates the meaning of words pretty well for common conversation; but nobody having an authority to establish the precise signification of words, nor determined to what ideas any one shall annex them, common use is not sufficient to adjust them to philosophical discourses; there being scarce any name of any very complex idea (to say nothing of others) which in common use has not a great latitude, and which keeping within the bounds of propriety, may not be made the sign of far different ideas. Besides, the rule and measure of propriety itself being no where established, it is often matter of dispute whether this or that way of using a word be propriety of speech or no.

3. *Essay*, 3.9.15

It is true, as to civil and common conversation, the general names of substances, regulated in their ordinary signification by some obvious qualities (as by the shape and figure in things of known seminal propogation, and in other substances, for the most part by colour, joined with some other sensible qualities) do well enough to design the things men would be understood to speak of: and so they usually conceive well enough the substances meant by the word gold, or apple, to distinguish the one from the other. But in philosophical inquiries and debates, where general truths are to be established, and consequences drawn from positions laid down; there the precise signification of the names of substances will be found, not only not to be well established, but also very hard to be so.

> These remarks of Locke bear upon the writing of philosophy or works in other special areas. He was also sensitive to the need for understanding an author's words in his own terms.

4. *Essay*, 3.9.22–3

Sure I am, that the signification of words in all languages depending very much on the thoughts, notions, and ideas of him that uses them, must unavoidably be of great uncertainty to men of the same language and country. This is so evident in the Greek authors, that he that shall peruse their writings will find in almost every one of them a distinct language, though the same words. But when to this natural difficulty in every country there shall be added different countries and remote ages, wherein the speakers and writers had very different notions, tempers, customs, ornaments and figures of speech, etc., every one of which influenced the signification of their words then, though to us now they are lost and unknown; it would become us to be charitable one to another in our interpretations or misunderstanding of those ancient writings: which though of great concernment to be understood, are liable to the unavoidable difficulties of speech, which (if we except the names of simple ideas, and some very obvious things) is not capable, without a constant defining the terms, of conveying the sense and intention of the speaker, without any manner of doubt and uncertainty, to the hearer. And in discourses of religion, law, and morality, as they are matters of the highest concernment, so there will be the greatest difficulty.

The volumes of interpreters and commentators on the old and new Testament are but too manifest proofs of this. Though every thing said in the text be infallibly true, yet the reader may be, nay cannot choose but be very fallible in the understanding of it. Nor is it to be wondered, that the will of God, when cloathed in words, should be liable to that doubt and uncertainty, which unavoidably attends that sort of conveyance; when even his Son, whilst cloathed in flesh, was subject to all the frailties and inconveniences of human nature, sin excepted. And we ought to magnify his goodness that he hath spread before all the world such legible characters of his works and providence, and given all mankind so sufficient a light of reason, that they to whom this written word never came, could not (whenever they set themselves to search) either doubt of the being of a God, or of the obedience due to him. Since then the precepts of natural religion are plain, and very intelligible to all mankind, and seldom come to be controverted; and other revealed truths, which are conveyed to us by books and languages, are liable to the common and natural obscurities and difficulties incident to words; methinks it would become us to be more careful and diligent in observing the former, and less magisterial, positive, and imperious, in imposing our own sense and interpretations of the latter.

> A more sustained hermeneutic is found in Locke's "An Essay for the Understanding of St. Paul's Epistles," the preface to his *A Paraphrase and Notes on the Epistles of St. Paul.*

5. *Works*, VIII, pp. 3–21

To go about to explain any of St. Paul's epistles, after so great a train of expositors and commentators, might seem an attempt of vanity, censurable for its needlessness, did not the daily and approved examples of pious and learned men justify it. This may be some excuse for me to the public, if ever these following papers should chance to come abroad: but to myself, for whose use this work was undertaken, I need make no apology. Though I had been conversant in these epistles, as well as in other parts of sacred Scripture, yet I found that I understood them not; I mean the doctrinal and discursive parts of them: though the practical directions, which are usually dropped in the latter part of each epistle, appeared to me very plain, intelligible, and instructive.

I did not, when I reflected on it, very much wonder that this part of sacred Scripture had difficulties in it: many causes of obscurity did readily occur to me. The nature of epistolary writings in general disposes the writer to pass by the mentioning of many things, as well known to him to whom his letter is addressed, which are necessary to be laid open to a stranger, to make him comprehend what is said: and it not seldom falls out that a well-penned letter, which is very easy and intelligible to the receiver, is very obscure to a stranger, who hardly knows what to make of it. The matters that St. Paul writ about were certainly things well known to those he writ to, and which they had some peculiar concern in; which made them easily apprehend his meaning, and see the tendency and force of his discourse. But we having now, at this distance, no information of the occasion of his writing, little or no knowledge of the temper and circumstances those he writ to were in, but what is to be gathered out of the epistles themselves; it is not strange that many things in them lie concealed to us, which, no doubt, they who were concerned in the letter understood at first sight. Add to this, that in many places it is manifest he answers letters sent, and questions proposed to him, which, if we had, would much better clear those passages that relate to them than all the learned notes of critics and commentators, who in aftertimes fill us with their conjectures; for very often, as to the matter in hand, they are nothing else.

The language wherein these epistles are writ is another, and that no small occasion of their obscurity to us now: the words are Greek; a language dead many ages since; a language of a very witty, volatile people, seekers after novelty, and abounding with variety of notions and sects, to which they applied the terms of their common tongue with great liberty and variety: and yet this makes but one small part of the difficulty in the language of these epistles; there is a peculiarity in it that much more obscures and perplexes the meaning of these writings than what can be occasioned by the looseness and variety of the Greek tongue. The terms are Greek, but the idiom, or turn of the phrases, may be truly said to be Hebrew or Syriac. The custom and familiarity of which tongues do sometimes so far influence the expressions in these epistles, that one may observe the force of the Hebrew conjugations, particularly that of Hiphil, given to Greek verbs, in a way unknown to the Grecians themselves. Nor is this all; the subject treated of in these epistles is so wholly new, and the doctrines contained in them so perfectly remote from the notions that mankind were acquainted with, that most of the important terms in it have quite another signification from what they have in other discourses. So that putting all together, we may truly say that the New Testament is a book written in a language peculiar to itself.

To these causes of obscurity, common to St. Paul, with most of the other penmen of the several books of the New Testament, we may add those that are peculiarly his, and owing to his style and temper. He was, as it is visible, a man of quick thought and warm temper, mighty well versed in the writings of the Old Testament, and full of the doctrine of the new. All this put together, suggested matter to him in abundance on those subjects which came in his way: so that one may consider him, when he was writing, as beset with a crowd of thoughts, all striving for utterance. In this posture of mind it was almost impossible for him to keep that slow pace, and observe minutely that order and method of ranging all he said, from which results an easy and obvious perspicuity. To this plenty and vehemence of his may be imputed those many large parentheses which a careful reader may observe in his epistles. Upon this account also it is, that he often breaks off in the middle of an argument, to let in some new thought suggested by his own words; which having pursued and explained, as far as conduced to his present purpose, he re-assumes again the thread of his discourse, and goes on with it, without taking any notice that he returns again to what he had been before saying; though sometimes it be so far off, that it may well have slipped out of his mind, and requires a very attentive reader to observe, and so bring the disjointed members together, as to make up the connexion, and see how the scattered parts of the discourse hang together in a coherent, well-agreeing sense, that makes it all of a piece.

Besides the disturbance in perusing St. Paul's epistles, from the plenty and vivacity of his thoughts, which may obscure his method, and often hide his sense from an unwary or over-hasty reader; the frequent changing of the personage he speaks in renders the sense very uncertain, and is apt to mislead one that has not some clue to guide him; sometimes by the pronoun, I, he means himself; sometimes any Christian; sometimes a Jew, and sometimes any man, &c. If speaking of himself, in the first person singular, has so various meanings; his use of the first person plural is with a far greater latitude, sometimes designing himself alone, sometimes those with himself, whom he makes partners to the epistles; sometimes with himself, comprehending the other apostles, or preachers of the Gospel, or Christians: nay, sometimes he in that way speaks of the converted Jews, other times of the converted Gentiles, and sometimes of others, in a more or less extended sense, every one of which varies the meaning of the place, and makes it to be differently understood. I have forborne to trouble the reader with examples of them here. If his own observation hath not already furnished him with them, the following Paraphrase and Notes, I suppose, will satisfy him in the point.

In the current also of his discourse he sometimes drops in the objections of others, and his answers to them, without any change in the scheme of his language, that might give notice of any other speaking besides himself. This requires great attention to observe; and yet, if it be neglected or overlooked, will make the reader very much mistake and misunderstand his meaning, and render the sense very perplexed.

These are intrinsic difficulties arising from the text itself, whereof there might be a great many other named, as the uncertainty, sometimes, who are the persons he speaks to, or the opinions, or practices, which he has in his eye, sometimes in alluding to them, sometimes in his exhortations and reproofs. But those above-mentioned being the chief, it may suffice to have opened our eyes a little upon them, which, well examined, may contribute towards our discovery of the rest.

To these we may subjoin two external causes, that have made no small increase of the native and original difficulties, that keep us from an easy and assured discovery of St. Paul's sense, in many parts of his epistles; and those are,

First, The dividing of them into chapters and verses, as we have done; whereby they are so chopped and minced, and, as they are now printed, stand so broken and divided, that not only the common people take the verses usually for distinct aphorisms; but even men of more advanced knowledge, in reading them, lose very much of the strength and force of the coherence and the light that depends on it. Our minds are so weak and narrow, that they have need of all the helps and assistances that can be procured, to lay before them undisturbedly the thread and coherence of any discourse; by which alone they are truly improved, and led into the genuine sense of the author. When the eye is constantly disturbed in loose sentences, that by their standing and separation appear as so many distinct fragments; the mind will have much ado to take in, and carry on in its memory, an uniform discourse of dependent reasonings; especially having from the cradle been used to wrong impressions concerning them, and constantly accustomed to hear them quoted as distinct sentences, without any limitation or explication of their precise meaning, from the place they stand in, and the relation they bear to what goes before, or follows. These divisions also have given occasion to the reading these epistles by parcels, and in scraps, which has farther confirmed the evil arising from such partitions. And I doubt not but every one will confess it to be a very unlikely way, to come to the understanding of any other letters, to read them piece-meal, a bit to-day, and another scrap to-morrow, and so on by broken intervals; especially if the pause and cessation should be made, as the chapters the apostle's epistles are divided into, do end sometimes in the middle of a discourse, and sometimes in the middle of a sentence. It cannot therefore but be wondered that that should be permitted to be done to holy writ, which would visibly disturb the sense, and hinder the understanding of any other book whatsoever. If Tully's epistles were so printed, and so used, I ask, Whether they would not be much harder to be understood, less easy, and less pleasant to be read, by much, than now they are?

How plain soever this abuse is, and what prejudice soever it does to the understanding of the sacred Scripture, yet if a Bible was printed as it should be, and as the several parts of it were writ, in continued discourses, where the argument is continued, I doubt not but the several parties would complain of it, as an innovation, and a dangerous change in the publishing those holy books. And indeed, those who are for maintaining their opinions, and the systems of parties, by sound of words, with a neglect of the true sense of Scripture, would have reason to make and foment the outcry. They would most of them be immediately disarmed of their great magazine of artillery, wherewith they defend themselves and fall upon others. If the holy Scripture were but laid before the eyes of Christians, in its connexion and consistency, it would not then be so easy to snatch out a few words, as if they were separate from the rest, to serve a purpose, to which they do not at all belong, and with which they have nothing to do. But as the matter now stands, he that has a mind to it, may at a cheap rate be a notable champion for the truth, that is, for the doctrines of the sect that chance or interest has cast him into. He need but be furnished with verses of sacred Scripture, containing words and expressions that are but flexible (as all general obscure and doubtful ones are), and his system, that has appropriated them to the orthodoxy of his church, makes them immediately strong and irrefragable arguments for his opinion. This is the benefit of loose sentences, and Scripture crumbled into verses, which quickly turn into independent aphorisms. But if the quotation in the verse produced were considered as a part of a continued coherent discourse, and so its sense were limited by the tenour of the context, most of these forward and warm disputants would be quite stripped of those, which they doubt not now to call spiritual weapons; and they would have often nothing to say, that would not show their weakness, and manifestly fly in their faces. I crave leave to set down a saying of the learned and judicious Mr. Selden: "In interpreting the Scripture," says he, "many do as if a man should see one have ten pounds, which he reckoned by 1, 2, 3, 4, 5, 6, 7, 8, 9, 10, meaning four was but four units, and five five units, &c. and that he had in all but ten pounds: the other that sees him, takes not the figures together as he doth, but picks here and there; and thereupon reports that he had five pounds in one bag, and six pounds in an another bag, and nine pounds in another bag, &c. when as, in truth, he has but ten pounds in all. So we pick out a text here and there, to make it serve our turn; whereas if we take it altogether, and consider what went before, and what followed after, we should find it meant no such thing."

I have heard sober Christians very much admire, why ordinary illiterate people, who were professors, that showed a concern for religion, seemed much more conversant in St. Paul's epistles than in the plainer, and (as it seemed to them) much more intelligible parts of the New Testament; they confessed, that, though they read St. Paul's epistles with their best attention, yet they generally found them too hard to be mastered; and they laboured in vain so far to reach the apostle's meaning, all along in the train of what he said, as to read them with that satisfaction that arises from a feeling that we understand and fully comprehend the force and reasoning of an author; and therefore they could not imagine what those saw in them, whose eyes they thought not much better than their own. But the case was plain; these sober inquisitive readers had a mind to see nothing in St. Paul's epistles but just what he meant; whereas those others, of a quicker and gayer sight, could see in them what they pleased. Nothing is more acceptable to fancy than pliant terms, and expressions that are not obstinate; in such it can find its account with delight, and with them be illuminated, orthodox, infallible at pleasure, and in its own way. But where the sense of the author goes visibly in its own train, and the words, receiving a determined sense from their companions and adjacents, will not consent to give countenance and colour to what is agreed to be right, and must be supported at any rate, there men of established orthodoxy do not so well find their satisfaction. And perhaps, if it were well examined, it would be no very extravagant paradox to say, that there are fewer that bring their opinions to the sacred Scripture, to be tried by that infallible rule, than bring the sacred Scripture to their opinions, to bend it to them, to make it, as they can, a cover and guard to them. And to this purpose, its being divided into verses, and brought, as much as may be, into loose and general aphorisms, makes it most useful and serviceable. And in this lies the other great cause of obscurity and perplexedness which has been cast upon St. Paul's epistles from without.

St. Paul's epistles, as they stand translated in our English Bibles, are now, by long and constant use, become a part of the English language, and common phraseology, especially in matters of religion: this every one uses familiarly, and thinks he understands; but it must be observed, that if he has a distinct meaning when he uses those words and phrases, and knows himself what he intends by them, it is always according to the sense of his own system, and the articles, or interpretations, of the society he is engaged in. So that all this knowledge and understanding, which he has in the use of these passages of sacred Scripture, reaches no farther than this, that he knows (and that is very well) what he himself says, but thereby knows nothing at all what St. Paul said in them. The apostle writ not by that man's system, and so his meaning cannot be known by it. This being the ordinary way of understanding the epistles, and every sect being perfectly orthodox in his own judgment; what a great and invincible darkness must this cast upon St. Paul's meaning, to all those of that way, in all those places where his thoughts and sense run counter to what any party has espoused for orthodox; as it must, unavoidably, to all but one of the different systems, in all those passages that any way relate to the points in controversy between them!

This is a mischief, which however frequent, and almost natural, reaches so far, that it would justly make all those who depend upon them wholly diffident of commentators, and let them see how little help was to be expected from them, in relying on them for the true sense of the sacred Scripture, did they not take care to help to cozen themselves, by choosing to use and pin their faith on such expositors as explain the sacred Scripture in favour of those opinions that they beforehand have voted orthodox, and bring to the sacred Scripture, not for trial, but confirmation. Nobody can think that any text of St. Paul's epistles has two contrary meanings; and yet so it must have, to two different men, who taking two commentators of different sects for their respective guides into the sense of any one of the epistles, shall build upon their respective expositions. We need go no further for a proof of it than the notes of the two celebrated commentators on the New Testament, Dr. Hammond and Beza, both men of parts and learning, and both thought, by their followers, men mighty in the sacred Scriptures. So that here we see the hopes of great benefit and light, from expositors and commentators, is in a great part abated; and those who have most need of their help can receive but little from them, and can have very little assurance of reaching the apostle's sense, by what they find in them, whilst matters remain in the same state they are in at present. For those who find they need help, and would borrow light from expositors, either consult only those who have the good luck to be thought sound and orthodox, avoiding those of different sentiments from themselves, in the great and approved points of their systems, as dangerous and not fit to be meddled with; or else with indifferency look into the notes of all commentators promiscuously. The first of these take pains only to confirm themselves in the opinions and tenets they have already, which whether it be the way to get the true meaning of what St. Paul delivered, is easy to determine. The others, with much more fairness to themselves, though with reaping little more advantage (unless they have something else to guide them into the apostle's meaning than the comments themselves), seek help on all hands, and refuse not to be taught by any one who offers to enlighten them in any of the dark passages. But here, though they avoid the mischief, which the others fall into, of being confined in their sense, and seeing nothing but that in St. Paul's writings, be it right or wrong; yet they run into as great on the other side, and instead of being confirmed in the meaning that they thought they saw in the text, are distracted with a hundred, suggested by those they advised with; and so, instead of that one sense of the Scripture, which they carried with them to their commentators, return from them with none at all.

This, indeed, seems to make the case desperate: for if the comments and expositions of pious and learned men cannot be depended on, whither shall we go for help? To which I answer, I would not be mistaken, as if I thought the labours of the learned in this case wholly lost and fruitless. There is great use and benefit to be made of them, when we have once got a rule to know which of their expositions, in the great variety there is of them, explains the words and phrases according to the apostle's meaning.

Until then it is evident, from what is above said, they serve for the most part to no other use, but either to make us find our own sense, and not his, in St. Pauls' words; or else to find in them no settled sense at all.

Here it will be asked, "How shall we come by this rule you mentioned? Where is that touchstone to be had, that will show us, whether the meaning we ourselves put, or take as put by others, upon St. Paul's words, in his epistles, be truly his meaning or no?" I will not say the way which I propose, and have in the following Paraphrase followed, will make us infallible in our interpretations of the apostle's text: but this I will own, that till I took this way, St. Paul's epistles, to me, in the ordinary way of reading and studying them, were very obscure parts of Scripture, that left me almost every where at a loss; and I was at a great uncertainty in which of the contrary senses, that were to be found in his commentators, he was to be taken. Whether what I have done has made it any clearer and more visible, now, I must leave others to judge. This I beg leave to say for myself, that if some very sober, judicious Christians, no strangers to the sacred Scriptures, nay, learned divines of the church of England, had not professed, that by the perusal of these following papers, they understood the epistles much better than they did before, and had not, with repeated instances, pressed me to publish them, I should not have consented they should have gone beyond my own private use, for which they were at first designed, and where they made me not repent my pains.

If any one be so far pleased with my endeavours, as to think it worth while to be informed, what was the clue I guided myself by, through all the dark passages of these epistles, I shall minutely tell him the steps by which I was brought into this way, that he may judge whether I proceed rationally, upon right grounds, or no; if so be any thing, in so mean an example as mine, may be worth his notice.

After I had found, by long experience, that the reading of the text and comments in the ordinary way proved not so successful as I wished, to the end proposed, I began to suspect, that in reading a chapter as was usual, and thereupon sometimes consulting expositors upon some hard places of it, which at that time most affected me, as relating to points then under consideration in my own mind, or in debate amongst others, was not a right method to get into the true sense of these epistles. I saw plainly, after I began once to reflect on it, that if any one now should write me a letter, as long as St. Paul's to the Romans, concerning such a matter as that is, in a style as foreign, and expressions as dubious, as his seem to be, if I should divide it into fifteen or sixteen chapters, and read of them one today, and another to-morrow, &c. it was ten to one I should never come to a full and clear comprehension of it. The way to understand the mind of him that writ it, every one would agree, was to read the whole letter through, from one end to the other, all at once, to see what was the main subject and tendency of it: or if it had several views and purposes in it, not dependent one of another, nor in a subordination to one chief aim and end, to discover what those different matters were, and where the author concluded one, and began another; and if there were any necessity of dividing the epistle into parts, to make these the boundaries of them.

In prosecution of this thought, I concluded it necessary, for the understanding of any one of St. Paul's epistles, to read it all through at one sitting; and to observe, as well as I could, the drift and design of his writing it. If the first reading gave me some light, the second gave me more; and so I persisted on, reading constantly the whole epistle over at once, till I came to have a good general view of the apostle's main purpose in writing the epistle, the chief branches of his discourse wherein he prosecuted it, the arguments he used, and the disposition of the whole.

This, I confess, is not to be obtained by one or two hasty readings; it must be repeated again and again, with a close attention to the tenour of the discourse, and a perfect neglect of the divisions into chapters and verses. On the contrary, the safest way is to suppose that the epistle has but one business, and one aim, until, by a frequent perusal of it, you are forced to see there are distinct independent matters in it, which will forwardly enough show themselves.

It requires so much more pains, judgment, and application, to find the coherence of obscure and abstruse writings, and makes them so much the more unfit to serve prejudice and pre-occupation, when found; that it is not to be wondered that St. Paul's epistles have, with many, passed rather for disjointed, loose, pious discourses, full of warmth and zeal and overflows of light, rather than for calm, strong, coherent reasonings, that carried a thread of argument and consistency all through them.

But this muttering of lazy or ill-disposed readers hindered me not from persisting in the course I had begun: I continued to read the same epistle over and over, and over again, until I came to discover, as appeared to me, what was the drift and aim of it, and by what steps and arguments St. Paul prosecuted his purpose. I remembered that St. Paul was miraculously called to the ministry of the Gospel, and declared to be a chosen vessel; that he had the whole doctrine of the Gospel from God, by immediate revelation; and was appointed to be the apostle of the Gentiles, for the propagating of it in the heathen world. This was enough to persuade me, that he was not a man of loose and shattered parts, incapable to argue, and unfit to convince those he had to deal with. God knows how to choose fit instruments for the business he employs them in. A large stock of Jewish learning he had taken in, at the feet of Gamaliel; and for his information in Christian knowledge, and the mysteries and depths of the dispensation of grace by Jesus Christ, God himself had condescended to be his instructor and teacher. The light of the Gospel he had received from the Fountain and Father of light himself, who, I concluded, had not furnished him in this extraordinary manner, if all this plentiful stock of learning and illumination had been in danger to have been lost, or proved useless, in a jumbled and confused head; nor have laid up such a store of admirable and useful knowledge in a man, who, for want of method and order, clearness of conception, or pertinency in discourse, could not draw it out into use with the greatest advantages of force and coherence. That he knew how to prosecute this purpose with strength of argument and close reasoning, without incoherent sallies, or the intermixing of things foreign to his business, was evident to me, from several speeches of his, recorded in the Acts: and it was hard to think, that a man, that could talk with so much consistency and clearness of conviction should not be able to write without confusion, inextricable obscurity, and perpetual rambling. The force, order, and perspicuity of those discourses, could not be denied to be very visible. How then came it, that the like was thought much wanting in his epistles? And of this there appeared to me this plain reason: the particularities of the history, in which these speeches are inserted, show St. Paul's end in speaking; which, being seen, casts a light on the whole, and shows the pertinency of all that he says. But his epistles not being so circumstantiated; there being no concurring history, that plainly declares the disposition St. Paul was in; what the actions, expectations, or demands of those to whom he writ required him to speak to, we are nowhere told. All this, and a great deal more, necessary to guide us into the true meaning of the epistles, is to be had only from the epistles themselves, and to be gathered from thence with stubborn attention, and more than common application.

This being the only safe guide (under the Spirit of God, that dictated these sacred writings) that can be relied on, I hope I may be excused, if I venture to say that the utmost ought to be done to observe and trace out St. Paul's reasonings; to follow the thread of his discourse in each of his epistles; to show how it goes on, still directed with the same view, and pertinently drawing the several incidents towards the same point. To understand him right, his inferences should be strictly observed; and it should be carefully examined, from what they are drawn, and what they tend to. He is certainly a coherent, argumentative, pertinent writer; and care, I think, should be taken, in expounding of him, to show that he is so. But though I say he has weighty aims in his epistles, which he steadily keeps in his eye, and drives at in all he says; yet I do not say, that he puts his discourses into an artificial method, or leads his reader into a distinction of his arguments, or gives them notice of new matter, by rhetorical or studied transitions. He has no ornaments borrowed from the Greek eloquence; no notions of their philosophy mixed with his doctrine, to set it off. The enticing words of man's wisdom, whereby he means all the studied rules of the Grecian schools, which made them such masters in the art of speaking, he, as he says himself, 1 Cor. ii. 4, wholly neglected. The reason whereof he gives in the next verse, and in other places. But though politeness of language, delicacy of style, fineness of expression, laboured periods, artificial transitions, and a very methodical ranging of the parts, with such other embellishments as make a discourse enter the mind smoothly, and strike the fancy at first hearing, have little or no place in his style; yet coherence of discourse, and a direct tendency of all the parts of it to the argument in hand, are most eminently to be found in him. This I take to be his character, and doubt not but it will be found to be so upon diligent examination. And in this, if it be so, we have a clue, if we will take the pains to find it, that will conduct us with surety through those seemingly dark places, and imagined intricacies, in which Christians have wandered so far one from another, as to find quite contrary senses.

Whether a superficial reading, accompanied with the common opinion of his invincible obscurity, has kept off some from seeking, in him, the coherence of a discourse, tending with close, strong reasoning to a point; or a seemingly more honourable opinion of one that had been rapt up into the third heaven, as if from a man so warmed and illuminated as he had been, nothing could be expected but flashes of light, and raptures of zeal, hindered others to look for a train of reasoning, proceeding on regular and cogent argumentation, from a man raised above the ordinary pitch of humanity, to a higher and brighter way of illumination; or else, whether others were loth to beat their heads about the tenour and coherence in St. Paul's discourses; which, if found out, possibly might set them at a manifest and irreconcileable difference with their systems; it is certain that, whatever hath been the cause, this way of getting the true sense of St. Paul's epistles seems not to have been much made use of, or at least so thoroughly as I am apt to think it deserves.

For, granting that he was full stored with the knowledge of the things he treated of; for he had light from heaven, it was God himself furnished him, and he could not want: allowing also that he had ability to make use of the knowledge had been given him, for the end for which it was given him, viz. the information, conviction, and conversion of others; and accordingly, that he knew how to direct his discourse to the point in hand: we cannot widely mistake the parts of his discourse employed about it, when we have any where found out the point he drives at: wherever we have got a view of his design, and the aim he proposed to himself in writing, we may be sure, that such or such an interpretation does not give us his genuine sense, it being nothing at all to his present purpose. Nay, among various meanings given a text, it fails not to direct us to the best, and very often to assure us of the true. For it is no presumption, when one sees a man arguing for this or that proposition, if he be a sober man, master of reason or common sense, and takes any care of what he says, to pronounce with confidence, in several cases, that he could not talk thus or thus.

I do not yet so magnify this method of studying. St. Paul's epistles, as well as other parts of sacred Scripture, as to think it will perfectly clear every hard place, and leave no doubt unresolved. I know, expressions now out of use, opinions of those times not heard of in our days, allusions to customs lost to us, and various circumstances and particularities of the parties, which we cannot come at, &c. must needs continue several passages in the dark, now to us, at this distance, which shone with full light to those they were directed to. But for all that, the studying of St. Paul's epistles, in the way I have proposed, will, I humbly conceive, carry us a great length in the right understanding of them, and make us rejoice in the light we receive from those most useful parts of divine revelation, by furnishing us with visible grounds that we are not mistaken, whilst the consistency of the discourse, and the pertinency of it to the design he is upon, vouches it worthy of our great apostle. At least I hope it may be my excuse, for having endeavoured to make St. Paul an interpreter to me of his own epistles.

To this may be added another help, which St. Paul himself affords us, towards the attaining the true meaning contained in his epistles. He that reads him with the attention I propose will easily observe, that as he was full of the doctrine of the Gospel, so it lay all clear and in order, open to his view. When he gave his thoughts utterance upon any point, the matter flowed like a torrent; but it is plain, it was a matter he was perfectly master of: he fully possessed the entire revelation he had received from God; had thoroughly digested it; all the parts were formed together in his mind, into one well-contracted harmonious body. So that he was no way at an uncertainty, nor ever, in the least, at a loss concerning any branch of it. One may see his thoughts were all of a piece in all his epistles, his notions were at all times uniform, and constantly the same, though his expressions very various. In them he seems to take great liberty. This at least is certain, that no one seems less tied up to a form of words. If then, having, by the method before proposed, got into the sense of the several epistles, we will but compare what he says, in the places where he treats of the same subject, we can hardly be mistaken in his sense, nor doubt what it was that he believed and taught, concerning those points of the Christian religion. I know it is not unusual to find a multitude of texts heaped up, for the maintaining of an espoused proposition; but in a sense often so remote from their true meaning, that one can hardly avoid thinking, that those, who so used them, either sought not, or valued not the sense; and were satisfied with the sound, where they could but get that to favour them. But a verbal concordance leads not always to texts of the same meaning; trusting too much thereto will furnish us but with slight proofs in many cases, and any one may observe, how apt that is to jumble together passages of Scripture, not relating to the same matter, and thereby to disturb and unsettle the true meaning of holy Scripture. I have therefore said, that we should compare together places of Scripture treating of the same point. Thus indeed, one part of the sacred text could not fail to give light unto another. And since the providence of God hath so ordered it, that St. Paul has writ a great number of epistles; which, though upon different occasions, and to several purposes, yet all confined within the business of his apostleship, and so contain nothing but points of Christian instruction, amongst which he seldom fails to drop in, and often to enlarge on, the great and distinguishing doctrines of our holy religion; which, if quitting our own infallibility in that analogy of faith, which we have made to ourselves, or have implicitly adopted from some other, we would carefully lay together, and diligently compare and study, I am apt to think, would give us

St. Paul's system in a clear and indisputable sense; which every one must acknowledge to be a better standard to interpret his meaning by, in any obscure and doubtful parts of his epistles, if any such should still remain, than the system, confession, or articles of any church, or society of Christians, yet known; which, however pretended to be founded on Scripture, are visibly the contrivances of men, fallible both in their opinions and interpretations; and, as is visible in most of them, made with partial views, and adapted to what the occasions of that time, and the present circumstances they were then in, were thought to require, for the support or justification of themselves. Their philosophy, also, has its part in misleading men from the true sense of the sacred Scripture. He that shall attentively read the Christian writers, after the age of the apostles, will easily find how much the philosophy they were tinctured with influenced them in their understanding of the books of the Old and New Testament. In the ages wherein Platonism prevailed, the converts to Christianity of that school, on all occasions, interpreted holy writ according to the notions they had imbibed from that philosophy. Aristotle's doctrine had the same effect in its turn; and when it degenerated into the peripateticism of the schools, that, too, brought its notions and distinctions into divinity, and affixed them to the terms of the sacred Scripture. And we may see still how, at this day, every one's philosophy regulates every one's interpretation of the word of God. Those who are possessed with the doctrine of aerial and ethereal vehicles, have thence borrowed an interpretation of the four first verses of 2 Cor. v. without having any ground to think that St. Paul had the least notion of any such vehicle. It is plain, that the teaching of men philosophy was no part of the design of divine revelation; but that the expressions of Scripture are commonly suited, in those matters, to the vulgar apprehensions and conceptions of the place and people where they were delivered. And, as to the doctrine therein directly taught by the apostles, that tends wholly to the setting up the kingdom of Jesus Christ in this world, and the salvation of men's souls: and in this it is plain their expressions were conformed to the ideas and notions which they had received from revelation, or were consequent from it. We shall, therefore, in vain go about to interpret their words by the notions of our philosophy, and the doctrines of men delivered in our schools. This is to explain the apostles' meaning by what they never thought of whilst they were writing; which is not the way to find their sense, in what they delivered, but our own, and to take up, from their writings, not what they left there for us, but what we bring along with us in ourselves. He that would understand St. Paul right, must understand his terms, in the sense he uses them, and not as they are appropriated, by each man's particular philosophy, to conceptions that never entered the mind of the apostle. For example, he that shall bring the philosophy now taught and received, to the explaining of spirit, soul, and body, mentioned 1 Thess. v. 23, will, I fear, hardly reach St. Paul's sense, or represent to himself the notions St. Paul then had in his mind. That is what we should aim at, in reading him, or any other author; and until we, from his words, paint his very ideas and thoughts in our minds, we do not understand him.

> What Locke urges for understanding Saint Paul applies as well to our understanding of Locke. One of the difficulties impeding the understanding of Saint Paul was, Locke suggested, that the epistles were "chopped and minced . . . broken and divided" by their being printed in chapters and verse. He urges us to read an author's work whole and all through. This is good advice, to be especially remembered when working with selections from the range of Locke's writings. There is always the danger that the selections will be one-sided, will be read differently from what they would in the body of the text. But these dangers can be greatly reduced if we follow the precautions and care Locke recommended for paying close attention to Locke's use of words, keeping out our contemporary meanings for similar words. There is an added precaution behind the selections in this *Locke Reader:* they are guided by Locke's own classification of knowledge at the end of his *Essay.*

6. *Essay*, 4.21.1–5

All that can fall within the compass of human understanding being either, first, the nature of things, as they are in themselves, their relations, and their manner of operation: or, secondly, that which man himself ought to do, as a rational and voluntary agent, for the attainment of any end, especially happiness; or, thirdly, the ways and means whereby the knowledge of both the one and the other of these is attained and communicated: I think science may be divided properly into these three sorts.

First, the knowledge of things, as they are in their own proper beings, their constitution, properties, and operations; whereby I mean not only matter and body, but spirits also, which have their proper natures, constitutions, and operations, as well as bodies. This, in a little more enlarged sense of the word, I call φυσική, or natural philosophy. The end of this is bare speculative truth; and whatsoever can afford the mind of man any such, falls under this branch, whether it be God himself, angels, spirits, bodies, or any of their affections, as number, and figure, etc.

Secondly, Πρακτική, the skill of right applying our own powers and actions for the attainment of things good and useful. The most considerable under this head is ethics, which is the seeking out those rules and measures of human actions which lead to happiness, and the means to practice them. The end of this is not bare speculation, and the knowledge of truth; but right, and a conduct suitable to it.

Thirdly, the third branch may be called σημειωτική, or the doctrine of signs, the most usual whereof being words, it is aptly enough termed also λογική, logic; the business whereof is to consider the nature of signs the mind makes use of for the understanding of things, or conveying its knowledge to others. For since the things the mind contemplates are none of them, besides itself, present to the understanding, it is necessary that something else, as a sign or representation of the thing it considers, should be present to it: and these are ideas. And because the scene of ideas that makes one man's thoughts cannot be laid open to the immediate view of another, nor laid up any where but in the memory, a no very sure repository; therefore to communicate our thoughts to one another, as well as record them for our own use, signs of our ideas are also necessary. Those which men have found most convenient, and therefore generally make use of, are articulate sounds. The consideration then of ideas and words, as the great instruments of knowledge, makes no despicable part of their contemplation who would take a view of human knowledge in the whole extent of it. And perhaps, if they were distinctly weighed, and duly considered, they would afford us another sort of logic and critic than what we have been hitherto acquainted with.

This seems to me the first and most general, as well as natural division of the objects of our understanding. For a man can employ his thoughts about nothing, but either the contemplation of things themselves for the discovery of truth; or about the things in his own power, which are his own actions, for the attainment of his own ends; or the signs the mind makes use of both in the one and the other, and the right ordering of them for its clearer information. All which three, viz. things as they are in themselves knowable;

actions as they depend on us, in order to happiness; and the right use of signs, in order to knowledge, being *toto caelo* different, they seemed to me to be the three great provinces of the intellectual world, wholly separate and distinct one from another.

This threefold division need not be used as a Procrustean bed, but the range of Locke's interests and writings can fairly well be fitted into this division. Within each of these divisions, selections from his texts are made around central themes and topics.

1

The Science of Nature

"The knowledge of things as they are in their own proper being."

Locke lived in an important age of science. Not only were developments in scientific knowledge and method in all fields moving rapidly ahead, but scientific activity was gaining social recognition and acceptance. The Royal Society was formed around 1660, with a charter from King Charles II. Locke was elected a member of this society in 1668. He was a close friend of Robert Boyle, the chemist, and of the medical doctor Thomas Sydenham; Newton was among later friends. Boyle's *The Origine of Formes and Qualities* (1666) had a strong influence on Locke. Locke's library contained an extensive collection of books in science. The relations between Locke's thought and the scientific activity of his day are now beginning to receive the attention of scholars.[10] The phrase *the science of nature* is ambiguous. It referred to speculation in theology and metaphysics as well as theories used by scientists, for example, the corpuscular theory. But *the science of nature* also for Locke encompassed the experimental, observational activities of Boyle, Sydenham, Hooke, and many others. Locke's account of knowledge was written against this background.

The definition of knowledge
Locke's *Essay* is frequently read as taking demonstrative, deductive knowledge as the model for knowledge. But if one keeps in mind Locke's interest in the observational knowledge being produced by the scientists of his day, the

10 See G. Buchdahl, *Metaphysics and the Philosophy of Science* (Oxford, 1969); F. Duchesneau, *L'Empirisme de Locke* (The Hague, 1973); R. Woolhouse, *Locke's Philosophy of Science and Knowledge* (Oxford, 1971); and J. W. Yolton, *Locke and the Compass of Human Understanding* (Cambridge, 1970).

definition of knowledge in his *Essay* can be seen as an attempt to include nondemonstrative as well as demonstrative knowledge. In the definition of knowledge, and in the account of the different knowledge relations (as well as throughout Book 2), it is useful to watch the occurrence of two words: *coexistence* and *observation* (and its cognates, e.g., *see*, *hear*, etc.). The word *idea* also is important to watch.

7. *Essay*, 4.1

Since the mind, in all its thoughts and reasonings, hath no other immediate object but its own ideas, which it alone does or can contemplate; it is evident, that our knowledge is only conversant about them.

Knowledge then seems to me to be nothing but the perception of the connexion and agreement, or disagreement and repugnancy, of any of our ideas. In this alone it consists. Where this perception is, there is knowledge; and where it is not, there, though we may fancy, guess, or believe, yet we always come short of knowledge. For when we know that white is not black, what do we else but perceive that these two ideas do not agree? When we possess ourselves with the utmost security of the demonstration, that the three angles of a triangle are equal to two right ones, what do we more but perceive, that equality to two right ones does necessarily agree to, and is inseparable from the three angles of a triangle?

But to understand a little more distinctly wherein this agreement or disagreement consists, I think we may reduce it all to these four sorts:

1. Identity, or diversity.
2. Relation.
3. Co-existence, or necessary connexion.
4. Real existence.

First, as to the first sort of agreement or disagreement, viz. identity or diversity. It is the first act of the mind, when it has any sentiments or ideas at all, to perceive its ideas; and so far as it perceives them, to know each what it is, and thereby also to perceive their difference, and that one is not another. This is so absolutely necessary, that without it there could be no knowledge, no reasoning, no imagination, no distinct thoughts, at all. By this the mind clearly and infallibly perceives each idea to agree with itself, and to be what it is; and all distinct ideas to disagree, i.e. the one not to be the other: and this it does without pains, labour, or deduction; but at first view, by its natural power of perception and distinction. And though men of art have reduced this into those general rules, "what is, is"; and "it is impossible for the same thing to be and not to be"; for ready application in all cases, wherein there may be occasion to reflect on it: yet it is certain, that the first exercise of this faculty is about particular ideas. A man infallibly knows, as soon as ever he has them in his mind, that the ideas he calls white and round, are the very ideas they are, and that they are not other ideas which he calls red or square. Nor can any maxim or proposition in the world make him know it clearer or surer than he did before, and without any such general rule. This then is the first agreement or disagreement, which the mind perceives in its ideas; which it always perceives at first sight: and if there ever happen any doubt about it, it will always be found to be about the names, and not the ideas themselves, whose identity and diversity will always be perceived, as soon and clearly as the ideas themselves are; nor can it possibly be otherwise.

Secondly, the next sort of agreement or disagreement, the mind perceives in any of its ideas, may, I think, be called relative, and is nothing but the perception of the relation between any two ideas, of what kind soever, whether substances, modes, or any other. For since all distinct ideas must eternally be known not to be the same, and so be universally and constantly denied one of another, there could be no room for any positive knowledge at all, if we could not perceive any relation between our ideas, and find out the agreement or disagreement they have one with another, in several ways the mind takes of comparing them.

Thirdly, the third sort of agreement, or disagreement, to be found in our ideas, which the perception of the mind is employed about, is co-existence, or non co-existence in the same subject; and this belongs particularly to substances. Thus when we pronounce concerning gold that it is fixed, our knowledge of this truth amounts to no more but this, that fixedness, or a power to remain in the fire unconsumed, is an idea that always accompanies, and is joined with that particular sort of yellowness, weight, fusibility, malleableness, and solubility in aqua regia, which make our complex idea, signified by the word gold.

Fourthly, the fourth and last sort is that of actual and real existence agreeing to any idea. Within these four sorts of agreement or disagreement, is, I suppose, contained all the knowledge we have, or are capable of: for all the inquiries we can make concerning any of our ideas, all that we know or can affirm concerning any of them, is, that it is, or is not, the same with some other; that it does or does not always co-exist with some other idea in the same subject; that it has this or that relation with some other idea; or that it has a real existence without the mind. Thus blue is not yellow; is of identity: two triangles upon equal bases between two parallels are equal; is of relation: iron is susceptible of magnetical impressions; is of co-existence: God is; is of real existence. Though identity and co-existence are truly nothing but relations, yet they are such peculiar ways of agreement or disagreement of our ideas, that they deserve well to be considered as distinct heads, and not under relation in general; since they are so different grounds of affirmation and negation, as will easily appear to any one, who will but reflect on what is said in several places of this essay. I should not proceed to examine the several degrees of our knowledge but that it is necessary first to consider the different acceptations of the word knowledge.

There are several ways wherein the mind is possessed of truth, each of which is called knowledge.

1. There is actual knowledge which is the present view the mind has of the agreement or disagreement of any of its ideas, or of the relation they have one to another.

2. A man is said to know any proposition, which having been once laid before his thoughts, he evidently perceived the agreement or disagreement of the ideas whereof it consists; and so lodged it in his memory, that whenever that proposition comes again to be reflected on, he, without doubt or hesitation, embraces the right side, assents to, and is certain of the truth of it. This, I think, one may call habitual knowledge: and thus a man may be said to know all those truths which are lodged in his memory, by a foregoing, clear and full perception, whereof the mind is assured past doubt, as often as it has occasion to reflect on them. For our finite understandings being able to think clearly and distinctly but on one thing at once, if men had no knowledge of any more than what they actually thought on, they would all be very ignorant; and he that knew most, would know but one truth, that being all he was able to think on at one time.

Of habitual knowledge, there are also, vulgarly speaking, two degrees:

First, the one is of such truths laid up in the memory, as, whenever they occur to the mind, it actually perceives the relation is between those ideas. And this is in all those truths whereof we have an intuitive knowledge; where the ideas themselves, by an immediate view, discover their agreement or disagreement one with another.

Secondly, the other is of such truths, whereof the mind having been convinced, it retains the memory of the conviction, without the proofs. Thus a man that remembers certainly that he once perceived the demonstration, that the three angles of a triangle are equal to two right ones, is certain that he knows it, because he cannot doubt the truth of it. In his adherence to a truth, where the demonstration by which it was at first known is forgot, though a man may be thought rather to believe his memory than really to know, and this way of entertaining a truth seemed formerly to me like something between opinion and knowledge; a sort of assurance which exceeds bare belief, for that relies on the testimony of another: yet upon a due examination I find it comes not short of perfect certainty, and is in effect true knowledge. That which is apt to mislead our first thoughts into a mistake in this matter is, that the agreement or disagreement of the ideas in this case is not perceived, as it was at first, by an actual view of all the intermediate ideas, whereby the agreement or disagreement of those in the proposition was at first perceived; but by other intermediate ideas, that show the agreement or disagreement of the ideas contained in the proposition whose certainty we remember. For example, in this proposition, that the three angles of a triangle are equal to two right ones, one who has seen and clearly perceived the demonstration of this truth knows it to be true, when that demonstration is gone out of his mind; so that at present it is not actually in view, and possibly cannot be recollected: but he knows it in a different way from what he did before. The agreement of the two ideas joined in that proposition is perceived, but it is by the intervention of other ideas than those which at first produced that perception. He remembers, i.e. he knows (for remembrance is but the reviving of some past knowledge) that he was once certain of the truth of this proposition, that the three angles of a triangle are equal to two right ones. The immutability of the same relations between the same immutable things, is now the idea that shows him that if the three angles of a triangle were once equal to two right ones, they will always be equal to two right ones. And hence he comes to be certain, that what was once true in the case, is always true; what ideas once agreed, will always agree; and consequently what he once knew to be true, he will always know to be true, as long as he can remember that he once knew it. Upon this ground it is, that

particular demonstrations in mathematics afford general knowledge. If then the perception that the same ideas will eternally have
the same habitudes and relations, be not a sufficient ground of
knowledge, there could be no knowledge of general propositions
in mathematics; for no mathematical demonstration would be any
other than particular: and when a man had demonstrated any
proposition concerning one triangle or circle, his knowledge would
not reach beyond that particular diagram. If he would extend it
further, he must renew his demonstration in another instance, before he could know it to be true in another like triangle, and so on:
by which means one could never come to the knowledge of any
general propositions. Nobody, I think, can deny that Mr. Newton
certainly knows any proposition, that he now at any time reads
in his book, to be true; though he has not in actual view that
admirable chain of intermediate ideas, whereby he at first discovered it to be true. Such a memory as that, able to retain such a train
of particulars, may be well thought beyond the reach of human
faculties; when the very discovery, perception, and laying together
that wonderful connexion of ideas, is found to surpass most readers' comprehension. But yet it is evident, the author himself knows
the proposition to be true, remembering he once saw the connexion of those ideas, as certainly as he knows such a man wounded
another, remembering that he saw him run him through. But because the memory is not always so clear as actual perception, and
does in all men more or less decay in length of time, this amongst
other differences is one, which shows that demonstrative knowledge is much more imperfect than intuitive, as we shall see in the
following chapter.

8. *Essay*, 4.2

All our knowledge consisting, as I have said, in the view the mind
has of its own ideas, which is the utmost light and greatest certainty
we, with our faculties, and in our way of knowledge, are capable
of; it may not be amiss to consider a little the degrees of its
evidence. The different clearness of our knowledge seems to me
to lie in the different way of perception the mind has of the agreement or disagreement of any of its ideas. For if we will reflect on
our own ways of thinking, we shall find that sometimes the mind
perceives the agreement or disagreement of two ideas immediately
by themselves, without the intervention of any other: and this, I
think, we may call intuitive knowledge. For in this the mind is at
no pains of proving or examining, but perceives the truth, as the eye

doth light, only by being directed toward it. Thus the mind perceives, that white is not black, that a circle is not a triangle, that three are more than two, and equal to one and two. Such kind of truths the mind perceives at the first sight of the ideas together, by bare intuition, without the intervention of any other idea; and this kind of knowledge is the clearest and most certain that human frailty is capable of. This part of knowledge is irresistible, and like bright sunshine forces itself immediately to be perceived, as soon as ever the mind turns its view that way; and leaves no room for hesitation, doubt, or examination, but the mind is presently filled with the clear light of it. It is on this intuition that depends all the certainty and evidence of all our knowledge; which certainty every one finds to be so great, that he cannot imagine, and therefore not require a greater: for a man cannot conceive himself capable of a greater certainty, than to know that any idea in his mind is such as he perceives it to be; and that two ideas, wherein he perceives a difference, are different and not precisely the same. He that demands a greater certainty than this, demands he knows not what, and shows only that he has a mind to be a sceptic, without being able to be so. Certainty depends so wholly on this intuition, that in the next degree of knowledge, which I call demonstrative, this intuition is necessary in all the connexions of the intermediate ideas, without which we cannot attain knowledge and certainty.

The next degree of knowledge is, where the mind perceives the agreement or disagreement of any ideas, but not immediately. Though wherever the mind perceives the agreement or disagreement of any of its ideas, there be certain knowledge; yet it does not always happen that the mind sees that agreement or disagreement of any of its ideas, there be certain knowledge; yet it does and in that case remains in ignorance, and at most gets no farther than a probable conjecture. The reason why the mind cannot always perceive presently the agreement or disagreement of two ideas is, because those ideas, concerning whose agreement or disagreement the inquiry is made, cannot by the mind be so put together as to show it. In this case then, when the mind cannot so bring its ideas together, as by their immediate comparison, and as it were juxta-position or application one to another, to perceive their agreement or disagreement, it is fain, by the intervention of other ideas (one or more, as it happens) to discover the agreement or disagreement which it searches; and this is that which we call reasoning. Thus the mind being willing to know the agreement or disagreement in bigness, between the three angles of a triangle and two right ones, cannot by an immediate view and comparing them do it: because the three angles of a triangle cannot be brought at once, and be compared with any one or two angles; and so of this the mind has no immediate, no intuitive knowledge. In this case the mind is fain to find out some other angles, to which the three angles of a triangle have an equality; and, finding those equal to two right ones, comes to know their equality to two right ones.

Those intervening ideas which serve to show the agreement of any two others, are called proofs; and where the agreement and disagreement is by this means plainly and clearly perceived, it is called demonstration, it being shown to the understanding, and the mind made to see that it is so. A quickness in the mind to find out these intermediate ideas (that shall discover the agreement or disagreement of any other) and to apply them right, is, I suppose, that which is called sagacity.

This knowledge by intervening proofs, though it be certain, yet the evidence of it is not altogether so clear and bright, nor the assent so ready, as in intuitive knowledge. For though, in demonstration, the mind does at last perceive the agreement or disagreement of the ideas it considers; yet it is not without pains and attention: there must be more than one transient view to find it. A steady application and pursuit are required to this discovery: and there must be a progression by steps and degrees, before the mind can in this way arrive at certainty, and come to perceive the agreement or repugnancy between two ideas that need proofs and the use of reason to show it.

Another difference between intuitive and demonstrative knowledge is, that though in the latter all doubt be removed, when by the intervention of the intermediate ideas the agreement or disagreement is perceived; yet before the demonstration there was a doubt, which in intuitive knowledge cannot happen to the mind, that has its faculty of perception left to a degree capable of distinct ideas, no more than it can be a doubt to the eye (that can distinctly see white and black) whether this ink and this paper be all of a colour. If there be sight in the eyes, it will at first glimpse, without hesitation, perceive the words printed on this paper different from the colour of the paper: and so if the mind have the faculty of distinct perceptions, it will perceive the agreement or disagreement of those ideas that produce intuitive knowledge. If the eyes have lost the faculty of seeing, or the mind of perceiving, we in vain inquire after the quickness of sight in one, or clearness of perception in the other.

It is true, the perception produced by demonstration is also very clear, yet it is often with a great abatement of that evident lustre and full assurance that always accompany that which I call intuitive; like a face reflected by several mirrors one to another, where as long as it retains the similitude and agreement with the object, it produces a knowledge; but it is still in every successive reflection with a lessening of that perfect clearness and distinctness which is in the first, till at last, after many removes, it has a great mixture of dimness, and is not at first sight so knowable, especially to weak eyes. Thus it is with knowledge made out by a long train of proof.

Now, in every step reason makes in demonstrative knowledge, there is an intuitive knowledge of that agreement or disagreement it seeks with the next intermediate idea, which it uses as a proof: for if it were not so, that yet would need a proof; since without the perception of such agreement or disagreement, there is no knowledge produced. If it be perceived by itself, it is intuitive knowledge: if it cannot be perceived by itself, there is need of some intervening idea, as a common measure to show their agreement or disagreement. By which it is plain, that every step in reasoning that produces knowledge has intuitive certainty; which when the mind perceives, there is no more required, but to remember it to make the agreement or disagreement of the ideas, concerning which we inquire, visible and certain. So that to make any thing a demonstration, it is necessary to perceive the immediate agreement of the intervening ideas, whereby the agreement or disagreement of the two ideas under examination (whereof the one is always the first, and the other the last in the account) is found. This intuitive perception of the agreement or disagreement of the intermediate ideas, in each step and progression of the demonstration, must also be carried exactly in the mind, and a man must be sure that no part is left out: which because in long deductions, and the use of many proofs, the memory does not always so readily and exactly retain; therefore it comes to pass, that this is more imperfect than intuitive knowledge, and men embrace often falsehood for demonstrations.

The necessity of this intuitive knowledge, in each step of scientifical or demonstrative reasoning, gave occasion, I imagine, to that mistaken axiom, that all reasoning was "ex praecognitis et praeconcessis"; which how far it is mistaken, I shall have occasion to show more at large, when I come to consider propositions, and particularly those propositions which are called maxims; and to show that it is by a mistake that they are supposed to be the foundations of all our knowledge and reasonings.

It has been generally taken for granted, that mathematics alone are capable of demonstrative certainty: but to have such an agreement or disagreement, as may intuitively be perceived, being, as I imagine, not the privilege of the ideas of number, extension, and figure alone, it may possibly be the want of due method and application in us, and not of sufficient evidence in things, that demonstration has been thought to have so little to do in other parts of knowledge, and been scarce so much as aimed at by any but mathematicians. For whatever ideas we have, wherein the mind can perceive the immediate agreement or disagreement that is between them, there the mind is capable of intuitive knowledge; and where it can perceive the agreement or disagreement of any two ideas, by an intuitive perception of the agreement or disagreement they have with any intermediate ideas, there the mind is capable of demonstration, which is not limited to ideas of extension, figure, number, and their modes.

The reason why it has been generally sought for, and supposed to be only in those, I imagine has been not only the general usefulness of those sciences; but because, in comparing their equality or excess, the modes of numbers have every the least difference very clear and perceivable: and though in extension every the least excess is not so perceptible, yet the mind has found out ways to examine and discover demonstratively the just equality of two angles, or extensions, or figures: and both these, i.e. numbers and figures, can be set down by visible and lasting marks, wherein the ideas under consideration are perfectly determined; which for the most part they are not, where they are marked only by names and words.

But in other simple ideas, whose modes and differences are made and counted by degrees, and not quantity, we have not so nice and accurate a distinction of their differences, as to perceive and find ways to measure their just equality, or the least differences. For those other simple ideas, being appearances of sensations, produced in us by the size, figure, number, and motion of minute corpuscles singly insensible; their different degrees also depend upon the variation of some or of all those causes: which since it cannot be observed by us in particles of matter, whereof each is too subtile to be perceived, it is impossible for us to have any exact measures of the different degrees of these simple ideas. For supposing the sensation or idea we name whiteness be produced in us by a certain number of globules, which, having a verticity about their own centres, strike upon the retina of the eye with a certain degree of rotation, as well as progressive swiftness; it will hence easily follow, that the more the superficial parts of any body are so ordered, as to reflect the greater number of globules of light, and to give them the proper rotation, which is fit to produce this sensation of white in us, the more white will that body appear, that from an equal space sends to the retina the greater number of such corpuscles, with that peculiar sort of motion. I do not say, that the nature of light consists in very small round globules, nor of whiteness in such a texture of parts as gives a certain rotation to these globules, when it reflects them; for I am not now treating physically of light or colours: but this, I think, I may say, that I cannot (and I would be glad any one would make intelligible that he did) conceive how bodies without us can any ways affect our senses, but by the immediate contact of the sensible bodies themselves, as in tasting and feeling, or the impulse of some insensible particles coming from them, as in seeing, hearing, and smelling; by the different impulse of which parts, caused by their different size, figure, and motion, the variety of sensations is produced in us.

Whether then they be globules, or no, – or whether they have a verticity about their own centres that produces the idea of whiteness in us, – this is certain, that the more particles of light are reflected from a body, fitted to give them that peculiar motion, which produces the sensation of whiteness in us, – and possibly too, the quicker that peculiar motion is, – the whiter does the body appear from which the greater number are reflected, as is evident in the same piece of paper put in the sun-beams, in the shade, and in a dark hole; in each of which it will produce in us the idea of whiteness in far different degrees.

Not knowing therefore what number of particles, nor what motion of them is fit to produce any precise degree of whiteness, we cannot demonstrate the certain equality of any two degrees of whiteness, because we have no certain standard to measure them by, nor means to distinguish every the least real difference, the only help we have being from our senses, which in this point fail us. But where the difference is so great as to produce in the mind clearly distinct ideas, whose differences can be perfectly retained, there these ideas or colours, as we see in different kinds, as blue and red, are as capable of demonstration as ideas of number and extension. What I have here said of whiteness and colours, I think, holds true in all secondary qualities, and their modes.

These two, viz. intuition and demonstration, are the degrees of our knowledge; whatever comes short of one of these, with what assurance soever embraced, is but faith, or opinion, but not knowledge, at least in all general truths. There is, indeed, another perception of the mind, employed about the particular existence of finite beings without us; which going beyond bare probability, and yet not reaching perfectly to either of the foregoing degrees of certainty, passes under the name of knowledge. There can be nothing more certain than that the idea we receive from an external object is in our minds; this is intuitive knowledge. But whether there be any thing more than barely that idea in our minds, whether we can thence certainly infer the existence of any thing without us, which corresponds to that idea, is that whereof some men think there may be a question made; because men may have such ideas in their minds, when no such thing exists, no such object affects their senses. But yet here, I think, we are provided with an evidence, that puts us past doubting: for I ask any one, whether he be not invincibly conscious to himself of a different perception, when he looks on the sun by day, and thinks on it by night; when he actually tastes wormwood, or smells a rose, or only thinks on that savour or odour? We as plainly find the difference there is between an idea revived in our minds by our own memory, and actually coming into our minds by our senses, as we do between any two distinct ideas. If any one say, a dream may do the same thing, and all these ideas may be produced in us without any external objects; he may please to dream that I make him this answer; 1. That it is no great matter, whether I remove this scruple or no: where all is but dream, reasoning and arguments are of no use, truth and knowledge nothing. 2. That I believe he will allow a very manifest difference between dreaming of being in the fire, and being actually in it. But yet if he be resolved to appear so sceptical as to maintain, that what I call being actually in the fire is nothing but a dream, and we cannot thereby certainly know that any such thing as fire actually exists without us; I answer, that we certainly finding that pleasure or pain follows upon the application of certain objects to us, whose existence we perceive, or dream that we perceive, by our senses; this certainty is as great as our happiness or misery, beyond which we have no concernment to know, or to be. So that, I think, we may add to the two former sorts of knowledge this also of the existence of particular external objects, by that perception and consciousness we have of the actual entrance of ideas from them, and allow these three degrees of knowledge, viz. intuitive, demonstrative, and sensitive: in each of which there are different degrees and ways of evidence and certainty.

But since our knowledge is founded on, and employed about, our ideas only, will it not follow from thence, that it is conformable to our ideas; and that where our ideas are clear and distinct, or obscure and confused, our knowledge will be so too? To which I answer, no: for our knowledge consisting in the perception of the agreement or disagreement of any two ideas, its clearness or obscurity consists in the clearness or obscurity of that perception, and not in the clearness or obscurity of the ideas themselves; v.g. a man that has as clear ideas of the angles of a triangle, and of equality to two right ones, as any mathematician in the world, may yet have but a very obscure perception of their agreement, and so have but a very obscure knowledge of it. But ideas, which by reason of their obscurity or otherwise are confused, cannot produce any clear or distinct knowledge; because as far as any ideas are confused, so far the mind cannot perceive clearly, whether they agree or disagree. Or to express the same thing in a way less apt to be misunderstood; he that hath not determined ideas to the words he uses, cannot make propositions of them, of whose truth he can be certain.

9. *Essay*, 4.3.6–9

From all which it is evident, that the extent of our knowledge comes not only short of the reality of things, but even of the extent of our own ideas. Though our knowledge be limited to our ideas, and cannot exceed them either in extent or perfection; and though these be very narrow bounds, in respect of the extent of all being, and far short of what we may justly imagine to be in some even created understandings, not tied down to the dull and narrow information which is to be received from some few, and not very acute ways of perception, such as are our senses; yet it would be well with us if our knowledge were but as large as our ideas, and there were not many doubts and inquiries concerning the ideas we have, whereof we are not, nor I believe ever shall be in this world resolved. Nevertheless I do not question but that human knowledge, under the present circumstances of our beings and constitutions, may be carried much farther than it has hitherto been, if men would sincerely, and with freedom of mind, employ all that industry and labour of thought, in improving the means of discovering truth, which they do for the colouring or support of falsehood, to maintain a system, interest, or party, they are once engaged in.

The affirmations or negations we make concerning the ideas we have, may, as I have before intimated in general, be reduced to these four sorts, viz. identity, co-existence, relation, and real existence. I shall examine how far our knowledge extends in each of these.

First, as to identity and diversity, in this way of agreement or disagreement of our ideas, our intuitive knowledge is as far extended as our ideas themselves: and there can be no idea in the mind, which it does not presently, by an intuitive knowledge, perceive to be what it is, and to be different from any other.

Secondly, as to the second sort, which is the agreement or disagreement of our ideas in co-existence; in this our knowledge is very short, though in this consists the greatest and most material part of our knowledge concerning substances. For our ideas of the species of substances being, as I have showed, nothing but certain collections of simple ideas united in one subject, and so co-existing together; v. g. our idea of flame is a body hot, luminous, and moving upward; of gold, a body heavy to a certain degree, yellow, malleable, and fusible: these, or some such complex ideas as these in men's minds, do these two names of the different substances, flame and gold, stand for. When we would know any thing farther concerning these, or any other sort of substances, what do we inquire, but what other qualities or power these substances have or have not? Which is nothing else but to know what other simple ideas do or do not co-exist with those that make up that complex idea.

10. *Essay*, 4.4

I doubt not but my reader by this time may be apt to think, that I have been all this while only building a castle in the air; and be ready to say to me, "To what purpose all this stir? Knowledge, say you, is only the perception of the agreement or disagreement of our own ideas: but who knows what those ideas may be? Is there any thing so extravagant, as the imaginations of men's brains? Where is the head that has no chimeras in it? Or if there be a sober and a wise man, what difference will there be, by your rules, between his knowledge and that of the most extravagant fancy in the world? They both have their ideas, and perceive their agreement and disagreement one with another. If there be any difference between them, the advantage will be on the warm-headed man's side, as having the more ideas and the more lively: and so, by your rules, he will be the more knowing. If it be true, that all knowledge lies only in the perception of the agreement or disagreement of our own ideas, the visions of an enthusiast, and the reasonings of a sober man, will be equally certain. It is no matter how things are; so a man observe but the agreement of his own imaginations, and talk conformably, it is all truth, all certainty. Such castles in the air will be as strong holds of truth, as the demonstrations of Euclid. That an harpy is not a centaur is by this way as certain knowledge, and as much a truth, as that a square is not a circle.

"But of what use is all this fine knowledge of men's own imaginations, to a man that inquires after the reality of things? It matters not what men's fancies are, it is the knowledge of things that is only to be prized; it is this alone gives a value to our reasonings, and preference to one man's knowledge over another's, that it is of things as they really are, and not of dreams and fancies."

To which I answer, that if our knowledge of our ideas terminate in them, and reach no farther, where there is something farther intended, our most serious thoughts will be of little more use, than the reveries of a crazy brain; and the truths built thereon of no more weight, than the discourses of a man, who sees things clearly in a dream, and with great assurance utters them. But, I hope, before I have done, to make it evident, that this way of certainty, by the knowledge of our own ideas, goes a little farther than bare imagination: and I believe it will appear, that all the certainty of general truths a man has, lies in nothing else.

It is evident the mind knows not things immediately, but only by the intervention of the ideas it has of them. Our knowledge therefore is real, only so far as there is a conformity between our ideas and the reality of things. But what shall be here the criterion? How shall the mind, when it perceives nothing but its own ideas, know that they agree with things themselves? This, though it seems not to want difficulty, yet, I think, there be two sorts of ideas, that, we may be assured, agree with things.

First, the first are simple ideas, which since the mind, as has been showed, can by no means make to itself, must necessarily be the product of things operating on the mind in a natural way, and producing therein those perceptions which by the wisdom and will of our maker they are ordained and adapted to. From whence it follows, that simple ideas are not fictions of our fancies, but the natural and regular productions of things without us, really operating upon us, and so carry with them all the conformity which is intended, or which our state requires: for they represent to us things under those appearances which they are fitted to produce in us, whereby we are enabled to distinguish the sorts of particular substances, to discern the states they are in, and so to take them for our necessities, and to apply them to our uses. Thus the idea of whiteness, or bitterness as it is in the mind, exactly answering that power which is in any body to produce it there, has all the real conformity it can, or ought to have, with things without us. And this conformity between our simple ideas, and the existence of things, is sufficient for real knowledge.

Secondly, all our complex ideas, except those of substances, being archetypes of the mind's own making, not intended to be the copies of any thing, nor referred to the existence of any thing, as to their originals; cannot want any conformity necessary to real knowledge. For that which is not designed to represent any thing but itself, can never be capable of a wrong representation, nor mislead us from the true apprehension of any thing, by its dislikeness to it; and such, excepting those of substances, are all our complex ideas: which, as I have showed in another place, are combinations of ideas, which the mind, by its free choice, puts together, without considering any connexion they have in nature. And hence it is, that in all these sorts the ideas themselves are considered as the archetypes, and things no otherwise regarded, but as they are conformable to them. So that we cannot but be infallibly certain, that all the knowledge we attain concerning these ideas is real, and reaches things themselves; because in all our thoughts, reasonings, and discourses of this kind, we intend things no farther than as they are conformable to our ideas. So that in these we cannot miss of a certain and undoubted reality.

I doubt not but it will be easily granted, that the knowledge we have of mathematical truths, is not only certain, but real knowledge; and not the bare empty vision of vain insignificant chimeras of the brain: and yet, if we will consider, we shall find that it is only of our own ideas. The mathematician considers the truth and properties belonging to a rectangle, or circle, only as they are in idea in his own mind. For it is possible he never found either of them existing mathematically, i.e. precisely true, in his life. But yet the knowledge he has of any truths or properties belonging to a circle, or any other mathematical figure, are nevertheless true and certain, even of real things existing; because real things are no farther concerned, nor intended to be meant by any such propositions, than as things really agree to those archetypes in his mind. Is it true of the idea of a triangle, that its three angles are equal to two right ones? It is true also of a triangle, wherever it really exists. Whatever other figure exists, that is not exactly answerable to the idea of a triangle in his mind, is not at all concerned in that proposition: and therefore he is certain all his knowledge concerning such ideas is real knowledge; because intending things no farther than they agree with those his ideas, he is sure what he knows concerning those figures, when they have barely an ideal existence in his mind, will hold true of them also, when they have real existence in matter; his consideration being barely of those figures, which are the same, wherever or however they exist.

And hence it follows that moral knowledge is as capable of real certainty, as mathematicks. For certainty being but the perception of the agreement or disagreement of our ideas; and demonstration nothing but the perception of such agreement, by the intervention of other ideas, or mediums; our moral ideas, as well as mathematical, being archetypes themselves, and so adequate and complete ideas; all the agreement or disagreement, which we shall find in them, will produce real knowledge, as well as in mathematical figures.

For the attaining of knowledge and certainty, it is requisite that we have determined ideas; and, to make our knowledge real, it is requisite that the ideas answer their archetypes. Nor let it be wondered, that I place the certainty of our knowledge in the consideration of our ideas, with so little care and regard (as it may seem) to the real existence of things: since most of those discourses, which take up the thoughts, and engage the disputes of those who pretend to make it their business to inquire after truth and certainty, will, I presume, upon examination be found to be general propositions, and notions in which existence is not at all concerned. All the discourses of the mathematicians about the squaring of a circle, conick sections, or any other part of mathematicks, concern not the existence of any of those figures; but their demonstrations, which depend on their ideas, are the same, whether there be any square or circle existing in the world, or no. In the same manner the truth and certainty of moral discourses abstracts from the lives of men, and the existence of those virtues in the world whereof they treat. Nor are Tully's offices less true, because there is nobody in the world that exactly practises his rules, and lives up to that pattern of a virtuous man which he has given us, and which existed no where, when he writ, but in idea. If it be true in speculation, i.e. in idea, that murder deserves death, it will also be true in reality of any action that exists conformable to that idea of murder. As for other actions, the truth of that proposition concerns them not. And thus it is of all other species of things, which have no other essences but those ideas, which are in the minds of men.

But it will here be said, that if moral knowledge be placed in the contemplation of our own moral ideas, and those, as other modes, be of our own making, what strange notions will there be of justice and temperance? What confusion of virtues and vices, if every one may make what ideas of them he pleases? No confusion or disorder in the things themselves, nor the reasonings about them; no more than (in mathematicks) there would be a disturbance in the demonstration, or a change in the properties of figures, and their relations one to another, if a man should make a triangle with four corners, or a trapezium with four right angles: that is, in plain English, change the names of the figures, and call that by one name, which mathematicians call ordinarily by another. For let a man make to himself the idea of a figure with three angles, whereof one is a right one, and call it, if he please, equilaterum or trapezium, or any thing else, the properties of and demonstrations about that idea will be the same, as if he called it a rectangular triangle. I confess the change of the name, by the impropriety of speech, will at first disturb him, who knows not what idea it stands for; but as soon as the figure is drawn, the consequences and demonstration are plain and clear. Just the same is it in moral knowledge, let a man have the idea of taking from others, without their consent, what their honest industry has possessed them of, and call this justice, if he please. He that takes the name here without the idea put to it, will be mistaken, by joining another idea of his own to that name: but strip the idea of that name, or take it such as it is in the speaker's mind, and the same things will agree to it, as if you called it injustice. Indeed wrong names in moral discourses breed usually more disorder, because they are not so easily rectified as in mathematicks, where the figure, once drawn and seen, makes the name useless and of no force. For what need of a sign, when the thing signified is present and in view? But in moral names that cannot be so easily and shortly done, because of the many decompositions that go to the making up the complex ideas of those modes. But yet for all this, miscalling of any of those ideas, contrary to the usual signification of the words of that language, hinders not but that we may have certain and demonstrative knowledge of their several agreements and disagreements, if we will carefully, as in mathematicks, keep to the same precise ideas, and trace them in their several relations one to another, without being led away by their names. If we but separate the idea under consideration from the sign that stands for it, our knowledge goes equally on in the discovery of real truth and certainty, whatever sounds we make use of.

One thing more we are to take notice of, that where God, or any other law-maker, hath defined any moral names, there they have made the essence of that species to which that name belongs; and there it is not safe to apply or use them otherwise: but in other cases it is bare impropriety of speech to apply them contrary to the common usage of the country. But yet even this too disturbs not the certainty of that knowledge, which is still to be had by a due contemplation, and comparing of those even nick-named ideas.

Thirdly, there is another sort of complex ideas, which being referred to archetypes without us, may differ from them, and so our knowledge about them may come short of being real. Such are our ideas of substances, which consisting of a collection of simple ideas, supposed taken from the works of nature, may yet vary from them, by having more or different ideas united in them, than are to be found united in the things themselves. From whence it comes to pass, that they may, and often do, fail of being exactly conformable to things themselves.

I say then, that to have ideas of substances, which, by being conformable to things, may afford us real knowledge, it is not enough, as in modes, to put together such ideas as have no inconsistence, though they did never before so exist; v. g. the ideas of sacrilege or perjury, &c. were as real and true ideas before, as after the existence of any such fact. But our ideas of substances being supposed copies, and referred to archetypes without us, must still be taken from something that does or has existed; they must not consist of ideas put together at the pleasure of our thoughts, without any real pattern they were taken from, though we can perceive no inconsistence in such a combination. The reason whereof is, because we knowing not what real constitution it is of substances, whereon our simple ideas depend, and which really is the cause of the strict union of some of them one with another, and the exclusion of others; there are very few of them, that we can be sure are, or are not, inconsistent in nature, any farther than experience and sensible observation reach. Herein therefore is founded the reality of our knowledge concerning substances, that all our complex ideas of them must be such, and such only, as are made up of such simple ones, as have been discovered to co-exist in nature. And our ideas being thus true: though not, perhaps, very exact copies, are yet the subjects of real (as far as we have any) knowledge of them. Which (as has been already shown) will not be found to reach very far: but so far as it does, it will still be real knowledge. Whatever ideas we have, the agreement we find they have with others, will still be knowledge. If those ideas be abstract, it will be general knowledge. But, to make it real concerning substances, the ideas must be taken from the real existence of things. Whatever simple ideas have been found to co-exist in any substance, these we may with confidence join together again, and so make abstract ideas of substances. For whatever have once had an union in nature, may be united again.

This, if we rightly consider, and confine not our thoughts and abstract ideas to names, as if there were, or could be no other sorts of things than what known names had already determined, and as it were set out; we should think of things with greater freedom and less confusion than perhaps we do. It would possibly be thought a bold paradox, if not a very dangerous falsehood, if I should say, that some changelings, who have lived forty years together without any appearance of reason, are something between a man and a beast: which prejudice is founded upon nothing else but a false supposition, that these two names, man and beast, stand for distinct species so set out by real essences, that there can come no other species between them: whereas if we will abstract from those names, and the supposition of such specifick essences made by nature, wherein all things of the same denominations did exactly and equally partake; if we would not fancy that there were a certain number of these essences, wherein all things, as in moulds, were cast and formed; we should find that the idea of the shape, motion, and life of a man without reason, is as much a distinct idea, and makes as much a distinct sort of things from man and beast, as the idea of the shape of an ass with reason would be different from either that of man or beast, and be a species of an animal between, or distinct from both.

Here every body will be ready to ask, If changelings may be supposed something between man and beast, pray what are they? I answer, changelings, which is as good a word to signify something different from the signification of man or beast, as the names man and beast are to have significations different one from the other. This, well considered, would resolve this matter, and show my meaning without any more ado. But I am not so unacquainted with the zeal of some men, which enables them to spin consequences, and to see religion threatened whenever any one ventures to quit their forms of speaking; as not to foresee what names such a proposition as this is like to be charged with: and without doubt it will be asked, If changelings are something between man and beast, what will become of them in the other world? To which I answer, 1. It concerns me not to know or inquire. To their own master they stand or fall. It will make their state neither better nor worse, whether we determine any thing of it or no. They are in the hands of a faithful creator and a bountiful father, who disposes not of his creatures according to our narrow thoughts or opinions, nor distinguishes them according to names and species of our contrivance. And we that know so little of this present world we are in, may, I think, content ourselves without being peremptory in defining the different states, which creatures shall come into when they go off this stage. It may suffice us, that he hath made known to all those, who are capable of instruction, discoursing, and reasoning, that they shall come to an account, and receive according to what they have done in this body.

But, secondly, I answer, the force of these men's question (viz. will you deprive changelings of a future state?) is founded on one of these two suppositions, which are both false. The first is, that all things that have the outward shape and appearance of a man must necessarily be designed to an immortal future being after this life: or, secondly, that whatever is of human birth must be so. Take away these imaginations, and such questions will be groundless and ridiculous. I desire then those who think there is no more but an accidental difference between themselves and changelings, the essence in both being exactly the same, to consider whether they can imagine immortality annexed to any outward shape of the body? the very proposing it, is, I suppose, enough to make them disown it. No one yet, that ever I heard of, how much soever immersed in matter, allowed that excellency to any figure of the gross sensible outward parts, as to affirm eternal life due to it, or a necessary consequence of it; or that any mass of matter should, after its dissolution here, be again restored hereafter to an everlasting state of sense, perception, and knowledge, only because it was moulded into this or that figure, and had such a particular frame of its visible parts. Such an opinion as this, placing immortality in a certain superficial figure, turns out of doors all consideration of soul or spirit, upon whose account alone some corporeal beings have hitherto been concluded immortal, and others not. This is to attribute more to the outside than inside of things; and to place the excellency of a man more in the external shape of his body, than internal perfections of his soul: which is but little better than to annex the great and inestimable advantage of immortality and life everlasting, which he has above other material beings, to annex it, I say, to the cut of his beard, or the fashion of his coat. For this or that outward mark of our bodies no more carries with it the hope of an eternal duration, than the fashion of a man's suit gives him reasonable grounds to imagine it will never wear out, or that it will make him immortal. It will perhaps be said, that no-body thinks that the shape makes any thing immortal, but it is the shape is the sign of a rational soul within, which is immortal. I wonder who made it the sign of any such thing: for barely saying it, will not make it so. It would require some proofs to persuade one of it. No figure that I know speaks any such language. For it may as rationally be concluded, that the dead body of a man, wherein there is to be found no more appearance or action of life than there is in a statue, has yet nevertheless a living soul in it because of its shape; as that there is a rational soul in a changeling, because he has the outside of a rational creature; when his actions carry far less marks of reason with them, in the whole course of his life, than what are to be found in many a beast.

But it is the issue of rational parents, and must therefore be concluded to have a rational soul. I know not by what logick you must so conclude. I am sure this is a conclusion, that men no where allow of. For if they did, they would not make bold, as every where they do, to destroy ill-formed and mis-shaped productions. Ay, but these are monsters. Let them be so; what will your driveling, unintelligent, intractable changeling be? Shall a defect in the body make a monster; a defect in the mind (the far more noble, and in the common phrase, the far more essential part) not? Shall the want of a nose, or a neck, make a monster, and put such issue out of the rank of men; the want of reason and understanding, not? This is to bring all back again to what was exploded just now: this is to place all in the shape, and to take the measure of a man only by his outside. To show that, according to the ordinary way of reasoning in this matter, people do lay the whole stress on the figure, and resolve the whole essence of the species of man (as they make it) into the outward shape, how unreasonable soever it be, and how much soever they disown it; we need but trace their thoughts and practice a little farther, and then it will plainly appear. The well-shaped changeling is a man, has a rational soul, though it appear not; this is past doubt, say you. Make the ears a little longer, and more pointed, and the nose a little flatter than ordinary, and then you begin to boggle; make the face yet narrower, flatter and longer, and then you are at a stand: add still more and more of the likeness of a brute to it, and let the head be perfectly that of some other animal, then presently it is a monster; and it is demonstration with you that it hath no rational soul, and must be destroyed. Where now (I ask) shall be the just measure of the utmost bounds of that shape, that carries with it a rational soul? For since there have been human foetuses produced, half beast, and half man; and others three parts one, and one part the other; and so it is possible they may be in all the variety of approaches to the one or the other shape, and may have several degrees of mixture of the likeness of a man or a brute; I would gladly know what are those precise lineaments, which, according to this hypothesis, are, or are not capable of a rational soul to be joined to them. What sort of outside is the certain sign that there is, or is not such an inhabitant within? For till that be done, we talk at random of man: and shall always, I fear, do so, as long as we give ourselves up to certain sounds, and the imaginations of settled and fixed species in nature, we know not what. But after all, I desire it may be considered, that those who think they have answered the difficulty by telling us, that a mis-shaped foetus is a monster, run into the same fault they are arguing against, by constituting a species between man and beast. For what else, I pray, is their monster in the case (if the word monster signifies any thing at all) but something neither man nor beast, but partaking somewhat of either? And just so is the changeling before-mentioned. So necessary is it to quit the common notion of species and essences, if we will truly look into the nature of things, and examine them, by what our faculties can discover in them as they exist, and not by groundless fancies, that have been taken up about them.

I have mentioned this here, because I think we cannot be too cautious that words and species, in the ordinary notions which we have been used to of them, impose not on us. For I am apt to think, therein lies one great obstacle to our clear and distinct knowledge, especially in reference to substances; and from thence has rose a great part of the difficulties about truth and certainty. Would we accustom ourselves to separate our contemplations and reasonings from words, we might, in a great measure, remedy this inconvenience within our own thoughts; but yet it would still disturb us in our discourse with others, as long as we retained the opinion, that species and their essences were any thing else but our abstract ideas (such as they are) with names annexed to them, to be the signs of them.

Wherever we perceive the agreement or disagreement of any of our ideas, there is certain knowledge: and wherever we are sure those ideas agree with the reality of things, there is certain real knowledge. Of which agreement of our ideas, with the reality of things, having here given the marks, I think I have shown wherein it is, that certainty, real certainty, consists: which, whatever it was to others, was, I confess, to me heretofore, one of those desiderata which I found great want of.

Deductive knowledge and real essence

In his account of human knowledge, Locke speaks of scientific knowledge as limited to experience and experiment. He also discusses demonstration. There lurks behind his remarks about the limitation of knowledge another kind of knowledge of what there is: a deductive or demonstrative knowledge of nature. This knowledge is not attainable by men because we cannot discover the real essence, the inner constitution, of objects on which the observable properties depend. Locke's account of real essence, and of the nominal essence that we must rely upon instead, is a reaction to an older doctrine of fixed, natural kinds (real classes) of things.

11. *Essay,* 2.31.6

What ideas we have of substances, I have above showed. Now those ideas have in the mind a double reference: 1. Sometimes they are referred to a supposed real essence of each species of things. 2. Sometimes they are only designed to be pictures and representations in the mind of things that do exist by ideas of those qualities that are discoverable in them. In both which ways, these copies of those originals and archetypes are imperfect and inadequate.

First, it is usual for men to make the names of substances stand for things, as supposed to have certain real essences, whereby they are of this or that species: and names standing for nothing but the ideas that are in men's minds, they must constantly refer their ideas to such real essences, as to their archetypes. That men (especially such as have been bred up in the learning taught in this part of the world) do suppose certain specific essences of substances, which each individual, in its several kinds, is made conformable to, and partakes of; is so far from needing proof, that it will be thought strange if any one should do otherwise. And thus they ordinarily apply the specific names they rank particular substances under to things, as distinguished by such specific real essences. Who is there almost, who would not take it amiss, if it should be doubted, whether he called himself a man, with any other meaning, than as having the real essence of a man? And yet if you demand what those real essences are, it is plain men are ignorant, and know them not. From whence it follows, that the ideas they have in their minds, being referred to real essences, as to archetypes which are unknown, must be so far from being adequate, that they cannot be supposed to be any representation of them at all. The complex ideas we have of substances are, as it has been shown, certain collections of simple ideas that have been observed or supposed constantly to exist together. But such a complex idea cannot be the real essence of any substance; for then the properties we discover in that body would depend on that complex idea, and be deducible from it, and their necessary connection with it be known; as all properties of a triangle depend on, and, as far as they are discoverable, are deducible from the complex idea of three lines, including a space. But it is plain, that in our complex ideas of substances are not contained such ideas, on which all the other qualities, that are to be found in them, do depend. The common idea men have of iron, is a body of a certain colour, weight and hardness; and a property that they look on as belonging to it, is malleableness. But yet this property has no necessary connection with that complex idea, or any part of it; and there is no more reason to think that malleableness depends on that colour, weight, and hardness, than that colour, or that weight depends on its malleableness. And yet, though we know nothing of these real essences, there is nothing more ordinary, than that men should attribute the sorts of things to such essences. The particular parcel of matter, which makes the ring I have on my finger, is forwardly, by most men, supposed to have a real essence, whereby it is gold; and from whence those qualities flow, which I find in it, viz. its peculiar colour, weight, hardness, fusibility, fixedness, and change of colour upon a slight touch of mercury, &c. This essence, from which all these properties flow, when I inquire into it and search after it, I plainly perceive I cannot discover: the farthest I can go is only to presume, that it being nothing but body, its real essence, or internal constitution, on which these qualities depend, can be nothing but the figure, size, and connection of its solid parts; of neither of which having any distinct perception at all, can I have any idea of its essence, which is the cause that it has that particular shining yellowness, a greater weight than any thing I know of the same bulk, and a fitness to have its colour changed by the touch of quicksilver. If any one will say, that the real essence and internal constitution, on which these properties depend, is not the figure, size, and arrangement or connexion of its solid parts, but something

else, called its particular form; I am farther from having any idea
of its real essence, than I was before: for I have an idea of figure,
size, and situation of solid parts in general, though I have none of
the particular figure, size, or putting together of parts, whereby the
qualities above-mentioned are produced; which qualities I find in
that particular parcel of matter that is on my finger, and not in
another parcel of matter, with which I cut the pen I write with.
But when I am told, that something besides the figure, size, and
posture of the solid parts of that body, is its essence, something
called substantial form; of that, I confess, I have no idea at all, but
only of the sound form, which is far enough from an idea of its real
essence, or constitution. The like ignorance as I have of the real
essence of this particular substance, I have also of the real essence
of all other natural ones; of which essences, I confess, I have no
distinct ideas at all; and I am apt to suppose others, when they
examine their own knowledge, will find in themselves, in this one
point, the same sort of ignorance.

12. *Essay*, 3.6.1–9, 14–21, 28–9

The common names of substances, as well as other general terms,
stand for sorts; which is nothing else but the being made signs of
such complex ideas, wherein several particular substances do, or
might agree, by virtue of which they are capable of being comprehended in one common conception, and signified by one name.
I say, do or might agree: for though there be but one sun existing
in the world, yet the idea of it being abstracted, so that more
substances (if there were several) might each agree in it; it is as
much a sort, as if there were as many suns as there are stars. They
want not their reasons who think there are, and that each fixed
star would answer the idea the name sun stands for, to one who
was placed in a due distance; which, by the way, may show us
how much the sorts, or, if you please, genera and species of things
(for those Latin terms signify to me no more than the English word
sort) depend on such collections of ideas as men have made, and
not on the real nature of things, since it is not impossible but that, in
propriety of speech that might be a sun to one, which is a star to
another.

The measure and boundary of each sort, or species, whereby
it is constituted that particular sort, and distinguished from others,
is that we call its essence, which is nothing but that abstract idea
to which the name is annexed: so that every thing contained in
that idea is essential to that sort. This, though it be all the essence

of natural substances that we know, or by which we distinguish them into sorts; yet I call it by a peculiar name, the nominal essence, to distinguish it from the real constitution of substances, upon which depends this nominal essence, and all the properties of that sort; which therefore, as has been said, may be called the real essence: v. g. the nominal essence of gold is that complex idea the word gold stands for, let it be, for instance, a body yellow, of a certain weight, malleable, fusible, and fixed. But the real essence is the constitution of the insensible parts of that body, on which those qualities, and all the other properties of gold depend. How far these two are different, though they are both called essence, is obvious at first sight to discover.

For though perhaps voluntary motion, with sense and reason, joined to a body of a certain shape, be the complex idea to which I, and others, annex the name man, and so be the nominal essence of the species so called; yet nobody will say that complex idea is the real essence and source of all those operations which are to be found in any individual of that sort. The foundation of all those qualities, which are the ingredients of our complex idea, is something quite different; and had we such a knowledge of that constitution of man, from which his faculties of moving, sensation, and reasoning, and other powers flow, and on which his so regular shape depends, as it is possible angels have, and it is certain his Maker has; we should have a quite other idea of his essence than what now is contained in our definition of that species, be it what it will: and our idea of any individual man would be as far different from what it is now, as is his who knows all the springs and wheels, and other contrivances within, of the famous clock at Strasburgh, from that which a gazing countryman has for it, who barely sees the motion of the hand, and hears the clock strike, and observes only some of the outward appearances.

That essence, in the ordinary use of the word, relates to sorts; and that it is considered in particular beings no farther than as they are ranked into sorts; appears from hence: that take but away the abstract ideas, by which we sort individuals, and rank them under common names, and then the thought of any thing essential to any of them instantly vanishes; we have no notion of the one without the other; which plainly shows their relation. It is necessary for me to be as I am; God and nature has made me so: but there is nothing I have is essential to me. An accident, or disease, may very much alter my colour, or shape; a fever, or fall, may take away my reason or memory, or both, and an apoplexy leave neither sense nor understanding, no nor life. Other creatures of my shape may be made with more and better, or fewer and worse faculties than I have; and others may have reason and sense in a shape and body very different from mine. None of these are essential to the one, or the other, or to any individual whatever, till the mind refers it to some sort or species of things; and then presently, according to the abstract idea of that sort, something is found essential. Let any one examine his own thoughts, and he will find that as soon as he supposes or speaks of essential, the consideration of some species, or the complex idea, signified by some general name, comes into his mind; and it is in reference to that, that this or that quality is said to be essential. So that if it be asked, whether it be essential to me or any other particular corporeal being to have reason? I say no; no more than it is essential to this white thing I write on to have words in it. But if that particular being be to be counted of the sort man, and to have the name man given it, then reason is essential to it, supposing reason to be a part of the complex idea the name man stands for: as it is essential to this thing I write on to contain words, if I will give it the name treatise, and rank it under that species. So that essential, and not essential, relate only to our abstract ideas, and the names annexed to them; which amounts to no more but this, that whatever particular thing has not in it those qualities, which are contained in the abstract idea, which any general term stands for, cannot be ranked under that species, nor be called by that name, since that abstract idea is the very essence of that species.

Thus if the idea of body, with some people, be bare extension or space, then solidity is not essential to body: if others make the idea, to which they give the name body, to be solidity and extension, then solidity is essential to body. That therefore, and that alone, is considered as essential, which makes a part of the complex idea the name of a sort stands for, without which no particular thing can be reckoned of that sort, nor be intitled to that name. Should there be found a parcel of matter that had all the other qualities that are in iron, but wanted obedience to the loadstone; and would neither be drawn by it, nor receive direction from it; would any one question, whether it wanted any thing essential? It would be absurd to ask, Whether a thing really existing wanted any thing essential to it? Or could it be demanded, Whether this made an essential or specific difference or no; since we have no other measure of essential or specific but our abstract ideas? And to talk of specific differences in nature, without reference to general ideas and names, is to talk unintelligibly. For I would ask any one, What is sufficient to make an essential difference in nature, between any two particular beings, without any regard had to some abstract idea, which is looked upon as the essence and standard of a species? All such patterns and standards being quite laid aside, particular beings, considered barely in themselves, will be found to have all their qualities equally essential; and every thing, in each individual, will be essential to it, or, which is more, nothing at all. For though it may be reasonable to ask, Whether obeying the magnet be essential to iron? yet, I think, it is very improper and insignificant to ask, Whether it be essential to the particular parcel of matter I cut my pen with, without considering it under the name iron, or as being of a certain species? And if, as has been said, our abstract ideas, which have names annexed to them, are the boundaries of species, nothing can be essential but what is contained in those ideas.

It is true, I have often mentioned a real essence, distinct in substances from those abstract ideas of them, which I call their nominal essence. By this real essence I mean the real constitution of anything, which is the foundation of all those properties that are combined in, and are constantly found to co-exist with the nominal essence; that particular constitution which every thing has within itself, without any relation to any thing without it. But essence, even in this sense, relates to a sort, and supposes a species; for being that real constitution, on which the properties depend, it necessarily supposes a sort of things, properties belonging only to species, and not to individuals; v. g. supposing the nominal essence of gold to be a body of such a peculiar colour and weight, with malleability and fusibility, the real essence is that constitution of the parts of matter, on which these qualities and their union depend; and is also the foundation of its solubility in aqua regia and other properties accompanying that complex idea. Here are essences and properties, but all upon supposition of a sort, or general abstract idea, which is considered as immutable; but there is no individual parcel of matter, to which any of these qualities are so annexed, as to be essential to it, or inseparable from it. That which is essential belongs to it as a condition, whereby it is of this or that sort; but take away the consideration of its being ranked under the name of some abstract idea, and then there is nothing necessary to it, nothing inseparable from it. Indeed, as to the real essences of substances, we only suppose their being, without precisely knowing what they are: but that which annexes them still to the species, is the nominal essence, of which they are the supposed foundation and cause.

The next thing to be considered, is, by which of those essences it is that substances are determined into sorts, or species; and that, it is evident, is by the nominal essence. For it is that alone that the name, which is the mark of the sort, signifies. It is impossible therefore that any thing should determine the sorts of things, which we rank under general names, but that idea which that name is designed as a mark for; which is that, as has been shown, which we call nominal essence. Why do we say, this is a horse, that a mule; this is an animal, that an herb? How comes any particular thing to be of this or that sort, but because it has that nominal essence, or, which is all one, agrees to that abstract idea that name is annexed to? And I desire any one but to reflect on his own thoughts, when he hears or speaks any of those, or other names of substances, to know what sort of essences they stand for.

And that the species of things to us are nothing but the ranking them under distinct names, according to the complex ideas in us, and not according to precise, distinct, real essences in them; is plain from hence, that we find many of the individuals that are ranked into one sort, called by one common name, and so received as being of one species, have yet qualities depending on their real constitutions, as far different one from another, as from others, from which they are accounted to differ specifically. This, as it is easy to be observed by all who have to do with natural bodies; so chemists especially are often, by sad experience, convinced of it, when they, sometimes in vain, seek for the same qualities in one parcel of sulphur, antimony, or vitriol, which they have found in others. For though they are bodies of the same species, having the same nominal essence, under the same name; yet do they often, upon severe ways of examination, betray qualities so different one from another, as to frustrate the expectation and labour of very wary chemists. But if things were distinguished into species, according to their real essences, it would be as impossible to find different properties in any two individual substances of the same species, as it is to find different properties in two circles, or two equilateral triangles. That is properly the essence to us, which determines every particular to this or that *classis*; or, which is the same thing, to this or that general name: and what can that be else, but that abstract idea, to which that name is annexed? and so has, in truth, a reference, not so much to the being of particular things, as to their general denominations.

Nor indeed can we rank and sort things, and consequently (which is the end of sorting) denominate them by their real essences, because we know them not. Our faculties carry us no farther towards the knowledge and distinction of substances, than a collection of those sensible ideas which we observe in them; which, however made with the greatest diligence and exactness we are capable of, yet is more remote from the true internal constitution, from which those qualities flow, than, as I said, a countryman's idea is from the inward contrivance of that famous clock at Strasburgh, whereof he only sees the outward figure and motions. There is not so contemptible a plant or animal, that does not confound the most enlarged understanding. Though the familiar use of things about us take off our wonder; yet it cures not our ignorance. When we come to examine the stones we tread on, or the iron we daily handle, we presently find we know not their make, and can give no reason of the different qualities we find in them. It is evident the internal constitution, whereon their properties depend, is unknown to us. For to go no farther than the grossest and most obvious we can imagine amongst them, what is that texture of parts, that real essence, that makes lead and antimony fusible; wood and stones not? What makes lead and iron malleable, antimony and stones not? And yet how infinitely these come short of the fine contrivances, and unconceivable real essences of plants or animals, every one knows. The workmanship of the all-wise and powerful God, in the great fabric of the universe, and every part thereof, farther exceeds the capacity and comprehension of the most inquisitive and intelligent man, than the best contrivance of the most ingenious man doth the conceptions of the most ignorant of rational creatures. Therefore we in vain pretend to range things into sorts, and dispose them into certain classes, under names, by their real essences, that are so far from our discovery or comprehension. A blind man may as soon sort things by their colours, and he that has lost his smell, as well distinguish a lily and a rose by their odours, as by those internal constitutions which he knows not. He that thinks he can distinguish sheep and goats by their real essences, that are unknown to him, may be pleased to try his skill in those species, called cassiowary and querechinchio; and by their internal real essences determine the boundaries of those species, without knowing the complex idea of sensible qualities, that each of those names stand for, in the countries where those animals are to be found.

To distinguish substantial beings into species, according to the usual supposition, that there are certain precise essences or forms of things, whereby all the individuals existing are by nature distinguished into species, these things are necessary:

First, To be assured that nature, in the production of things, always designs them to partake of certain regulated established essences, which are to be the models of all things to be produced. This, in that crude sense it is usually proposed, would need some better explication before it can fully be assented to.

Secondly, It would be necessary to know whether nature always attains that essence it designs in the production of things. The irregular and monstrous births, that in divers sorts of animals have been observed, will always give us reason to doubt of one or both of these.

Thirdly, It ought to be determined whether those we call monsters be really a distinct species, according to the scholastic notion of the word species; since it is certain, that every thing that exists has its particular constitution: and yet we find that some of these monstrous productions have few or none of those qualities, which are supposed to result from, and accompany the essence of that species, from whence they derive their originals, and to which, by their descent, they seem to belong.

Fourthly, The real essences of those things, which we distinguish into species, and as so distinguished we name, ought to be known; i.e. we ought to have ideas of them. But since we are ignorant in these four points, the supposed real essences of things stand us not in stead for the distinguishing substances into species.

Fifthly, The only imaginable help in this case would be, that having framed perfect complex ideas of the properties of things, flowing from their different real essences, we should thereby distinguish them into species. But neither can this be done; for being ignorant of the real essence itself, it is impossible to know all those properties that flow from it, and are so annexed to it, that any one of them being away, we may certainly conclude, that that essence is not there, and so the thing is not of that species. We can never know what is the precise number of properties depending on the real essence of gold, any one of which failing, the real essence of gold, and consequently gold, would not be there, unless we knew the real essence of gold itself, and by that determined that species. By the word gold here, I must be understood to design a particular piece of matter; v. g. the last guinea that was coined. For if it should stand here in its ordinary signification for that complex idea, which I or any one else calls gold; i. e. for the nominal essence of gold, it would be jargon: so hard is it to show the various meaning and imperfection of words, when we have nothing else but words to do it by.

By all which it is clear, that our distinguishing substances into species by names, is not at all founded on their real essences; nor can we pretend to range and determine them exactly into species, according to internal essential differences.

But since, as has been remarked, we have need of general words, though we know not the real essences of things; all we can do is to collect such a number of simple ideas, as by examination we find to be united together in things existing, and thereof to make one complex idea: which, though it be not the real essence of any substance that exists, is yet the specific essence, to which our name belongs, and is convertible with it; by which we may at least try the truth of these nominal essences. For example, there be that say, that the essence of body is extension: if it be so, we can never mistake in putting the essence of any thing for the thing itself. Let us then in discourse put extension for body; and when we would say that body moves, let us say that extension moves, and see how ill it will look. He that should say that one extension by impulse moves another extension, would, by the bare expression, sufficiently show the absurdity of such a notion. The essence of anything, in respect of us, is the whole complex idea, comprehended and marked by that name; and in substances, besides the several distinct simple ideas that make them up, the confused one of substance, or of an unknown support and cause of their union, is always a part: and therefore the essence of body is not bare extension, but an extended solid thing; and so to say an extended solid thing moves, or impels another, is all one, and as intelligible as to say, body moves or impels. Likewise to say, that a rational animal is capable of conversation, is all one as to say a man. But no one will say, that rationality is capable of conversation, because it makes not the whole essence to which we give the name man.

But though these nominal essences of substances are made by the mind, they are not yet made so arbitrarily as those of mixed modes. To the making of any nominal essence, it is necessary, First, that the ideas whereof it consists have such an union as to make but one idea, how compounded soever. Secondly, that the particular idea so united be exactly the same, neither more nor less. For if two abstract complex ideas differ either in number or sorts of their component parts, they make two different, and not one and the same essence. In the first of these, the mind, in making its complex ideas of substances, only follows nature; and puts none together, which are not supposed to have an union in nature. Nobody joins the voice of a sheep with the shape of a horse; nor the colour of lead, with the weight and fixedness of gold; to be the complex ideas of any real substances: unless he has a mind to fill his head with chimeras, and his discourse with unintelligible words. Men observing certain qualities always joined and existing together, therein copied nature; and of ideas so united, made their complex ones of substances. For though men may make what complex ideas they please, and give what names to them they will; yet if they will be understood, when they speak of things really existing, they must in some degree conform their ideas to the things they would speak of: or else men's language will be like that of Babel; and every man's words being intelligible only to himself, would no longer serve to conversation, and the ordinary affairs of life, if the ideas they stand for be not some way answering the common appearances and agreement of substances, as they really exist.

Secondly, though the mind of man, in making its complex ideas of substances, never puts any together that do not really or are not supposed to co-exist; and so it truly borrows that union from nature: yet the number it combines depends upon the various care, industry, or fancy of him that makes it. Men generally content themselves with some few sensible obvious qualities; and often, if not always, leave out others as material, and as firmly united, as those that they take. Of sensible substances there are two sorts; one of organized bodies, which are propagated by seed; and in these, the shape is that, which to us is the leading quality and most characteristical part that determines the species. And therefore in vegetables and animals, an extended solid substance of such a certain figure usually serves the turn. For however some men seem to prize their definition of "animal rationale," yet should there a creature be found, that had language and reason, but partook not of the usual shape of a man, I believe it would hardly pass for a man, how much soever it were "animal rationale." And if Balaam's ass had, all his life, discoursed as rationally as he did once with his master, I doubt yet whether any one would have thought him worthy the name man, or allowed him to be of the same species with himself. As in vegetables and animals it is the shape, so in most other bodies, not propagated by seed, it is the colour we most fix on, and are most led by. Thus where we find the colour of gold, we are apt to imagine all the other qualities, comprehended in our complex idea, to be there also: and we commonly take these two

obvious qualities, viz. shape and colour, for so presumptive ideas of
several species, that in a good picture we readily say this is a lion,
and that a rose; this is a gold, and that a silver goblet, only by the
different figures and colours represented to the eye by the pencil.

13. *Essay,* 4.3.10–29
This, how weighty and considerable a part soever of human science,
is yet very narrow, and scarce any at all. The reason whereof is,
that the simple ideas, whereof our complex ideas of substances are
made up, are, for the most part, such as carry with them in their
own nature, no visible necessary connexion or inconsistency with
any other simple ideas, whose co-existence with them we would
inform ourselves about.

The ideas that our complex ones of substances are made up of,
and about which our knowledge concerning substances is most
employed, are those of their secondary qualities: which depending
all (as has been shown) upon the primary qualities of their minute
and insensible parts; or if not upon them, upon something yet more
remote from our comprehension; it is impossible we should know
which have a necessary union or inconsistency one with another:
for not knowing the root they spring from, not knowing what size,
figure, and texture of parts they are, on which depend, and from
which result, those qualities which make our complex idea of gold;
it is impossible we should know what other qualities result from,
or are incompatible with, the same constitution of the insensible
parts of gold, and so consequently must always co-exist with that
complex idea we have of it, or else are inconsistent with it.

Besides this ignorance of the primary qualities of the insensible
parts of bodies, on which depend all their secondary qualities, there
is yet another and more incurable part of ignorance, which sets us
more remote from a certain knowledge of the co-existence or in-
co-existence (if I may so say) of different ideas in the same subject; and that is that there is no discoverable connexion between
any secondary quality and those primary qualities that it depends
on.

That the size, figure, and motion of one body should cause a
change in the size, figure, and motion of another body is not beyond
our conception; the separation of the parts of one body upon the
intrusion of another, and the change from rest to motion upon
impulse; these, and the like, seem to us to have some connexion
one with another. And if we knew these primary qualities of bodies,
we might have reason to hope we might be able to know a great

deal more of these operations of them one with another: but our minds not being able to discover any connexion betwixt these primary qualities of bodies and the sensations that are produced in us by them, we can never be able to establish certain and undoubted rules of the consequences or co-existence of any secondary qualities, though we could discover the size, figure, or motion of those invisible parts which immediately produce them. We are so far from knowing what figure, size, or motion of parts produce a yellow colour, a sweet taste, or a sharp sound, that we can by no means conceive how any size, figure, or motion of any particles, can possibly produce in us the idea of any colour, taste, or sound whatsoever; there is no conceivable connexion betwixt the one and the other.

In vain, therefore shall we endeavour to discover by our ideas (the only true way of certain and universal knowledge) what other ideas are to be found constantly joined with that of our complex idea of any substance: since we neither know the real constitution of the minute parts on which their qualities do depend; nor, did we know them, could we discover any necessary connexion between them and any of the secondary qualities; which is necessary to be done before we can certainly know their necessary co-existence. So that let our complex idea of any species of substances be what it will, we can hardly, from the simple ideas contained in it, certainly determine the necessary co-existence of any other quality whatsoever. Our knowledge in all these inquiries reaches very little farther than our experience. Indeed, some few of the primary qualities have a necessary dependence and visible connexion one with another, as figure necessarily supposes extension: receiving or communicating motion by impulse, supposes solidity. But though these and perhaps some other of our ideas have, yet there are so few of them, that have a visible connexion one with another, that we can by intuition or demonstration discover the co-existence of very few of the qualities are to be found united in substances: and we are left only to the assistance of our senses, to make known to us what qualities they contain. For of all the qualities that are co-existent in any subject, without this dependence and evident connexion of their ideas one with another, we cannot know certainly any two to co-exist any farther than experience, by our senses, informs us. Thus though we see the yellow colour, and upon trial find the weight, malleableness, fusibility, and fixedness, that are united in a piece of gold; yet because no one of these ideas has any evident dependence, or necessary connexion with the other, we cannot certainly know, that where any four of these are, the fifth will be there also, how highly probable soever it may be; because the highest probability amounts not to certainty, without which there can be no true knowledge. For this co-existence can be no farther known than it is perceived; and it cannot be perceived but either in particular subjects, by the observation of our senses, or, in general, by the necessary connexion of the ideas themselves.

As to the incompatibility or repugnancy to co-existence we may know, that any subject may have of each sort of primary qualities but one particular at once; v. g. each particular extension, figure, number of parts, motion, excludes all other of each kind. The like also is certain of all sensible ideas peculiar to each sense; for whatever of each kind is present in any subject, excludes all other of that sort; v. g. no one subject can have two smells or two colours at the same time. To this perhaps will be said, Has not an opal, or the infusion of lignum nephriticum, two colours at the same time? To which I answer, that these bodies, to eyes differently placed, may at the same time afford different colours: but I take liberty also to say, that to eyes differently placed, it is different parts of the object that reflect the particles of light: and therefore it is not the same part of the object, and so not the very same subject, which at the same time appears both yellow and azure. For it is as impossible that the very same particle of any body should at the same time differently modify or reflect the rays of light, as that it should have two different figures and textures at the same time.

But as to the powers of substances to change the sensible qualities of other bodies, which make a great part of our inquiries about them, and is no inconsiderable branch of our knowledge; I doubt, as to these, whether our knowledge reaches much farther than our experience; or whether we can come to the discovery of most of these powers, and be certain that they are in any subject, by the connexion with any of those ideas which to us make its essence. Because the active and passive powers of bodies, and their ways of operating, consisting in a texture and motion of parts, which we cannot by any means come to discover; it is but in very few cases, we can be able to perceive their dependence on, or repugnance to, any of those ideas which make our complex one of that sort of things. I have here instanced in the corpuscularian hypothesis, as that which is thought to go farthest in an intelligible explication of those qualities of bodies; and I fear the weakness of human understanding is scarce able to substitute another, which will afford us a fuller and clearer discovery of the necessary connexion and co-existence of the powers which are to be observed united in several sorts of them. This at least is certain, that whichever hypothesis be clearest and truest, (for of that it is not my business to determine) our knowledge concerning corporeal substances will be very little advanced by any of them, till we are made to see what qualities and powers of bodies have a necessary connexion or repugnancy one with another; which in the present state of philosophy, I think, we know but to a very small degree: and I doubt whether, with those faculties we have, we shall ever be able to carry our general knowledge (I say not particular experience) in this part much farther. Experience is that which in this part we must depend on. And it were to be wished that it were more improved. We find the advantages some men's generous pains have this way brought to the stock of natural knowledge. And if others, especially the philosophers by fire, who pretend to it, had been so wary in their observations, and sincere in their reports, as those who call themselves philosophers ought to have been; our acquaintance with the bodies here about us, and our insight into their powers and operations, had been yet much greater.

If we are at a loss in respect of the powers and operations of bodies, I think it is easy to conclude, we are much more in the dark in reference to the spirits; whereof we naturally have no ideas, but what we draw from that of our own, by reflecting on the operations of our own souls within us, as far as they can come within our observation. But how inconsiderable a rank the spirits that inhabit our bodies hold amongst those various and possible innumerable kinds of nobler beings; and how far short they come of the endowments and perfections of cherubims and seraphims, and infinite sorts of spirits above us; is what by a transient hint, in another place, I have offered to my reader's consideration.

As to the third sort of our knowledge, viz. the agreement or disagreement of any of our ideas in any other relation: this, as it is the largest field of our knowledge, so it is hard to determine how far it may extend; because the advances that are made in this part of knowledge, depending on our sagacity in finding intermediate ideas, that may show the relations and habitudes of ideas, whose co-existence is not considered, it is a hard matter to tell when we are at an end of such discoveries; and when reason has all the helps it is capable of, for the finding of proofs, or examining the agreement or disagreement of remote ideas. They that are ignorant of algebra cannot imagine the wonders in this kind are to be done by it: and what farther improvements and helps, advantageous to other parts of knowledge, the sagacious mind of man may yet find out, it is not easy to determine. This at least I believe, that the ideas of quantity are not those alone that are capable of demonstration and knowledge; and that other, and perhaps more useful parts of contemplation, would afford us certainty, if vices, passions, and domineering interest did not oppose or menace such endeavours.

The idea of a supreme being, infinite in power, goodness, and wisdom, whose workmanship we are, and on whom we depend; and the idea of ourselves, as understanding rational beings, being such as are clear in us, would, I suppose, if duly considered and pursued, afford such foundations of our duty and rules of action, as might place morality amongst the sciences capable of demonstration: wherein I doubt not but from self-evident propositions, by necessary consequences, as incontestable as those in mathematicks, the measures of right and wrong might be made out to any one that will apply himself with the same indifferency and attention to the one, as he does to the other of these sciences. The relation of other modes may certainly be perceived, as well as those of number and extension: and I cannot see why they should not also be capable of demonstration, if due methods were thought on to examine or pursue their agreement or disagreement. Where there is no property, there is no injustice, is a proposition as certain as any demonstration in Euclid: for the idea of property being a right to any thing; and the idea to which the name injustice is given, being the invasion or violation of that right; it is evident, that these ideas being thus established, and these names annexed to them, I can as certainly know this proposition to be true, as that a triangle has three angles equal to two right ones. Again, "no government allows absolute liberty." The idea of government being the establishment of society upon certain rules or laws which require conformity to them; and the idea of absolute liberty being for any one to do whatever he pleases; I am as capable of being certain of the truth of this proposition, as of any in the mathematicks.

That which in this respect has given the advantage to the ideas of quantity, and made them thought more capable of certainty and demonstration, is,

First, that they can be set down and represented by sensible marks, which have a greater and nearer correspondence with them than any words or sounds whatsoever. Diagrams drawn on paper are copies of the ideas in the mind, and not liable to the uncertainty that words carry in their signification. An angle, circle, or square, drawn in lines, lies open to the view, and cannot be mistaken: it remains unchangeable, and may at leisure be considered and examined, and the demonstration be revised, and all the parts of it may be gone over more than once without any danger of the least change in the ideas. This cannot be thus done in moral ideas, we have no sensible marks that resemble them, whereby we can set them down; we have nothing but words to express them by: which though, when written, they remain the same, yet the ideas they stand for may change in the same man; and it is very seldom that they are not different in different persons.

Secondly, another thing that makes the greater difficulty in ethicks, is, that moral ideas are commonly more complex than those of the figures ordinarily considered in mathematicks. From whence these two inconveniences follow: First, that their names are of more uncertain signification, the precise collection of simple ideas they stand for not being so easily agreed on, and so the sign that is used for them in communication always, and in thinking often, does not steadily carry with it the same idea. Upon which the same disorder, confusion and error follow, as would if a man, going to demonstrate something of an heptagon, should, in the diagram he took to do it, leave out one of the angles, or by oversight make the figure with one angle more than the name ordinarily imported, or he intended it should, when at first he thought of his demonstration. This often happens, and is hardly avoidable in very complex moral ideas, where the same name being retained, one angle, i. e. one simple idea is left out or put in the complex one, (still called by the same name) more at one time than another. Secondly, from the complexedness of these moral ideas, there follows another inconvenience, viz. that the mind cannot easily retain those precise combinations, so exactly and perfectly as is necessary in the examination of the habitudes and correspondencies, agreements or disagreements, of several of them one with another; especially where it is to be judged of by long deductions, and the intervention of several other complex ideas, to show the agreement or disagreement of two remote ones.

The great help against this which mathematicians find in diagrams and figures, which remain unalterable in their draughts, is very apparent, and the memory would often have great difficulty otherwise to retain them so exactly, whilst the mind went over the parts of them step by step, to examine their several correspondencies. And though in casting up a long sum either in addition, multiplication, or division, every part be only a progression of the mind, taking a view of its own ideas, and considering their agreement or disagreement; and the resolution of the question be nothing but the result of the whole, made up of such particulars, whereof the mind has a clear perception: yet without setting down the several parts by marks, whose precise significations are known, and by marks that last and remain in view when the memory had let them go, it would be almost impossible to carry so many different ideas in the mind, without confounding or letting slip some parts of the reckoning, and thereby making all our reasonings about it useless. In which case, the cyphers or marks help not the mind at all to perceive the agreement of any two or more numbers, their equalities or proportions: that the mind has only by intuition of its own ideas of the numbers themselves. But the numerical characters are helps to the memory, to record and retain the several ideas about which the demonstration is made, whereby a man may know how far his intuitive knowledge, in surveying several of the particulars has proceeded; that so he may without confusion go on to what is yet unknown, and at last have in one view before him the result of all his perceptions and reasonings.

One part of these disadvantages in moral ideas, which has made them be thought not capable of demonstration, may in a good measure be remedied by definitions, setting down that collection of simple ideas, which every term shall stand for, and then using the terms steadily and constantly for that precise collection. And what methods algebra, or something of that kind, may hereafter suggest, to remove the other difficulties, it is not easy to foretel. Confident I am, that if men would, in the same method, and with the same indifferency, search after moral, as they do mathematical truths, they would find them have a stronger connexion one with another, and a more necessary consequence from our clear and distinct ideas, and to come nearer perfect demonstration than is commonly imagined. But much of this is not to be expected, whilst the desire of esteem, riches, or power, makes men espouse the well-endowed opinions in fashion, and then seek arguments either to make good their beauty, or varnish over and cover their deformity: nothing being so beautiful to the eye, as truth is to the mind; nothing so deformed and irreconcileable to the understanding as a lye. For though many a man can with satisfaction enough own a no very handsome wife in his bosom; yet who is bold enough openly to avow, that he has espoused a falsehood, and received into his breast so ugly a thing as a lye? Whilst the parties of men cram their tenets down all men's throats, whom they can get into their power, without permitting them to examine their truth or falsehood, and will not let truth have fair play in the world, nor men the liberty to search after it; what improvements can be expected of this kind? What greater light can be hoped for in the moral sciences? The subject part of mankind in most places might, instead thereof, with *Egyptian* bondage expect *Egyptian* darkness, were not the candle of the Lord set up by himself in men's minds, which it is impossible for the breath or power of man wholly to extinguish.

As to the fourth sort of our knowledge, viz. of the real actual existence of things, we have an intuitive knowledge of our own existence; and a demonstrative knowledge of the existence of a God; of the existence of any thing else, we have no other but a sensitive knowledge, which extends not beyond the objects present to our senses.

Our knowledge being so narrow, as I have showed, it will perhaps give us some light into the present state of our minds, if we look a little into the dark side, and take a view of our ignorance; which, being infinitely larger than our knowledge, may serve much to the quieting of disputes, and improvement of useful knowledge; if discovering how far we have clear and distinct ideas, we confine our thoughts within the contemplation of those things that are within the reach of our understandings, and launch not out into that abyss of darkness (where we have not eyes to see, nor faculties to perceive any thing) out of a presumption, that nothing is beyond our comprehension. But to be satisfied of the folly of such a conceit, we need not go far. He that knows any thing, knows this in the first place, that he need not seek long for instances of his ignorance. The meanest and most obvious things that come in our way have dark sides, that the quickest sight cannot penetrate into. The clearest and most enlarged understandings of thinking men find themselves puzzled, and at a loss, in every particle of matter. We shall the less wonder to find it so, when we consider the causes of our ignorance; which, from what has been said, I suppose, will be found to be these three:

First, want of ideas.

Secondly, want of a discoverable connexion between the ideas we have.

Thirdly, want of tracing and examining our ideas.

First, there are some things, and those not a few, that we are ignorant of, for want of ideas.

First; all the simple ideas we have, are confined (as I have shown) to those we receive from corporeal objects by sensation, and from the operations of our own minds as the objects of reflection. But how much these few and narrow inlets are disproportionate to the vast whole extent of all beings, will not be hard to persuade those, who are not so foolish as to think their span the measure of all things. What other simple ideas it is possible the creatures in other parts of the universe may have, by the assistance of senses and faculties more, or perfecter, than we have, or different from ours, it is not for us to determine. But to say, or think there are no such, because we conceive nothing of them, is no better an argument, than if a blind man should be positive in it, that there was no such thing as sight and colours, because he had no manner of idea of any such thing, nor could by any means frame to himself any notions about seeing. The ignorance and darkness that is in us, no more hinders nor confines the knowledge that is in others, than the blindness of a mole is an argument against the quicksightedness of an eagle. He that will consider the infinite power, wisdom, and goodness of the Creator of all things, will find reason to think it was not all laid out upon so inconsiderable, mean, and impotent a creature, as he will find man to be; who, in all probability, is one of the lowest of all intellectual beings. What faculties therefore other species of creatures have, to penetrate into the nature and inmost constitutions of things; what ideas they may receive of them, far different from ours; we know not. This we know, and certainly find, that we want several other views of them, besides those we have, to make discoveries of them more perfect. And we may be convinced that the ideas we can attain to by our faculties, are very disproportionate to things themselves, when a positive, clear, distinct one of substance itself, which is the foundation of all the rest, is concealed from us. But want of ideas of this kind being a part, as well as cause of our ignorance, cannot be described. Only this, I think, I may confidently say of it, that the intellectual and sensible world are in this perfectly alike; that that part, which we see of either of them, holds no proportion with what we see not; and whatsoever we can reach with our eyes, or our thoughts, of either of them, is but a point, almost nothing in comparison of the rest.

Secondly, another great cause of ignorance is the want of ideas we are capable of. As the want of ideas, which our faculties are not able to give us, shuts us wholly from those views of things, which it is reasonable to think other beings, perfecter than we, have, of which we know nothing; so the want of ideas I now speak of keeps us in ignorance of things we conceive capable of being known to us. Bulk, figure, and motion, we have ideas of. But though we are not without ideas of these primary qualities of bodies in general, yet not knowing what is the particular bulk, figure, and motion, of the greatest part of the bodies of the universe; we are ignorant of the several powers, efficacies, and ways of operation, whereby the effects, which we daily see, are produced. These are hid from us in some things, by being too remote; and in others, by being too minute. When we consider the vast distance of the known and visible parts of the world, and the reasons we have to think, that what lies within our ken is but a small part of the universe, we shall then discover an huge abyss of ignorance. What are the particular fabricks of the great masses of matter, which make up the whole stupendous frame of corporeal beings, how far they are extended, what is their motion, and how continued or communicated, and what influence they have one upon another, are contemplations that at first glimpse our thoughts lose themselves in. If we narrow our contemplations, and confine our thoughts to this little canton, I mean this system of our sun, and the grosser masses of matter, that visibly move about it; what several sorts of vegetables, animals, and intellectual corporeal beings, infinitely different from those of our little spot of earth, may there probably be in the other planets, to the knowledge of which, even of their outward figures and parts, we can no way attain, whilst we are confined to this earth; there being no natural means, either by sensation or reflection, to convey their certain ideas into our minds? They are out of the reach of those inlets of all our knowledge: and what sorts of furniture and inhabitants those mansions contain in them, we cannot so much as guess, much less have clear and distinct ideas of them.

If a great, nay, far the greatest part of the several ranks of bodies in the universe, escape our notice by their remoteness, there are others that are no less concealed from us by their minuteness. These insensible corpuscles being the active parts of matter, and the great instruments of nature, on which depend not only all their secondary qualities, but also most of their natural operations; our want of precise distinct ideas of their primary qualities, keeps us in an incurable ignorance of what we desire to know about them. I doubt not but if we could discover the figure, size, texture, and motion of the minute constituent parts of any two bodies, we should know without trial several of their operations one upon another, as we do now the properties of a square or a triangle. Did we know the mechanical affections of the particles of rhubarb, hemlock, opium, and a man; as a watch-maker does those of a watch, whereby it performs its operations, and of a file which by rubbing on them will alter the figure of any of the wheels; we should be able to tell before-hand, that rhubarb will purge, hemlock kill, and opium make a man sleep; as well as a watch maker can, that a little piece of paper laid on the balance will keep the watch from going, till it be removed; or that, some small part of it being rubbed by a file, the machine would quite lose its motion, and the watch go no more. The dissolving of silver in aqua fortis, and gold in aqua regia and not vice versa, would be then perhaps no more difficult to know, than it is to a smith to understand why the turning of one key will open a lock, and not the turning of another. But whilst we are destitute of senses acute enough to discover the minute particles of bodies, and to give us ideas of their mechanical affections, we must be content to be ignorant of their properties and ways of operation; nor can we be assured about them any farther, than some few trials we make are able to reach. But whether they will succeed again another time, we cannot be certain. This hinders our certain knowledge of universal truths concerning natural bodies: and our reason carries us herein very little beyond particular matter of fact.

And therefore I am apt to doubt, that how far soever human industry may advance useful and experimental philosophy in physical things, scientifical will still be out of our reach; because we want perfect and adequate ideas of those very bodies which are nearest to us, and most under our command. Those which we have ranked into classes under names, and we think ourselves best acquainted with, we have but very imperfect and incomplete ideas of. Distinct ideas of the several sorts of bodies that fall under the examination of our senses perhaps we may have: but adequate ideas, I suspect, we have not of any one amongst them. And though the former of these will serve us for common use and discourse, yet whilst we want the latter, we are not capable of scientifical knowledge; nor shall ever be able to discover general, instructive, unquestionable truths concerning them. Certainty and demonstration are things we must not, in these matters, pretend to. By the colour, figure, taste, and smell, and other sensible qualities, we have as clear and distinct ideas of sage and hemlock, as we have of a circle and a triangle: but having no ideas of the particular primary qualities of the minute parts of either of these plants, nor of other bodies which we would apply them to, we cannot tell what effects they will produce; nor when we see those effects, can we so much as guess, much less know, their manner of production. Thus having no ideas of the particular mechanical affections of the minute parts of bodies that are within our view and reach, we are ignorant of their constitutions, powers, and operations: and of bodies more remote we are yet more ignorant, not knowing so much as their very outward shapes or the sensible and grosser parts of their constitutions.

This, at first, will show us how disproportionate our knowledge is to the whole extent even of material beings; to which if we add the consideration of that infinite number of spirits that may be and probably are, which are yet more remote from our knowledge, whereof we have no cognizance, nor can frame to ourselves any distinct ideas of their several ranks and sorts, we shall find this cause of ignorance conceal from us, in an impenetrable obscurity, almost the whole intellectual world; a greater certainly, and more beautiful world than the material. For bating some very few, and those, if I may so call them, superficial ideas of spirit, which by reflection we get of our own, and from thence the best we can collect of the father of all spirits, the eternal independent author of them and us and all things; we have no certain information, so much as of the existence of other spirits, but by revelation. Angels of all sorts are naturally beyond our discovery: and all those intelligences whereof it is likely there are more orders than of corporeal substances, are things whereof our natural faculties give us no certain account at all. That there are minds and thinking beings in other men as well as himself, every man has a reason, from their words and actions, to be satisfied: and the knowledge of his own mind cannot suffer a man, that considers, to be ignorant, that there is a God. But that there are degrees of spiritual beings between us and the great God, who is there that by his own search and ability can come to know? Much less have we distinct ideas of their different natures, conditions, states, powers, and several constitutions wherein they agree or differ from one another, and from us. And therefore in what concerns their different species and properties, we are under an absolute ignorance.

Secondly, what a small part of the substantial beings that are in the universe, the want of ideas leaves open to our knowledge, we have seen. In the next place, another cause of ignorance, of no less moment, is a want of a discoverable connexion between those ideas we have. For wherever we want that, we are utterly incapable of universal and certain knowledge; and are, in the former case, left only to observation and experiment: which, how narrow and confined it is, how far from general knowledge, we need not be told.

I shall give some few instances of this cause of our ignorance, and so leave it. It is evident that the bulk, figure, and motion of several bodies about us, produce in us several sensations, as of colours, sounds, tastes, smells, pleasure and pain, &c. These mechanical affections of bodies having no affinity at all with those ideas they produce in us (there being no conceivable connexion between any impulse of any sort of body and any perception of a colour or smell, which we find in our minds) we can have no distinct knowledge of such operations beyond our experience; and can reason no otherwise about them, than as effects produced by the appointment of an infinitely wise agent, which perfectly surpass our comprehensions. As the ideas of sensible secondary qualities which we have in our minds, can by us be no way deduced from bodily causes, nor any correspondence or connexion be found between them and those primary qualities which (experience shows us) produce them in us; so on the other side, the operation of our minds upon our bodies is as inconceivable. How any thought should produce a motion in body is as remote from the nature of our ideas, as how any body should produce any thought in the mind. That it is so, if experience did not convince us, the consideration of the things themselves would never be able in the least to discover to us. These, and the like, though they have a constant and regular connexion, in the ordinary course of things; yet that connexion being not discoverable in the ideas themselves, which appearing to have no necessary dependence one on another, we can attribute their connexion to nothing else but the arbitrary determination of that all-wise agent, who has made them to be, and to operate as they do, in a way wholly above our weak understandings to conceive.

In some of our ideas there are certain relations, habitudes, and connexions, so visibly included in the nature of the ideas themselves, that we cannot conceive them separable from them by any power whatsoever. And in these only we are capable of certain and universal knowledge. Thus the idea of a right-lined triangle necessarily carries with it an equality of its angles to two right ones. Nor can we conceive this relation, this connexion of these two ideas, to be possibly mutable, or to depend on any arbitrary power, which of choice made it thus, or could make it otherwise. But the coherence and continuity of the parts of matter; the production of sensation in us of colours and sounds, &c. by impulse and motion; nay, the original rules and communication of motion being such, wherein we can discover no natural connexion with any ideas we have; we cannot but ascribe them to the arbitrary will and good pleasure of the wise architect. I need not, I think, here mention the resurrection of the dead, the future state of this globe of earth, and such other things, which are by every one acknowledged to depend wholly on the determination of a free agent. The things that, as far as our observation reaches, we constantly find to proceed regularly, we may conclude do act by a law set them; but yet by a law, that we know not: whereby, though causes work steadily, and effects constantly flow from them, yet their connexions and dependencies being not discoverable in our ideas, we can have but an experimental knowledge of them. From all which it is easy to perceive what a darkness we are involved in, how little it is of being, and the things that are, that we are capable to know. And therefore we shall do no injury to our knowledge, when we modestly think with ourselves, that we are so far from being able to comprehend the whole nature of the universe, and all the things contained in it, that we are not capable of a philosophical knowledge of the bodies that are about us, and make a part of us: concerning their secondary qualities, powers, and operations, we can have no universal certainty. Several effects come every day within the notice of our senses, of which we have so far sensitive knowledge; but the causes, manner, and certainty of their production, for the two foregoing reasons, we must be content to be very ignorant of. In these we can go no farther than particular experience informs us of matter of fact, and by analogy to guess what effects the like bodies are, upon other trials, like to produce. But as to a perfect science of natural bodies (not to mention spiritual beings) we are, I think, so far from being capable of any such thing, that I conclude it lost labour to seek after it.

14. *Essay*, 4.6.9–16

As there is no discoverable connexion between fixedness and the colour, weight, and other simple ideas of that nominal essence of gold; so if we make our complex idea of gold a body yellow, fusible, ductile, weighty and fixed, we shall be at the same uncertainty concerning solubility in aqua regia, and for the same reason: since we can never, from consideration of the ideas themselves, with certainty affirm or deny of a body, whose complex idea is made up of yellow, very weighty, ductile, fusible, and fixed, that it is soluble in aqua regia; and so on, of the rest of its qualities. I would gladly meet with one general affirmation concerning any quality of gold, that any one can certainly know is true. It will, no doubt, be presently objected, is not this an universal proposition, "all gold is malleable?" To which I answer, it is a very certain proposition, if malleableness be a part of the complex idea the word gold stands for. But then here is nothing affirmed of gold, but that that sound stands for an idea in which malleableness is contained: and such a sort of truth and certainty as this, it is to say a centaur is four-footed. But if malleableness makes not a part of the specific essence the name of gold stands for, it is plain, "all gold is malleable" is not a certain proposition. Because let the complex idea of gold be made up of which soever of its other qualities you please, malleableness will not appear to depend on that complex idea, nor follow from any simple one contained in it: the connexion that malleableness has (if it has any) with those other qualities, being only by the intervention of the real constitution of its insensible parts; which, since we know not, it is impossible we should perceive that connexion, unless we could discover that which ties them together.

The more, indeed, of these co-existing qualities we unite into one complex idea, under one name, the more precise and determinate we make the signification of that word; but never yet make it thereby more capable of universal certainty, in respect of other qualities not contained in our complex idea; since we perceive not their connexion or dependence on one another, being ignorant both of that real constitution in which they are all founded, and also how they flow from it. For the chief part of our knowledge concerning substances is not, as in other things, barely of the relation of two ideas that may exist separately; but is of the necessary connexion and co-existence of several distinct ideas in the same subject, or of their repugnancy so to co-exist. Could we begin at the other end, and discover what it was, wherein that colour consisted, what made a body lighter or heavier, what texture of parts made it malleable, fusible, and fixed, and fit to be dissolved in this sort of liquor, and not in another; if (I say) we had such an idea as this of bodies, and could perceive wherein all sensible qualities originally consist, and how they are produced; we might frame such ideas of them, as would furnish us with matter of more general knowledge, and enable us to make universal propositions, that should carry general truth and certainty with them. But whilst our complex ideas of the sorts of substances are so remote from that internal real constitution, on which their sensible qualities depend, and are made up of nothing but an imperfect collection of those apparent qualities our senses can discover; there can be few general propositions concerning substances, of whose real truth we can be certainly assured: since there are but few simple ideas, of whose connexion and necessary co-existence we can have certain and undoubted knowledge. I imagine, amongst all the secondary qualities of substances, and the powers relating to them, there cannot any two be named, whose necessary co-existence, or repugnance to co-exist, can certainly be known, unless in those of the same sense, which necessarily exclude one another, as I have elsewhere showed. No one, I think, by the colour that is in any body, can certainly know what smell, taste, sound, or tangible qualities it has, nor what alterations it is capable to make or receive, on or from other bodies. The same may be said of the sound or taste, &c. Our specific names of substances standing for any collections of such ideas, it is not to be wondered, that we can with them make very few general propositions of undoubted real certainty. But yet so far as any complex idea of any sort of substances contains in it any simple idea, whose necessary co-existence with any other may be discovered, so far universal propositions may with certainty be made concerning it: v. g. could any one discover a necessary connexion between malleableness, and the colour or weight of gold, or any other part of the complex idea signified by that name, he might make a certain universal proposition concerning gold in this respect; and the real truth of this proposition, "that all gold is malleable," would be as certain as of this, "the three angles of all right-lined triangles are all equal to two right ones."

Had we such ideas of substances, as to know what real constitutions produce those sensible qualities we find in them, and how those qualities flowed from thence, we could, by the specific ideas of their real essences in our own minds, more certainly find out their properties, and discover what qualities they had or had not, than we can now by our senses: and to know the properties of gold, it would be no more necessary that gold should exist, and that we should make experiments upon it, than it is necessary for the knowing the properties of a triangle, that a triangle should exist in any matter; the idea in our minds would serve for the one as well as the other. But we are so far from being admitted into the secrets of nature, that we scarce so much as ever approach the first entrance towards them. For we are wont to consider the substances we meet with, each of them as an entire thing by itself, having all its qualities in itself, and independent of other things; overlooking, for the most part, the operations of those invisible fluids they are encompassed with, and upon whose motions and operations depend the greatest part of those qualities which are taken notice of in them, and are made by us the inherent marks of distinction whereby we know and denominate them. Put a piece of gold any where by itself, separate from the reach and influence of all other bodies, it will immediately lose all its colour and weight, and perhaps malleableness too; which, for aught I know, would be changed into a perfect friability. Water, in which to us fluidity is an essential quality, left to itself, would cease to be fluid. But if inanimate bodies owe so much of their present state to other bodies without them, that they would not be what they appear to us, were those bodies that environ them removed; it is yet more so in vegetables, which are nourished, grow, and produce leaves, flowers, and seeds, in a constant succession. And if we look a little nearer into the state of animals, we shall find that their dependence, as to life, motion, and the most considerable qualities to be observed in them, is so wholly on extrinsical causes and qualities of other bodies that make no part of them, that they cannot subsist a moment without them: though yet those bodies on which they depend, are little taken notice of, and make no part of the complex ideas we frame of those animals. Take the air but for a minute from the greatest part of living creatures, and they presently lose sense, life, and motion. This the necessity of breathing has forced into our knowledge. But how many other extrinsical, and possibly very remote bodies, do the springs of these admirable machines depend on, which are not vulgarly observed, or so much as thought on; and how many are there, which the severest inquiry can never discover? The inhabitants of this spot of the universe, though removed so many millions of miles from the sun, yet depend so much on the duly tempered motion of particles coming from, or agitated by it, that were this earth removed but a small part of the distance out of its present situation, and placed a little farther or nearer that source of heat, it is more than probable that the greatest part of the animals in it would immediately perish: since we find them so often destroyed by an excess or defect of the sun's warmth, which an accidental position, in some parts of this our little globe, exposes them to. The qualities observed in a loadstone must needs have their source far beyond the confines of that body; and the ravage made often on several sorts of animals by invisible causes, the certain death (as we are told) of some of them, by barely passing the line, or, as it is certain of other, by being removed into a neighbouring country; evidently show that the concurrence and operations of several bodies, with which they are seldom thought to have any thing to do, is absolutely necessary to make them be what they appear to us, and to preserve those qualities by which we know and distinguish them. We are then quite out of the way, when we think that things contain within themselves the qualities that appear to us in them; and we in vain search for that constitution within the body of a fly, or an elephant, upon which depend those qualities and powers we observe in them. For which perhaps, to understand them aright, we ought to look not only beyond this our earth and atmosphere, but even beyond the sun, or remotest star our eyes have yet discovered. For how much the being and operation of particular substances in this our globe depends on causes utterly beyond our view, is impossible for us to determine. We see and perceive some of the motions and grosser operations of things here about us; but whence the streams come that keep all these curious machines in motion and repair, how conveyed and modified, is beyond our notice and apprehension; and the great parts and wheels, as I may so say, of this stupendous structure of the universe, may, for aught we know, have such a connexion and dependence in their influences and operations one upon another, that perhaps things in this our mansion would put on quite another face, and cease to be what they are, if some one of the stars or great bodies, incomprehensibly remote from us, should cease to be or move as it does. This is certain, things however absolute and entire they seem in themselves, are but retainers to other parts of nature, for that which they are most taken notice of by us. Their observable qualities, actions, and powers, are owing to something without them; and there is not so complete and perfect a part that we know of nature, which does not owe the being it has, and the excellencies of it, to its neighbours; and we must not confine our thoughts within the surface of any body, but look a great deal farther, to comprehend perfectly those qualities that are in it.

If this be so, it is not to be wondered, that we have very imperfect ideas of substances; and that the real essences, on which depend their properties and operations are unknown to us. We cannot discover so much as that size, figure, and texture of their minute and active parts, which is really in them; much less the different motions and impulses made in and upon them by bodies from without, upon which depends, and by which is formed, the greatest and most remarkable part of those qualities we observe in them, and of which our complex ideas of them are made up. This consideration alone is enough to put an end to all our hopes of ever having the ideas of their real essences; which whilst we want, the nominal essences we make use of instead of them will be able to furnish us but very sparingly with any general knowledge, or universal propositions capable of real certainty.

We are not therefore to wonder, if certainty be to be found in very few general propositions made concerning substances: our knowledge of their qualities and properties goes very seldom farther than our senses reach and inform us. Possibly inquisitive, and observing men may, by strength of judgment, penetrate farther, and on probabilities taken from wary observation, and hints well laid together, often guess right at what experience has not yet discovered to them. But this is but guessing still; it amounts only to opinion, and has not that certainty which is requisite to knowledge. For all general knowledge lies only in our own thoughts, and consists barely in the contemplation of our own abstract ideas. Wherever we perceive any agreement or disagreement amongst them, there we have general knowledge; and, by putting the names of those ideas together accordingly in propositions, can with certainty pronounce general truths. But because the abstract ideas of substances, for which their specific names stand, whenever they have any distinct and determinate signification, have a discoverable connexion or inconsistency with but a very few other ideas: the certainty of universal propositions concerning substances is very narrow and scanty in that part, which is our principal inquiry concerning them: and there are scarce any of the names of substances, let the idea it is applied to be what it will, of which we can generally and with certainty pronounce, that it has or has not this or that other quality belonging to it, and constantly co-existing or inconsistent with that idea, wherever it is to be found.

Before we can have any tolerable knowledge of this kind, we must first know what changes the primary qualities of one body do regularly produce in the primary qualities of another, and how. Secondly, we must know what primary qualities of any body produce certain sensations or ideas in us. This is in truth no less than to know all the effects of matter, under its divers modifications of bulk, figure, cohesion of parts, motion and rest. Which, I think every body will allow, is utterly impossible to be known by us without revelation. Nor if it were revealed to us, what sort of figure, bulk, and motion of corpuscles, would produce in us the sensation of a yellow colour, and what sort of figure, bulk, and texture of parts, in the superficies of any body, were fit to give such corpuscles their due motion to produce that colour; would that be enough to make universal propositions with certainty, concerning the several sorts of them, unless we had faculties acute enough to perceive the precise bulk, figure, texture, and motion of bodies in those minute parts, by which they operate on our senses, so that we might by those frame our abstract ideas of them. I have mentioned here only corporeal substances, whose operations seem to lie more level to our understandings: for as to the operations of spirits, both their thinking and moving of bodies, we at first sight find ourselves at a loss; though perhaps, when we have applied our thoughts a little nearer to the consideration of bodies, and their operations, and examined how far our notions, even in these, reach, with any clearness, beyond sensible matter of fact, we shall be bound to confess, that even in these too our discoveries amount to very little beyond perfect ignorance and incapacity.

This is evident, the abstract complex ideas of substances, for which their general names stand, not comprehending their real constitutions, can afford us very little universal certainty. Because our ideas of them are not made up of that, on which those qualities we observe in them, and would inform ourselves about, do depend, or with which they have any certain connexion: v. g. let the ideas to which we give the name man, be, as it commonly is, a body of the ordinary shape, with sense, voluntary motion, and reason joined to it. This being the abstract idea, and consequently the essence of our species man, we can make but very few general certain propositions concerning man, standing for such an idea. Because not knowing the real constitution on which sensation, power of motion, and reasoning, with that peculiar shape, depend, and whereby they are united together in the same subject, there are very few other qualities, with which we can perceive them to have a necessary connexion: and therefore we cannot with certainty affirm, that all men sleep by intervals; that no man can be nourished by wood or stones; that all men will be poisoned by hemlock: because these ideas have no connexion nor repugnancy with this our nominal essence of man, with this abstract idea that name stands for. We must, in these and the like, appeal to trial in particular subjects, which can reach but a little way. We must content ourselves with probability in the rest; but can have no general certainty, whilst our specific idea of man contains not that real constitution, which is the root, wherein all his inseparable qualities are united, and from whence they flow. Whilst our idea, the word man stands for, is only an imperfect collection of some sensible qualities and powers in him, there is no discernible connexion or repugnance between our specific idea, and the operation of either the parts of hemlock or stones, upon his constitution. There are animals that safely eat hemlock, and others that are nourished by wood and stones: but as long as we want ideas of those real constitutions of different sorts of animals, wherein these and the like qualities and powers depend, we must not hope to reach certainty in universal propositions concerning them. Those few ideas only, which have a discernible connexion with our nominal essence, or any part of it, can afford us such propositions. But these are so few, and of so little moment, that we may justly look on our certain general knowledge of substances, as almost none at all.

To conclude, general propositions, of what kind soever, are then only capable of certainty, when the terms used in them stand for such ideas, whose agreement or disagreement, as there expressed, is capable to be discovered by us. And we are then certain of their truth or falsehood, when we perceive the ideas the terms stand for to agree or not agree, according as they are affirmed or denied one of another. Whence we may take notice, that general certainty is never to be found but in our ideas. Whenever we go to seek it elsewhere in experiment, or observations without us, our knowledge goes not beyond particulars. It is the contemplation of our own abstract ideas that alone is able to afford us general knowledge.

Observational knowledge of nature

At the time Locke was writing his *Essay*, the move among most of the writers on science was toward experiment and observation, the gathering of data prior to the formation of general laws or explanations. Typical expressions of this attitude are found in two of Locke's contemporaries. Former opinions are now being put to the test of "matter of Fact, in *Experiments;* and what is found consonant to *Truth*, made forth by collateral *Observations*, is approved, the rest . . . is rejected."[11] Robert Hooke cites as an important fundamental step in science finding a way "for collecting the Phenomena of Nature, and for compiling of a Philosophical History, Consisting of an exact Description of all sorts of Natural and Artificial Operations."[12]

11 W. Simpson, *Hydrologia Chymica* (London, 1669), p. 214.
12 Robert Hooke, "The Present State of Natural Philosophy," in *Posthumous Works* (London, 1705), pp. 7–8.

The role of what Locke called the *nominal essence* – that set of properties collected from the phenomena and made to stand for a kind of thing – is found in Boyle also. "We may now advance somewhat farther and consider, that Men having taken notice that certain conspicuous accidents were to be found associated in some Bodies, and other Conventions of accidents in other Bodies, they did for conveniency, and for more expeditious Expression of their Conceptions agree to distinguish them into several Sorts, which they call *Genders* or *Species*."[13]

15. *Essay*, 3.11.19–21

For the explaining the signification of the names of substances, as they stand for the ideas we have of their distinct species, both the fore-mentioned ways, viz. of showing and defining, are requisite in many cases to be made use of. For there being ordinarily in each sort some leading qualities, to which we suppose the other ideas, which make up our complex idea of that species, annexed; we forwardly give the specifick name to that thing, wherein that characteristical mark is found, which we take to be the most distinguishing idea of that species. These leading or characteristical (as I may call them) ideas, in the sorts of animals and vegetables, are mostly figure, and in inanimate bodies, colour, and in some both together. Now,

These leading sensible qualities are those which make the chief ingredients of our specifick ideas, and consequently the most observable and invariable part in the definitions of our specifick names, as attributed to sorts of substances coming under our knowledge. For though the sound man, in its own nature, be as apt to signify a complex idea made up of animality and rationality, united in the same subject, as to signify any other combination; yet used as a mark to stand for a sort of creatures we count of our own kind, perhaps, the outward shape is as necessary to be taken into our complex idea, signified by the word man, as any other we find in it: and therefore why Plato's "animal implume bipes latis unguibus" should not be a good definition of the name man, standing for that sort of creatures, will not be easy to show: for it is the shape, as the leading quality, that seems more to determine that species, than a faculty of reasoning, which appears not at first,

13 *Origine of Formes and Qualities* (Oxford, 1666), p. 39. There are many other passages of this sort, as well as other ways in which Locke is anticipated by Boyle in this work.

and in some never. And if this be not allowed to be so, I do not know how they can be excused from murder, who kill monstrous births, (as we call them) because of an unordinary shape, without knowing whether they have a rational soul or no; which can be no more discerned in a well-formed than ill-shaped infant, as soon as born. And who is it has informed us, that a rational soul can inhabit no tenement, unless it has just such a sort of frontispiece; or can join itself to, and inform no sort of body but one that is just of such an outward structure?

Now these leading qualities are best made known by showing, and can hardly be made known otherwise. For the shape of an horse, or cassuary, will be but rudely and imperfectly imprinted on the mind by words; the sight of the animals doth it a thousand times better: and the idea of the particular colour of gold is not to be got by any description of it, but only by the frequent exercise of the eyes about it, as is evident in those who are used to this metal, who will frequently distinguish true from counterfeit, pure from adulterate, by the sight; where others (who have as good eyes, but yet by use have not got the precise nice idea of that peculiar yellow) shall not perceive any difference. The like may be said of those other simple ideas, peculiar in their kind to any substance; for which precise ideas there are no peculiar names. The particular ringing sound there is in gold, distinct from the sound of other bodies, has no particular name annexed to it, no more than the particular yellow that belongs to that metal.

16. *Essay,* 3.11.25

It were therefore to be wished, that men, versed in physical inquiries, and acquainted with the several sorts of natural bodies, would set down those simple ideas, wherein they observe the individuals of each sort constantly to agree. This would remedy a great deal of that confusion which comes from several persons applying the same name to a collection of a smaller or greater number of sensible qualities, proportionably as they have been more or less acquainted with, or accurate in examining the qualities of any sort of things which come under one denomination. But a dictionary of this sort containing, as it were, a natural history, requires too many hands, as well as too much time, cost, pains, and sagacity, ever to be hoped for; and till that be done, we must content ourselves with such definitions of the names of substances as explain the sense men use them in. And it would be well, where there is occasion, if they would afford us so much. This yet is not usually done; but men talk to one another, and dispute in words, whose meaning is not agreed between them, out of a mistake, that the significations of common words are certainly established, and the precise ideas they stand for perfectly known; and that it is a shame to be ignorant of them. Both which suppositions are false: no names of complex ideas having so settled determined significations, that they are constantly used for the same precise ideas. Nor is it a shame for a man not to have a certain knowledge of any thing, but by the necessary ways of attaining it; and so it is no discredit not to know what precise idea any sound stands for in another man's mind, without he declare it to me by some other way than barely using that sound; there being no other way, without such a declaration, certainly to know it. Indeed the necessity of communication by language brings men to an agreement in the signification of common words, within some tolerable latitude, that may serve for ordinary conversation: and so a man cannot be supposed wholly ignorant of the ideas which are annexed to words by common use, in a language familiar to him. But common use, being but a very uncertain rule, which reduces itself at last to the ideas of particular men, proves often but a very variable standard. But though such a dictionary, as I have above-mentioned, will require too much time, cost, and pains, to be hoped for in this age; yet methinks it is not unreasonable to propose, that words standing for things, which are known and distinguished by their outward shapes, should be expressed by little draughts and prints made of them. A vocabulary made after this fashion would perhaps, with more ease, and in less time, teach the true signification of many terms, especially in languages of remote countries or ages, and settle truer ideas in men's minds of several things, whereof we read the names in ancient authors, than all the large and laborious comments of learned criticks. Naturalists, that treat of plants and animals, have found the benefit of this way: and he that has had occasion to consult them, will have reason to confess, that he has a clearer idea of apium or ibex, from a little print of that herb or beast, than he could have from a long definition of the names of either of them. And so no doubt he would have of strigil and sistrum, if instead of curry comb and cymbal, which are the English names dictionaries render them by, he could see stamped in the margin small pictures of these instruments, as they were in use amongst the ancients. "Toga, tunica, pallium," are words easily translated by gown, coat, and cloak: but we have thereby no more true ideas of the fashion of those habits amongst the Romans, than we have of the faces of the taylors who made them. Such things as these, which the eye distinguishes by their shapes, would be best let into the mind by draughts made of them, and more determine the signification of such words than any other words set for them, or made use of to define them.

17. *Essay*, 4.12.9

In our search after the knowledge of substances, our want of ideas, that are suitable to such a way of proceeding, obliges us to a quite different method. We advance not here, as in the other (where our abstract ideas are real as well as nominal essences) by contemplating our ideas, and considering their relations and correspondencies; that helps us very little, for the reasons, that in another place we have at large set down. By which I think it is evident, that substances afford matter of very little general knowledge; and the bare contemplation of their abstract ideas will carry us but a very little way in the search of truth and certainty. What then are we to do for the improvement of our knowledge in substantial beings? Here we are to take a quite contrary course; the want of ideas of their real essences, sends us from our own thoughts to the things themselves, as they exist. Experience here must teach me what reason cannot; and it is by trying alone, that I can certainly know, what other qualities co-exist with those of my complex idea, v. g. whether that yellow, heavy, fusible body, I call gold, be malleable, or no; which experience (which way ever it prove, in that particular body, I examine) makes me not certain, that it is so in all, or any other yellow, heavy, fusible bodies, but that which I have tried. Because it is no consequence one way or the other from my complex idea; the necessity or inconsistence of malleability hath no visible connexion with the combination of that colour, weight, and fusibility in any body. What I have said here of the nominal essence of gold, supposed to consist of a body of such a determinate colour, weight, and fusibility, will hold true, if malleableness, fixedness and solubility in aqua regia be added to it. Our reasonings from these ideas will carry us but a little way in the certain discovery of the other properties in those masses of matter wherein all these are to be found. Because the other properties of such bodies, depending not on these, but on that unknown real essence, on which these also depend, we cannot by them discover the rest; we can go no farther than the simple ideas of our nominal essence will carry us, which is very little beyond themselves; and so afford us but very sparingly any certain, universal, and useful truths. For

upon trial having found that particular piece (and all others of that
colour, weight, and fusibility, that I ever tried) malleable, that also
makes now perhaps a part of my complex idea, part of my nominal
essence of gold: whereby though I make my complex idea, to which
I affix the name gold, to consist of more simple ideas than before;
yet still, it not containing the real essence of any species of bodies,
it helps me not certainly to know (I say to know, perhaps it may
to conjecture) the other remaining properties of that body, farther
than they have a visible connexion with some or all of the simple
ideas, that make up my nominal essence. For example, I cannot be
certain from this complex idea, whether gold be fixed, or no; because, as before, there is no necessary connexion or inconsistence to
be discovered betwixt a complex idea of a body yellow, heavy,
fusible, malleable; betwixt these, I say, and fixedness; so that I may
certainly know, that in whatsoever body these are found, there
fixedness is sure to be. Here again for assurance, I must apply myself to experience; as far as that reaches, I may have certain knowledge, but no farther.

18. *Essay*, 4.12.12

I would not therefore be thought to disesteem, or dissuade the
study of nature. I readily agree the contemplation of his works gives
us occasion to admire, revere, and glorify their author: and, if
rightly directed, may be of greater benefit to mankind, than the
monuments of exemplary charity, that have at so great charge been
raised by the founders of hospitals and alms-houses. He that first
invented printing, discovered the use of the compass, or made
public the virtue and right use of kin kina, did more for the propa-
gation of knowledge, for the supply and increase of useful commodities, and saved more from the grave, than those who built
colleges, work-houses, and hospitals. All that I would say, is, that
we should not be too forwardly possessed with the opinion, or expectation of knowledge, where it is not to be had; or by ways that
will not attain to it: that we should not take doubtful systems for
complete sciences, nor unintelligible notions for scientifical demonstrations. In the knowledge of bodies, we must be content to glean
what we can from particular experiments: since we cannot, from a
discovery of their real essences, grasp at a time whole sheaves, and
in bundles comprehend the nature and properties of whole species
together. Where our enquiry is concerning co-existence, or repugnancy to co-exist, which by contemplation of our ideas we cannot
discover; there experience, observation, and natural history must

give us by our senses, and by retail, an insight into corporeal substances. The knowledge of bodies we must get by our senses, warily
employed in taking notice of their qualities and operations on one
another: and what we hope to know of separate spirits in this world,
we must, I think, expect only from revelation. He that shall consider
how little general maxims, precarious principles, and hypotheses
laid down at pleasure, have promoted true knowledge, or helped
to satisfy the inquiries of rational men after real improvements:
how little, I say, the setting out at that end has, for many ages
together, advanced men's progress towards the knowledge of natural philosophy; will think we have reason to thank those, who in
this latter age have taken another course, and have trod out to us,
though not an easier way to learned ignorance, yet a surer way to
profitable knowledge.

19. *Essay*, 4.12.2

There is also another thing in a man's power, and that is, though
he turns his eyes sometimes towards an object, yet he may choose
whether he will curiously survey it, and with an intent application
endeavour to observe accurately all that is visible in it. But yet
what he does see, he cannot see otherwise than he does. It depends
not on his will to see that black which appears yellow; nor to persuade himself, that what actually scalds him, feels cold. The earth
will not appear painted with flowers, nor the fields covered with
verdure, whenever he has a mind to it: in the cold winter he cannot help seeing it white and hoary, if he will look abroad. Just thus
is it with our understanding: all that is voluntary in our knowledge,
is the employing or withholding any of our faculties, from this or
that sort of objects, and a more or less accurate survey of them: but
they being employed, our will hath no power to determine the
knowledge of the mind one way or other; that is done only by the
objects themselves, as far as they are clearly discovered. And therefore, as far as men's senses are conversant about external objects,
the mind cannot but receive those ideas which are presented by
them, and be informed of the existence of things without: and so
far as men's thoughts converse with their own determined ideas,
they cannot but, in some measure, observe the agreement or disagreement that is to be found amongst some of them, which is so
far knowledge: and if they have names for those ideas which they
have thus considered, they must needs be assured of the truth of
those propositions, which express that agreement or disagreement
they perceive in them, and be undoubtedly convinced of those

truths. For what a man sees, he cannot but see; and what he perceives, he cannot but know that he perceives.

Hypotheses in science

After the step of collecting the phenomena (the making of natural histories), Robert Hooke saw the next step as that of finding a "Method of describing, registring, and ranging these particulars so collected, as that they may become the most adopted Materials for the raising of axioms and the Perfecting of Natural Philosophy."[14] Locke was properly cautious about the use of hypotheses in science, but he recognized the need for hypotheses grounded in observation: "he that would not deceive himself ought to build his hypothesis on matter of fact and make it out by sensible experience, and not presume on matter of fact because of his hypothesis" (2.1.10).

20. Essay, 4.12.10

I deny not but a man, accustomed to rational and regular experiments, shall be able to see farther into the nature of bodies, and guess righter at their yet unknown properties, than one that is a stranger to them: but yet, as I have said, this is but judgment and opinion, not knowledge and certainty. This way of getting and improving our knowledge in substances only by experience and history, which is all that the weakness of our faculties in this state of mediocrity which we are in in this world can attain to, makes me suspect that natural philosophy is not capable of being made a science. We are able, I imagine, to reach very little general knowledge concerning the species of bodies, and their several properties. Experiments and historical observations we may have, from which we may draw advantages of ease and health, and thereby increase our stock of conveniences for this life; but beyond this I fear our talents reach not, nor are our faculties, as I guess, able to advance.

21. Essay, 4.12.13

Not that we may not, to explain any phaenomena of nature, make use of any probable hypothesis whatsoever: hypotheses, if they are well made, are at least great helps to the memory, and often direct us to new discoveries. But my meaning is, that we should not take up any one too hastily (which the mind, that would

14 Hooke, *op. cit.*, p. 8.

always penetrate into the causes of things, and have principles
to rest on, is very apt to do) till we have very well examined
particulars, and made several experiments in that thing which we
would explain by our hypothesis, and see whether it will agree to
them all; whether our principles will carry us quite through, and
not be as inconsistent with one phaenomenon of nature as they
seem to accommodate and explain another. And at least that we
take care, that the name of principles deceive us not, nor impose
on us, by making us receive that for an unquestionable truth which
is really at best but a very doubtful conjecture, such as are most
(I had almost said all) of the hypotheses in natural philosophy.

22. *Conduct,* section 13

Particular matters of fact are the undoubted foundations on which
our civil and natural knowledge is built: the benefit the understanding makes of them, is to draw from them conclusions, which
may be as standing rules of knowledge, and consequently of practice. The mind often makes not that benefit it should of the information it receives from the accounts of civil or natural historians,
by being too forward or too slow in making observations on the
particular facts recorded in them.

There are those who are very assiduous in reading, and yet do
not much advance their knowledge by it. They are delighted with
the stories that are told, and perhaps can tell them again, for they
make all they read nothing but history to themselves; but not
reflecting on it, not making to themselves observations from what
they read, they are very little improved by all that crowd of particulars, that either pass through, or lodge themselves in their
understandings. They dream on in a constant course of reading
and cramming themselves; but not digesting any thing, it produces nothing but an heap of crudities.

If their memories retain well, one may say, they have the materials of knowledge; but, like those for building, they are of no
advantage, if there be no other use made of them but to let them
lie heaped up together. Opposite to these, there are others who
lose the improvement they should make of matters of fact by a
quite contrary conduct. They are apt to draw general conclusions,
and raise axioms from every particular they meet with. These make
as little true benefit of history as the other; nay, being of forward
and active spirits, receive more harm by it; it being of worse consequence to steer one's thoughts by a wrong rule, than to have
none at all; errour doing to busy men much more harm, than

ignorance to the slow and sluggish. Between these, those seem
to do best, who taking material and useful hints, sometimes from
single matters of fact, carry them in their minds to be judged of,
by what they shall find in history, to confirm or reverse their imperfect observations; which may be established into rules fit to be
relied on, when they are justified by a sufficient and wary induc-
tion of particulars. He that makes no such reflections on what he
reads, only loads his mind with a rhapsody of tales, fit, in winter-
nights, for the entertainment of others: and he that will improve
every matter of fact into a maxim, will abound in contrary observations, that can be of no other use but to perplex and pudder
him, if he compares them; or else to misguide him, if he gives himself up to the authority of that, which for its novelty, or for some
other fancy, best pleases him.

23. *Conduct*, section 25

The eagerness and strong bent of the mind after knowledge, if not
warily regulated, is often an hindrance to it. It still presses into
further discoveries and new objects, and catches at the variety of
knowledge; and therefore often stays not long enough on what is
before it, to look into it as it should, for haste to pursue what is yet
out of sight. He that rides post through a country, may be able,
from the transient view, to tell how in general the parts lie, and
may be able to give some loose description of here a mountain, and
there a plain; here a morass, and there a river; woodland in one
part, and savannahs in another. Such superficial ideas and observations as these he may collect in gallopping over it: but the
more useful observations of the soil, plants, animals, and inhabitants, with their several sorts and properties, must necessarily escape him; and it is seldom men ever discover the rich mines
without some digging. Nature commonly lodges her treasure and
jewels in rocky ground. If the matter be knotty, and the sense
lies deep, the mind must stop and buckle to it, and stick upon it
with labour and thought, and close contemplation; and not leave it
till it has mastered the difficulty, and got possession of truth. But
here care must be taken to avoid the other extreme: a man must
not stick at every useless nicety, and expect mysteries of science
in every trivial question, or scruple, that he may raise. He that will
stand to pick up and examine every pebble that comes in his way,
is as unlikely to return enriched and loaden with jewels, as the
other that travelled full speed. Truths are not the better nor the
worse for their obviousness or difficulty, but their value is to be

measured by their usefulness and tendency. Insignificant observations should not take up any of our minutes; and those that enlarge our view, and give light towards farther and useful discoveries, should not be neglected, though they stop our course, and spend some of our time in a fixed attention.

There is another haste that does often, and will mislead the mind if it be left to itself, and its own conduct. The understanding is naturally forward, not only to learn its knowledge by variety (which makes it skip over one to get speedily to another part of knowledge) but also eager to enlarge its views, by running too fast into general observations and conclusions, without a due examination of particulars enough whereon to found those general axioms. This seems to enlarge their stock, but it is of fancies, not realities; such theories built upon narrow foundations stand but weakly, and, if they fall not of themselves, are at least very hardly to be supported against the assaults of opposition. And thus men being too hasty to erect to themselves general notions and ill-grounded theories, find themselves deceived in their stock of knowledge, when they come to examine their hastily assumed maxims themselves, or to have them attacked by others. General observations drawn from particulars, are the jewels of knowledge, comprehending great store in a little room; but they are therefore to be made with the greater care and caution, lest, if we take counterfeit for true, our loss and shame be the greater when our stock comes to a severe scrutiny. One or two particulars may suggest hints of inquiry, and they do well to take those hints; but if they turn them into conclusions, and make them presently general rules, they are forward indeed, but it is only to impose on themselves by propositions assumed for truths without sufficient warrant. To make such observations is, as has been already remarked, to make the head a magazine of materials, which can hardly be called knowledge; or at least it is but like a collection of lumber not reduced to use or order; and he that makes every thing an observation, has the same useless plenty and much more falsehood mixed with it. The extremes on both sides are to be avoided, and he will be able to give the best account of his studies who keeps his understanding in the right mean between them.

24. *Conduct*, sections 43–4

There are fundamental truths that lie at the bottom, the basis upon which a great many others rest, and in which they have their consistency. These are teeming truths, rich in store, with which they furnish the mind, and, like the lights of heaven, are not only beau-

tiful and entertaining in themselves, but give light and evidence to
other things, that without them could not be seen or known. Such
is that admirable discovery of Mr. Newton, that all bodies gravitate
to one another, which may be counted as the basis of natural
philosophy; which, of what use it is to the understanding of the
great frame of our solar system, he has to the astonishment of the
learned world shown; and how much farther it would guide us in
other things, if rightly pursued, is not yet known. Our Saviour's
great rule, that "we should love our neighbour as ourselves," is such
a fundamental truth for the regulating human society, that, I think,
by that alone, one might without difficulty determine all the cases
and doubts in social morality. These and such as these are the
truths we should endeavour to find out, and store our minds with.
Which leads me to another thing in the conduct of the understanding that is no less necessary, viz.

To accustom ourselves, in any question proposed, to examine and
find out upon what it bottoms. Most of the difficulties that come
in our way, when well considered and traced, lead us to some
proposition, which, known to be true, clears the doubt, and gives
an easy solution of the question; whilst topical and superficial arguments, of which there is store to be found on both sides, filling
the head with variety of thoughts, and the mouth with copious
discourse, serve only to amuse the understanding, and entertain
company without coming to the bottom of the question, the only
place of rest and stability for an inquisitive mind, whose tendency
is only to truth and knowledge.

For example, if it be demanded, whether the grand seignior can
lawfully take what he will from any of his people? This question
cannot be resolved without coming to a certainty, whether all
men are naturally equal; for upon that it turns; and that truth well
settled in the understanding, and carried in the mind through the
various debates concerning the various rights of men in society, will
go a great way in putting an end to them, and showing on which
side the truth is.

25. *Conduct,* sections 34–5

Men deficient in knowledge are usually in one of these three states;
either wholly ignorant, or as doubting of some proposition they
have either embraced formerly, or are at present inclined to; or
lastly, they do with assurance hold and profess without ever having
examined, and being convinced by well grounded arguments.

The first of these are in the best state of the three, by having their minds yet in their perfect freedom and indifferency; the likelier to pursue truth the better, having no bias yet clapped on to mislead them.

For ignorance, with an indifferency for truth, is nearer to it than opinion with ungrounded inclination, which is the great source of errour; and they are more in danger to go out of the way, who are marching under the conduct of a guide, that it is an hundred to one will mislead them, than he that has not yet taken a step, and is likelier to be prevailed on to inquire after the right way. The last of the three sorts are in the worst condition of all; for if a man can be persuaded and fully assured of any thing for a truth, without having examined, what is there that he may not embrace for truth? and if he has given himself up to believe a lye, what means is there left to recover one who can be assured without examining? To the other two this I crave leave to say, that as he that is ignorant is in the best state of the two, so he should pursue truth in a method suitable to that state; i. e. by inquiring directly into the nature of the thing itself, without minding the opinions of others, or troubling himself with their questions or disputes about it; but to see what he himself can, sincerely searching after truth, find out. He that proceeds upon other principles in his inquiry into any sciences, though he be resolved to examine them and judge of them freely, does yet at least put himself on that side, and post himself in a party which he will not quit till he be beaten out; by which the mind is insensibly engaged to make what defence it can, and so is unawares biassed. I do not say but a man should embrace some opinion when he has examined, else he examines to no purpose; but the surest and safest way is to have no opinion at all till he has examined, and that without any the least regard to the opinions or systems of other men about it. For example, were it my business to understand physic, would not the safe and readier way be to consult nature herself, and inform myself in the history of diseases and their cures; than espousing the principles of the dogmatists, methodists, or chemists, to engage in all the disputes concerning either of those systems, and suppose it to be true, till I have tried what they can say to beat me out of it? Or, supposing that Hippocrates, or any other book, infallibly contains the whole art of physic; would not the direct way be to study, read, and consider that book, weigh and compare the parts of it to find the truth, rather than espouse the doctrines of any party? who, though they acknowledge his authority, have already interpreted and wire-drawn all his text to their own sense; the tincture whereof, when

I have imbibed, I am more in danger to misunderstand his true meaning, than if I had come to him with a mind unprepossessed by doctors and commentators of my sect; whose reasonings, interpretation, and language, which I have been used to, will of course make all chime that way, and make another, and perhaps the genuine meaning of the author seem harsh, strained, and uncouth to me. For words having naturally none of their own, carry that signification to the hearer, that he is used to put upon them, whatever be the sense of him that uses them. This, I think, is visibly so; and if it be, he that begins to have any doubt of any of his tenets, which he received without examination, ought, as much as he can, to put himself wholly into this state of ignorance in reference to that question; and throwing wholly by all his former notions, and the opinions of others, examine, with a perfect indifferency, the question in its source; without any inclination to either side, or any regard to his or others' unexamined opinions. This I own is no easy thing to do; but I am not inquiring the easy way to opinion, but the right way to truth; which they must follow who will deal fairly with their own understandings and their own souls.

26. *Essay,* 4.16.12

The probabilities we have hitherto mentioned are only such as concern matter of fact, and such things as are capable of observation and testimony. There remains that other sort, concerning which men entertain opinions with variety of assent, though the things be such, that, falling not under the reach of our senses, they are not capable of testimony. Such are, 1. The existence, nature, and operations of finite immaterial beings without us; as spirits, angels, devils, &c. or the existence of material beings; which either for their smallness in themselves, or remoteness from us, our senses cannot take notice of; as whether there be any plants, animals, and intelligent inhabitants in the planets, and other mansions of the vast universe. 2. Concerning the manner of operation in most parts of the works of nature; wherein though we see the sensible effects, yet their causes are unknown, and we perceive not the ways and manner how they are produced. We see animals are generated, nourished, and move; the loadstone draws iron; and the parts of a candle, successively melting, turn into flame, and give us both light and heat. These and the like effects we see and know; but the causes that operate, and the manner they are produced in, we can only guess and probably conjecture. For these and the like, coming not within the scrutiny of human senses, cannot be examined by them, or be attested by any body; and therefore can appear more or less probable, only as they more or less agree to truths that are established in our minds, and as they hold proportion to other parts of our knowledge and observation. Analogy in these matters is the only help we have, and it is from that alone we draw all our grounds of probability. Thus observing that the bare rubbing of two bodies violently one upon another produces heat, and very often fire itself, we have reason to think that what we call heat and fire consists in a violent agitation of the imperceptible minute parts of the burning matter: observing likewise that the different refractions of pellucid bodies produce in our eyes the different appearances of several colours, and also that the different ranging and laying the superficial parts of several bodies, as of velvet, watered silk, &c. does the like, we think it probable that the colour and shining of bodies is in them nothing but the different arrangement and refraction of their minute and insensible parts. Thus finding in all parts of the creation, that fall under human observation, that there is a gradual connexion of one with another, without any great or discernible gaps between, in all that great variety of things we see in the world, which are so closely linked together, that in the several ranks of beings it is not easy to discover the bounds betwixt them; we have reason to be persuaded, that by such gentle steps things ascend upwards in degrees of perfection. It is a hard matter to say where sensible and rational begin, and where insensible and irrational end: and who is there quick-sighted enough to determine precisely which is the lowest species of living things, and which the first of those which have no life? Things, as far as we can observe, lessen and augment as the quantity does in a regular cone; where, though there be a manifest odds betwixt the bigness of the diameter at a remote distance, yet the difference between the upper and under, where they touch one another, is hardly discernible. The difference is exceeding great between some men and some animals; but if we will compare the understanding and abilities of some men and some brutes, we shall find so little difference, that it will be hard to say, that that of the man is either clearer or larger. Observing, I say, such gradual and gentle descents downwards in those parts of the creation that are beneath man, the rule of analogy may make it probable, that it is so also in things above us and our observation; and that there are several ranks of intelligent beings, excelling us in several degrees of perfection, ascending upwards towards the infinite perfection of the Creator, by gentle steps and differences, that are every one at no great distance from the next to it. This sort of probability, which is the best conduct of rational experiments, and the rise of hypothesis, has also its use and influence; and a wary reasoning from analogy leads us often into the discovery of truths and useful productions which would otherwise lie concealed.

27. Letter to Molyneux, *Works*, IX, pp. 463–5

Sir,   Oates, Jan. 20, 1692–3.

I must acknowledge the care you take of my health, in a way wherein you so kindly apply to my mind; and if I could persuade myself that my weak constitution was owing to that strength of mind you ascribe to me, or accompanied with it, I should find therein, if not a remedy, yet a great relief against the infirmities of my body. However, I am not the less obliged to you for so friendly an application; and if the cordial you prescribe be not to be had (for I know none equal to a judicious and capacious mind) your kindness is not to be blamed, who I am confident wish me that satisfaction, or any thing else that could contribute to my health.

The doctor, concerning whom you inquire of me, had, I remember, when I lived in town, and conversed among the physicians there, a good reputation amongst those of his own faculty. I can say nothing of his late book of fevers, having not read it myself, nor heard it spoke of by others: but I perfectly agree with you concerning general theories, that they are, for the most part, but a sort of waking dreams, with which, when men have warmed their own heads, they pass into unquestionable truths, and then the ignorant world must be set right by them. Though this be, as you rightly observe, beginning at the wrong end, when men lay the foundation in their own fancies, and then endeavour to suit the phenomena of diseases, and the cure of them, to those fancies. I wonder that, after the pattern Dr. Sydenham has set them of a better way, men should return again to that romance way of physic. But I see it is easier and more natural, for men to build castles in the air, of their own, than to survey well those that are to be found standing. Nicely to observe the history of diseases in all their changes and circumstances, is a work of time, accurateness, attention, and judgment, and wherein if men, through prepossession or oscitancy, mistake, they may be convinced of their errour by unerring nature and matter of fact, which leaves less room for the subtlety and dispute of words, which serves very much instead of knowledge, in the learned world, where, methinks, wit and invention has much the preference to truth. Upon such grounds as are the established history of diseases, hypotheses might with less danger be erected, which I think are so far useful, as they serve as an art of memory to direct the physician in particular cases, but not to be relied on as foundations of reasoning, or verities to be contended for; they being, I think I may say all of them, suppositions taken up gratis, and will so remain, till we can discover how the natural functions of the body are performed, and by what alteration of the humours, or defects in the parts, they are hindered or disordered. To which purpose, I fear the Galenists four humours, or the chemists sal, sulphur, and mercury, or the late prevailing invention of acid and alcali, or whatever hereafter shall be substituted to these with new applause, will, upon examination, be found to be but so many learned empty sounds, with no precise determinate signification. What we know of the works of nature, especially in the constitution of health, and the operations of our own bodies, is only by the sensible effects, but not by any certainty we can have of the tools she uses, or the ways she works by. So that there is nothing left for a physician to do, but to observe well, and so, by analogy, argue to like cases, and thence make to himself rules of practice: and he that is this way most sagacious, will, I imagine, make the best physician, though he should entertain distinct hypotheses concerning distinct species of diseases, subservient to this end, that were inconsistent one with another; they being made use of in those several sorts of diseases, but as distinct arts of memory, in those cases. And I the rather say this, that they might be relied on only as artificial helps to a physician, and not as philosophical truths to a naturalist. But, sir, I run too far, and must beg your pardon for talking so freely on a subject you understand so much better than I do. I hoped the way of treating of diseases, which, with so much approbation, Dr. Sydenham had introduced into the world, would have beaten the other out, and turned men from visions and wrangling to observation, and endeavouring after settled practices in more diseases; such as I think he has given us in some. If my zeal for the saving men's lives, and preserving their health (which is infinitely to be preferred to any speculations ever so fine in physic) has carried me too far, you will excuse it in one who wishes well to the practice of physic, though he meddles not with it. I wish you and your brother, and all yours, a very happy new-year, and am,

Sir,

Your most humble and faithful servant,

JOHN LOCKE

There was one hypothesis that Locke accepted as the most probable explanation of sense perception: the corpuscular theory. This was also a theory about the nature of matter. It held that bulk, figure, motion, or rest "belong to a Body, as it is consider'd in it self, without relation to sensative Beings or to other Natural bodies."[15] Colors, tastes, and so on, belong to bodies only, Boyle says, "dispositively"; that is, these qualities are "nothing of real and Physical [in the body] but the Size, Shape and Motion or Rest of its component Particles" (p. 27). The theory is developed with great detail by Boyle. Versions of it can be found in Descartes, Galileo, Newton, and many others. Locke gives the theory a prominent place in Book 2.

28. *Essay*, 2.8.1–2, 7–23

Concerning the simple ideas of sensation it is to be considered that whatsoever is so constituted in nature as to be able, by affecting our senses, to cause any perception in the mind, doth thereby produce in the understanding a simple idea; which, whatever be the external cause of it, when it comes to be taken notice of by our discerning faculty, it is by the mind looked on and considered there to be a real positive idea in the understanding as much as any other whatsoever; though perhaps the cause of it be but a privation of the subject.

Thus the ideas of heat and cold, light and darkness, white and black, motion and rest, are equally clear and positive ideas in the mind; though perhaps some of the causes which produce them are barely privations in subjects, from whence our senses derive those ideas. These the understanding, in its view of them, considers all as distinct positive ideas, without taking notice of the causes that produce them: which is an inquiry not belonging to the idea, as it is in the understanding, but to the nature of the things existing without us. These are two very different things, and carefully to be distinguished; it being one thing to perceive and know the idea of white or black, and quite another to examine what kind of

15 Boyle, *op. cit.*, p. 65.

particles they must be, and how ranged in the superficies, to make any object appear white or black.

To discover the nature of our ideas the better, and to discourse of them intelligibly, it will be convenient to distinguish them as they are ideas or perceptions in our minds, and as they are modifications of matter in the bodies that cause such perceptions in us: that so we may not think (as perhaps usually is done) that they are exactly the images and resemblances of something inherent in the subject; most of those of sensation being in the mind no more the likeness of something existing without us, than the names that stand for them are the likeness of our ideas, which yet upon hearing they are apt to excite in us.

Whatsoever the mind perceives in itself, or is the immediate object of perception, thought, or understanding, that I call idea; and the power to produce any idea in our mind I call quality of the subject wherein that power is. Thus a snow-ball having the power to produce in us the ideas of white, cold, and round, the powers to produce those ideas in us, as they are in the snow-ball, I call qualities; and as they are sensations or perceptions in our understandings, I call them ideas: which ideas, if I speak of sometimes, as in the things themselves, I would be understood to mean those qualities in the objects which produce them in us.

Qualities thus considered in bodies are, first, such as are utterly inseparable from the body, in what estate soever it be; such as in all the alterations and changes it suffers, all the force can be used upon it, it constantly keeps; and such as sense constantly finds in every particle of matter which has bulk enough to be perceived, and the mind finds inseparable from every particle of matter, though less than to make itself singly be perceived by our senses, v. g. Take a grain of wheat, divide it into two parts, each part has still solidity, extension, figure, and mobility; divide it again, and it retains still the same qualities; and so divide it on till the parts become insensible, they must retain still each of them all those qualities. For division (which is all that a mill, or pestle, or any other body does upon another, in reducing it to insensible parts) can never take away either solidity, extension, figure, or mobility from any body, but only makes two or more distinct separate masses of matter, of that which was but one before: all which distinct masses, reckoned as so many distinct bodies, after division make a certain number. These I call original or primary qualities of body, which I think we may observe to produce simple ideas in us, viz. solidity, extension, figure, motion or rest, and number.

Secondly, such qualities which in truth are nothing in the objects themselves, but powers to produce various sensations in us by their primary qualities, i. e. by the bulk, figure, texture, and motion of their insensible parts, as colours, sounds, tastes, &c. these I call secondary qualities. To these might be added a third sort, which are allowed to be barely powers, though they are as much real qualities in the subject, as those which I, to comply with the common way of speaking, call qualities, but for distinction, secondary qualities. For the power in fire to produce a new colour, or consistency, in wax or clay, by its primary qualities, is as much a quality in fire, as the power it has to produce in me a new idea or sensation of warmth or burning, which I felt not before by the same primary qualities, viz. the bulk, texture, and motion of its insensible parts.

The next thing to be considered is, how bodies produce ideas in us; and that is manifestly by impulse, the only way which we can conceive bodies to operate in.

If then external objects be not united to our minds, when they produce ideas therein, and yet we perceive these original qualities in such of them as singly fall under our senses, it is evident that some motion must be thence continued by our nerves or animal spirits, by some parts of our bodies, to the brain, or the seat of sensation, there to produce in our minds the particular ideas we have of them. And since the extension, figure, number and motion of bodies, of an observable bigness, may be perceived at a distance by the sight, it is evident some singly imperceptible bodies must come from them to the eyes, and thereby convey to the brain some motion, which produces these ideas which we have of them in us.

After the same manner that the ideas of these original qualities are produced in us, we may conceive that the ideas of secondary qualities are also produced, viz. by the operations of insensible particles on our senses. For it being manifest that there are bodies and good store of bodies, each whereof are so small, that we cannot, by any of our senses, discover either their bulk, figure, or motion as is evident in the particles of the air and water, and others extremely smaller than those, perhaps as much smaller than the particles of air and water, as the particles of air and water are smaller than pease or hail-stones: let us suppose at present, that the different motions and figures, bulk and number of such particles, affecting the several organs of our senses, produce in us those different sensations, which we have from the colours and smells of bodies; v. g. that a violet, by the impulse of such insensible particles of matter of peculiar figures and bulks, and in different

degrees and modifications of their motions, causes the ideas of the
blue colour and sweet scent of that flower, to be produced in
our minds; it being no more impossible to conceive that God
should annex such ideas to such motions, with which they have
no similitude, than that he should annex the idea of pain to the
motion of a piece of steel dividing our flesh, with which that idea
hath no resemblance.

What I have said concerning colours and smells may be understood also of tastes and sounds, and other the like sensible qualities; which, whatever reality we by mistake attribute to them, are
in truth nothing in the objects themselves, but powers to produce
various sensations in us, and depend on those primary qualities,
viz. bulk, figure, texture, and motion of parts; as I have said.

From whence I think it easy to draw this observation, that the
ideas of primary qualities of bodies are resemblances of them, and
their patterns do really exist in the bodies themselves; but the ideas,
produced in us by these secondary qualities, have no resemblance
of them at all. There is nothing like our ideas existing in the bodies
themselves. They are in the bodies, we denominate from them, only
a power to produce those sensations in us: and what is sweet,
blue or warm in idea, is but the certain bulk, figure, and motion
of the insensible parts in the bodies themselves, which we call so.

Flame is denominated hot and light; snow, white and cold; and
manna, white and sweet, from the ideas they produce in us: which
qualities are commonly thought to be the same in those bodies
that those ideas are in us, the one the perfect resemblance of the
other, as they are in a mirror; and it would by most men be
judged very extravagant, if one should say otherwise. And yet he
that will consider that the same fire, that at one distance produces
in us the sensation of warmth, does at a nearer approach produce
in us the far different sensation of pain, ought to bethink himself
what reason he has to say, that his idea of warmth, which was
produced in him by the fire, is actually in the fire; and his idea of
pain, which the same fire produced in him the same way, is not
in the fire. Why are whiteness and coldness in snow, and pain not,
when it produces the one and the other idea in us; and can do
neither, but by the bulk, figure, number, and motion of its solid
parts?

The particular bulk, number, figure, and motion of the parts of
fire, or snow, are really in them, whether any one's senses perceive
them or no; and therefore they may be called real qualities, because they really exist in those bodies: but light, heat, whiteness

or coldness, are no more really in them, than sickness or pain is in manna. Take away the sensation of them; let not the eyes see light, or colours, nor the ears hear sounds; let the palate not taste, nor the nose smell; and all colours, tastes, odours, and sounds, as they are such particular ideas, vanish and cease, and are reduced to their causes, i. e. bulk, figure, and motion of parts.

A piece of manna of a sensible bulk is able to produce in us the idea of a round or square figure, and, by being removed from one place to another, the idea of motion. This idea of motion represents it as it really is in the manna moving: a circle or square are the same, whether in idea or existence, in the mind, or in the manna; and this both motion and figure are really in the manna, whether we take notice of them or no: this every body is ready to agree to. Besides, manna by the bulk, figure, texture, and motion of its parts, has a power to produce the sensations of sickness, and sometimes of acute pains or gripings in us. That these ideas of sickness and pain are not in the manna, but effects of its operations on us, and are nowhere when we feel them not; this also every one readily agrees to. And yet men are hardly to be brought to think, that sweetness and whiteness are not really in manna; which are but the effects of the operations of manna by the motion, size, and figure of its particles on the eyes and palate; as the pain and sickness caused by manna are confessedly nothing but the effects of its operations on the stomach and guts, by the size, motion and figure of its insensible parts (for by nothing else can a body operate as has been proved:) as if it could not operate on the eyes and palate, and thereby produce in the mind particular distinct ideas, which in itself it has not, as well as we allow it can operate on the guts and stomach, and thereby produce distinct ideas, which in itself it has not. These ideas being all effects of the operations of manna, on several parts of our bodies, by the size, figure, number, and motion of its parts; why those produced by the eyes and palate should rather be thought to be really in the manna, than those produced by the stomach and guts; or why the pain and sickness, ideas that are the effect of manna, should be thought to be no-where when they are not felt; and yet the sweetness and whiteness, effects of the same manna on other parts of the body, by ways equally as unknown, should be thought to exist in the manna, when they are not seen or tasted, would need some reason to explain.

Let us consider the red and white colours in porphyry: hinder light from striking on it, and its colours vanish, it no longer produces any such ideas in us; upon the return of light, it produces these appearances on us again. Can any one think any real alterations are made in the porphyry, by the presence or absence of light; and that those ideas of whiteness and redness are really in porphyry in the light, when it is plain it has no colour in the dark? it has, indeed, such a configuration of particles, both night and day, as are apt, by the rays of light rebounding from some parts of that hard stone, to produce in us the idea of redness, and from others the idea of whiteness; but whiteness or redness are not in it at any time, but such a texture, that hath the power to produce such a sensation in us.

Pound an almond, and the clear white colour will be altered into a dirty one, and the sweet taste into an oily one. What real alteration can the beating of the pestle make in any body, but an alteration of the texture of it?

Ideas being thus distinguished and understood, we may be able to give an account how the same water, at the same time, may produce the idea of cold by one hand and of heat by the other; whereas it is impossible that the same water, if those ideas were really in it, should at the same time be both hot and cold: for if we imagine warmth, as it is in our hands, to be nothing but a certain sort and degree of motion in the minute particles of our nerves, or animal spirits, we may understand how it is possible that the same water may, at the same time, produce the sensations of heat in one hand, and cold in the other; which yet figure never does, that never producing the idea of a square by one hand, which has produced the idea of a globe by another. But if the sensation of heat and cold be nothing but the increase or diminution of the motion of the minute parts of our bodies, caused by the corpuscles of any other body, it is easy to be understood, that if that motion be greater in one hand than in the other; if a body be applied to the two hands, which has in its minute particles a greater motion, than in those of one of the hands, and a less than in those of the other; it will increase the motion of the one hand, and lessen it in the other, and so cause the different sensations of heat and cold that depend thereon.

I have in what just goes before been engaged in physical inquiries a little farther than perhaps I intended. But it being necessary to make the nature of sensation a little understood, and to make the difference between the qualities in bodies, and the ideas produced by them in the mind, to be distinctly conceived, without which it were impossible to discourse intelligibly of them; I hope I shall be pardoned this little excursion into natural philosophy, it being necessary in our present inquiry to distinguish the primary and real qualities of bodies, which are always in them (viz. solidity, extension, figure, number, and motion, or rest; and are sometimes perceived by us, viz. when the bodies they are in are big enough singly to be discerned) from those secondary and imputed qualities, which are but the powers of several combinations of those primary ones, when they operate, without being distinctly discerned; whereby we may also come to know what ideas are, and what are not, resemblances of something really existing in the bodies we denominate from them.

The qualities then that are in bodies, rightly considered, are of three sorts.

First, the bulk, figure, number, situation, and motion, or rest of their solid parts; those are in them, whether we perceive them or no; and when they are of that size, that we can discover them, we have by these an idea of the thing, as it is in itself, as is plain in artificial things. These I call primary qualities.

Secondly, the power that is in any body, by reason of its insensible primary qualities, to operate after a peculiar manner on any of our senses, and thereby produce in us the different ideas of several colours, sounds, smells, tastes, &c. These are usually called sensible qualities.

Thirdly, the power that is in any body, by reason of the particular constitution of its primary qualities, to make such a change in the bulk, figure, texture, and motion of another body, as to make it operate on our senses, differently from what it did before. Thus the sun has a power to make wax white, and fire to make lead fluid. These are usually called powers.

The first of these, as has been said, I think, may be properly called real, original, or primary qualities, because they are in the things themselves, whether they are perceived or no; and upon their different modifications it is, that the secondary qualities depend.

The other two are only powers to act differently upon other things, which powers result from the different modifications of those primary qualities.

2

The Doctrine of Signs

*"The consideration . . . of *ideas* and *words* as the great instruments of knowledge"*

The division of knowledge called "the doctrine of signs" considers "the nature of signs the mind makes use of for the understanding of things, or conveying its knowledge to others" (4.21.4). We understand through attending to our ideas. Words that stand for ideas enable us to communicate our knowledge.

Two concepts of ideas
Two themes about the nature of ideas can be found in the *Essay*, themes that reflect debates among Locke's Cartesian predecessors. (1) Most often Locke writes of ideas as objects, the immediate object of the mind when it thinks or is aware. This theme appears to lead to a representative theory of knowledge, where ideas as objects stand proxy for things that cannot be immediately known. (2) There are other passages where Locke identifies ideas with perceptions, where *ideas* and *perceptions* are used interchangeably. In these passages, Locke is echoing, if not following, Arnauld, who said an idea is the same as the perception of an object.[16] The difference between these two themes or concepts of idea is the subject of a long exchange Arnauld had with Malebranche. Malebranche had clearly made ideas into things – entities that existed separate from our mind. He insisted that to know anything other than ourselves or our states, we need to have something united to our mind that is different from our mind. A modality of mind cannot lead to knowledge of that which is not mind. Malebranche's ideas were separately existing

16 Antoine Arnauld, *Des Vraies et des Fausses Idées* (Cologne, 1683), Definition 3, vol. 38, p. 198, of his Collected Works.

entities in God's mind that God unites to our mind when specific physical and physiological processes occur in the world and in our bodies. These entities must be (1) different from our minds in order to represent things, and they must be (2) united to our mind when we know, because cognition cannot operate over distance. Arnauld attacked both requirements insisted upon by Malebranche. Perception and idea are, Arnauld argued, one and the same: *to have an idea* and *to perceive* say the same. Thus, ideas are not objects. To insist that what is known must be united with the mind is to confuse, or run the danger of confusing, *spatial* with *cognitive* presence. Arnauld thought he was just following Descartes in this account of ideas. To say that an object is present to our mind just means that we apprehend or understand that object: "I say that a thing is *objectively* in my mind, when I conceive it."[17]

In this last remark, Arnauld is using Descartes' language. Descartes' third *Meditation* distinguishes ideas as modes of mind from ideas as representations of things. In this latter capacity, ideas have objective reality; that is, "the entity or being of the thing represented" is in the idea or in the mind. In the Preface to his *Meditations*, Descartes drew the distinction between ideas as operations of the understanding and ideas "taken objectively for the thing which is represented by that operation."

There are thus available to Locke these two concepts of ideas: ideas as operations of the understanding and ideas as objects in the mind. Both concepts give to ideas a representative function, although the precise way in which ideas of either sort do represent objects was not worked out in much detail. It is the second of these two concepts that is usually ascribed to Locke, but both are to be found in the *Essay*. It is useful to remind ourselves of some passages where this second concept is present in Locke's writing.

In Book 2, which is entitled "Of Ideas," Locke sets out his program for the origin and derivation of ideas. He tells us in 2.1.3 that our senses convey into the mind "several distinct *perceptions* of things" or, more precisely, the senses "from external objects convey into the mind what produces there those *perceptions*." Later, in 2.1.23, he says that sen-

17 *Ibid.*, Definition 5.

sation "produces some perception in the understanding." Elsewhere, we find not just the interchange of the two words *idea* and *perception,* but the identification of them. For example, "Whatever *idea* is in the mind is either an actual perception or else, having been an actual perception, is so in the mind that by the memory it can be made an actual perception again" (1.4.21). The answer to the question "At what time does a man first have any ideas?" is "when he begins to perceive: having *ideas* and perception being the same thing" (2.1.9). (Compare 2.10.2: "our *ideas* being nothing but actual perceptions in the mind.") In other writings, Locke accepts the Arnauld concept of idea in opposition to that of Malebranche.

29. *Examination,* sections 3–5, 17–18, 42

That P. Malebranche's Recherche de la Vérité, 1. 3. p. 2. c. 1. tells us, that whatever the mind perceives "must be actually present and intimately united to it." That the things that the mind perceives are its own sensations, imaginations, or notions; which, being in the soul the modifications of it, need no ideas to represent them. But all things exterior to the soul we cannot perceive but by the intervention of ideas, supposing that the things themselves cannot be intimately united to the soul. But because spiritual things may possibly be united to the soul, therefore he thinks it probable that they can discover themselves immediately without ideas; though of this he doubts, because he believes not there is any substance purely intelligible but that of God; and that though spirits can possibly unite themselves to our minds; yet at present we cannot entirely know them. But he speaks here principally of material things, which he says certainly cannot unite themselves to our souls in such a manner, as is necessary that it should perceive them; because, being extended, the soul not being so, there is no proportion between them.

This is the sum of his doctrine contained in the first chapter of the second part of the third book, as far as I can comprehend it; wherein, I confess, there are many expressions, which carrying with them, to my mind, no clear ideas, are like to remove but little of my ignorance by their sounds. v. g. "What it is to be intimately united to the soul"; what it is for two souls or spirits to be intimately united; for intimate union being an idea taken from bodies when the parts of one get within the surface of the other, and touch their inward parts; what is the idea of intimate union, I must have, between two beings that have neither of them any extension or surface? And if it be not so explained as to give me a clear idea of that union, it will make me understand very little more of the nature of the ideas in my mind, when it is said I see them in God, who being "intimately united to the soul" exhibits them to it; than when it is only said they are by the appointment of God produced in the mind by certain motions of our bodies, to which our minds are united. Which, however imperfect a way of explaining this matter, will still be as good as any other that does not by clear ideas remove my ignorance of the manner of my perception.

But he says that "certainly material things cannot unite themselves to our souls." Our bodies are united to our souls, yes; but, says he, not after "a manner which is necessary that the soul may perceive them." Explain this manner of union, and show wherein the difference consists betwixt the union necessary and not necessary to perception, and then I shall confess this difficulty removed.

The reason that he gives why "material things cannot be united to our souls after a manner" that is necessary to the soul's perceiving them, is this, viz. That, "material things being extended, and the soul not, there is no proportion between them." This, if it shows any thing, shows only that a soul and a body cannot be united, because one has surface to be united by, and the other none. But it shews not why soul, united to a body as ours is, cannot, by that body, have the idea of a triangle excited in it, as well as by being united to God, (between whom and the soul there is as little proportion, as between any creature immaterial or material, and the soul,) see in God the idea of a triangle that is in him, since we cannot conceive a triangle, whether seen in matter, or in God, to be without extension.

The mind cannot produce ideas, says he, because they are "real spiritual beings," i. e. substances; for so is the conclusion of that paragraph, where he mentions it as an absurdity to think they are "annihilated when they are not present to the mind." And the whole force of this argument would persuade one to understand him so; though I do not remember that he any-where speaks it out, or in direct terms calls them substances.

I shall here only take notice how inconceivable it is to me, that a spiritual, i. e. an unextended substance, should represent to the mind an extended figure, v. g. a triangle of unequal sides, or two triangles of different magnitudes. Next, supposing I could conceive an unextended substance to represent a figure, or be the idea of a figure, the difficulty still remains to conceive how it is my soul sees it. Let this substantial being be ever so sure, and the picture ever so clear; yet how we see it, is to me inconceivable. Intimate union, were it as intelligible of two unextended substances as of two bodies, would not yet reach perception, which is something beyond union. But yet a little lower he agrees, that an idea "is not a substance," but yet affirms it is "a spiritual thing": this "spiritual thing" therefore must either be a "spiritual substance," or a mode of a spiritual substance, or a relation; for besides these I have no conception of any thing. And if any shall tell me it is a "mode," it must be a mode of the substance of God; which, besides that it will be strange to mention any modes in the simple essence of God; whosoever shall propose any such modes, as a way to explain the nature of our ideas, proposes to me something inconceivable, as a means to conceive what I do not yet know; and so bating a new phrase, teaches me nothing, but leaves me as much in the dark as one can be where he conceives nothing. So that supposing ideas real spiritual things ever so much, if they are neither substances nor modes, let them be what they will, I am no more instructed in their nature, than when I am told they are perceptions such as I find them. And I appeal to my reader, whether that hypothesis be to be preferred for its easiness, to be understood, which is explained by real beings, that are neither substances nor modes.

The reader must not blame me for making use here all along of the word 'sentiment,' which is our author's own, and I understood it so little, that I knew not how to translate it to any other. He concludes, "that he believes there is no appearance of truth in any other ways of explaining these things, and that this of seeing all things in God, is more than probable." I have considered with as much indifferency and attention as is possible; and I must own it appears to me as little or less intelligible than any of the rest; and the summary of his doctrine, which he here subjoins, is to me wholly incomprehensible. His words are, "Thus our souls depend on God all manner of ways: for as it is he which makes them feel pleasure and pain, and all other sensations, by the natural union which he has made between them and our bodies, which is nothing else but his decree and general will: so it is he, who by the natural union which he has made betwixt the will of man and the representation of ideas, which the immensity of the divine being contains, makes them know all that they know; and this natural union is also nothing but his general will." This phrase of the union of our wills to the ideas contained in God's immensity, seems to me a very strange one; and what light it gives to his doctrine I truly cannot find. It seemed so unintelligible to me, that I guessed it an errour in the print of the edition I used, which was the 4to printed at Paris, 78, and therefore consulted the 8vo, printed also at Paris, and found it "will" in both of them. Here again the "immensity of the divine being" is mentioned as that which contains in it the ideas to which our wills are united; which ideas being only those of quantity, as I shall show hereafter, seems to me to carry with it a very gross notion of this matter, as we have above remarked. But that which I take notice of principally here, is, that this union of our wills to the ideas contained in God's immensity does not at all explain our seeing of them. This union of our wills to the ideas, or, as in other places, of our souls to God, is, says he, nothing but the will of God. And, after this union, our seeing them is only when God discovers them, i. e. our having them in our minds, is nothing but the will of God; all which is brought about in a way we comprehend not. And what then does this explain more than when one says, our souls are united to our bodies by the will of God, and by the motion of some parts of our bodies? V. g. the nerves or animal spirits have ideas or perceptions produced in them, and this is the will of God. Why is not this as intelligible and as clear as the other? Here is by the will of God given union and perception in both cases; but how that perception is made in both ways, seems to me equally incomprehensible. In one, God discovers ideas in himself to the soul united to him when he pleases; and in the other, he discovers ideas to the soul, or produces perception in the soul united to the body by motion, according to laws established by the good pleasure of his will; but how it is done in the one or the other, I confess my incapacity to comprehend. So that I agree perfectly with him in his conclusion, that "there is nothing but God that can enlighten us": but a clear comprehension of the manner how he does it, I doubt I shall not have, till I know a great deal more of him and myself, than in this state of darkness and ignorance our souls are capable of.

In his *Remarks upon Some of Mr. Norris' Books* (*Works*, vol. X), Locke repeats his charge that Malebranche's theory tells us nothing at all about the nature of the act of perceiving. Whether we follow the corpuscular account of the production of ideas or Malebranche's divine volition theory, both accounts are extrinsical to the mind and to

perceiving. Locke asks Norris and Malebranche to explain
to him "what the alteration in the mind is, [when we per-
ceive] besides saying, as we vulgar do, it is having a perception" (section 2, pp. 248–9). Locke also repeats to Norris the objections he has against Malebranche's talk of ideas
as real entities (section 17, p. 256). He professes ignorance
as to what ideas are "any further than as they are perceptions we experiment in ourselves" (section 18, p. 256).

The debate over the nature of ideas continued through
the eighteenth century. More often there was no debate,
only the different concepts were used. Toward the end of
the eighteenth century, Thomas Reid succinctly stated the
second concept, in contrast with the first.

> To think of a thing, and to have a thought of it; to be-
> lieve a thing, and to have a belief of it; to see a thing,
> and have a sight of it; to conceive a thing, and to have a
> conception, notion, or idea of it, are phrases perfectly
> synonymous. In these phrases, the thought means noth-
> ing but the act of thinking; the belief, the act of believ-
> ing; and the conception, notion, or idea, the act of con-
> ceiving. To have a clear and distinct idea, is, in this
> sense, nothing else but to conceive the thing clearly and
> distinctly. When the word *idea* is taken in this popular
> sense, there can be no doubt of our having ideas in our
> minds. To think without ideas would be to think without
> thought, which is a manifest contradiction.[18]

For Reid, the first concept of idea (which he called the
"philosopher's idea") was a fiction that, if real, would mean
that "we perceive not external objects immediately, and
that the immediate objects of perception are only certain
shadows of the external objects."[19] Locke's definition of
knowledge in 4.1.2, as *"the perception of the connexion
and agreement, or disagreemnt and repugnancy,* of any
of *our ideas,"* can, if *idea* is taken in the first sense and if
the relation of coexistence is either overlooked or made
equivalent with necessary connection, raise the skeptical
challenge. Locke himself puts the question of skepticism
to himself (see selection 10) and to Malebranche.

18 *Essays on the Intellectual Powers of Man* (Dublin, 1786), vol. 1,
   p. 174.
19 *Ibid.,* p. 133.

30. *Examination*, section 20

He farther says, that had we a magazine of all ideas that are necessary for seeing things, they would be of no use, since the mind could not know which to choose, and set before itself to see the sun. What he here means by the sun is hard to conceive, and according to his hypothesis of "seeing all things in God," how can he know that there is any such real being in the world as the sun? Did he ever see the sun? No, but on occasion of the presence of the sun to his eyes, he has seen the idea of the sun in God, which God has exhibited to him; but the sun, because it cannot be united to his soul, he cannot see. How then does he know that there is a sun which he never saw? And since God does all things by the most compendious ways, what need is there that God should make a sun that we might see its idea in him when he pleased to exhibit it, when this might as well be done without any real sun at all.

> Each reader will have to decide this much-debated issue in Locke: which concept of idea did he mean? And has he avoided skepticism? Many things he says about ideas would seem to be neutral between the two concepts

The origin of ideas
Locke's account of the origin of ideas contains five components. (a) First, there is his rejection of innate ideas and principles. (b) Second, there is a brief, truncated genetic account of the order of acquisition of ideas in children. (c) Then there is his generalized doctrine about experience being the only source of ideas. (d) Fourthly, there is his acceptance, with varying degrees of conviction, of the physical and physiological processes accompanying perception. (e) Finally, there is an account of how specific ideas are generated.

(a) Rejection of innate ideas
The second to fifth components above obviously contain Locke's alternative to innatism, the belief commonly held that we are born with some ideas or truths.

31. *Essay*, 1.2.1–9

It is an established opinion amongst some men, that there are in the understanding certain innate principles; some primary notions, χοιναὶ ἔννοιαι, characters, as it were, stamped upon the mind of man, which the soul receives in its very first being; and brings into the world with it. It would be sufficient to convince unprejudiced readers of the falseness of this supposition, if I should only shew (as I hope I shall in the following parts of this discourse) how men, barely by the use of their natural faculties, may attain to all the knowledge they have, without the help of any innate impressions; and may arrive at certainty, without any such original notions or principles. For I imagine any one will easily grant, that it would be impertinent to suppose, the ideas of colours innate in a creature, to whom God hath given sight, and a power to receive them by the eyes, from external objects: and no less unreasonable would it be to attribute several truths to the impressions of nature, and innate characters, when we may observe in ourselves faculties, fit to attain as easy and certain knowledge of them, as if they were originally imprinted on the mind.

But because a man is not permitted without censure to follow his own thoughts in the search of truth, when they lead him ever so little out of the common road; I shall set down the reasons, that made me doubt of the truth of that opinion, as an excuse for my mistake, if I be in one; which I leave to be considered by those, who, with me, dispose themselves to embrace truth, wherever they find it.

There is nothing more commonly taken for granted, than that there are certain principles, both speculative and practical (for they speak of both) universally agreed upon by all mankind: which therefore, they argue, must needs be constant impressions, which the souls of men receive in their first beings, and which they bring into the world with them, as necessarily and really as they do any of their inherent faculties.

This argument, drawn from universal consent, has this misfortune in it, that if it were true in matter of fact, that there were certain truths, wherein all mankind agreed, it would not prove them innate, if there can be any other way shewn, how men may come to that universal agreement, in the things they do consent in; which I presume may be done.

But, which is worse, this argument of universal consent, which is made use of to prove innate principles, seems to me a demonstration that there are none such; because there are none to which all mankind give an universal assent. I shall begin with the speculative, and instance in those magnified principles of demonstration; "whatsoever is, is"; and, "it is impossible for the same thing to be, and not to be"; which, of all others, I think have the most allowed title to innate. These have so settled a reputation of maxims universally received, that it will, no doubt, be thought strange, if any one should seem to question it. But yet I take liberty to say, that these propositions are so far from having an universal assent, that there are great part of mankind to whom they are not so much as known.

For, first, it is evident, that all children and idiots have not the least apprehension or thought of them; and the want of that is enough to destroy that universal assent, which must needs be the necessary concomitant of all innate truths: it seeming to me near a contradiction, to say, that there are truths imprinted on the soul, which it perceives or understands not; imprinting, if it signify any thing, being nothing else, but the making certain truths to be perceived. For to imprint any thing on the mind, without the mind's perceiving it, seems to me hardly intelligible. If therefore children and idiots have souls, have minds, with those impressions upon them, they must unavoidably perceive them, and necessarily know and assent to these truths; which since they do not, it is evident that there are no such impressions. For if they are not notions naturally imprinted, how can they be innate? and if they are notions imprinted, how can they be unknown? To say a notion is imprinted on the mind, and yet at the same time to say, that the mind is ignorant of it, and never yet took notice of it, is to make this impression nothing. No proposition can be said to be in the mind, which it never yet knew, which it was never yet conscious of. For if any one may, then, by the same reason, all propositions that are true, and the mind is capable of ever assenting to, may be said to be in the mind, and to be imprinted: since, if any one can be said to be in the mind, which it never yet knew, it must be only, because it is capable of knowing it, and so the mind is of all truths it ever shall know. Nay, thus truths may be imprinted on the mind, which it never did, nor ever shall know: for a man may live long, and die at last in ignorance of many truths, which his mind was capable of knowing, and that with certainty. So that if the capacity of knowing, be the natural impression contended for, all the truths a man ever comes to know, will, by this account, be every one of them innate; and this great point will amount to no more, but only to a very improper way of speaking; which, whilst it pretends to assert the contrary, says nothing different from those, who deny innate principles. For nobody, I think, ever denied that the mind was capable of knowing several truths. The capacity, they say, is innate, the knowledge acquired. But then to what end such contest for certain innate maxims? If truths can be imprinted on the understanding without being perceived, I can see no difference there can be, between any truths the mind is capable of knowing, in respect of their original: they must all be innate, or all adventitious: in vain shall a man go about to distinguish them. He therefore, that talks of innate notions in the understanding, cannot (if he intend thereby any distinct sort of truths) mean such truths to be in the understanding, as it never perceived, and is yet wholly ignorant of. For if these words (to be in the understanding) have any propriety, they signify to be understood: so that, to be in the understanding, and not to be understood; to be in the mind, and never to be perceived; is all one, as to say, any thing is, and is not, in the mind or understanding. If therefore these two propositions, "whatsoever is, is"; and "it is impossible for the same thing to be, and not to be," are by nature imprinted, children cannot be ignorant of them; infants, and all that have souls, must necessarily have them in their understandings, know the truth of them, and assent to it.

To avoid this, it is usually answered, That all men know and assent to them, when they come to the use of reason, and this is enough to prove them innate. I answer,

Doubtful expressions, that have scarce any signification, go for clear reasons, to those, who being prepossessed, take not the pains to examine, even what they themselves say. For to apply this answer with any tolerable sense to our present purpose, it must signify one of these two things; either, that, as soon as men come to the use of reason, these supposed native inscriptions come to be known, and observed by them: or else, that the use and exercise of men's reason assists them in the discovery of these principles, and certainly makes them known to them.

If they mean, that by the use of reason men may discover these principles; and that this is sufficient to prove them innate: their way of arguing will stand thus, (viz.) that, whatever truths reason can certainly discover to us, and make us firmly assent to, those are all naturally imprinted on the mind: since that universal assent, which is made the mark of them, amounts to no more but this; that by the use of reason, we are capable to come to a certain knowledge of, and assent to them; and, by this means, there will be no difference between the maxims of the mathematicians, and theorems they deduce from them; all must be equally allowed innate; they being all discoveries made by the use of reason, and truths that a rational creature may certainly come to know, if he apply his thoughts rightly that way.

But how can these men think the use of reason necessary, to

discover principles that are supposed innate, when reason (if we may believe them) is nothing else but the faculty of deducing unknown truths from principles, or propositions, that are already known? That certainly can never be thought innate, which we have need of reason to discover; unless, as I have said, we will have all the certain truths, that reason ever teaches us, to be innate. We may as well think the use of reason necessary to make our eyes discover visible objects, as that there should be need of reason, or the exercise thereof, to make the understanding see what is originally engraven on it, and cannot be in the understanding before it be perceived by it. So that to make reason discover those truths thus imprinted, is to say, that the use of reason discovers to a man what he knew before: and if men have those innate impressed truths originally, and before the use of reason, and yet are always ignorant of them, till they come to the use of reason; it is in effect to say, that men know, and know them not, at the same time.

32. *Essay,* 1.3.1–4, 10–11

If those speculative maxims, whereof we discoursed in the foregoing chapter, have not an actual universal assent from all mankind, as we there proved, it is much more visible concerning practical principles, that they come short of an universal reception: and I think it will be hard to instance any one moral rule, which can pretend to so general and ready an assent as, "what is, is"; or to be so manifest a truth as this, "that it is impossible for the same thing to be, and not to be." Whereby it is evident, that they are farther removed from a title to be innate; and the doubt of their being native impressions on the mind, is stronger against those moral principles than the other. Not that it brings their truth at all in question: they are equally true, though not equally evident. Those speculative maxims carry their own evidence with them; but moral principles require reasoning and discourse, and some exercise of the mind, to discover the certainty of their truth. They lie not open as natural characters engraven on the mind; which, if any such were, they must needs be visible by themselves, and by their own light be certain and known to every body. But this is no derogation to their truth and certainty, no more than it is to the truth or certainty of the three angles of a triangle being equal to two right ones; because it is not so evident, as "the whole is bigger than a part"; nor so apt to be assented to at first hearing. It may suffice, that these moral rules are capable of demonstration; and therefore it is our own fault, if we come not to a certain knowledge of them. But the ignorance wherein many men are of them, and the slowness of assent wherewith others receive them, are manifest proofs that they are not innate, and such as offer themselves to their view without searching.

Whether there be any such moral principles, wherein all men do agree, I appeal to any, who have been but moderately conversant in the history of mankind, and looked abroad beyond the smoke of their own chimnies. Where is that practical truth, that is universally received without doubt or question, as it must be, if innate? Justice, and keeping of contracts, is that which most men seem to agree in. This is a principle, which is thought to extend itself to the dens of thieves, and the confederacies of the greatest villains; and they who have gone farthest towards the putting off of humanity itself, keep faith and rules of justice one with another. I grant that outlaws themselves do this one amongst another; but it is without receiving these as the innate laws of nature. They practise them as rules of convenience within their own communities: but it is impossible to conceive, that he embraces justice as a practical principle, who acts fairly with his fellow highwayman, and at the same time plunders or kills the next honest man he meets with. Justice and truth are the common ties of society; and therefore, even outlaws and robbers, who break with all the world besides, must keep faith and rules of equity amongst themselves, or else they cannot hold together. But will any one say, that those that live by fraud or rapine, have innate principles of truth and justice which they allow and assent to?

Perhaps it will be urged, that the tacit assent of their minds agrees to what their practice contradicts. I answer, first, I have always thought the actions of men the best interpreters of their thoughts. But since it is certain, that most men's practices, and some men's open professions, have either questioned or denied these principles, it is impossible to establish an universal consent, (though we should look for it only amongst grown men) without which it is impossible to conclude them innate. Secondly, it is very strange and unreasonable to suppose innate practical principles, that terminate only in contemplation. Practical principles derived from nature are there for operation, and must produce conformity of action, not barely speculative assent to their truth, or else they are in vain distinguished from speculative maxims. Nature, I confess, has put into man a desire of happiness, and an aversion to misery: these indeed are innate practical principles, which (as

practical principles ought) do continue constantly to operate and
influence all our actions without ceasing: these may be observed
in all persons and all ages, steady and universal; but these are
inclinations of the appetite to good, not impressions of truth on
the understanding. I deny not, that there are natural tendencies
imprinted on the minds of men; and that, from the very first instances of sense and perception, there are some things that are
grateful, and others unwelcome to them; some things, that they
incline to, and others that they fly: but this makes nothing for
innate characters on the mind, which are to be the principles of
knowledge, regulating our practice. Such natural impressions on
the understanding are so far from being confirmed hereby, that this
is an argument against them; since, if there were certain characters imprinted by nature on the understanding, as the principles
of knowledge, we could not but perceive them constantly operate
in us and influence our knowledge, as we do those others on the
will and appetite; which never cease to be the constant springs
and motives of all our actions, to which we perpetually feel them
strongly impelling us.

Another reason that makes me doubt of any innate practical
principles, is, that I think there cannot any one moral rule be
proposed, whereof a man may not justly demand a reason: which
would be perfectly ridiculous and absurd, if they were innate, or
so much as self-evident; which every innate principle must needs
be, and not need any proof to ascertain its truth, nor want any
reason to gain it approbation. He would be thought void of common
sense, who asked on the one side, or on the other side went to
give a reason, why it is impossible for the same thing to be, and
not to be. It carries its own light and evidence with it, and needs
no other proof: he that understands the terms, assents to it for its
own sake, or else nothing will ever be able to prevail with him to
do it. But should that most unshaken rule of morality, and foundation of all social virtue, "that one should do as he would be done
unto," be proposed to one who never heard it before, but yet is of
capacity to understand its meaning, might he not without any
absurdity ask a reason why? and were not he that proposed it
bound to make out the truth and reasonableness of it to him?
which plainly shows it not to be innate.

He that will carefully peruse the history of mankind, and look
abroad into the several tribes of men, and with indifferency survey
their actions, will be able to satisfy himself, that there is scarce
that principle of morality to be named, or rule of virtue to be

thought on (those only excepted that are absolutely necessary to hold society together, which commonly, too, are neglected betwixt distinct societies) which is not, somewhere or other, slighted and condemned by the general fashion of whole societies of men, governed by practical opinions and rules of living, quite opposite to others.

Here, perhaps, it will be objected, that it is no argument that the rule is not known, because it is broken. I grant the objection good, where men, though they transgress, yet disown not the law; where fear of shame, censure, or punishment, carries the mark of some awe it has upon them. But it is impossible to conceive, that a whole nation of men should all publicly reject and renounce what every one of them, certainly and infallibly, knew to be a law: for so they must, who have it naturally imprinted on their minds. It is possible men may sometimes own rules of morality, which, in their private thoughts, they do not believe to be true, only to keep themselves in reputation and esteem amongst those, who are persuaded of their obligation. But it is not to be imagined, that a whole society of men should publicly and professedly disown, and cast off a rule, which they could not, in their own minds, but be infallibly certain was a law; nor be ignorant that all men they should have to do with, knew it to be such: and therefore must every one of them apprehend from others, all the contempt and abhorrence due to one, who professes himself void of humanity; and one, who, confounding the known and natural measures of right and wrong, cannot but be looked on as the professed enemy of their peace and happiness. Whatever practical principle is innate, cannot but be known to every one to be just and good.

33. *Essay*, 1.4.1–7

Had those, who would persuade us that there are innate principles, not taken them together in gross, but considered separately the parts out of which those propositions are made; they would not, perhaps, have been so forward to believe they were innate: since, if the ideas which made up those truths were not, it was impossible that the propositions made up of them should be innate, or the knowledge of them be born with us. For if the ideas be not innate, there was a time when the mind was without those principles; and then they will not be innate, but be derived from some other original. For where the ideas themselves are not, there can be no knowledge, no assent, no mental or verbal propositions about them.

If we will attentively consider new-born children, we shall have little reason to think, that they bring many ideas into the world with them. For bating perhaps some faint ideas of hunger and thirst, and warmth, and some pains which they may have felt in the womb, there is not the least appearance of any settled ideas at all in them; especially of ideas, answering the terms which make up those universal propositions, that are esteemed innate principles. One may perceive how, by degrees, afterwards, ideas come into their minds; and that they get no more, nor no other, than what experience, and the observation of things, that come in their way, furnish them with: which might be enough to satisfy us, that they are not original characters stamped on the mind.

"It is impossible for the same thing to be, and not to be," is certainly (if there be any such) an innate principle. But can any one think, or will any one say, that impossibility and identity are two innate ideas? Are they such as all mankind have, and bring into the world with them? And are they those which are the first in children, and antecedent to all acquired ones? If they are innate, they must needs be so. Hath a child an idea of impossibility and identity, before it has of white or black, sweet or bitter? And is it from the knowledge of this principle, that it concludes, that wormwood rubbed on the nipple hath not the same taste that it used to receive from thence? Is it the actual knowledge of "impossibile est idem esse, & non esse," that makes a child distinguish between its mother and a stranger? or, that makes it fond of the one, and fly the other? Or does the mind regulate itself and its assent by ideas, that it never yet had? Or the understanding draw conclusions from principles, which it never yet knew or understood? The names impossibility and identity stand for two ideas, so far from being innate, or born with us, that I think it requires great care and attention to form them right in our understandings. They are so far from being brought into the world with us, so remote from the thoughts of infancy and childhood; that, I believe, upon examination it will be found, that many grown men want them.

If identity (to instance in that alone) be a native impression, and consequently so clear and obvious to us, that we must needs know it even from our cradles; I would gladly be resolved by one of seven, or seventy years old, whether a man, being a creature consisting of soul and body, be the same man when his body is changed? Whether Euphorbus and Pythagoras, having had the same soul, were the same men, though they lived several ages asunder? Nay, whether the cock too, which had the same soul, were not the same with both of them? Whereby, perhaps, it will appear, that our idea of sameness is not so settled and clear, as to deserve to be thought innate in us. For if those innate ideas are not clear and distinct, so as to be universally known, and naturally agreed on, they cannot be subjects of universal and undoubted truths; but will be the unavoidable occasion of perpetual uncertainty. For, I suppose, every one's idea of identity will not be the same that Pythagoras, and others of his followers have: And which then shall be true? Which innate? Or are there two different ideas of identity, both innate?

Nor let any one think, that the questions I have here proposed about the identity of man, are bare empty speculations; which if they were, would be enough to show, that there was in the understandings of men no innate idea of identity. He that shall, with a little attention, reflect on the resurrection, and consider that divine justice will bring to judgment, at the last day, the very same persons, to be happy or miserable in the other, who did well or ill in this life; will find it perhaps not easy to resolve with himself, what makes the same man, or wherein identity consists; and will not be forward to think he, and every one, even children themselves, have naturally a clear idea of it.

Let us examine that principle of mathematicks, viz. "that the whole is bigger than a part." This, I take it, is reckoned amongst innate principles. I am sure it has as good a title as any to be thought so; which yet nobody can think it to be, when he considers the ideas it comprehends in it, "whole and part," are perfectly relative: but the positive ideas, to which they properly and immediately belong, are extension and number, of which alone whole and part are relations. So that if whole and part are innate ideas, extension and number must be so too; it being impossible to have an idea of a relation, without having any at all of the thing to which it belongs, and in which it is founded. Now whether the minds of men have naturally imprinted on them the ideas of extension and number, I leave to be considered by those, who are the patrons of innate principles.

"That God is to be worshipped," is, without doubt, as great a truth as any can enter into the mind of man, and deserves the first place amongst all practical principles. But yet it can by no means be thought innate, unless the ideas of God and worship are innate. That the idea the term worship stands for, is not in the understanding of children, and a character stamped on the mind in its first original, I think, will be easily granted, by any one that considers how few there be, amongst grown men, who have a clear and distinct notion of it. And, I suppose, there cannot be any thing more ridiculous, than to say that children have this practical principle innate, "that God is to be worshipped"; and yet, that they know not what that worship of God is, which is their duty.

(b) Genetic account of ideas in children
The genetic account was not elaborated by Locke, but it is clear that he had a notion of the gradual acquisition of ideas by children. This account is perhaps more relevant to his interests in education than it is to his theory of knowledge, although of course the generalized doctrine assumes a notion of learning and idea acquisition.

34. *Essay,* 1.2.15

The senses at first let in particular ideas, and furnish the yet empty cabinet; and the mind by degrees growing familiar with some of them, they are lodged in the memory, and names got to them. Afterwards the mind, proceeding farther, abstracts them, and by degrees learns the use of general names. In this manner the mind comes to be furnished with ideas and language, the materials about which to exercise its discursive faculty: and the use of reason becomes daily more visible, as these materials that give it employment increase. But though the having of general ideas, and the use of general words and reason, usually grow together; yet, I see not, how this any way proves them innate. The knowledge of some truths, I confess, is very early in the mind; but in a way that shows them not to be innate. For, if we will observe, we shall find it still to be about ideas, not innate, but acquired: It being about those first which are imprinted by external things, with which infants have earliest to do, which make the most frequent impressions on their senses. In ideas thus got, the mind discovers that some agree, and others differ, probably as soon as it has any use of memory; as soon as it is able to retain and perceive distinct ideas.

35. *Essay,* 1.2.25

Whether we can determine it or no, it matters not, there is certainly a time when children begin to think, and their words and actions do assure us that they do so.

36. *Essay,* 1.4.13

He that shall observe in children the progress whereby their minds attain the knowledge they have, will think that the objects they do first and most familiarly converse with, are those that make the first impressions on their understandings: nor will he find the least foot-steps of any other. It is easy to take notice, how their thoughts enlarge themselves, only as they come to be acquainted with a greater variety of sensible objects, to retain the ideas of them in their memories; and to get the skill to compound and enlarge them, and several ways put them together.

37. *Essay*, 2.1.6, 21–2

He that attentively considers the state of a child, at his first coming into the world, will have little reason to think him stored with plenty of ideas, that are to be the matter of his future knowledge: It is by degrees he comes to be furnished with them. And though the ideas of obvious and familiar qualities imprint themselves be-fore the memory begins to keep a register of time or order, yet it is often so late before some unusual qualities come in the way, that there are few men that cannot recollect the beginning of their acquaintance with them: and if it were worth while, no doubt a child might be so ordered as to have but a very few even of the ordinary ideas, till he were grown up to a man. But all that are born into the world being surrounded with bodies that perpetually and diversely affect them; variety of ideas, whether care be taken of it or no, are imprinted on the minds of children. Light and colours are busy at hand everywhere, when the eye is but open; sounds and some tangible qualities fail not to solicit their proper senses, and force an entrance to the mind: but yet, I think, it will be granted easily, that if a child were kept in a place where he never saw any other but black and white till he were a man, he would have no more ideas of scarlet or green, than he that from his childhood never tasted an oyster or a pineapple has of those particular relishes.

He that will suffer himself to be informed by observation and experience, and not make his own hypothesis the rule of nature, will find few signs of a soul accustomed to much thinking in a new-born child, and much fewer of any reasoning at all. And yet it is hard to imagine, that the rational soul should think so much, and not reason at all. And he that will consider, that infants, newly come into the world, spend the greatest part of their time in sleep, and are seldom awake, but when either hunger calls for the teat, or some pain (the most importunate of all sensations) or some other violent impression upon the body forces the mind to perceive, and attend to it: he, I say, who considers this, will, perhaps, find reason to imagine, that a foetus in the mother's womb differs not much from the state of a vegetable; but passes the greatest part of its time without perception or thought, doing very little but sleep in a place where it needs not seek for food, and is surrounded with liquor, always equally soft, and near of the same temper; where the eyes have no light, and the ears, so shut up, are not very susceptible of sounds; and where there is little or no variety or change of objects to move the senses.

Follow a child from its birth, and observe the alterations that time makes, and you shall find, as the mind by the senses comes more and more to be furnished with ideas, it comes to be more and more awake; thinks more, the more it has matter to think on. After some time it begins to know the objects, which, being most familiar with it, have made lasting impressions. Thus it comes by degrees to know the persons it daily converses with, and distinguish them from strangers; which are instances and effects of its coming to retain and distinguish the ideas the senses convey to it. And so we may observe how the mind, by degrees, improves in these, and advances to the exercise of those other faculties of enlarging, compounding, and abstracting its ideas, and of reasoning about them, and reflecting upon all these; of which I shall have occasion to speak more hereafter.

38. Essay, 2.9.5, 7

Therefore I doubt not but children, by the exercise of their senses about objects that affect them in the womb, receive some few ideas before they are born; as the unavoidable effects, either of the bodies that environ them, or else of those wants or diseases they suffer: amongst which (if one may conjecture concerning things not very capable of examination) I think the ideas of hunger and warmth are two; which probably are some of the first that children have, and which they scarce ever part with again.

As there are some ideas which we may reasonably suppose may be introduced into the minds of children in the womb, subservient to the necessities of their life and being there; so after they are born, those ideas are the earliest imprinted, which happen to be the sensible qualities which first occur to them: amongst which, light is not the least considerable, nor of the weakest efficacy. And how covetous the mind is to be furnished with all such ideas as have no pain accompanying them, may be a little guessed, by what is observable in children new-born, who always turn their eyes to that part from whence the light comes, lay them how you please. But the ideas that are most familiar at first being various, according to the divers circumstances of children's first entertainment in the world; the order wherein the several ideas come at first into the mind is very various and uncertain also.

(c) Experience as the source
The statement of the generalized theory is straightforward, though it must be read in the context of the next two components.

39. Essay, 1.4.25

To show how the understanding proceeds herein, is the design of the following discourse; which I shall proceed to, when I have first premised, that hitherto, to clear my way to those foundations, which I conceive are the only true ones whereon to establish those notions we can have of our own knowledge, it hath been necessary for me to give an account of the reasons I had to doubt of innate principles. And since the arguments which are against them do some of them rise from common received opinions, I have been forced to take several things for granted, which is hardly avoidable to any one, whose task is to show the falsehood or improbability of any tenet; it happening in controversial discourses, as it does in assaulting of towns, where if the ground be but firm whereon the batteries are erected, there is no farther inquiry of whom it is borrowed, nor whom it belongs to, so it affords but a fit rise for the present purpose. But in the future part of this discourse, designing to raise an edifice uniform and consistent with itself, as far as my own experience and observation will assist me, I hope to erect it on such a basis, that I shall not need to shore it up with props and buttresses, leaning on borrowed or begged foundations; or at least, if mine prove a castle in the air, I will endeavour it shall be all of a piece, and hang together. Wherein I warn the reader not to expect undeniable cogent demonstrations, unless I may be allowed the privilege, not seldom assumed by others, to take my principles for granted: and then, I doubt not, but I can demonstrate too. All that I shall say for the principles I proceed on is, that I can only appeal to men's own unprejudiced experience and observation, whether they be true or no; and this is enough for a man who professes no more, than to lay down candidly and freely his own conjectures, concerning a subject lying somewhat in the dark, without any other design than an unbiased inquiry after truth.

Every man being conscious to himself that he thinks, and that which his mind is applied about, whilst thinking, being the ideas that are there, it is past doubt, that men have in their minds several ideas, such as are those expressed by the words, Whiteness, Hardness, Sweetness, Thinking, Motion, Man, Elephant, Army, Drunkenness, and others. It is in the first place then to be inquired, how he comes by them. I know it is a received doctrine, that men have native ideas, and original characters, stamped upon their minds, in their very first being. This opinion I have, at large, examined already; and, I suppose, what I have said in the foregoing book, will be much more easily admitted, when I have shown, whence the understanding may get all the ideas it has, and by what ways and degrees they may come into the mind; for which I shall appeal to every one's own observation and experience.

Let us then suppose the mind to be, as we say, white paper, void of all characters, without any ideas; how comes it to be furnished? Whence comes it by that vast store which the busy and boundless fancy of man has painted on it, with an almost endless variety? Whence has it all the materials of reason and knowledge? To this I answer, in one word, from experience; in all that our knowledge is founded, and from that it ultimately derives itself. Our observation employed either about external sensible objects, or about the internal operations of our minds, perceived and reflected on by ourselves, is that which supplies our understandings with all the materials of thinking. These two are the fountains of knowledge, from whence all the ideas we have, or can naturally have, do spring.

First, Our senses, conversant about particular sensible objects, do convey into the mind several distinct perceptions of things, according to those various ways wherein those objects do affect them: and thus we come by those ideas we have, of Yellow, White, Heat, Cold, Soft, Hard, Bitter, Sweet, and all those which we call sensible qualities; which when I say the senses convey into the mind, I mean, they from external objects convey into the mind what produces there those perceptions. This great source of most of the ideas we have, depending wholly upon our senses, and derived by them to the understanding, I call SENSATION.

Secondly, The other fountain, from which experience furnisheth the understanding with ideas, is the perception of the operations of our own mind within us, as it is employed about the ideas it has got; which operations when the soul comes to reflect on and consider, do furnish the understanding with another set of ideas, which could not be had from things without; and such are Perception, Thinking, Doubting, Believing, Reasoning, Knowing, Willing, and all the different actings of our own minds; which we being conscious of and observing in ourselves, do from these receive into our understandings as distinct ideas, as we do from bodies affecting our senses. This source of ideas every man has wholly in himself; and though it be not sense, as having nothing to do with external objects, yet it is very like it, and might properly enough be called internal sense. But as I call the other sensation, so I call this REFLECTION, the ideas it affords being such only as the mind gets by reflecting on its own operations within itself. By reflection then, in the following part of this discourse, I would be understood to mean that notice which the mind takes of its own operations, and the manner of them; by reason whereof there come to be ideas of these operations in the understanding. These two, I say, viz. external material things, as the objects of sensation; and the operations of our own minds within, as the objects of reflection; are to me the only originals from whence all our ideas take their beginnings. The term operations here I use in a large sense, as comprehending not barely the actions of the mind about its ideas, but some sort of passions arising sometimes from them, such as is the satisfaction or uneasiness arising from any thought.

The understanding seems to me not to have the least glimmering of any ideas, which it doth not receive from one of these two. External objects furnish the mind with the ideas of sensible qualities, which are all those different perceptions they produce in us: and the mind furnishes the understanding with ideas of its own operations.

These, when we have taken a full survey of them and their several modes, combinations, and relations, we shall find to contain all our whole stock of ideas; and that we have nothing in our minds which did not come in one of these two ways. Let any one examine his own thoughts, and thoroughly search into his understanding; and then let him tell me, whether all the original ideas he has there, are any other than of the objects of his senses, or of the operations of his mind, considered as objects of his reflection; and how great a mass of knowledge soever he imagines to be lodged there, he will, upon taking a strict view, see that he has not any idea in his mind, but what one of these two have imprinted; though perhaps, with infinite variety compounded and enlarged by the understanding, as we shall see hereafter.

In time the mind comes to reflect on its own operations about
the ideas got by sensation, and thereby stores itself with a new set
of ideas, which I call ideas of reflection. These are the impressions
that are made on our senses by outward objects that are extrinsical
to the mind, and its own operations, proceeding from powers in-
trinsical and proper to itself; which when reflected on by itself,
becoming also objects of its contemplation, are, as I have said, the
original of all knowledge. Thus the first capacity of human intellect
is, that the mind is fitted to receive the impressions made on it;
either through the senses by outward objects; or by its own operations when it reflects on them. This is the first step a man makes
towards the discovery of any thing, and the ground-work whereon
to build all those notions which ever he shall have naturally in this
world. All those sublime thoughts which tower above the clouds,
and reach as high as heaven itself, take their rise and footing here:
in all that good extent wherein the mind wanders, in those remote
speculations, it may seem to be elevated with, it stirs not one jot
beyond those ideas which sense or reflection have offered for its
contemplation.

(d) Physiology

When, early in his Introduction (1.1.2), Locke announced
his intention to "inquire into the original, certainty, and
extent of human knowledge, together with the grounds
and degrees of belief, opinion, and assent," he hastened
to add: "I shall not at present meddle with the physical
consideration of the mind; or trouble myself to examine,
wherein its essence consists, or by what motions of our
spirits, or alterations of our bodies, we come to have any
sensation by our organs, or any ideas in our understandings; and whether those ideas do in their formation, any,
or all of them, depend on matter or no." However, he is
forced to resort to the physical and physiological account
from time to time in the *Essay*. Some passages in his *Examination of P. Malebranche's Opinion* go into considerable
detail on the physical causes of perception.

41. *Examination*, sections 9–16

Though the peripatetic doctrine of the species does not at all satisfy
me, yet I think it were not hard to show, that it is as easy to
account for the difficulties he charges on it, as for those his own
hypothesis is laden with. But it being not my business to defend

what I do not understand, nor to prefer the learned gibberish of the schools to what is yet unintelligible to me in P. M. I shall only take notice of so much of his objections, as concerns what I guess to be the truth. Though I do not think any material species, carrying the resemblance of things by a continual flux from the body we perceive, bring the perception of them to our senses; yet I think the perception we have of bodies at a distance from ours, may be accounted for, as far as we are capable of understanding it, by the motion of particles of matter coming from them and striking on our organs. In feeling and tasting there is immediate contact. Sound is not unintelligibly explained by a vibrating motion communicated to the medium, and the effluvia of odorous bodies will, without any great difficulties, account for smells. And therefore P. M. makes his objections only against visible species, as the most difficult to be explained by material causes, as indeed they are. But he that shall allow extreme smallness in the particles of light, and exceeding swiftness in their motion; and the great porosity that must be granted in bodies, if we compare gold, which wants them not, with air, the medium wherein the rays of light come to our eyes, and that of a million of rays that rebound from any visible area of any body, perhaps the 1/1000 or 1/10000 part coming to the eye, are enough to move the retina, sufficiently to cause a sensation in the mind, will not find any great difficulty in the objections which are brought from the impenetrability of matter, and these rays ruffling and breaking one another in the medium which is full of them. As to what is said, that from one point we can see a great number of objects, that is no objection against the species, or visible appearances of bodies, being brought into the eye by the rays of light; for the bottom of the eye or retina, which, in regard of these rays, is the place of vision, is far from being a point. Nor is it true, that though the eye be in any one place; yet that the sight is performed in one point, i. e. that the rays that bring those visible species do all meet at a point; for they cause their distinct sensations by striking on distinct parts of the retina, as is plain in optics: and the figure they paint there must be of some considerable bigness, since it takes up on the retina an area whose diameter is at least thirty seconds of a circle, whereof the circumference is in the retina, and the centre somewhere in the crystalline; as a little skill in optics will manifest to any one that considers, that few eyes can perceive an object less than thirty minutes of a circle, whereof the eye is the centre. And he that will but reflect on that seeming odd experiment of seeing only the two outward ones of three bits of paper stuck up against a wall, at about half a foot, or a foot one from another, without seeing the middle one at all, whilst his eye remains fixed in the same posture, must confess that vision is not made in a point, when it is plain, that looking with one eye there is always one part between the extremes of the area that we see, which is not seen at the same time that we perceive the extremes of it; though the looking with two eyes, or the quick turning of the axis of the eye to the part we would distinctly view, when we look but with one, does not let us take notice of it.

What I have here said I think sufficient to make intelligible, how by material rays of light visible species may be brought into the eye, notwithstanding any of P. M.'s objections against so much of material causes, as my hypothesis is concerned in. But when by this means an image is made on the retina, how we see it, I conceive no more than when I am told we see it in God. How we see it, is, I confess, what I understand not in the one or in the other, only it appears to me more difficult to conceive a distinct visible image in the uniform invariable essence of God, than in variously modifiable matter; but the manner how I see either, still escapes my comprehension. Impressions made on the retina by rays of light, I think I understand; and motions from thence continued to the brain may be conceived, and that these produce ideas in our minds I am persuaded, but in a manner to me incomprehensible. This I can resolve only into the good pleasure of God, whose ways are past finding out. And I think I know it as well when I am told these are ideas that the motion of the animal spirits by a law established by God, produces in me; as when I am told they are ideas I see in God. The ideas it is certain I have, and God both ways is the original cause of my having them; but the manner how I come by them, how it is that I perceive, I confess I understand not; though it be plain motion has to do in the producing of them: and motion so modified, is appointed to be the cause of our having them; as appears by the curious and artificial structure of the eye, accommodated to all the rules of refraction and dioptrics, that so visible objects might be exactly and regularly painted on the bottom of the eye.

The change of bigness in the ideas of visible objects, by distance and optic-glasses, which is the next argument he uses against visible species, is a good argument against them, as supposed by the peripatetics; but when considered, would persuade one that we see the figures and magnitudes of things rather in the bottom of our eyes than in God: the idea we have of them and their grandeur being still proportioned to the bigness of the area, on the bottom of our eyes, that is affected by the rays which paint the image there; and we may be said to see the picture in the retina, as, when it is pricked, we are truly said to feel the pain in our finger.

In the next place where he says, that when we look on a cube "we see all its sides equal." This, I think, is a mistake; and I have in another place shown, how the idea we have from a regular solid, is not the true idea of that solid, but such an one as by custom (as the name of it does) serves to excite our judgment to form such an one.

What he says of seeing an object several millions of leagues, the very same instant that it is uncovered, I think may be shown to be a mistake in matter of fact. For by observations made on the satellites of Jupiter, it is discovered that light is successively propagated and is about ten minutes coming from the sun to us.

By what I have said, I think it may be understood how we may conceive, that from remote objects material causes may reach our senses, and therein produce several motions that may be the causes of ideas in us; notwithstanding what P. M. has said in his second chapter against material species. I confess his arguments are good against those species as usually understood by the peripatetics: but, since my principles have been said to be conformable to the Aristotelian philosophy, I have endeavoured to remove the difficulties it is charged with, as far as my opinion is concerned in them.

His third chapter is to confute the "opinion of those who think our minds have a power to produce the ideas of things on which they would think, and that they are excited to produce them by the impressions which objects make on the body." One who thinks ideas are nothing but perceptions of the mind annexed to certain motions of the body by the will of God, who hath ordered such perceptions always to accompany such motions, though we know not how they are produced; does in effect conceive those ideas or perceptions to be only passions of the mind, when produced in it, whether we will or no, by external objects. But he conceives them to be a mixture of action and passion when the mind attends to them, or revives them in the memory. Whether the soul has such a power as this, we shall perhaps have occasion to consider hereafter; and this power our author does not deny, since in this very chapter he says, "When we conceive a square by pure understanding, we can yet imagine it, *i. e.* perceive it in ourselves by tracing an image of it on the brain." Here then he allows the soul power to trace images on the brain, and perceive them. This, to me, is matter of new perplexity in his hypothesis; for if the soul be so united to the brain as to trace images on it, and perceive them, I do not see how this consists with what he says a little before in the first chapter, viz. "that certainly material things cannot be united to our souls after a manner necessary to its perceiving them."

That which is said about objects exciting ideas in us by motion; and our reviving the ideas we have once got in our memories, does not, I confess, fully explain the manner how it is done. In this I frankly avow my ignorance, and should be glad to find in him any thing that would clear it to me; but in his explications I find these difficulties which I cannot get over.

> There are a number of references to the physiology of nerves and brain, of the activity of animal spirits (the seventeenth- and eighteenth-century term for an active fluid thought to be in the brain and nerves) in the *Essay*. Locke's references to this doctrine (a doctrine that had detailed exposition in Descartes and Malebranche) vary from acceptance of it as a probable explanation of some specific phenomenon to skepticism of it as explaining another mental event. In 2.1.15, he refers to it as a possible explanation of memory and of the loss of memory. In 2.8 (see selection 28) he cites it as the way ideas are caused. Elsewhere, he refers to it as an explanation of action and thought.

42. *Essay*, 2.8.4

If it were the design of my present undertaking to inquire into the natural causes and manner of perception, I should offer this as a reason why a privative cause might, in some cases at least, produce a positive idea, viz. that all sensation being produced in us only by different degrees and modes of motion in our animal spirits, variously agitated by external objects, the abatement of any former motion must as necessarily produce a new sensation, as the variation or increase of it; and so introduce a new idea, which depends only on a different motion of the animal spirits in that organ.

43. *Essay*, 2.10.5

Thus many of those ideas, which were produced in the minds of children, in the beginning of their sensation (some of which perhaps, as of some pleasures and pains, were before they were born, and others in their infancy) if in the future course of their lives they are not repeated again, are quite lost, without the least glimpse remaining of them. This may be observed in those who by some mischance have lost their sight when they were very young, in whom the ideas of colours having been but slightly taken notice of, and ceasing to be repeated, do quite wear out: so that some years after there is no more notion nor memory of colours left in their minds, than in those of people born blind. The memory of some, it is true, is very tenacious, even to a miracle: but yet there seems to be a constant decay of all our ideas, even of those which are struck deepest, and in minds the most retentive; so that if they be not sometimes renewed by repeated exercise of the senses, or reflection on those kind of objects which at first occasioned them, the print wears out, and at last there remains nothing to be seen. Thus the ideas, as well as children, of our youth, often die before us: and our minds represent to us those tombs, to which we are approaching; where though the brass and marble remain, yet the inscriptions are effaced by time, and the imagery moulders away. The pictures drawn in our minds are laid in fading colours, and, if not sometimes refreshed, vanish and disappear. How much the constitution of our bodies and the make of our animal spirits are concerned in this, and whether the temper of the brain make this difference, that in some it retains the characters drawn on it like marble, in others like free-stone, and in others little better than sand; I shall not here inquire: though it may seem probable that the constitution of the body does sometimes influence the memory; since we oftentimes find a disease quite strip the mind of all its ideas, and the flames of a fever in a few days calcine all those images to dust and confusion, which seemed to be as lasting as if graved in marble.

44. *Essay*, 2.33.6

Custom settles habits of thinking in the understanding, as well as of determining in the will, and of motions in the body; all which seems to be but trains of motion in the animal spirits, which once set a-going, continue in the same steps they have been used to: which, by often treading, are worn into a smooth path, and the motion in it becomes easy, and as it were natural. As far as we can comprehend thinking, thus ideas seem to be produced in our minds; or if they are not, this may serve to explain their following one another in an habitual train, when once they are put into their track, as well as it does to explain such motions of the body. A musician used to any tune will find, that let it but once begin in his head, the ideas of the several notes of it will follow one another orderly in his understanding, without any care or attention, as regularly as his fingers move orderly over the keys of the organ to play out the tune he has begun, though his unattentive thoughts be elsewhere a-wandering. Whether the natural cause of these ideas, as well as of the regular dancing of his fingers, be the motion of his animal spirits, I will not determine, how probable soever, by this instance, it appears to be so: but this may help us a little to conceive of intellectual habits, and of the tying together of ideas.

(e) Specific ideas

45. *Essay,* 2.4.1–3

The idea of solidity we receive by our touch; and it arises from the resistance which we find in body, to the entrance of any other body into the place it possesses, till it has left it. There is no idea which we receive more constantly from sensation, than solidity. Whether we move or rest, in what posture soever we are, we always feel something under us that supports us, and hinders our farther sinking downwards; and the bodies which we daily handle make us perceive, that, whilst they remain between them, they do by an insurmountable force hinder the approach of the parts of our hands that press them. That which thus hinders the approach of two bodies, when they are moved one towards another, I call solidity. I will not dispute, whether this acceptation of the word solid be nearer to its original signification, than that which mathematicians use it in: it suffices, that I think the common notion of solidity will allow, if not justify, this use of it; but, if any one think it better to call it impenetrability, he has my consent. Only I have thought the term solidity the more proper to express this idea, not only because of its vulgar use in that sense, but also because it carries something more of positive in it than impenetrability, which is negative, and is perhaps more a consequence of solidity, than solidity itself. This, of all other, seems the idea most intimately connected with and essential to body, so as nowhere else to be found or imagined, but only in matter. And though our senses take no notice of it, but in masses of matter, of a bulk sufficient to cause a sensation in us; yet the mind, having once got this idea from such grosser sensible bodies, traces it farther; and considers it, as well as figure, in the minutest particle of matter that can exist: and finds it inseparably inherent in body, wherever or however modified.

This is the idea which belongs to body, whereby we conceive it to fill space. The idea of which filling of space is, that, where we imagine any space taken up by a solid substance, we conceive it so to possess it, that it excludes all other solid substances; and will for ever hinder any other two bodies, that move towards one another in a straight line, from coming to touch one another, unless it removes from between them, in a line not parallel to that which they move in. This idea of it the bodies which we ordinarily handle sufficiently furnish us with.

This resistance, whereby it keeps other bodies out of the space which it possesses, is so great, that no force, how great soever, can surmount it. All the bodies in the world, pressing a drop of water on all sides, will never be able to overcome the resistance which it will make, soft as it is, to their approaching one another, till it be removed out of their way: whereby our idea of solidity is distinguished both from pure space, which is capable neither of resistance nor motion; and from the ordinary idea of hardness. For a man may conceive two bodies at a distance, so as they may approach one another, without touching or displacing any solid thing, till their superficies come to meet: whereby, I think, we have the clear idea of space without solidity. For (not to go so far as annihilation of any particular body) I ask, whether a man cannot have the idea of the motion of one single body alone without any other succeeding immediately into its place? I think it is evident he can: the idea of motion in one body no more including the idea of motion in another, than the idea of a square figure in one body includes the idea of a square figure in another. I do not ask, whether bodies do so exist that the motion of one body cannot really be without the motion of another? To determine this either way, is to beg the question for or against a vacuum. But my question is, whether one cannot have the idea of one body moved whilst others are at rest? And I think this no one will deny. If so, then the place it deserted gives us the idea of pure space without solidity, whereinto any other body may enter, without either resistance or protrusion of any thing. When the sucker in a pump is drawn, the space it filled in the tube is certainly the same whether any other body follows the motion of the sucker or not: nor does it imply a contradiction that, upon the motion of one body, another that is only contiguous to it, should not follow it. The necessity of such a motion is built only on the supposition that the world is full, but not on the distinct ideas of space and solidity: which are as different as resistance and not resistance; protrusion and not protrusion. And that men have ideas of space without a body, their very disputes about a vacuum plainly demonstrate; as is showed in another place.

46. *Essay*, 2.7.7

Existence and unity are two other ideas that are suggested to the understanding by every object without, and every idea within. When ideas are in our minds, we consider them as being actually there, as well as we consider things to be actually without us; which is, that they exist, or have existence: and whatever we can consider as one thing, whether a real being or idea, suggests to the understanding the idea of unity.

47. *Essay*, 2.13.7

Another idea coming under this head, and belonging to this tribe, is that we call place. As in simple space, we consider the relation of distance between any two bodies or points; so in our idea of place, we consider the relation of distance betwixt any thing, and any two or more points, which are considered as keeping the same distance one with another, and so considered as at rest: for when we find any thing at the same distance now, which it was yesterday, from any two or more points, which have not since changed their distance one with another, and with which we then compared it, we say it hath kept the same place; but if it hath sensibly altered its distance with either of those points, we say it hath changed its place: though vulgarly speaking, in the common notion of place, we do not always exactly observe the distance from these precise points; but from larger portions of sensible objects, to which we consider the thing placed to bear relation, and its distance from which we have some reason to observe.

48. *Essay*, 2.14.3–6

To understand time and eternity aright, we ought with attention to consider what idea it is we have of duration, and how we came by it. It is evident to any one, who will but observe what passes in his own mind, that there is a train of ideas which constantly succeed one another in his understanding, as long as he is awake. Reflection on these appearances of several ideas, one after another, in our minds, is that which furnishes us with the idea of succession; and the distance between any parts of that succession, or between the appearance of any two ideas in our minds, is that we call duration. For whilst we are thinking, or whilst we receive successively several ideas in our minds, we know that we do exist; and so we call the existence, or the continuation of the existence of ourselves, or any thing else, commensurate to the succession of any ideas in our minds, the duration of ourselves, or any such other thing coexistent with our thinking.

That we have our notion of succession and duration from this original, viz. from reflection on the train of ideas which we find to appear one after another in our own minds, seems plain to me, in that we have no perception of duration, but by considering the train of ideas that take their turns in our understandings. When that succession of ideas ceases, our perception of duration ceases with it; which every one clearly experiments in himself, whilst he sleeps soundly, whether an hour or a day, a month or a year: of which duration of things, while he sleeps or thinks not, he has no perception at all, but it is quite lost to him; and the moment wherein he leaves off to think, till the moment he begins to think again, seems to him to have no distance. And so I doubt not it would be to a waking man, if it were possible for him to keep only one idea in his mind, without variation and the succession of others. And we see, that one who fixes his thoughts very intently on one thing, so as to take but little notice of the succession of ideas that pass in his mind, whilst he is taken up with that earnest contemplation, lets slip out of his account a good part of that duration, and thinks that time shorter than it is. But if sleep commonly unites the distant parts of duration, it is because during that time we have no succession of ideas in our minds. For if a man, during his sleep, dreams, and variety of ideas make themselves perceptible in his mind one after another; he hath then, during such dreaming, a sense of duration, and of the length of it. By which it is to me very clear, that men derive their ideas of duration from their reflections, on the train of the ideas they observe to succeed one another in their own understandings; without which observation they can have no notion of duration, whatever may happen in the world.

Indeed, a man having, from reflecting on the succession and number of his own thoughts, got the notion or idea of duration, he can apply that notion to things which exist while he does not think; as he that has got the idea of extension from bodies by his sight or touch, can apply it to distances, where no body is seen or felt. And therefore though a man has no perception of the length of duration, which passed whilst he slept or thought not; yet having observed the revolution of days and nights, and found the length of their duration to be in appearance regular and constant, he can, upon the supposition that that revolution has proceeded after the same manner, whilst he was asleep or thought not, as it used to do at other times; he can, I say, imagine and make allowance for the length of duration, whilst he slept. But if Adam and Eve (when they were alone in the world) instead of their ordinary night's sleep, had passed the whole twenty-four hours in one continued sleep, the duration of that twenty-four hours had been irrecoverably lost to them, and been for ever left out of their account of time.

Thus by reflecting on the appearing of various ideas one after another in our understandings, we get the notion of succession; which, if any one would think we did rather get from our observation of motion by our senses, he will perhaps be of my mind, when he considers that even motion produces in his mind an idea of succession, no otherwise than as it produces there a continued train of distinguishable ideas. For a man looking upon a body really moving, perceives yet no motion at all, unless that motion produces a constant train of successive ideas: v. g. a man becalmed at sea, out of sight of land, in a fair day, may look on the sun, or sea, or ship, a whole hour together, and perceive no motion at all in either; though it be certain that two, and perhaps all of them, have moved during that time a great way. But as soon as he perceives either of them to have changed distance with some other body, as soon as this motion produces any new idea in him, then he perceives that there has been motion. But wherever a man is, with all things at rest about him, without perceiving any motion at all; if during this hour of quiet he has been thinking, he will perceive the various ideas of his own thoughts in his own mind, appearing one after another, and thereby observe and find succession where he could observe no motion.

49. *Essay,* 2.16.1–2

Amongst all the ideas we have, as there is none suggested to the mind by more ways, so there is none more simple, than that of unity, or one. It has no shadow of variety or composition in it: every object our senses are employed about, every idea in our understandings, every thought of our minds, brings this idea along with it. And therefore it is the most intimate to our thoughts, as well as it is, in its agreement to all other things, the most universal idea we have. For number applies itself to men, angels, actions, thoughts, every thing that either doth exist, or can be imagined.

By repeating this idea in our minds, and adding the repetitions together, we come by the complex ideas of the modes of it. Thus, by adding one to one, we have the complex idea of a couple; by putting twelve units together, we have the complex idea of a dozen; and so of a score, or a million, or any other number.

50. *Essay*, 2.21.1

The mind being every day informed, by the senses, of the alteration of those simple ideas it observes in things without, and taking notice how one comes to an end, and ceases to be, and another begins to exist which was not before; reflecting also on what passes within himself, and observing a constant change of its ideas, sometimes by the impression of outward objects on the senses, and sometimes by the determination of its own choice; and concluding from what it has so constantly observed to have been, that the like changes will for the future be made in the same things by like agents, and by the like ways; considers in one thing the possibility of having any of its simple ideas changed, and in another the possibility of making that change: and so comes by that idea which we call power. Thus we say, fire has a power to melt gold, i. e. to destroy the consistency of its insensible parts, and consequently its hardness, and make it fluid; and gold has a power to be melted: that the sun has a power to blanch wax, and wax a power to be blanched by the sun, whereby the yellowness is destroyed, and whiteness made to exist in its room. In which, and the like cases, the power we consider is in reference to the change of perceivable ideas: for we cannot observe any alteration to be made in, or operation upon, any thing, but by the observable change of its sensible ideas; nor conceive any alteration to be made, but by conceiving a change of some of its ideas.

51. *Essay*, 2.23.1

The mind being, as I have declared, furnished with a great number of the simple ideas, conveyed in by the senses, as they are found in exterior things, or by reflection on its own operations, takes notice also, that a certain number of these simple ideas go constantly together; which being presumed to belong to one thing, and words being suited to common apprehensions, and made use of for quick dispatch, are called, so united in one subject, by one name: which, by inadvertency, we are apt afterward to talk of, and consider as one simple idea, which indeed is a complication of many ideas together; because, as I have said, not imagining how

these simple ideas can subsist by themselves, we accustom ourselves to suppose some substratum wherein they do subsist, and
from which they do result; which therefore we call substance.

Two features of Locke's account of the origin of ideas
are important to note. The first is that his account is not
limited to simple ideas of sense and reflection, where the
mind plays a more or less passive role in idea acquisition.
Locke's account extends as well to more complex and so-
phisticated ideas, such as those in selections 42–51, above.
Here, the activity of the mind in the origin of ideas is
both prominent and important. However we characterize
Locke's program of the origin of ideas, his account of experience as the source of ideas clearly includes mental
operations acting on features of experience. Locke warned
the Bishop of Worcester about misreading his account on
just this point.

52. *Letter to the Bishop of Worcester, Works,* IV, p. 11
Your lordship here argues against a proposition that I know nobody
that holds; I am sure the author of the *Essay of Human Understanding* never thought, nor in that *Essay* hath any where said, that
the ideas that come into the mind by sensation and reflection are
all the ideas that are necessary to reason, or that reason is exercised
about; for then he must have laid by all the ideas of simple and
mixed modes and relations, and the complex ideas of the species
of substances, about which he has spent so many chapters; and
must have denied that these complex ideas are the objects of men's
thoughts or reasonings, which he is far enough from. All that he has
said about sensation and reflection is, that all our simple ideas
are received by them, and that these simple ideas are the foundation of all our knowledge, for as much as all our complex, relative,
and general ideas are made by the mind, abstracting, enlarging,
comparing, compounding, and referring, etc. these simple ideas,
and their several combinations, one to another; whereby complex
and general ideas are formed of modes, relations, and the several
species of substances, all which are made use of by reason, as well
as the other faculties of the mind.

The second important feature of Locke's account of the
origin of ideas is that it was offered as an alternative to the
claims, made by many of his contemporaries, that some

ideas are innate, born with us, and not derived in any way
from experience. Locke's derivation program has thus
given a detailed account in opposition to innatism.[20]

Word signs

Remarks on the nature and function of language are found
throughout the *Essay*, but the most sustained account is in
Book 3. This book not only contains reflections on language,
its origins and use, but a careful application of Locke's
views on language to the account of ideas and knowledge.
The following selections pick out three of the basic features
of his account of words and language.

(a) The relation of words to ideas

53. *Essay*, 3.2.1–5, 8

Man, though he has great variety of thoughts, and such, from
which others, as well as himself, might receive profit and delight;
yet they are all within his own breast, invisible and hidden from
others, nor can of themselves be made appear. The comfort and
advantage of society not being to be had without communication
of thoughts, it was necessary that man should find out some external sensible signs, whereof those invisible ideas, which his
thoughts are made up for, might be made known to others. For
this purpose nothing was so fit, either for plenty or quickness, as
those articulate sounds, which with so much ease and variety he
found himself able to make. Thus we may conceive how words
which were by nature so well adapted to that purpose, come to
be made use of by men, as the signs of their ideas; not by any
natural connexion that there is between particular articulate sounds
and certain ideas, for then there would be but one language
amongst all men; but by a voluntary imposition, whereby such a

20 For an account of the doctrine of innate ideas and principles against
which Locke wrote, see my *John Locke and the Way of Ideas* (Oxford). For an interesting study in Descartes' theory of rational psychology (a theory similar to that of Locke's) that traces the role and
function of mental processes in cognition, see Zeno Vendler, *Res Cogi-
tans* (Ithaca, N.Y., 1972), especially Chapter III, "Thoughts." The
debate over innateness has been revived by Chomsky; see his *Cartesian Linguistics* (New York, 1966) and *Language and Mind* (New
York, 1972). There is an extensive literature of debate on Chomsky's
theory. Two essays of especial importance and relevance are "Innate
Ideas," by R. Edgley, in *Knowledge and Necessity*, ed. G. Vesey
(London, 1970) and "Mr. Locke's Darling Notion," by Jonathan
Barnes, in *The Philosophical Quarterly* (July, 1972).

word is made arbitrarily the mark of such an idea. The use then of words is to be sensible marks of ideas; and the ideas they stand for are their proper and immediate signification.

The use men have of these marks being either to record their own thoughts for the assistance of their own memory, or as it were to bring out their ideas, and lay them before the view of others; words in their primary or immediate signification stand for nothing but the ideas in the mind of him that uses them, how imperfectly soever or carelessly those ideas are collected from the things which they are supposed to represent. When a man speaks to another, it is that he may be understood; and the end of speech is, that those sounds, as marks, may make known his ideas to the hearer. That then which words are the marks of are the ideas of the speaker: nor can any one apply them as marks, immediately to any thing else, but the ideas that he himself hath. For this would be to make them signs of his own conceptions, and yet apply them to other ideas; which would be to make them signs, and not signs, of his ideas at the same time; and so in effect to have no signification at all. Words being voluntary signs, they cannot be voluntary signs imposed by him on things he knows not. That would be to make them signs of nothing, sounds without signification. A man cannot make his words the signs either of qualities in things, or of conceptions in the mind of another, whereof he has none in his own. Till he has some ideas of his own, he cannot suppose them to correspond with the conceptions of another man; nor can he use any signs for them: for thus they would be the signs of he knows not what, which is in truth to be the signs of nothing. But when he represents to himself other men's ideas by some of his own, if he consent to give them the same names that other men do, it is still to his own ideas; to ideas that he has, and not to ideas that he has not.

This is so necessary in the use of language, that in this respect the knowing and the ignorant, the learned and unlearned, use the words they speak (with any meaning) all alike. They, in every man's mouth, stand for the ideas he has, and which he would express by them. A child having taken notice of nothing in the metal he hears called gold, but the bright shining yellow colour, he applies the word gold only to his own idea of that colour, and nothing else; and therefore calls the same colour in a peacock's tail gold. Another that hath better observed, adds to shining yellow great weight: and then the sound gold when he uses it, stands for a complex idea of a shining yellow and very weighty substance. Another adds to those qualities fusibility: and then the word gold signifies to him a body, bright, yellow, fusible, and very heavy. Another adds malleability. Each of these uses equally the word gold when they have occasion to express the idea which they have applied it to: but it is evident, that each can apply it only to his own idea; nor can he make it stand as a sign of such a complex idea as he has not.

But though words, as they are used by men, can properly and immediately signify nothing but the ideas that are in the mind of the speaker; yet they in their thoughts give them a secret reference to two other things.

First, they suppose their words to be marks of the ideas in the minds also of other men, with whom they communicate: for else they should talk in vain, and could not be understood, if the sounds they applied to one idea were such as by the hearer were applied to another; which is to speak two languages. But in this, men stand not usually to examine, whether the idea they and those they discourse with have in their minds, be the same; but think it enough that they use the word, as they imagine, in the common acceptation of that language; in which they suppose, that the idea they make it a sign of is precisely the same, to which the understanding men of that country apply that name.

Secondly, Because men would not be thought to talk barely of their own imaginations, but of things as really they are; therefore they often suppose the words to stand also for the reality of things. But this relating more particularly to substances, and their names, as perhaps the former does to simple ideas and modes, we shall speak of these two different ways of applying words more at large, when we come to treat of the names of mixed modes, and substances in particular: though give me leave here to say, that it is a perverting the use of words, and brings unavoidable obscurity and confusion into their signification, whenever we make them stand for any thing, but those ideas we have in our own minds.

Words by long and familiar use, as has been said, come to excite in men certain ideas so constantly and readily, that they are apt to suppose a natural connexion between them. But that they signify only men's peculiar ideas, and that by a perfect arbitrary imposition, is evident in that they often fail to excite in others (even that use the same language) the same ideas we take them to be the signs of: and every man has so inviolable a liberty to make words stand for what ideas he pleases, that no one hath the power to make others have the same ideas in their minds that he has, when they use the same words that he does. And therefore the great Augustus himself, in the possession of that power which ruled the world, acknowledged he could not make a new Latin word: which was as much as to say, that he could not arbitrarily appoint what idea any sound should be a sign of, in the mouths and common language of his subjects. It is true, common use by a tacit consent appropriates certain sounds to certain ideas in all languages, which so far limits the signification of that sound, that unless a man applies it to the same idea, he does not speak properly: and let me add, that unless a man's words excite the same ideas in the hearer, which he makes them stand for in speaking, he does not speak intelligibly. But whatever be the consequence of any man's using of words differently, either from their general meaning, or the particular sense of the person to whom he addresses them, this is certain, their signification, in his use of them, is limited to his ideas, and they can be signs of nothing else.

54. *Essay*, 3.3.6, 11

The next thing to be considered is, how general words come to be made. For since all things that exist are only particulars, how come we by general terms, or where find we those general natures they are supposed to stand for? Words become general, by being made the signs of general ideas; and ideas become general, by separating from them the circumstances of time, and place, and any other ideas, that may determine them to this or that particular existence. By this way of abstraction they are made capable of representing more individuals than one; each of which, having in it a conformity to that abstract idea, is (as we call it) of that sort.

To return to general words, it is plain by what has been said, that general and universal belong not to the real existence of things; but are the inventions and creatures of the understanding, made by it for its own use, and concern only signs, whether words or ideas. Words are general, as has been said, when used for signs of general ideas, and so are applicable indifferently to many particular things: and ideas are general, when they are set up as the representatives of many particular things: but universality belongs not to things themselves, which are all of them particular in their existence; even those words and ideas, which in their signification are general. When therefore we quit particulars, the generals that rest are only creatures of our own making; their general nature being nothing but the capacity they are put into by the understanding, of signifying or representing many particulars. For the signification they have is nothing but a relation, that by the mind of man is added to them.

55. Essay, 4.5.4

And that which makes it yet harder to treat of mental and verbal propositions separately, is, that most men, if not all, in their thinking and reasonings, within themselves, make use of words instead of ideas: at least when the subject of their meditation contains in it complex ideas. Which is a great evidence of the imperfection and uncertainty of our ideas of that kind, and may, if attentively made use of, serve for a mark to show us, what are those things we have clear and perfect established ideas of, and what not. For if we will curiously observe the way our mind takes in thinking and reasoning, we shall find, I suppose, that when we make any propositions within our own thoughts about white or black, sweet or bitter, a triangle or a circle, we can and often do frame in our minds the ideas themselves, without reflecting on the names. But when we would consider, or make propositions about the more complex ideas as of a man, vitriol, fortitude, glory, we usually put the name for the idea: because the ideas these names stand for, being for the most part imperfect, confused, and undetermined, we reflect on the names themselves, because they are more clear, certain, and distinct, and readier occur to our thoughts than the pure ideas: and so we make use of these words instead of the ideas themselves, even when we would meditate and reason within ourselves, and make tacit mental propositions. In substances, as has been already noticed, this is occasioned by the imperfection of our ideas: we making the name stand for the real essence, of which we have no idea at all. In modes, it is occasioned by the great number of simple ideas, that go to the making them up. For many of them being compounded, the name occurs much easier than the complex idea itself, which requires time and attention to be recollected, and exactly represented to the mind, even in those men who have formerly been at the pains to do it; and is utterly impossible to be done by those, who, though they have ready in their memory the greatest part of the common words of that language, yet perhaps never troubled themselves in all their lives to consider what precise ideas the most of them stood for. Some confused or obscure notions have served their turns, and many who talk very much of religion and conscience, of church and faith, of power and right, of obstructions and humours, melan-

choly and choler, would perhaps have little left in their thoughts
and meditations, if one should desire them to think only of the
things themselves, and lay by those words, with which they so
often confound others, and not seldom themselves also.

56. *Essay*, 4.6.1

Though the examining and judging of ideas by themselves, their
names being quite laid aside, be the best and surest way to clear
and distinct knowledge; yet, through the prevailing custom of using
sounds for ideas, I think it is very seldom practised. Every one
may observe how common it is for names to be made use of,
instead of the ideas themselves, even when men think and reason
within their own breasts: especially if the ideas be very complex,
and made up of a great collection of simple ones. This makes the
consideration of words and propositions so necessary a part of the
treatise of knowledge, that it is very hard to speak intelligibly of
the one, without explaining the other.

(b) The distinction between words as signs and words as sounds

57. *Essay*, 3.1.1–2

God having designed man for a sociable creature, made him not
only with an inclination, and under a necessity to have fellowship
with those of his own kind; but furnished him also with language,
which was to be the great instrument and common tie of society.
Man therefore had by nature his organs so fashioned, as to be fit
to frame articulate sounds, which we call words. But this was not
enough to produce language; for parrots, and several other birds,
will be taught to make articulate sounds distinct enough, which
yet, by no means, are capable of language.

Besides articulate sounds therefore, it was farther necessary, that
he should be able to use these sounds as signs of internal conceptions; and to make them stand as marks for the ideas within his
own mind, whereby they might be made known to others, and the
thoughts of men's minds be conveyed from one to another.

58. *Essay*, 3.4.11

Simple ideas, as has been shown, are only to be got by those impressions objects themselves make on our minds, by the proper
inlets appointed to each sort. If they are not received this way, all
the words in the world, made use of to explain or define any of their
names, will never be able to produce in us the idea it stands

for. For words being sounds can produce in us no other simple
ideas, than of those very sounds; nor excite any in us, but by that
voluntary connexion which is known to be between them and
those simple ideas, which common use has made them signs of.
He that thinks otherwise, let him try if any words can give him
the taste of a pine-apple, and make him have the true idea of the
relish of that celebrated delicious fruit. So far as he is told it has
a resemblance with any tastes, whereof he has the ideas already
in his memory, imprinted there by sensible objects not strangers
to his palate, so far may he approach that resemblance in his
mind. But this is not giving us that idea by a definition, but
exciting in us other simple ideas by their known names; which will
be still very different from the true taste of that fruit itself. In
light and colours, and all other simple ideas, it is the same thing;
for the signification of sounds is not natural, but only imposed
and arbitrary. And no definition of light, or redness, is more fitted,
or able to produce either of those ideas in us, than the sound
light or red by itself. For to hope to produce an idea of light,
or colour, by a sound, however formed, is to expect that sounds
should be visible, or colours audible, and to make the ears do the
office of all the other senses. Which is all one as to say, that we
might taste, smell, and see by the ears; a sort of philosophy worthy
only of Sancho Pança, who had the faculty to see Dulcinea by
hearsay. And therefore he that has not before received into his
mind, by the proper inlet, the simple idea which any word stands
for, can never come to know the signification of that word by any
other words or sounds whatsoever, put together according to any
rules of definition. The only way is by applying to his senses the
proper object, and so producing that idea in him, for which he has
learned the name already. A studious blind man, who had mightily
beat his head about visible objects, and made use of the explication
of his books and friends, to understand those names of light and
colours, which often came in his way, bragged one day, that he now
understood what scarlet signified. Upon which his friend demand-
ing, what scarlet was? the blind man answered, It was like the
sound of a trumpet. Just such an understanding of the name of any
other simple idea will he have, who hopes to get it only from a
definition, or other words made use of to explain it.

59. *Essay,* 3.10.26

First, he that hath words of any language, without distinct ideas
in his mind to which he applies them, does, so far as he uses them

in discourse, only make a noise without any sense or signification; and how learned soever he may seem by the use of hard words or learned terms, is not much more advanced thereby in knowledge, than he would be in learning, who had nothing in his study but the bare titles of books, without possessing the contents of them. For all such words, however put into discourse, according to the right construction of grammatical rules, or the harmony of well-turned periods, do yet amount to nothing but bare sounds, and nothing else.

60. *Essay*, 3.11.5–6

This inconvenience, in an ill use of words, men suffer in their own private meditations: but much more manifest are the disorders which follow from it, in conversation, discourse, and arguings with others. For language being the great conduit, whereby men convey their discoveries, reasonings, and knowledge, from one to another; he that makes an ill use of it, though he does not corrupt the fountains of knowledge, which are in things themselves; yet he does, as much as in him lies, break or stop the pipes, whereby it is distributed to the public use and advantage of mankind. He that uses words without any clear and steady meaning, what does he but lead himself and others into errors? And he that designedly does it, ought to be looked on as an enemy to truth and knowledge. And yet who can wonder, that all the sciences and parts of knowledge have been so overcharged with obscure and equivocal terms, and insignificant and doubtful expressions, capable to make the most attentive or quick-sighted very little or not at all the more knowing or orthodox; since subtilty, in those who make profession to teach or defend truth, hath passed so much for a virtue: a virtue, indeed, which consisting for the most part in nothing but the fallacious and illusory use of obscure or deceitful terms, is only fit to make men more conceited in their ignorance, and more obstinate in their errors.

Let us look into the books of controversy of any kind: there we shall see, that the effect of obscure, unsteady or equivocal terms, is nothing but noise and wrangling about sounds, without convincing or bettering a man's understanding. For if the idea be not agreed on betwixt the speaker and hearer, for which the words stand, the argument is not about things, but names. As often as such a word, whose signification is not ascertained betwixt them, comes in use, their understandings have no other object wherein they agree, but barely the sound; the things that they think on at that time, as expressed by that word, being quite different.

61. *Essay*, 4.8.7, 13

Before a man makes any proposition, he is supposed to understand the terms he uses in it, or else he talks like a parrot, only making a noise by imitation, and framing certain sounds, which he has learnt of others: but not as a rational creature, using them for signs of ideas which he has in his mind. The hearer also is supposed to understand the terms as the speaker uses them, or else he talks jargon, and makes an unintelligible noise. And therefore he trifles with words, who makes such a proposition, which, when it is made, contains no more than one of the terms does, and which a man was supposed to know before; v. g. a triangle hath three sides, or saffron is yellow. And this is no farther tolerable, than where a man goes to explain his terms, to one who is supposed or declares himself not to understand him: and then it teaches only the signification of that word, and the use of that sign.

Secondly, all propositions wherein a part of the complex idea, which any term stands for, is predicated of that term, are only verbal; v. g. to say that gold is a metal or heavy. And thus all propositions, wherein more comprehensive words, called genera, are affirmed of subordinate or less comprehensive, called species, or individuals, are barely verbal.

When by these two rules we have examined the propositions that make up the discourses we ordinarily meet with both in and out of books, we shall, perhaps, find that a greater part of them, than is usually suspected, are purely about the signification of words, and contain nothing in them, but the use and application of these signs.

This, I think, I may lay down for an infallible rule, that wherever the distinct idea any word stands for is not known and considered, and something not contained in the idea is not affirmed or denied of it; there our thoughts stick wholly in sounds, and are able to attain no real truth or falsehood. This, perhaps, if well heeded, might save us a great deal of useless amusement and dispute, and very much shorten our trouble and wandering, in the search of real and true knowledge.

62. *Essay*, 4.18.3

First then I say, that no man inspired by God can by any revelation communicate to others any new simple ideas, which they had not before from sensation or reflection. For whatsoever impressions he himself may have from the immediate hand of God, this revelation, if it be of new simple ideas, cannot be conveyed to another, either by words, or any other signs. Because words, by their immediate operation on us, cause no other ideas, but of their natural sounds: and it is by the custom of using them for signs, that they excite and revive in our minds latent ideas; but yet only such ideas as were there before. For words seen or heard, recall to our thoughts those ideas only, which to us they have been wont to be signs of; but cannot introduce any perfectly new, and formerly unknown simple ideas. The same holds in all other signs, which cannot signify to us things, of which we have before never had any idea at all.

Thus, whatever things were discovered to St. Paul, when he was rapt up into the third heaven, whatever new ideas his mind there received, all the description he can make to others of that place, is only this, that there are such things, "as eye hath not seen, nor ear heard, nor hath it entered into the heart of man to conceive." And supposing God should discover to any one, supernaturally, a species of creatures inhabiting, for example, Jupiter or Saturn, (for that it is possible there may be such, nobody can deny) which had six senses; and imprint on his mind the ideas conveyed to theirs by that sixth sense; he could no more, by words, produce in the minds of other men those ideas, imprinted by that sixth sense, than one of us could convey the idea of any colour by the sounds of words into a man, who, having the other four senses perfect, had always totally wanted the fifth of seeing. For our simple ideas then, which are the foundation and sole matter of all our notions and knowledge, we must depend wholly on our reason, I mean our natural faculties; and can by no means receive them, or any of them, from traditional revelation; I say, traditional revelation, in distinction to original revelation. By the one, I mean that first impression, which is made immediately by God, on the mind of any man, to which we cannot set any bounds; and by the other, those impressions delivered over to others in words, and the ordinary ways of conveying our conceptions one to another.

(c) Defects of language and their remedies

63. *Essay*, 3.9.1, 2, 4, 5

From what has been said in the foregoing chapters, it is easy to perceive what imperfection there is in language, and how the very nature of words makes it almost unavoidable for many of them to be doubtful and uncertain in their significations. To examine the perfection or imperfection of words, it is necessary first to consider their use and end: for as they are more or less fitted to attain that, so they are more or less perfect. We have, in the former part of this discourse, often upon occasion mentioned a double use of words.

First, one for the recording of our own thoughts.

Secondly, the other for the communicating of our thoughts to others.

As to the first of these, for the recording our own thoughts for the help of our own memories, whereby, as it were, we talk to ourselves, any words will serve the turn. For since sounds are voluntary and indifferent signs of any ideas, a man may use what words he pleases, to signify his own ideas to himself: and there will be no imperfection in them, if he constantly use the same sign for the same idea; for then he cannot fail of having his meaning understood, wherein consists the right use and perfection of language.

The chief end of language is communication being to be understood, words serve not well for that end, neither in civil nor philosophical discourse, when any word does not excite in the hearer the same idea which it stands for in the mind of the speaker. Now since sounds have no natural connexion with our ideas, but have all their signification from the arbitrary imposition of men, the doubtfulness and uncertainty of their signification, which is the imperfection we here are speaking of, has its cause more in the ideas they stand for, than in any incapacity there is in one sound more than in another, to signify any idea: for in that regard they are all equally perfect.

That then which makes doubtfulness and uncertainty in the signification of some more than other words, is the difference of ideas they stand for.

Words having naturally no signification, the idea which each stands for must be learned and retained by those who would exchange thoughts, and hold intelligible discourse with others in any language. But this is hardest to be done, where,

First, the ideas they stand for are very complex, and made up of a great number of ideas put together.

Secondly, where the ideas they stand for have no certain connexion in nature; and so no settled standard, any where in nature existing, to rectify and adjust them by.

Thirdly, when the signification of the word is referred to a standard, which standard is not easy to be known.

Fourthly, where the signification of the word, and the real essence of the thing, are not exactly the same.

These are difficulties that attend the signification of several words that are intelligible. Those which are not intelligible at all, such as names standing for any simple ideas, which another has not organs or faculties to attain; as the names of colours to a blind man, or sounds to a deaf man; need not here be mentioned.

In all these cases we shall find an imperfection in words, which I shall more at large explain, in their particular application to our several sorts of ideas: for if we examine them, we shall find that the names of mixed modes are most liable to doubtfulness and imperfection, for the two first of these reasons; and the names of substances chiefly for the two latter.

64. *Essay*, 3.10.1–6, 9, 12, 23–5

Besides the imperfection that is naturally in language, and the obscurity and confusion that is so hard to be avoided in the use of words, there are several wilful faults and neglects which men are guilty of in this way of communication, whereby they render these signs less clear and distinct in their signification, than naturally they need to be.

First, in this kind, the first and most palpable abuse is, the using of words without clear and distinct ideas; or, which is worse, signs without any thing signified. Of these there are two sorts:

I. One may observe, in all languages, certain words, that if they be examined, will be found, in their first original and their appropriated use, not to stand for any clear and distinct ideas. These, for the most part, the several sects of philosophy and religion have introduced. For their authors, or promoters, either affecting something singular and out of the way of common apprehensions, or to support some strange opinions, or cover some weakness of their hypothesis, seldom fail to coin new words, and such as, when they come to be examined, may justly be called insignificant terms. For having either had no determinate collection of ideas annexed to them, when they were first invented; or at least such as, if well examined, will be found inconsistent; it is no wonder if afterwards, in the vulgar use of the same party, they remain empty sounds, with little or no signification, amongst those who think it enough to have them often in their mouths, as the distinguishing characters of their church, or school, without much troubling their heads to examine what are the precise ideas they stand for. I shall not need here to heap up instances; every man's reading and conversation will sufficiently furnish him; or if he wants to be better stored, the great mint-masters of this kind of terms, I mean the school-men and metaphysicians (under which, I think, the disputing natural and moral philosophers of these latter ages may be comprehended) have wherewithal abundantly to content him.

II. Others there be, who extend this abuse yet farther, who take so little care to lay by words, which in their primary notation have scarce any clear and distinct ideas which they are annexed to, that by an unpardonable negligence they familiarly use words, which the propriety of language has affixed to very important ideas, without any distinct meaning at all. Wisdom, glory, grace, &c. are words frequent enough in every man's mouth; but if a great many of those who use them, should be asked what they mean by them, they would be at a stand, and not know what to answer: a plain proof, that though they have learned those sounds, and have them ready at their tongue's end, yet there are no determined ideas laid up in their minds, which are to be expressed to others by them.

Men having been accustomed from their cradles to learn words, which are easily got and retained, before they knew, or had framed the complex ideas, to which they were annexed, or which were to be found in the things they were thought to stand for; they usually continue to do so all their lives; and without taking the pains necessary to settle in their minds determined ideas, they use their words for such unsteady and confused notions as they have, contenting themselves with the same words other people use: as if their very sound necessarily carried with it constantly the same meaning. This, though men make a shift with, in the ordinary occurrences of life, where they find it necessary to be understood, and therefore they make signs till they are so; yet this insignificancy in their words, when they come to reason concerning either their tenets or interest, manifestly fills their discourse with abundance of empty unintelligible noise and jargon; especially in moral matters, where the words for the most part standing for arbitrary and numerous collections of ideas, not regularly and permanently united in nature, their bare sounds are often only thought on, or at least very obscure and uncertain notions annexed to them. Men take the words they find in use amongst their neighbours; and that they may not seem ignorant what they stand for, use them confidently, without much troubling their heads about a certain fixed meaning: whereby, besides the ease of it, they obtain this advantage; that as in such discourses they seldom are in the right, so they are as seldom to be convinced that they are in the wrong; it being all one to go about to draw those men out of their mistakes, who have no settled notions, as to dispossess a vagrant of his habitation, who has no settled abode. This I guess to be so; and every one may observe in himself and others whether it be or no.

Secondly, another great abuse of words is inconstancy in the use of them. It is hard to find a discourse written of any subject, especially of controversy, wherein one shall not observe, if he read with attention, the same words (and those commonly the most material in the discourse, and upon which the argument turns) used sometimes for one collection of simple ideas, and sometimes for another; which is a perfect abuse of language. Words being intended for signs of my ideas, to make them known to others, not by any natural signification, but by a voluntary imposition—it is plain cheat and abuse, when I make them stand sometimes for one thing and sometimes for another; the wilful doing whereof can be imputed to nothing but great folly, or greater dishonesty: and a man, in his accounts with another, may, with as much fairness, make the characters of numbers stand sometimes for one and sometimes for another collection of units, (v.g. this character 3 stand sometimes for three, sometimes for four, and sometimes for eight) as in his discourse, or reasoning, make the same words stand for different collections of simple ideas. If men should do so in their reckonings, I wonder who would have to do with them? One who would speak thus, in the affairs and business of the world, and call eight sometimes seven, and sometimes nine, as best served his advantage, would presently have clapped upon him one of the two names men are commonly disgusted with: and yet in arguings and learned contests, the same sort of proceedings passes commonly for wit and learning: but to me it appears a greater dishonesty than the misplacing of counters in the casting up a debt; and the cheat the greater, by how much truth is of greater concernment and value than money.

Thirdly, another abuse of language is an affected obscurity, by either applying old words to new and unusual significations, or introducing new and ambiguous terms, without defining either; or else putting them so together, as may confound their ordinary meaning. Though the Peripatetic philosophy has been most eminent in this way, yet other sects have not been wholly clear of it. There are scarce any of them that are not cumbered with some difficulties (such is the imperfection of human knowledge) which they have been fain to cover with obscurity of terms, and to confound the signification of words, which, like a mist before people's eyes, might hinder their weak parts from being discovered. That body and extension, in common use, stand for two distinct ideas, is plain to any one that will but reflect a little: for were their signification precisely the same, it would be proper, and as intelligible to say, the body of an extension, as the extension of a body;

and yet there are those who find it necessary to confound their signification. To this abuse, and the mischiefs of confounding the signification of words, logic and the liberal sciences, as they have been handled in the schools, have given reputation; and the admired art of disputing hath added much to the natural imperfection of languages, whilst it has been made use of and fitted to perplex the signification of words, more than to discover the knowledge and truth of things: and he that will look into that sort of learned writings, will find the words there much more obscure, uncertain, and undetermined in their meaning than they are in ordinary conversation.

For notwithstanding these learned disputants, these all-knowing doctors, it was to the unscholastic statesman, that the governments of the world owed their peace, defence, and liberties; and from the illiterate and contemned mechanick (a name of disgrace) that they received the improvements of useful arts. Nevertheless, this artificial ignorance, and learned gibberish, prevailed mightily in these last ages, by the interest and artifice of those who found no easier way to that pitch of authority and dominion they have attained, than by amusing the men of business and ignorant with hard words, or employing the ingenious and idle in intricate disputes about unintelligible terms, and holding them perpetually entangled in that endless labyrinth. Besides, there is no such way to gain admittance, or give defence to strange and absurd doctrines, as to guard them round about with legions of obscure, doubtful, and undefined words: which yet make these retreats more like the dens of robbers, or holes of foxes, than the fortresses of fair warriors; which if it be hard to get them out of, it is not for the strength that is in them, but the briars and thorns, and the obscurity of the thickets they are beset with. For untruth being unacceptable to the mind of man, there is no other defence left for absurdity, but obscurity.

Nor hath this mischief stopped in logical niceties, or curious empty speculations; it hath invaded the great concernments of human life and society, obscured and perplexed the material truths of law and divinity; brought confusion, disorder, and uncertainty into the affairs of mankind; and if not destroyed, yet in a great measure rendered useless, these two great rules, religion and justice. What have the greatest part of the comments and disputes upon the laws of God and man served for, but to make the meaning more doubtful, and perplex the sense? What have been the effect of those multiplied curious distinctions and acute niceties, but obscurity and uncertainty, leaving the words more unintelligible, and the reader more at a loss? How else comes it to pass that princes, speaking or writing to their servants, in their ordinary commands, are easily understood; speaking to their people, in their laws, are not so? And, as I remarked before, doth it not often happen, that a man of an ordinary capacity very well understands a text or a law that he reads, till he consults an expositor, or goes to counsel; who, by that time he hath done explaining them, makes the words signify either nothing at all, or what he pleases.

To conclude this consideration of the imperfection and abuse of language; the ends of language in our discourse with others, being chiefly these three: first, to make known one man's thoughts or ideas to another; secondly, to do it with as much ease and quickness as is possible; and, thirdly, thereby to convey the knowledge of things: language is either abused or deficient, when it fails of any of these three.

First, words fail in the first of these ends, and lay not open one man's ideas to another's view: 1. When men have names in their mouths without any determinate ideas in their minds, whereof they are the signs; or, 2. When they apply the common received names of any language to ideas, to which the common use of that language does not apply them; or, 3. When they apply them very unsteadily, making them stand now for one, and by and by for another idea.

Secondly, men fail of conveying their thoughts with all the quickness and ease that may be, when they have complex ideas without having any distinct names for them. This is sometimes the fault of the language itself, which has not in it a sound yet applied to such a signification; and sometimes the fault of the man, who has not yet learned the name for that idea he would show another.

Thirdly, there is no knowledge of things conveyed by men's words, when their ideas agree not to the reality of things. Though it be a defect, that has its original in our ideas, which are not so conformable to the nature of things, as attention, study, and application might make them; yet it fails not to extend itself to our words too, when we use them as signs of real beings, which yet never had any reality or existence.

65. *Essay,* 3.11.1–6, 11–12

The natural and improved imperfections of languages we have seen above at large; and speech being the great bond that holds society together, and the common conduit whereby the improve-

ments of knowledge are conveyed from one man, and one generation to another; it would well deserve our most serious thoughts
to consider what remedies are to be found for the inconveniences
above-mentioned.

I am not so vain to think, that any one can pretend to attempt
the perfect reforming the languages of the world, no not so much
as of his own country, without rendering himself ridiculous. To
require that men should use their words constantly in the same
sense, and for none but determined and uniform ideas, would be
to think that all men should have the same notions, and should
talk of nothing but what they have clear and distinct ideas of;
which is not to be expected by any one, who hath not vanity
enough to imagine he can prevail with men to be very knowing
or very silent. And he must be very little skilled in the world,
who thinks that a voluble tongue shall accompany only a good
understanding; or that men's talking much or little should hold
proportion only to their knowledge.

But though the market and exchange must be left to their own
ways of talking, and gossipings not be robbed of their ancient
privilege; though the schools and men of argument would perhaps
take it amiss to have any thing offered to abate the length, or
lessen the number, of their disputes: yet methinks those who
pretend seriously to search after or maintain truth, should think
themselves obliged to study how they might deliver themselves
without obscurity, doubtfulness, or equivocation, to which men's
words are naturally liable, if care be not taken.

For he that shall well consider the errors and obscurity, the
mistakes and confusion, that are spread in the world by an ill use
of words, will find some reason to doubt whether language, as it
has been employed, has contributed more to the improvement or
hindrance of knowledge amongst mankind. How many are there
that, when they would think on things, fix their thoughts only on
words, especially when they would apply their minds to moral
matters? And who then can wonder, if the result of such contemplations and reasonings, about little more than sounds, whilst
the ideas they annexed to them are very confused and very unsteady, or perhaps none at all; who can wonder, I say, that such
thoughts and reasonings end in nothing but obscurity and mistake,
without any clear judgment or knowledge?

This inconvenience, in an ill use of words, men suffer in their
own private meditations, but much more manifest are the disorders
which follow from it, in conversation, discourse, and arguings with

others. For language being the great conduit, whereby men convey their discoveries, reasonings, and knowledge, from one to another; he that makes an ill use of it, though he does not corrupt the fountains of knowledge, which are in things themselves; yet he does, as much as in him lies, break or stop the pipes, whereby it is distributed to the public use and advantage of mankind. He that uses words without any clear and steady meaning, what does he but lead himself and others into errors? And he that designedly does it, ought to be looked on as an enemy to truth and knowledge. And yet who can wonder, that all the sciences and parts of knowledge have been so overcharged with obscure and equivocal terms, and insignificant and doubtful expressions, capable to make the most attentive or quick-sighted very little or not at all the more knowing or orthodox; since subtilty, in those who make profession to teach or defend truth, hath passed so much for a virtue, a virtue, indeed, which consisting for the most part in nothing but the fallacious and illusory use of obscure or deceitful terms, is only fit to make men more conceited in their ignorance, and more obstinate in their errors.

Let us look into the books of controversy of any kind; there we shall see, that the effect of obscure, unsteady or equivocal terms, is nothing but noise and wrangling about sounds, without convincing or bettering a man's understanding. For if the idea be not agreed on betwixt the speaker and hearer, for which the words stand, the argument is not about things, but names. As often as such a word, whose signification is not ascertained betwixt them, comes in use, their understandings have no other object wherein they agree, but barely the sound; the things that they think on at that time, as expressed by that word, being quite different.

Thirdly, it is not enough that men have ideas, determined ideas, for which they make these signs stand; but they must also take care to apply their words, as near as may be, to such ideas as common use has annexed them to. For words, especially of languages already framed, being no man's private possession, but the common measure of commerce and communication, it is not for any one, at pleasure, to change the stamp they are current in, nor alter the ideas they are affixed to; or at least, when there is a necessity to do so, he is bound to give notice of it. Men's intentions in speaking are, or at least should be, to be understood; which cannot be without frequent explanations, demands, and other the like incommodious interruptions, where men do not follow common use. Propriety of speech is that which gives our thoughts entrance into other men's

minds with the greatest ease and advantage; and therefore deserves
some part of our care and study, especially in the names of moral
words. The proper signification and use of terms is best to be
learned from those, who in their writings and discourses appear to
have had the clearest notions, and applied to them their terms with
the exactest choice and fitness. This way of using a man's words,
according to the propriety of the language, though it have not
always the good fortune to be understood; yet most commonly
leaves the blame of it on him, who is so unskilful in the language
he speaks, as not to understand it, when made use of as it ought
to be.

Fourthly, but because common use has not so visibly annexed
any signification to words, as to make men know always certainly
what they precisely stand for; and because men, in the improvement of their knowledge, come to have ideas different from the
vulgar and ordinary received ones, for which they must either make
new words (which men seldom venture to do, for fear of being
thought guilty of affectation or novelty) or else must use old ones,
in a new signification: therefore after the observation of the foregoing rules, it is sometimes necessary, for the ascertaining the signification of words, to declare their meaning; where either common
use has left it uncertain and loose (as it has in most names of
very complex ideas) or where the term, being very material in the
discourse, and that upon which it chiefly turns, is liable to any
doubtfulness or mistake.

66. *Conduct*, section 29

I have copiously enough spoken of the abuse of words in another
place, and therefore shall upon this reflection, that the sciences
are full of them, warn those that would conduct their understandings right, not to take any term, howsoever authorised by the language of the schools, to stand for any thing till they have an idea
of it. A word may be of frequent use, and great credit, with
several authors, and be by them made use of as if it stood for some
real being; but yet, if he that reads cannot frame any distinct idea
of that being, it is certainly to him a mere empty sound without a meaning; and he learns no more by all that is said of it, or
attributed to it, than if it were affirmed only of that bare empty
sound. They who would advance in knowledge, and not deceive
and swell themselves with a little articulated air, should lay down
this as a fundamental rule, not to take words for things, nor suppose
that names in books signify real entities in nature, till they can

frame clear and distinct ideas of those entities. It will not perhaps be allowed, if I should set down "substantial forms" and "intentional species," as such that may justly be suspected to be of this kind of insignificant terms. But this I am sure, to one that can form no determined ideas of what they stand for, they signify nothing at all; and all that he thinks he knows about them, is to him so much knowledge about nothing, and amounts at most but to be a learned ignorance. It is not without all reason supposed, that there are many such empty terms to be found in some learned writers, to which they had recourse to etch out their systems, where their understandings could not furnish them with conceptions from things. But yet I believe the supposing of some realities in nature, answering those and the like words, have much perplexed some, and quite misled others in the study of nature. That which in any discourse signifies, "I know not what," should be considered "I know not when." Where men have any conceptions, they can, if they are never so abstruse or abstracted, explain them, and the terms they use for them. For our conceptions being nothing but ideas, which are all made up of simple ones: if they cannot give us the ideas their words stand for, it is plain they have none. To what purpose can it be, to hunt after his conceptions, who has none, or none distinct: He that knew not what he himself meant by a learned term, cannot make us know any thing by his use of it, let us beat our heads about it never so long. Whether we are able to comprehend all the operations of nature, and the manners of them, it matters not to inquire; but this is certain, that we can comprehend no more of them, than we can distinctly conceive; and therefore to obtrude terms where we have no distinct conceptions, as if they did contain, or rather conceal something; is but an artifice of learned vanity to cover a defect in an hypothesis or our understandings. Words are not made to conceal, but to declare and show something; where they are by those, who pretend to instruct, otherwise used, they conceal indeed something; but that that they conceal is nothing but the ignorance, errour, or sophistry of the talker; for there is, in truth, nothing else under them.

Moral words

One other group of selections from Locke's views on language is useful by way of transition to the final division of the sciences, that division covering action, the individual, society, politics, religion, and ethics. This group reveals Locke's views on moral concepts and the language of morals. Such concepts were called *mixed modes*.

67. *Essay*, 3.10.33

In modes and relations generally we are liable only to the four first of these inconveniences; viz. 1. I may have in my memory the names of modes, as gratitude or charity, and yet not have any precise ideas annexed in my thoughts to those names. 2. I may have ideas, and not know the names that belong to them; v. g. I may have the idea of a man's drinking till his colour and humour be altered, till his tongue trips, and his eyes look red, and his feet fail him; and yet not know, that it is to be called drunkenness. 3. I may have the ideas of virtues or vices, and names also, but apply them amiss: v. g. when I apply the name frugality to that idea which others call and signify by this sound, covetousness. 4. I may use any of those names with inconstancy. 5. But, in modes and relations, I cannot have ideas disagreeing to the existence of things: for modes being complex ideas, made by the mind at pleasure; and relation being but by way of considering or comparing two things together, and so also an idea of my own making; these ideas can scarce be found to disagree with any thing existing, since they are not in the mind as the copies of things regularly made by nature, nor as properties inseparably flowing from the internal constitution or essence of any substance; but as it were patterns lodged in my memory, with names annexed to them, to denominate actions and relations by, as they come to exist. But the mistake is commonly in my giving a wrong name to my conceptions; and so using words in a different sense from other people, I am not understood, but am thought to have wrong ideas of them, when I give wrong names to them. Only if I put in my ideas of mixed modes or relations any inconsistent ideas together, I fill my head also with chimeras; since such ideas, if well examined, cannot so much as exist in the mind, much less any real being ever be denominated from them.

68. *Essay*, 3.11.15–18

Secondly, mixed modes, especially those belonging to morality, being most of them such combinations of ideas, as the mind puts together of its own choice, and whereof there are not always standing patterns to be found existing; the signification of their names cannot be made known, as those of simple ideas, by any showing; but, in recompense thereof, may be perfectly and exactly defined. For they being combinations of several ideas, that the mind of man has arbitrarily put together, without reference to any archetypes, men may, if they please, exactly know the ideas that go to each composition, and so both use these words in a certain and undoubted signification, and perfectly declare, when there is occasion, what they stand for. This, if well considered, would lay great blame on those, who make not their discourses about moral things very clear and distinct. For since the precise signification of the names of mixed modes, or, which is all one, the real essence of each species is to be known, they being not of nature's but man's making, it is a great negligence and perverseness to discourse of moral things with uncertainty and obscurity; which is more pardonable in treating of natural substances, where doubtful terms are hardly to be avoided, for a quite contrary reason, as we shall see by and by.

Upon this ground it is, that I am bold to think, that morality is capable of demonstration, as well as mathematicks: since the precise real essence of the things moral words stand for may be perfectly known; and so the congruity and incongruity of the things themselves be certainly discovered; in which consists perfect knowledge. Nor let any one object, that the names of substances are often to be made use of in morality, as well as those of modes, from which will arise obscurity. For as to substances, when concerned in moral discourses, their divers natures are not so much inquired into, as supposed; v. g. when we say that man is subject to law, we mean nothing by man, but a corporeal rational creature: what the real essence or other qualities of that creature are, in this case, is no way considered. And therefore whether a child or changeling be a man in a physical sense, may amongst the naturalists be as disputable as it will, it concerns not at all the moral man, as I may call him, which is this immovable unchangeable idea, a corporeal rational being. For were there a monkey, or any other creature to be found, that has the use of reason to such a degree as to be able to understand general signs, and to deduce consequences about general ideas, he would no doubt be subject to law, and in that sense be a man, how much soever he differed in shape from others of that name. The names of substances, if they be used in them as they should, can no more disturb moral than they do mathematical discourses: where, if the mathematician speaks of a cube or globe of gold, or any other body, he has his clear settled idea which varies not, though it may by mistake be applied to a particular body to which it belongs not.

This I have here mentioned by the by, to show of what consequence it is for men, in their names of mixed modes, and consequently in all their moral discoures, to define their words when there is occasion: since thereby moral knowledge may be brought to so great clearness and certainty. And it must be great want of ingenuity (to say no worse of it) to refuse to do it: since a definition is the only way whereby the precise meaning of moral words can be known; and yet a way whereby their meaning may be known certainly, and without leaving any room for any contest about it. And therefore the negligence or perverseness of mankind cannot be excused, if their discourses in morality be not much more clear than those in natural philosophy: since they are about ideas in the mind, which are none of them false or disproportionate: they having no external beings for the archetypes which they are referred to, and must correspond with. It is far easier for men to frame in their minds an idea which shall be the standard to which they will give the name justice, with which pattern so made, all actions that agree shall pass under that denomination; than, having seen Aristides, to frame an idea that shall in all things be exactly like him; who is as he is, let men make what idea they please of him. For the one, they need but know the combination of ideas that are put together in their own minds; for the other, they must inquire into the whole nature, and abstruse hidden constitution, and various qualities of a thing existing without them.

Another reason that makes the defining of mixed modes so necessary, especially of moral words, is what I mentioned a little before, viz. that it is the only way whereby the signification of the most of them can be known with certainty. For the ideas they stand for, being for the most part such whose component parts no where exist together, but scattered and mingled with others, it is the mind alone that collects them, and gives them the union of one idea: and it is only by words, enumerating the several simple ideas which the mind has united, that we can make known to others what their names stand for; the assistance of the senses in this case not helping us, by the proposal of sensible objects, to show the ideas which our names of this kind stand for, as it does often in the names of sensible simple ideas, and also to some degree in those of substances.

69. *Conduct,* section 9

Outward corporeal objects, that constantly importune our senses and captivate our appetites, fail not to fill our heads with lively and lasting ideas of that kind. Here the mind needs not to be set upon getting greater store; they offer themselves fast enough, and are usually entertained in such plenty, and lodged so carefully, that the mind wants room, or attention, for others that it has more use and need of. To fit the understanding, therefore, for such reasoning as I have been above speaking of, care should be taken to fill it with moral and more abstract ideas; for these not offering themselves to the senses, but being to be framed to the understanding, people are generally so neglectful of a faculty they are apt to think wants nothing, that I fear most men's minds are more unfurnished with such ideas than is imagined. They often use the words, and how can they be suspected to want the ideas? What I have said in the third book of my essay, will excuse me from any other answer to this question. But to convince people of what moment it is to their understandings to be furnished with such abstract ideas, steady and settled in them, give me leave to ask, how any one shall be able to know whether he be obliged to be just, if he has not established ideas in his mind of obligation and of justice; since knowledge consists in nothing but the perceived agreement or disagreement of those ideas? and so of all others the like, which concern our lives and manners. And if men do find a difficulty to see the agreement or disagreement of two angles, which lie before their eyes, unalterable in a diagram; how utterly impossible will it be to perceive it in ideas that have no other sensible object to represent them to the mind but sounds; with which they have no manner of conformity, and therefore had need to be clearly settled in the mind themselves, if we would make any clear judgment about them? This, therefore, is one of the first things the mind should be employed about, in the right conduct of the understanding, without which it is impossible it should be capable of reasoning right about those matters. But in these, and all other ideas, care must be taken that they harbour no inconsistencies, and that they have a real existence where real existence is supposed; and are not mere chimeras with a supposed existence.

3

The Science of Action

"The skill of applying our own powers and actions"

The last of the three main divisions of human knowledge
Locke characterizes as "that which man himself ought to
do, as a rational and voluntary agent, for the attainment
of any end, especially happiness." He also refers to this
area as involving the "skill of right applying our own powers and actions, for the attainment of things good and useful." Ethics is one subject matter in this division, but under
it belong also education, religion, and politics. Embedded
in ethics, religion, and politics are the concepts of the person, of action, of moral good and evil. It is the concept of
the person that is central to these areas, as well as basic to
Locke's views on education. Locke's concept of the person
is centered in action rather than in knowledge. He works
with an agent, rather than with a cognitive theory of the
person. The agent-centered person should not obscure from
us, however, the detailed psychological and cognitive account of the knower. What is most important for understanding Locke's views of the individual and society is that,
when he came to articulate a concept of person, he looked
to action and agency (especially to *moral* agency) as the
basis for that elaboration. It is misleading to suggest that
the moral concerns dominate his thought. Locke is too
complex and catholic in his interests to justify fixing on any
one concern as dominant. The moral and social philosophy
is important in the overall understanding of Locke. There
are also interconnections between the moral and social
and the epistemological interests.

The selections that follow do not cover all of the topics
and issues found in Locke's writings on ethics, education,
religion, or politics, but they are grouped around some of
the basic concepts at work in his writings in these areas.

169

Character traits and natural tendencies

A person is both a knower and a doer, a cognizer and an actor. For both, the person has indigenous or even inherited equipment. As cognizer, we have an array of faculties ready to operate on the data of sense and introspection. We also have dispositions to seek pleasure and avoid pain. As actor or agent, we are also equipped with traits and tendencies that have a particular significance for the educator. The list of traits or dispositions given by Locke – most of which he says are *given* for the educator and cannot be changed – suggest an observant nature of his own.

70. *Essay*, 1.3.3

Nature, I confess, has put into man a desire of happiness and an aversion to misery: these indeed are innate practical principles, which (as practical principles ought) do continue constantly to operate and influence all our actions without ceasing: these may be observed in all persons and all ages, steady and universal; but these are inclinations of the appetite to good, not impressions of truth on the understanding. I deny not, that there are natural tendencies imprinted on the minds of men; and that, from the very first instances of sense and perception, there are some things that are grateful, and others unwelcome to them; some things, that they incline to, and others unwelcome to them; some things, that they incline to, and others that they fly: but this makes nothing for innate characters on the mind, which are to be the principles of knowledge, regulating our practice. Such natural impressions on the understanding are so far from being confirmed hereby, that this is an argument against them; since, if there were certain characters imprinted by nature on the understanding, as the principles of knowledge, we could not but perceive them constantly operate in us and influence our knowledge, as we do those others on the will and appetite; which never cease to be the constant springs and motives of all our actions, to which we perpetually feel them strongly impelling us.

71. *Two Treatises*, I, section 86

God having made man, and planted in him, as in all other animals, a strong desire of self-preservation, and furnished the world with things fit for food and raiment, and other necessaries of life, subservient to his design, that man should live and abide for some time upon the face of the earth, and not that so curious and wonderful

a piece of workmanship, by his own negligence, or want of necessaries, should perish again, presently after a few moments continuance; God, I say, having made man and the world thus, spoke
to him, (that is) directed him by his senses and reason, as he did
the inferior animals by their sense and instinct, which were serviceable for his subsistence, and given him as the means of his preservation; and therefore I doubt not, but before these words were
pronounced, Gen. i. 28, 29, (if they must be understood literally
to have been spoken) and without any such verbal donation, man
had a right to an use of the creatures, by the will and grant of God:
for the desire, strong desire, of preserving his life and being, having
been planted in him as a principle of action by God himself, reason,
"which was the voice of God in him," could not but teach him and
assure him that pursuing that natural inclination he had to preserve
his being, he followed the will of his Maker, and therefore had a
right to make use of those creatures which by his reason or senses
he could discover would be serviceable thereunto.

72. *Education*, sections 66, 101–2

But pray remember, children are not to be taught by rules, which
will be always slipping out of their memories. What you think
necessary for them to do, settle in them by an indispensable practice, as often as the occasion returns; and, if it be possible, make
occasions. This will beget habits in them, which, being once established, operate of themselves, easily and naturally, without the
assistance of the memory. But here let me give two cautions: 1. The
one is, that you keep them to the practice of what you would have
grow into a habit in them, by kind words and gentle admonitions,
rather as minding them of what they forget, than by harsh rebukes
and chiding as if they were wilfully guilty. 2dly, Another thing
you are to take care of, is, not to endeavour to settle too many
habits at once, lest by a variety you confound them, and so perfect
none. When constant custom has made any one thing easy and
natural to them, and they practise it without reflection, you may
then go on to another.

This method of teaching children by a repeated practice, and the
same action done over and over again, under the eye and direction of the tutor, till they have got the habit of doing it well,
and not by relying on rules trusted to their memories; has so many
advantages, which way soever we consider it, that I cannot but
wonder (if ill customs could be wondered at in any thing) how it
could possibly be so much neglected. I shall name one more that

comes now in my way. By this method we shall see, whether what is required of him be adapted to his capacity, and any way suited to the child's natural genius and constitution: for that too must be considered in a right education. We must not hope wholly to change their original tempers, nor make the gay pensive and grave, nor the melancholy sportive, without spoiling them. God has stamped certain characters upon men's minds, which, like their shapes, may perhaps be a little mended; but can hardly be totally altered and transformed into the contrary.

He therefore that is about children, should well study their natures and aptitudes, and see, by often trials, what turn they easily take, and what becomes them; observe what their native stock is, how it may be improved, and what it is fit for: he should consider what they want, whether they be capable of having it wrought into them by industry, and incorporated there by practice; and whether it be worth while to endeavour it. For in many cases, all that we can do, or should aim at, is, to make the best of what nature has given, to prevent the vices and faults to which such a constitution is most inclined, and give it all the advantages it is capable of. Every one's natural genius should be carried as far as it could; but to attempt the putting another upon him, will be but labour in vain; and what is so plaistered on, will at best sit but untowardly, and have always hanging to it the ungracefulness of constraint and affectation.

Having thus very early set up your authority, and, by the gentler applications of it, shamed him out of what leads towards any immoral habit; as soon as you have observed it in him, (for I would by no means have chiding used, much less blows, till obstinacy and incorrigibleness make it absolutely necessary,) it will be fit to consider which way the natural make of his mind inclines him. Some men, by the unalterable frame of their constitutions, are stout, others timorous; some confident, others modest, tractable or obstinate, curious or careless, quick or slow. There are not more differences in men's faces, and the outward lineaments of their bodies, than there are in the makes and tempers of their minds: only there is this difference, that the distinguishing characters of the face, and the lineaments of the body, grow more plain and visible with time and age, but the peculiar physiognomy of the mind is most discernible in children, before art and cunning have taught them to hide their deformities, and conceal their ill inclinations under a dissembled outside.

Begin therefore betimes nicely to observe your son's temper;

and that, when he is under least restraint, in his play, and, as he thinks, out of your sight. See what are his predominant passions, and prevailing inclinations; whether he be fierce or mild, bold or bashful, compassionate or cruel, open or reserved, &c. For as these are different in him, so are your methods to be different, and your authority must hence take measures to apply itself different ways to him. These native propensities, these prevalencies of constitution, are not to be cured by rules, or a direct contest; especially those of them that are the humbler and meaner sort, which proceed from fear and lowness of spirit; though with art they may be much mended, and turned to good purposes. But this be sure of, after all is done, the bias will always hang on that side where nature first placed it: and, if you carefully observe the characters of his mind now in the first scenes of his life, you will ever after be able to judge which way his thoughts lean, and what he aims at even hereafter, when, as he grows up, the plot thickens, and he puts on several shapes to act it.

73. *Conduct,* sections 2, 4

There is, it is visible, great variety in men's understandings, and their natural constitutions put so wide a difference between some men, in this respect, that art and industry would never be able to master; and their very natures seem to want a foundation to raise on it that which other men easily attain unto. – Amongst men of equal education there is great inequality of parts. And the woods of America, as well as the schools of Athens, produce men of several abilities in the same kind. Though this be so, yet I imagine most men come very short of what they might attain unto, in their several degrees, by a neglect of their understandings. A few rules of logic are thought sufficient, in this case, for those who pretend to the highest improvement; whereas I think there are a great many natural defects in the understanding, capable of amendment, which are overlooked and wholly neglected. And it is easy to perceive, that men are guilty of a great many faults, in the exercise and improvement of this faculty of the mind, which hinder them in their progress, and keep them in ignorance and errour all their lives. Some of them I shall take notice of, and endeavour to point out proper remedies for, in the following discourse.

We are born with faculties and powers capable almost of any thing, such at least as would carry us farther than can easily be imagined: but it is only the exercise of those powers, which gives us ability and skill in any thing, and leads us towards perfection.

A middle-aged ploughman will scarce ever be brought to the carriage and language of a gentleman, though his body be as well proportioned, and his joints as supple, and his natural parts not any way inferior. The legs of a dancing-master, and the fingers of a musician, fall as it were naturally, without thought, or pains, into regular and admirable motions. Bid them change their parts, and they will in vain endeavour to produce like motions in the members not used to them, and it will require length of time and long practice to attain but some degrees of a like ability. What incredible and astonishing actions do we find rope-dancers and tumblers bring their bodies to! Not but that sundry, in almost all manual arts, are as wonderful; but I name those which the world takes notice of for such, because, on that very account, they give money to see them. All these admired motions, beyond the reach and almost conception of unpractised spectators, are nothing but the mere effects of use and industry in men, whose bodies have nothing peculiar in them from those of the amazed lookers-on.

As it is in the body, so it is in the mind; practice makes it what it is, and most even of those excellencies, which are looked on as natural endowments, will be found, when examined into more narrowly, to be the product of exercise, and to be raised to that pitch, only by repeated actions. Some men are remarked for pleasantness in raillery; others for apologues and apposite diverting stories. This is apt to be taken for the effect of pure nature, and that the rather, because it is not got by rules, and those who excel in either of them, never purposely set themselves to the study of it, as an art to be learnt. But yet it is true, that at first some lucky hit, which took with somebody, and gained him commendation, encouraged him to try again, inclined his thoughts and endeavours that way, till at last he insensibly got a facility in it, without perceiving how; and that is attributed wholly to nature, which was much more the effect of use and practice. I do not deny, that natural disposition may often give the first rise to it, but that never carries a man far, without use and exercise; and it is practice alone, that brings the powers of the mind, as well as those of the body, to their perfection. Many a good poetic vein is buried under a trade, and never produces any thing for want of improvement. We see the ways of discourse and reasoning are very different, even concerning the same matter, at court and in the university. And he that will go but from Westminster-hall to the Exchange, will find a different genius and turn in their ways of talking; and yet one cannot think that all whose lot fell in the city, were born with different parts from those who were bred at the university, or inns of court.

To what purpose all this, but to show that the difference, so observable in men's understandings and parts, does not arise so much from their natural faculties, as acquired habits. He would be laughed at, that should go about to make a fine dancer out of a country hedger, at past fifty. And he will not have much better success, who shall endeavour, at that age, to make a man reason well, or speak handsomely, who has never been used to it, though you should lay before him a collection of all the best precepts of logic or oratory. Nobody is made any thing by hearing of rules, or laying them up in his memory; practice must settle the habit of doing, without reflecting on the rule; and you may as well hope to make a good painter, or musician, extempore, by a lecture and instruction in the arts of music and painting, as a coherent thinker, or a strict reasoner, by a set of rules, showing him wherein right reasoning consists.

This being so, that defects and weakness in men's understandings, as well as other faculties, come from want of a right use of their own minds; I am apt to think, the fault is generally mislaid upon nature, and there is often a complaint of want of parts, when the fault lies in want of a due improvement of them. We see men frequently dexterous and sharp enough in making a bargain, who, if you reason with them about matters of religion, appear perfectly stupid.

Just as Locke's account of the origin of ideas relies upon many native faculties (but no native ideas or truths), so his account of education urges the tutor to work with the natural tendencies and traits of the child. The educator must study children's natures and adjust the goal of education to what these natures make possible: "the business of Education" is "either to take off, or counter-balance" those natural traits. The final section of his *Education* says that "there are possibly scarce two children, who can be conducted by exactly the same method." Other writers in the seventeenth century were taking the same view of teaching. John Dury, for example,[21] said that the tutor should discover the "predominant quality" of each child's

21.John Dury, *The Reformed School and Reformed Librarie-Keeper* (London, 1651).

humor or temper, "contemplate rationally the inward disposition and frame of his spirit, to find out the Principles by which he is led." In a 1677 essay, "Of Study," Locke stressed the same point: "There are peculiar endowments and natural fitnesses, as well as defects and weaknesses, almost in every man's mind."[22] We must learn how to "follow the bent and tendency of the mind itself" by recognizing these natural "sympathies and antipathies." From the opening section of his treatise on *Education*, Locke stressed the natural talents and tempers of all men, but it was training and education that bring out what is latent, what is possible. We begin with different character traits but with more or less equal natural faculties.

Action and the person

Actions, as opposed to events, come under Locke's concept of mixed modes. The concepts that are formed in any society to designate actions, to which are attached praise and blame, may vary and depend upon the customs of that society. Even those concepts that are found in a wide variety of societies pick out features of people's behavior, which, without those concepts, would be viewed as different actions. An early recognition of the role concepts play in indicating what actions can be performed is found in one of the early drafts of Locke's *Essay:* "a man holding a gun in his hand and pulling down the triger may be either Rebellion, Parricide, Murther, Homicide, Duty, Justice, Valer, or recreation, and be thus variously diversified, when all the circumstances put together are compared to a rule, though the simple action of holding the gun and pulling the triger may be exactly the same."[23] The same point is made in the *Essay* itself.

74. *Essay,* 2.22.4, 6

Every mixed mode consisting of many distinct simple ideas, it seems reasonable to inquire, "whence it has its unity, and how such a precise multitude comes to make but one idea, since that combination does not always exist together in nature?" To which

22 In *The Educational Writings of John Locke,* ed. James Axtell (Cambridge, 1968). For a discussion of Locke's views on education, see my *John Locke and Education* (New York, 1971).
23 See Aaron and Gibb, *op. cit.,* p. 35.

I answer, it is plain it has its unity from an act of the mind combining those several simple ideas together, and considering them as one complex one, consisting of those parts; and the mark of this union, or that which is looked on generally to complete it, is one name given to that combination. For it is by their names that men commonly regulate their account of their distinct species of mixed modes, seldom allowing or considering any number of simple ideas to make one complex one, but such collections as there be names for. Thus, though the killing of an old man be as fit in nature to be united into one complex idea, as the killing a man's father; yet there being no name standing precisely for the one, as there is the name of parricide to mark the other, it is not taken for a particular complex idea, nor a distinct species of actions from that of killing a young man, or any other man.

This shows us how it comes to pass, that there are in every language many particular words, which cannot be rendered by any one single word of another. For the several fashions, customs and manners of one nation, making several combinations of ideas familiar and necessary in one, which another people have had never any occasion to make, or perhaps so much as taken notice of; names come of course to be annexed to them, to avoid long periphrases in things of daily conversation; and so they become so many distinct complex ideas in their minds.

75. *Essay*, 3.5.10–11

The near relation that there is between species, essences, and their general name, at least in mixed modes, will farther appear, when we consider that it is the name that seems to preserve those essences, and give them their lasting duration. For the connexion between the loose parts of those complex ideas being made by the mind, this union, which has no particular foundation in nature, would cease again, were there not something that did, as it were, hold it together, and keep the parts from scattering. Though therefore it be the mind that makes the collection, it is the name which is as it were the knot that ties them fast together. What a vast variety of different ideas does the word triumphus hold together, and deliver to us as one species? Had this name been never made, or quite lost, we might, no doubt, have had descriptions of what passed in that solemnity: but yet, I think, that which holds those different parts together, in the unity of one complex idea, is that very word annexed to it; without which the several parts of that would no more be thought to make one thing, than any other show, which having never been made but once, had never been united into one complex idea, under one denomination. How much therefore, in mixed modes, the unity necessary to any essence depends on the mind, and how much the continuation and fixing of that unity depends on the name in common use annexed to it, I leave to be considered by those who look upon essences and species as real established things in nature.

Suitable to this, we find, that men speaking of mixed modes, seldom imagine or take any other for species of them, but such as are set out by name: because they being of man's making only, in order to naming, no such species are taken notice of, or supposed to be, unless a name be joined to it, as the sign of man's having combined into one idea several loose ones; and by that name giving a lasting union to the parts, which could otherwise cease to have any, as soon as the mind laid by that abstract idea, and ceased actually to think on it. But when a name is once annexed to it, wherein the parts of that complex idea have a settled and permanent union; then is the essence as it were established, and the species looked on as complete. For to what purpose should the memory charge itself with such compositions, unless it were by abstraction to make them general? And to what purpose make them general, unless it were that they might have general names for the convenience of discourse and communication? Thus we see, that killing a man with a sword or a hatchet, are looked on as no distinct species of action: but if the point of the sword first enter the body, it passes for a distinct species, where it has a distinct name; as in England, in whose language it is called stabbing; but in another country, where it has not happened to be specified under a peculiar name, it passes not for a distinct species. But in the species of corporeal substances, though it be the mind that makes the nominal essence; yet since those ideas which are combined in it are supposed to have an union in nature, whether the mind joins them or no, therefore those are looked on as distinct species, without any operation of the mind, either abstracting or giving a name to that complex idea.

76. *Essay*, 3.9.7

Because the names of mixed modes, for the most part, want standards in nature, whereby men may rectify and adjust their significations; therefore they are very various and doubtful. They are assemblages of ideas put together at the pleasure of the mind, pursuing its own ends of discourse, and suited to its own notions; whereby it designs not to copy any thing really existing, but to

denominate and rank things, as they come to agree with those
archetypes or forms it has made. He that first brought the word
sham, or wheedle, or banter, in use, put together, as he thought fit,
those ideas he made it stand for: and as it is with any new names
of modes, that are now brought into any language; so it was with
the old ones, when they were first made use of. Names therefore
that stand for collections of ideas which the mind makes at pleasure, must needs be of doubtful signification, when such collections are no where to be found constantly united in nature, nor any
patterns to be shown whereby men may adjust them. What the
word murder, or sacrilege, &c. signifies, can never be known from
things themselves: there be many of the parts of those complex
ideas, which are not visible in the action itself; the intention of
the mind, or the relation of holy things, which make a part of murder or sacrilege, have no necessary connexion with the outward
and visible action of him that commits either: and the pulling the
trigger of the gun, with which the murder is committed, and is all
the action that perhaps is visible, has no natural connexion with
those other ideas that make up the complex one, named murder.
They have their union and combination only from the understanding, which unites them under one name: but uniting them without
any rule or pattern, it cannot be but that the signification of the
name that stands for such voluntary collections should be often
various in the minds of different men, who have scarce any standing
rule to regulate themselves and their notions by, in such arbitrary
ideas.

> Our action concepts designate what movements of my
> body made by me will fall under those concepts, will count
> as stabbing, parricide, triumph. It is the person who does
> the acting. There was no clear account of *how I move my
> body* in the seventeenth and eighteenth centuries. Many
> writers discussed the problem; some said, "I move my body
> by activating the animal spirits in the brain": a physiologi-
> cal term that designated the active element in nerves and
> brain (what we might today call the firing of neurons). But
> no one professed to understand how we do activate the
> mechanism of the body. Locke simply tried to state the
> obvious; I can, he said, "by a thought directing the motion
> of my finger, make it move when it was at rest" (*Essay*,
> 2.21.21). He thought it was a "matter of fact which cannot
> be denied" that by taking thought, I can and do move my
> hand (*Essay*, 4.10.19).

The difficulties attendant upon trying to understand
how we move our bodies led many writers in the eighteenth century toward a biological or organic materialism.
Joseph Priestley, near the end of that century, said that
there is as much reason to say the brain thinks as that it
is white and soft. Recognition of the complex organization
of the brain, and of the fundamental role played by the
neurophysiological mechanism, was forcing some writers
to give up the more traditional notion of man as two substances, mind and body, an immaterial and a material substance. Locke did not move so far as to give up the two-
substance doctrine (although his passing suggestions that
God might be able to add to matter the power of thinking
unleashed a storm of reactions in the eighteenth century),
but he did not think any light was shed on the concept of
person by appealing to an immaterial substance. In trying
to say what it is to be the same person (a different question from the criterion one of *how can we tell he is the
same*), Locke first distinguished three different kinds of
identity.

77. *Essay,* 2.27.3–6

From what has been said, it is easy to discover what is so much
inquired after, the principium individuationis; and that, it is plain,
is existence itself, which determines a being of any sort to a particular time and place, incommunicable to two beings of the same
kind. This, though it seems easier to conceive in simple substances
or modes, yet when reflected on is not more difficult in compound
ones, if care be taken to what it is applied: v. g. let us suppose an
atom, i. e. a continued body under one immutable superficies,
existing in a determined time and place; it is evident that, considered in any instant of its existence, it is in that instant the same
with itself. For being at that instant what it is, and nothing else,
it is the same, and so must continue as long as its existence is
continued; for so long it will be the same, and no other. In like
manner, if two or more atoms be joined together into the same
mass, every one of those atoms will be the same, by the foregoing
rule: and whilst they exist united together, the mass, consisting
of the same atoms, must be the same mass, or the same body, let
the parts be ever so differently jumbled. But if one of these atoms
be taken away, or one new one added, it is no longer the same
mass, or the same body. In the state of living creatures, their
identity depends not on a mass of the same particles, but on some-

thing else. For in them the variation of great parcels of matters alters not the identity: an oak growing from a plant to a great tree, and then lopped, is still the same oak; and a colt grown up to a horse, sometimes fat, sometimes lean, is all the while the same horse: though in both these cases, there may be a manifest change of the parts; so that truly they are not either of them the same masses of matter, though they be truly one of them the same oak, and the other the same horse. The reason whereof is, that in these two cases, a mass of matter, and a living body, identity is not applied to the same thing.

We must therefore consider wherein an oak differs from a mass of matter, and that seems to me to be in this, that the one is only the cohesion of particles of matter any how united, the other such a disposition of them as constitutes the parts of an oak; and such an organization of those parts as is fit to receive and distribute nourishment, so as to continue and frame the wood, bark, and leaves, &c. of an oak, in which consists the vegetable life. That being then one plant which has such an organization of parts in one coherent body partaking of one common life, it continues to be the same plant as long as it partakes of the same life, though that life be communicated to new particles of matter vitally united to the living plant, in a like continued organization conformable to that sort of plants. For this organization being at any one instant in any one collection of matter, is in that particular concrete distinguished from all other, and is that individual life which existing constantly from that moment both forwards and backwards, in the same continuity of insensibly succeeding parts united to the living body of the plant, it has that identity, which makes the same plant, and all the parts of it parts of the same plant, during all the time that they exist united in that continued organization, which is fit to convey that common life to all the parts so united.

The case is not so much different in brutes, but that any one may hence see what makes an animal, and continues it the same. Something we have like this in machines, and may serve to illustrate it. For example, what is a watch? It is plain it is nothing but a fit organization, or construction of parts to a certain end, which when a sufficient force is added to it, it is capable to attain. If we would suppose this machine one continued body, all whose organized parts were repaired, increased, or diminished by a constant addition or separation of insensible parts, with one common life, we should have something very much like the body of an animal; with this difference, that in an animal the fitness of the organization, and the motion wherein life consists, begin together, the motion coming from within; but in machines, the force coming sensibly from without, is often away when the organ is in order, and well fitted to receive it.

This also shows wherein the identity of the same man consists: viz. in nothing but a participation of the same continued life, by constantly fleeting particles of matter, in succession vitally united to the same organized body. He that shall place the identity of man in any thing else, but like that of other animals in one fitly organized body, taken in any one instant, and from thence continued under one organization of life in several successively fleeting particles of matter united to it, will find it hard to make an embryo, one of years, mad and sober, the same man, by any supposition, that will not make it possible for Seth, Ismael, Socrates, Pilate, St. Austin, and Caesar Borgia, to be the same man. For if the identity of soul alone makes the same man, and there be nothing in the nature of matter why the same individual spirit may not be united to different bodies, it will be possible that those men living in distant ages, and of different tempers, may have been the same man: which way of speaking must be, from a very strange use of the word man, applied to an idea, out of which body and shape are excluded. And that way of speaking would agree yet worse with the notions of those philosophers who allow of transmigration, and are of opinion that the souls of men may, for their miscarriages, be detruded into the bodies of beasts, as fit habitations, with organs suited to the satisfaction of their brutal inclinations. But yet I think nobody, could he be sure that the soul of Heliogabalus were in one of his hogs, would yet say that hog were a man or Heliogabalus.

Locke then proceeds to lay out his account of sameness of consciousness, as what makes man a person. He also raises various puzzle cases about different consciousnesses in the same body or different bodies with the same consciousness. The question of sameness of body was believed by many to be essential for the resurrection. Locke received some criticisms from the Bishop of Worcester on this point, which Locke answered neatly.

78. *Essay*, 2.27.9, 16–17, 26

This being premised, to find wherein personal identity consists, we must consider what person stands for; which, I think, is a thinking intelligent being, that has reason and reflection, and can consider itself as itself, the same thinking thing in different times and places; which it does only by that consciousness which is inseparable from thinking, and, as it seems to me, essential to it: it being impossible for any one to perceive, without perceiving that he does perceive. When we see, hear, smell, taste, feel, meditate, or will any thing, we know that we do so. Thus it is always as to our present sensations and perceptions: and by this every one is to himself that which he calls self; it not being considered in this case whether the same self be continued in the same or divers substances. For since consciousness always accompanies thinking, and it is that which makes every one to be what he calls self, and thereby distinguishes himself from all other thinking things; in this alone consists personal identity, i. e. the sameness of a rational being: and as far as this consciousness can be extended backwards to any past action or thought, so far reaches the identity of that person; it is the same self now it was then; and it is by the same self with this present one that now reflects on it, that that action was done.

But though the same immaterial substance or soul does not alone, wherever it be, and in whatsoever state, make the same man; yet it is plain consciousness, as far as ever it can be extended, should it be to ages past, unites existences and actions, very remote in time, into the same person, as well as it does the existences and actions of the immediately preceding moment; so that whatever has the consciousness of present and past actions, is the same person to whom they both belong. Had I the same consciousness that I saw the ark and Noah's flood, as that I saw an overflowing of the Thames last winter, or as that I write now; I could no more doubt that I who write this now, that saw the Thames overflowed last winter, and that viewed the flood at the general deluge, was the same self, place that self in what substance you please, than that I who write this am the same myself now whilst I write (whether I consist of all the same substance, material or immaterial, or no) that I was yesterday. For as to this point of being the same self, it matters not whether this present self be made up of the same or other substances; I being as much concerned, and as justly accountable for any action that was done a thousand years since, appropriated to me now by this self-consciousness, as I am for what I did the last moment.

Self is that conscious thinking thing, whatever substance made up of (whether spiritual or material, simple or compounded, it mat-

ters not), which is sensible, or conscious of pleasure and pain, capable of happiness or misery, and so is concerned for itself, as far as
that consciousness extends. Thus every one finds, that whilst
comprehended under that consciousness, the little finger is as much
a part of himself as what is most so. Upon separation of this little
finger, should this consciousness go along with the little finger, and
leave the rest of the body, it is evident the little finger would be
the person, the same person; and self then would have nothing to
do with the rest of the body. As in this case it is the consciousness
that goes along with the substance, when one part is separate from
another, which makes the same person, and constitutes this inseparable self; so it is in reference to substances remote in time. That
with which the consciousness of this present thinking thing can
join itself, makes the same person, and is one self with it, and with
nothing else; and so attributes to itself, and owns all the actions
of that thing as its own, as far as that consciousness reaches, and no
farther; as every one who reflects will perceive.

Person, as I take it, is the name for this self. Wherever a man
finds what he calls himself, there I think another may say is the
same person. It is a forensick term appropriating actions and their
merit; and so belongs only to intelligent agents capable of a law,
and happiness and misery. This personality extends itself beyond
present existence to what is past, only by consciousness, whereby
it becomes concerned and accountable, owns and imputes to itself past actions, just upon the same ground, and for the same reason
that it does the present. All which is founded in a concern for happiness, the unavoidable concomitant of consciousness; that which is
conscious of pleasure and pain, desiring that that self that is conscious should be happy. And therefore whatever past actions it
cannot reconcile or appropriate to that present self by consciousness, it can be no more concerned in, than if they had never been
done: and to receive pleasure or pain, i. e. reward or punishment,
on the account of any such action, is all one as to be made happy
or miserable in its first being, without any demerit at all. For supposing a man punished now for what he had done in another life,
whereof he could be made to have no consciousness at all, what
difference is there between that punishment, and being created
miserable? And therefore conformable to this the apostle tells us,
that at the great day, when every one shall "receive according to
his doings, the secrets of all hearts shall be laid open." The sentence
shall be justified by the consciousness all persons shall have, that
they themselves, in what bodies soever they appear, or what sub-

stances soever that consciousness adheres to, are the same that committed those actions, and deserve that punishment for them.

79. *Essay, 2.27.15*

And thus we may be able, without any difficulty, to conceive the same person at the resurrection, though in a body not exactly in make or parts the same which he had here, the same consciousness going along with the soul that inhabits it. But yet the soul alone, in the change of bodies, would scarce to any one, but to him that makes the soul the man, be enough to make the same man. For should the soul of a prince, carrying with it the consciousness of the prince's past life, enter and inform the body of a cobler, as soon as deserted by his own soul, every one sees he would be the same person with the prince, accountable only for the prince's actions: but who would say it was the same man? The body too goes to the making the man, and would, I guess, to every body determine the man in this case; wherein the soul, with all its princely thoughts about it, would not make another man: but he would be the same cobler to every one besides himself. I know that, in the ordinary way of speaking, the same person, and the same man, stand for one and the same thing. And indeed every one will always have a liberty to speak as he pleases, and to apply what articulate sounds to what ideas he thinks fit, and change them as often as he pleases. But yet when we will inquire what makes the same spirit, man, or person, we must fix the ideas of spirit, man, or person in our minds; and having resolved with ourselves what we mean by them, it will not be hard to determine in either of them, or the like, when it is the same, and when not.

80. *Second Reply to the Bishop of Worcester, Works,* IV, pp. 303–8

The article of the Christian faith your lordship begins with, is that of the resurrection of the dead; and concerning that, you say, "the reason of believing the resurrection of the same body, upon my grounds, is from the idea of identity." Answ. Give me leave, my lord, to say that the reason of believing any article of the Christian faith (such as your lordship is here speaking of) to me and upon my grounds, is its being a part of divine revelation. Upon this ground I believed it, before I either writ that chapter of identity and diversity, and before I ever thought of those propositions which your lordship quotes out of that chapter, and upon the same ground I believe it still; and not from my idea of identity. This saying of your lordship's therefore, being a proposition neither self-evident, nor allowed by me to be true, remains to be proved. So that your foundation failing, all your large superstructure built thereupon comes to nothing.

But, my lord, before we go any farther, I crave leave humbly to represent to your lordship, that I thought you undertook to make out that my notion of ideas was inconsistent with the articles of the Christian faith. But that which your lordship instances in here, is not, that I yet know, any article of the Christian faith. The resurrection of the dead I acknowledge to be an article of the Christian faith: but that the resurrection of the same body, in your lordship's sense of the same body, is an article of the Christian faith, is what, I confess, I do not yet know.

In the New Testament (wherein, I think, are contained all the articles of the Christian faith) I find our Saviour and the apostles to preach the resurrection of the dead, and the resurrection from the dead, in many places: but I do not remember any place, where the resurrection of the same body is so much as mentioned. Nay, which is very remarkable in the case, I do not remember in any place of the New Testament (where the general resurrection at the last day is spoken of) any such expression as the resurrection of the body, much less of the same body. And it may seem to be, not without some special reason, that where St. Paul's discourse was particularly concerning the body, and so led him to name it; yet when he speaks of the resurrection, he says, you, and not your bodies. (1 Cor. vi. 14.)

I say, the general resurrection at the last day; because where the resurrection of some particular persons, presently upon our Saviour's resurrection, is mentioned, the words are, "The graves were opened, and many bodies of saints, which slept, arose and came out of the graves after his resurrection, and went into the holy city, and appeared to many" (Matt. xxvii. 52, 53). Of which peculiar way of speaking of this resurrection, the passage itself gives a reason in these words, "appeared to many"; i. e. those who slept appeared, so as to be known to be risen. But this could not be known, unless they brought with them the evidence, that they were those who had been dead, whereof there were these two proofs; their graves were opened, and their bodies not only gone out of them, but appeared to be the same to those who had known them formerly alive, and knew them to be dead and buried. For if they had been those who had been dead so long, that all who knew them once alive were now gone, those to whom they appeared might have known them to be men, but could not have known they were risen from the dead, because they never knew they had been dead. All that by their appearing they could have known, was, that they were so many living strangers, of whose resurrection they knew nothing. It was necessary therefore, that they should come in such bodies, as might in make and size, &c. appear to be the same they had before, that they might be known to those of their acquaintance whom they appeared to. And it is probable they were such as were newly dead, whose bodies were not dissolved and dissipated; and therefore it is particularly said here (differently from what is said of the general resurrection) that their bodies arose: because they were the same that were then lying in their graves the moment before they rose.

But your lordship endeavours to prove it must be the same body: and let us grant, that your lordship, nay, and others too, think you have proved it must be the same body; will you therefore say, that he holds what is inconsistent with an article of faith, who having never seen this your lordship's interpretation of the Scripture, nor your reasons for the same body, in your sense of same body; or, if he has seen them, yet not understanding them, or not perceiving the force of them; believes what the Scripture proposes to him, viz. that at the last day "the dead shall be raised," without determining whether it should be with the very same bodies or no?

I know your lordship pretends not to erect your particular interpretations of Scripture into articles of faith; and if you do not, he that believes "the dead shall be raised," believes that article of faith which the Scripture proposes; and cannot be accused of holding any thing inconsistent with it, if it should happen, that what he holds is inconsistent with another proposition, viz. "that the dead shall be raised with the same bodies," in your lordship's sense; which I do not find proposed in holy writ as an article of faith.

But your lordship argues, "it must be the same body"; which, as you explain same body, "is not the same individual particles of matter which were united at the point of death, nor the same particles of matter that the sinner had at the time of the commission of his sins: but that it must be the same material substance which was vitally united to the soul here"; i. e. as I understand it, the same individual particles of matter, which were, some time during his life here, vitally united to the soul.

Your first argument, to prove that it must be the same body, in this sense of the same body, is taken from these words of our Saviour: "All that are in the graves shall hear his voice, and shall come forth" (John v. 28, 29). From whence your lordship argues, that these words, "all that are in the graves," relate to no other substance than what was united to the soul in life; because "a different substance cannot be said to be in the graves, and to come out of them." Which words of your lordship's, if they prove any thing, prove that the soul too is lodged in the grave, and raised out of it at the last day. For your lordship says, "can a different substance be said to be in their graves, and come out of them?" So that, according to this interpretation of these words of our Saviour, no other substance being raised but what hears his voice; and no other substance hearing his voice but what, being called, comes out of the grave; and no other substance coming out of the grave but what was in the grave, any one must conclude, that the soul, unless it be in the grave, will make no part of the person that is raised, unless, as your lordship argues against me, "you can make it out, that a substance which never was in the grave may come out of it," or that the soul is no substance.

But setting aside the substance of the soul, another thing that will make any one doubt, whether this your interpretation of our Saviour's words be necessarily to be received as their true sense, is, that it will not be very easily reconciled to your saying, you do not mean by the same body "the same individual particles which were united at the point of death." And yet by this interpretation of our Saviour's words, you can mean no other particles but such as were united at the point of death: because you mean no other substance but what comes out of the grave; and no substance, no particles come out, you say, but what were in the grave: and I think your lordship will not say, that the particles that were separate from the body by perspiration, before the point of death, were laid up in the grave.

But your lordship, I find, has an answer to this; viz. "that by comparing this with other places, you find that the words [of our Saviour above quoted] are to be understood of the substance of the body, to which the soul was united; and not to (I suppose your lordship writ of) those individual particles," i. e. those individual particles that are in the grave at the resurrection: for so they must be read, to make your lordship's sense entire, and to have the purpose of your answer here. And then methinks this last sense of our Saviour's words given by your lordship wholly overturns the sense which you have given of them above; where from those words you press the belief of the resurrection of the same body, by this strong argument, that a substance could not, upon hearing the voice of

Christ, "come out of the grave which was never in the grave." There (as far as I can understand your words) your lordship argues, that our Saviour's words must be understood of the particles in the grave, "unless," as your lordship says, "one can make it out that a substance which was never in the grave may come out of it." And here your lordship expressly says, "that our Saviour's words are to be understood of the substance of that body, to which the soul was [at any time] united, and not to those individual particles that are in the grave." Which put together, seems to me to say, that our Saviour's words are to be understood of those particles only that are in the grave, and not of those particles only which are in the grave, but of others also which have at any time been vitally united to the soul, but never were in the grave.

The next text your lordship brings, to make the resurrection of the same body, in your sense, an article of faith, are these words of St. Paul: "For we must all appear before the judgment-seat of Christ, that every one may receive the things done in his body, according to that he hath done, whether it be good or bad" (2 Cor. v. 10). To which your lordship subjoins this question: "Can these words be understood of any other material substance, but that body in which these things were done?" Answ. A man may suspend his determining the meaning of the apostle to be, that a sinner shall suffer for his sins in the very same body wherein he committed them; because St. Paul does not say he shall have the very same body when he suffers that he had when he sinned. The apostle says, indeed, "done in his body." The body he had, and did things in, at five or fifteen, was no doubt his body, as much as that which he did things in at fifty was his body, though his body were not the very same body at those different ages: and so will the body which he shall have after the resurrection be his body, though it be not the very same with that which he had at five, or fifteen, or fifty. He that at threescore is broke on the wheel, for a murder he committed at twenty, is punished for what he did in his body; though the body he has, i. e. his body at threescore, be not the same, i. e. made up of the same individual particles of matter that that body was which he had forty years before. When your lordship has resolved with yourself what that same immutable he is, which at the last judgment shall receive the things done in his body; your lordship will easily see, that the body he had, when an embryo in the womb, when a child playing in coats, when a man marrying a wife, and when bed-rid, dying of a consumption, and at last, which he shall have after his resurrection; are each of them his body, though neither of them be the same body, the one with the other.

Virtue and law

Locke elaborates the concept of the person in terms of action, especially responsible action. Actions take place in society; the actions that can be performed are in fact governed by the available descriptions of possible actions in that society. Descriptive action terms carry a prescriptive content. Actions can be right or wrong, the measure of rightness being the moral law. The person subject to moral law is not "man in a physical sense" but "the *moral man, as I may call him, which is this immoveable unchangeable idea, a corporeal rational being*" (*Essay,* 3.11.16). The concept of the moral man, the corporeal rational being, is a fundamental one for Locke's ethical, social, political, and religious thought. Of equal importance is his notion of the true measure of moral rightness. Locke distinguishes three measures of moral rightness. Many of his own contemporaries, and many subsequent critics, took Locke's own preference to be the rule of custom. Locke emphatically rejected the rule of custom as the ultimate or basic measure of moral action. He retained the notion of laws of nature, God's laws, which reason can discover and which the Bible reveals. Rationality requires certain religious beliefs as well. The true measure of right and wrong has God's sanctions.

81. *Essay,* 1.3.5–8, 12–13, 18

That men should keep their compacts, is certainly a great and undeniable rule in morality. But yet, if a christian, who has the view of happiness and misery in another life, be asked why a man must keep his word, he will give this as a reason; because God, who has the power of eternal life and death, requires it of us. But if an Hobbist be asked why, he will answer, because the public requires it, and the Leviathan will punish you, if you do not. And if one of the old philosophers had been asked, he would have answered, because it was dishonest, below the dignity of a man, and opposite to virtue, the highest perfection of human nature, to do otherwise.

Hence naturally flows the great variety of opinions concerning moral rules, which are to be found among men, according to the different sorts of happiness they have a prospect of, or propose to themselves: which could not be if practical principles were innate, and imprinted in our minds immediately by the hand of God. I grant the existence of God is so many ways manifest, and the obedience we owe him so congruous to the light of reason, that a great part of mankind give testimony to the law of nature; but yet I think it must be allowed, that several moral rules may receive from mankind a very general approbation, without either knowing or admitting the true ground of morality; which can only be the will and law of a God, who sees men in the dark, has in his hand rewards and punishments, and power enough to call to account the proudest offender. For God having, by an inseparable connexion, joined virtue and public happiness together, and made the practice thereof necessary to the preservation of society, and visibly beneficial to all with whom the virtuous man has to do; it is no wonder, that every one should not only allow, but recommend and magnify those rules to others, from whose observance of them he is sure to reap advantage to himself. He may, out of interest, as well as conviction, cry up that for sacred, which if once trampled on and profaned, he himself cannot be safe nor secure. This, though it takes nothing from the moral and eternal obligation which these rules evidently have; yet it shows that the outward acknowledgment men pay to them in their words, proves not that they are innate principles; nay, it proves not so much, as that men assent to them inwardly in their own minds, as the inviolable rules of their own practice: since we find that self-interest, and the conveniencies of this life, make many men own an outward profession and approbation of them, whose actions sufficiently prove, that they very little consider the law-giver that prescribed these rules, nor the hell that he has ordained for the punishment of those that transgress them.

For, if we will not in civility allow too much sincerity to the professions of most men, but think their actions to be the interpreters of their thoughts, we shall find that they have no such internal veneration for these rules, nor so full a persuasion of their certainty and obligation. The great principle of morality, "to do as one would be done to," is more commended than practised. But the breach of this rule cannot be a greater vice, than to teach others, that it is no moral rule, nor obligatory, would be thought madness, and contrary to that interest men sacrifice to, when they break it themselves. Perhaps conscience will be urged as checking us for such breaches, and so the internal obligation and establishment of the rule be preserved.

To which I answer, that I doubt not but, without being written on their hearts, many men may, by the same way that they come to the knowledge of other things, come to assent to several moral rules, and be convinced of their obligation. Others also may come to be of the same mind, from their education, company, and customs of their country; which persuasion, however got, will serve to set conscience on work, which is nothing else, but our own opinion or judgment of the moral rectitude or pravity of our own actions. And if conscience be a proof of innate principles, contraries may be innate principles; since some men, with the same bent of conscience, prosecute what others avoid.

The breaking of a rule, say you, is no argument that it is unknown. I grant it: but the generally allowed breach of it any where, I say, is a proof that it is not innate. For example: let us take any of these rules, which being the most obvious deductions of human reason, and conformable to the natural inclination of the greatest part of men, fewest people have had the impudence to deny, or inconsideration to doubt of. If any can be thought to be naturally imprinted, none, I think can have a fairer pretence to be innate than this: "Parents, preserve and cherish your children." When therefore you say, that this is an innate rule, what do you mean? Either, that it is an innate principle, which upon all occasions excites and directs the actions of all men: or else, that it is a truth, which all men have imprinted on their minds, and which therefore they know and assent to. But in neither of these senses is it innate. First that it is not a principle which influences all men's actions, is what I have proved by the examples before cited: nor need we seek so far as Mingrelia or Peru, to find instances of such as neglect, abuse, nay and destroy their children; or look on it only as the more than brutality of some savage and barbarous nations, when we remember, that it was a familiar and uncondemned practice amongst the Greeks and Romans, to expose, without pity or remorse, their innocent infants. Secondly, that it is an innate truth, known to all men, is also false. For, "parents, preserve your children," is so far from an innate truth, that it is no truth at all; it being a command, and not a proposition, and so not capable of truth or falsehood. To make it capable of being assented to as true, it must be reduced to some such proposition as this: "it is the duty of parents to preserve their children." But what duty is, cannot be understood without a law; nor a law be known, or supposed, without a law-maker, or without reward and punishment: so that it is impossible, that this, or any other practical principle should be innate; i. e. be imprinted on the mind as a duty, without supposing the ideas of God, of law, of obligation, of punishment, of a life after this, innate: For that punishment follows not, in this life, the breach of this rule; and consequently, that it has not the force of a law in countries, where the generally allowed practice runs counter to it, is in itself evident. But these ideas (which must be all of them innate, if any thing as a duty be so) are so far from being innate, that it is not every studious or thinking man, much less every one that is born, in whom they are to be found clear and distinct; and that one of them, which of all others seems most likely to be innate, is not so, (I mean the idea of God) I think, in the next chapter, will appear very evident to any considering man.

From what has been said, I think we may safely conclude, that whatever practical rule is, in any place, generally and with allowance broken, cannot be supposed innate; it being impossible that men should, without shame or fear, confidently and serenely break a rule, which they could not but evidently know, that God had set up, and would certainly punish the breach of (which they must, if it were innate) to a degree, to make it a very ill bargain to the transgressor. Without such a knowledge as this, a man can never be certain that any thing is his duty. Ignorance, or doubt of the law, hopes to escape the knowledge or power of the law-maker, or the like, may make men give way to a present appetite: but let any one see the fault, and the rod by it, and with the transgression, a fire ready to punish it; a pleasure tempting, and the hand of the Almighty visibly held up, and prepared to take vengeance (for this must be the case, where any duty is imprinted on the mind) and then tell me, whether it be possible for people, with such a prospect, such a certain knowledge as this, wantonly, and without scruple, to offend against a law, which they carry about them in indelible characters, and that stares them in the face, whilst they are breaking it? whether men, at the same time that they feel in themselves the imprinted edicts of an omnipotent law-maker, can with assurance and gaiety slight and trample under foot his most sacred injunctions? and lastly, whether it be possible, that whilst a man thus openly bids defiance to this innate law and supreme law-giver, all the by-standers, yea, even the governors and rulers of the people, full of the same sense both of the law and law-maker, should silently connive, without testifying their dislike, or laying the least blame on it? Principles of actions indeed there are lodged in men's appetites, but these are so far from being innate moral principles, that if they were left to their full swing, they would carry men to the overturning of all morality. Moral laws are set as a curb and restraint to these exorbitant desires, which they cannot be but by rewards and punishments, that will over-balance the satisfaction any one shall propose to himself in the breach of the law. If therefore any thing be imprinted on the mind of all men as a law, all men must have a certain and unavoidable knowledge, that certain and unavoidable punishment will attend the breach of it. For, if men can be ignorant or doubtful of what is innate, innate principles are insisted on, and urged to no purpose; truth and certainty (the things pretended) are not at all secured by them: but men are in the same uncertain, floating estate with, as without them. An evident indubitable knowledge of unavoidable punishment, great enough to make the transgression very uneligible, must accompany an innate law; unless, with an innate law, they can suppose an innate gospel too. I would not here be mistaken, as if, because I deny an innate law, I thought there were none but positive laws. There is a great deal of difference between an innate law, and a law of nature; between something imprinted on our minds in their very original, and something that we being ignorant of may attain to the knowledge of, by the use and due application of our natural faculties. And I think they equally forsake the truth, who, running into the contrary extremes, either affirm an innate law, or deny that there is a law knowable by the light of nature, i.e., without the help of positive revelation.

For let us consider this proposition as to its meaning (for it is the sense, and not sound, that is, and must be the principle or common notion) viz. 'virtue is the best worship of God'; i.e. is most acceptable to him; which if virtue be taken, as most commonly it is, for those actions, which, according to the different opinions of several countries, are accounted laudable, will be a proposition so far from being certain, that it will not be true. If virtue be taken for actions conformable to God's will, or to the rule prescribed by God, which is the true and only measure of virtue, when virtue is used to signify what is in its own nature right and good; then this proposition, 'that virtue is the best worship of God,' will be most true and certain, but of very little use in human life: since it will amount to no more but this, viz. 'that God is pleased with the doing of what he commands'; which a man may certainly know to be true, without knowing what it is that God doth command; and so be as far from any rule or principle of his actions, as he was before. And I think very few will take a proposition, which amounts to no more than this, viz. that God is pleased with the doing of what he himself commands, for an innate moral principle writ on the minds of all men (however true and certain it may be) since it teaches so little. Whosoever does so, will have reason to think hundreds of propositions, innate principles; since there are many which have as good a title as this, to be received for such, which nobody yet ever put into that rank of innate principles.

82. *Essay*, 2.28.4–16

Fourthly, There is another sort of relation, which is the conformity, or disagreement, men's voluntary actions have to a rule to which they are referred, and by which they are judged of; which, I think, may be called moral relation, as being that which denominates our moral actions, and deserves well to be examined; there being no part of knowledge wherein we should be more careful to get determined ideas, and avoid, as much as may be, obscurity and confusion. Human actions, when with their various ends, objects, manners, and circumstances, they are framed into distinct complex ideas, are, as has been shown, so many mixed modes, a great part whereof have names annexed to them. Thus, supposing gratitude to be a readiness to acknowledge and return kindness received, polygamy to be the having more wives than one at once; when we frame these notions thus in our minds, we have there so many determined ideas of mixed modes. But this is not all that concerns our actions; it is not enough to have determined ideas of them, and to know what names belong to such and such combinations of ideas. We have a farther and greater concernment, and that is, to know whether such actions so made up are morally good or bad.

Good and evil, as hath been shown, b. ii. chap. 20 §. 2. and chap. 21. §. 42. are nothing but pleasure or pain, or that which occasions or procures pleasure or pain to us. Moral good and evil then is only the conformity or disagreement of our voluntary actions to some law, whereby good or evil is drawn on us by the will and power of the law-maker; which good and evil, pleasure or pain, attending our observance, or breach of the law, by the decree of the law-maker, is that we call reward and punishment.

Of these moral rules, or laws, to which men generally refer, and by which they judge of the rectitude or pravity of their actions, there seem to me to be three sorts, with their three different enforcements, or rewards and punishments. For since it would be utterly in vain to suppose a rule set to the free actions of men, without annexing to it some enforcement of good and evil to determine his will, we must, wherever we suppose a law, suppose also some reward or punishment annexed to that law. It would be in vain for one intelligent being to set a rule to the actions of another, if he had it not in his power to reward the compliance with, and punish deviation from his rule, by some good and evil, that is not the natural product and consequence of the action itself. For that being a natural convenience or inconvenience, would operate of itself without a law. This, if I mistake not, is the true nature of all law, properly so called.

The laws that men generally refer their actions to, to judge of their rectitude or obliquity, seem to me to be these three. 1. The divine law. 2. The civil law. 3. The law of opinion or reputation, if I may so call it. By the relation they bear to the first of these, men judge whether their actions are sins or duties; by the second, whether they be criminal or innocent; and by the third, whether they be virtues or vices.

First, the divine law, whereby I mean that law which God has set to the actions of men, whether promulgated to them by the light of nature, or the voice of revelation. That God has given a rule whereby men should govern themselves, I think there is nobody so brutish as to deny. He has a right to do it, we are his creatures: he has goodness and wisdom to direct our actions to that which is best; and he has power to enforce it by rewards and punishments, of infinite weight and duration in another life: for nobody can take us out of his hands. This is the only true touchstone of moral rectitude; and by comparing them to this law it is, that men judge of the most considerable moral good or evil of their actions: that is, whether as duties or sins, they are like to procure them happiness or misery from the hands of the Almighty.

Secondly, the civil law, the rule set by the commonwealth to the actions of those who belong to it, is another rule to which men refer their actions, to judge whether they be criminal or no. This law nobody overlooks, the rewards and punishments that enforce it being ready at hand, and suitable to the power that makes it; which is the force of the commonwealth, engaged to protect the lives, liberties, and possessions of those who live according to its law; and has power to take away life, liberty, or goods from him who disobeys: which is the punishment of offences committed against this law.

Thirdly, the law of opinion or reputation. Virtue and vice are names pretended and supposed every-where to stand for actions in their own nature right and wrong; and as far as they really are so applied, they so far are co-incident with the divine law above-mentioned. But yet whatever is pretended, this is visible, that these names virtue and vice, in the particular instances of their application, through the several nations and societies of men in the world, are constantly attributed only to such actions as in each country and society are in reputation or discredit. Nor is it to be thought strange, that men every-where should give the name of virtue to those actions, which amongst them are judged praise worthy; and call that vice, which they account blameable; since otherwise they would condemn themselves, if they should think any thing right, to which they allowed not commendation: any thing wrong, which they let pass without blame. Thus the measure of what is every-where called and esteemed virtue and vice, is the approbation or dislike, praise or blame, which by a secret and tacit consent establishes itself in the several societies, tribes, and clubs of men in the world; whereby several actions come to find credit or disgrace amongst them, according to the judgment, maxims, or fashion of that place. For though men uniting into politic societies have resigned up to the public the disposing of all their force, so that they cannot employ it against any fellow-citizens, any farther than the law of the country directs; yet they retain still the power of thinking well or ill, approving or disapproving of the actions of those whom they live amongst, and converse with; and by this approbation and dislike they establish amongst themselves what they will call virtue and vice.

That this is the common measure of virtue and vice, will appear to any one who considers, that though that passes for vice in one country, which is counted a virtue, or at least not vice in another; yet, every-where, virtue and praise, vice and blame go together. Virtue is every-where that which is thought praise-worthy; and nothing else but that which has the allowance of public esteem is called virtue. Virtue and praise are so united, that they are called often by the same name. "Sunt sua praemia laudi," says Virgil; and so Cicero, "nihil habet natura praestantius, quam honestatem, quam lauden, quam dignitatem, quam decus"; which, he tells you, are all names for the same thing. (Tusc. *lib.* ii) This is the language of the heathen philosophers, who well understood wherein their notions of virtue and vice consisted, and though perhaps by the different temper, education, fashion, maxims, or interests of different sorts of men, it fell out that what was thought praiseworthy in one place, escaped not censure in another; and so in different societies, virtues and vices were changed; yet, as to the main, they for the most part kept the same everywhere. For since nothing can be more natural, than to encourage with esteem and reputation that wherein every one finds his advantage, and to blame and discountenance the contrary; it is no wonder that esteem and discredit, virtue and vice, should in a great measure every-where correspond with the unchangeable rule of right and wrong, which the law of God hath established: there being nothing that so directly and visibly secures and advances the general good of mankind in this world, as obedience to the laws he has set them, and nothing that breeds such mischiefs and confusion, as the neglect of them. And therefore men, without renouncing all sense and reason, and their own interest, which they are so constantly true to, could not generally mistake in placing their commendation and blame on that side that really deserved it not. Nay, even those men whose practice was otherwise, failed not to give their approbation right; few being depraved to that degree, as not to condemn, at least in others, the faults they themselves were guilty of: whereby, even in the corruption of manners, the true boundaries of the law of nature, which ought to be the rule of virtue and vice, were pretty well preferred. So that even the exhortations of inspired teachers have not feared to appeal to common repute: "Whatsoever is lovely, whatsoever is of good report, if there be any virtue, if there be any praise," &c. Phil. iv. 8.

If any one shall imagine that I have forgot my own notion of a law, when I make the law, whereby men judge of virtue and vice, to be nothing else but the consent of private men, who have not authority enough to make a law: especially wanting that, which is so necessary and essential to a law, a power to enforce it: I think I may say, that he who imagines commendation and disgrace not to be strong motives to men, to accommodate themselves to the opinions and rules of those with whom they converse, seems little skilled in the nature or history of mankind: the greatest part whereof he shall find to govern themselves chiefly, if not solely, by this law of fashion; and so they do that which keeps them in reputation with their company, little regard the laws of God, or the magistrate. The penalties that attend the breach of God's laws, some, nay, perhaps most men, seldom seriously reflect on; and amongst those that do, many, whilst they break the law, entertain thoughts of future reconciliation, and making their peace for such breaches. And as to the punishments due from the laws of the commonwealth, they frequently flatter themselves with the hopes of impunity. But no man escapes the punishment of their censure and dislike, who offends against the fashion and opinion of the company he keeps, and would recommend himself to. Nor is there one of ten thousand, who is stiff and insensible enough to bear up under the constant dislike and condemnation of his own club. He must be of a strange and unusual constitution, who can content himself to live in constant disgrace and disrepute with his own particular society. Solitude many men have sought, and been reconciled to: but nobody, that has the least thought or sense of a man about him, can live in society under the constant dislike and ill opinion of his familiars, and those he converses with. This is a burden too heavy for human sufferance: and he must be made up of irreconcileable contradictions, who can take pleasure in company, and yet be insensible of contempt and disgrace from his companions.

These three then, first, the law of God; secondly, the law of politic societies; thirdly, the law of fashion, or private censure; are those to which men variously compare their actions; and it is by their conformity to one of these laws that they take their measures, when they would judge of their moral rectitude, and denominate their actions good or bad.

Whether the rule, to which, as to a touchstone, we bring our voluntary actions, to examine them by, and try their goodness, and accordingly to name them: which is, as it were, the mark of the value we set upon them: whether, I say, we take that rule from the fashion of the country, or the will of a law-maker, the mind is easily able to observe the relation any action hath to it, and to judge whether the action agrees or disagrees with the rule; and so hath a notion of moral goodness or evil, which is either conformity or not conformity of any action to that rule: and therefore is often called moral rectitude. This rule being nothing but a collection of several simple ideas, the conformity thereto is but so ordering the action, that the simple ideas belonging to it may correspond to those which the law requires. And thus we see how moral beings and notions are founded on, and terminated in these simple ideas we have received from sensation or reflection. For example, let us consider the complex idea we signify by the word murder; and when we have taken it asunder, and examined all the particulars, we shall find them to amount to a collection of simple ideas derived from reflection or sensation, viz. first, from reflection on the operations of our own minds, we have the ideas of willing, considering, purposing before-hand, malice, or wishing ill to another; and also of life, or perception, and self-motion. Secondly, from sensation we have the collection of those simple sensible ideas which are to be found in a man, and of some action, whereby we put an end to perception and motion in the man; all which simple ideas are comprehended in the word murder. This collection of simple ideas being found by me to agree or disagree with the esteem of the country I have been bred in, and to be held by most men there worthy praise or blame, I call the action virtuous or vicious: if I have the will of a supreme invisible law-giver for my rule; then, as I supposed the action commanded or forbidden by God, I call it good or evil, sin or duty: and if I compare it to the civil law, the rule made by the legislative power of the country, I call it lawful or unlawful, a crime or no crime. So that whence-soever we take the rule of moral actions, or by what standard soever we frame in our minds the ideas of virtues or vices, they consist only and are made up of collections of simple ideas, which we originally received from sense or reflection, and their rectitude or obliquity consists in the agreement or disagreement with those patterns prescribed by some law.

To conceive rightly of moral actions, we must take notice of them under this two-fold consideration. First, as they are in themselves each made up of such a collection of simple ideas. Thus drunkenness, or lying, signify such or such a collection of simple ideas, which I call mixed modes, and in this sense they are as much positive absolute ideas, as the drinking of a horse, or speaking of a parrot. Secondly, our actions are considered as good, bad, or indifferent; and in this respect they are relative, it being their conformity to, or disagreement with some rule that makes them to be regular or irregular, good or bad: and so, as far as they are compared with a rule, and thereupon denominated, they come under relation. Thus the challenging and fighting with a man, as it is a certain positive mode, or particular sort of action, by particular ideas, distinguished from all others, is called duelling: which, when considered in relation to the law of God, will deserve the name sin; to the law of fashion, in some countries, valour and virtue; and to the municipal laws of some governments, a capital crime. In this case, when the positive mode has one name, and another name as it stands in relation to the law, the distinction may as easily be observed, as it is in substances, where one name, v. g. man, is used to signify the thing; another, v. g. father, to signify the relation.

But because very frequently the positive idea of the action, and its moral relation, are comprehended together under one name, and the same word made use of to express both the mode or action, and its moral rectitude or obliquity; therefore the relation itself is less taken notice of, and there is often no distinction made between the positive idea of the action, and the reference it has to a rule. By which confusion of these two distinct considerations under one term, those who yield too easily to the impressions of sounds, and are forward to take names for things, are often misled in their judgment of actions. Thus, the taking from another what is his, without his knowledge or allowance, is properly called stealing; but that name being commonly understood to signify also the moral pravity of the action, and to denote its contrariety to the law, men are apt to condemn whatever they hear called stealing as an ill action, disagreeing with the rule of right. And yet the private taking away his sword from a madman, to prevent his doing mischief, though it be properly denominated stealing, as the name of such a mixed mode; yet when compared to the law of God, and considered in its relation to that supreme rule, it is no sin, or transgression, though the name stealing ordinarily carries such an intimation with it.

83. *Essay*, 2.21.60

Their aptness, therefore, to conclude that they can be happy without it, is one great occasion that men often are not raised to the desire of the greatest absent good. For whilst such thoughts possess them, the joys of a future state move them not: they have little concern or uneasiness about them; and the will, free from the determination of such desires, is left to the pursuit of nearer satisfactions, and to the removal of those uneasinesses which it then feels, in its want of and longings after them. Change but a man's view of these things; let him see, that virtue and religion are necessary to his happiness; let him look into the future state of bliss or misery, and see there God, the righteous judge, ready to "render to every man according to his deeds; to them who by patient continuance in well-doing seek for glory, and honour, and immortality, eternal life; but unto every soul that doth evil, indignation and wrath, tribulation and anguish": to him, I say, who hath a prospect of the different state of perfect happiness, or misery, that attends all men after this life, depending on their behaviour here, the measures of good and evil, that govern his choice, are mightily changed. For since nothing of pleasure and pain in this life can bear any proportion to the endless happiness, or exquisite misery, of an immortal soul hereafter; actions in his power will have their preference, not according to the transient pleasure or pain that accompanies or follows them here, but as they serve to secure that perfect durable happiness hereafter.

84. *Reasonableness, Works,* VII, pp. 10–15

On the other side, it seems the unalterable purpose of the divine justice, that no unrighteous person, no one that is guilty of any breach of the law, should be in paradise: but that the wages of sin should be to every man, as it was to Adam, an exclusion of him out of that happy state of immortality, and bring death upon him. And this is so conformable to the eternal and established law of right and wrong, that it is spoken of too, as if it could not be otherwise. St. James says, chap. i. 15, "Sin, when it is finished, bringeth forth death," as it were by a natural and necessary production. "Sin entered into the world, and death by sin," says St. Paul, Rom. v. 12; and vi. 23, "The wages of sin is death." Death is the purchase of any, of every sin. Gal. iii. 10, "Cursed is every one, who continueth not in all things which are written in the book of the law to do them." And of this St. James gives a reason, chap. ii. 10, 11, "Whosoever shall keep the whole law, and yet offend in one point, he is guilty of all: for he that said, Do not commit adultery, said also, Do not kill": i. e. he that offends in any one point, sins against the authority which established the law.

Here then we have the standing and fixed measures of life and death. Immortality and bliss belong to the righteous; those who have lived in an exact conformity to the law of God, are out of the reach of death; but an exclusion from paradise and loss of immortality is the portion of sinners; of all those who have any way broke that law, and failed of a complete obedience to it, by the guilt of any one transgression. And thus mankind by the law, are put upon the issues of life or death, as they are righteous or unrighteous, just or unjust; i. e. exact performers or transgressors of the law.

But yet, "All having sinned," Rom. iii. 23, "and come short of the glory of God," i. e. the kingdom of God in heaven (which is often called his glory) "both Jews and Gentiles"; ver. 22, so that, "by the deeds of the law," no one could be justified, ver. 20, it follows, that no one could then have eternal life and bliss.

Perhaps it will be demanded, "Why did God give so hard a law to mankind, that, to the apostle's time, no one of Adam's issue had kept it? As appears by Rom. iii. and Gal. iii. 21, 22."

Answ. It was such a law as the purity of God's nature required, and must be the law of such a creature as man; unless God would have made him a rational creature, and not required him to have lived by the law of reason; but would have countenanced in him irregularity and disobedience to that light which he had, and that rule which was suitable to his nature; which would have been to have authorised disorder, confusion, and wickedness in his creatures: for that this law was the law of reason, or, as it is called, of nature, we shall see by and by; and if rational creatures will not live up to the rule of their reason, who shall excuse them? If you will admit them to forsake reason in one point, why not in another? Where will you stop? To disobey God in any part of his commands (and it is he that commands what reason does) is direct rebellion; which, if dispensed with in any point, government and order are at an end; and there can be no bounds set to the lawless exorbitancy of unconfined man. The law therefore was, as St. Paul tells us, Rom. vii. 12, "holy, just, and good," and such as it ought and could not otherwise be.

This then being the case, that whoever is guilty of any sin should certainly die, and cease to be; the benefit of life, restored by Christ at the resurrection, would have been no great advantage (for as much as, here again, death must have seized upon all mankind, because all had sinned; for the wages of sin is everywhere death, as well after as before the resurrection) if God had not found out a way to justify some, i. e. so many as obeyed another law, which God gave; which in the New Testament is called "the law of faith," Rom. iii. 27, and is opposed to "the law of works." And therefore the punishment of those, who would not follow him, was to lose their souls, i. e. their lives, Mark viii. 35–38, as is plain, considering the occasion it was spoke on.

The better to understand the law of faith, it will be convenient, in the first place, to consider the law of works. The law of works then, in short, is that law which requires perfect obedience, without any remission or abatement; so that, by that law, a man cannot be just, or justified, without an exact performance of every title. Such a perfect obedience, in the New Testament, is termed δικαιοσύνη, which we translate righteousness.

The language of this law is, "Do this and live, transgress and die." Lev. xviii. 5, "Ye shall keep my statutes and my judgments, which if a man do, he shall live in them." Ezek. xx. 11, "I gave them my statutes, and showed them my judgments, which if a man do, he shall even live in them." "Moses," says St. Paul, Rom. x. 5, "describeth the righteousness, which is of the law, that the man, which doth those things, shall live in them." Gal. iii. 12, "The law is not of faith; but that man that doth them shall live in them." On the other side, transgress and die; no dispensation, no atonement. Ver. 10, "Cursed is every one that continueth not in all things which are written in the book of the law to do them."

Where this law of works was to be found, the New Testament tells us, viz. in the law delivered by Moses. John i. 17, "The law was given by Moses, but grace and truth came by Jesus Christ." Chap. vii. 19, "Did not Moses give you the law?" says our Saviour, "and yet none of you keep the law." And this is the law which he speaks of, where he asks the lawyer, Luke x. 26, "What is written in the law? How readest thou?" ver. 28, "This do, and thou shall live." This is that which St. Paul so often styles the law, without any other distinction, Rom. ii. 13, "Not the hearers of the law are just before God, but the doers of the law are justified." It is needless to quote any more places; his epistles are full of it, especially this of the Romans.

"But the law given by Moses, being not given to all mankind, how are all men sinners; since, without a law, there is no transgression?" To this the apostle, ver. 14, answers, "For when the Gentiles, which have not the law, do, (i. e. find it reasonable to do) by nature the things contained in the law; these, having not the law, are a law unto themselves: which show the work of the law written in their hearts; their consciences also bearing witness, and amongst themselves their thoughts accusing or excusing one another." By which, and other places in the following chapter, it is plain, that under the law of works, is comprehended also the law of nature, knowable by reason, as well as the law given by Moses. For, says St. Paul, Rom. iii. 9, 23, "We have proved both Jews and Gentiles, that they are all under sin: for all have sinned, and come short of the glory of God": which they could not do without a law.

Nay, whatever God requires any where to be done, without making any allowance for faith, that is a part of the law of works: so that forbidding Adam to eat of the tree of knowledge was part of the law of works. Only we must take notice here, that some of God's positive commands, being for peculiar ends, and suited to particular circumstances of times, places, and persons; have a limited and only temporary obligation, by virtue of God's positive injunction; such as was that part of Moses's law, which concerned the outward worship, or political constitution of the Jews; and is called the ceremonial and judicial law, in contradistinction to the moral part of it; which being conformable to the eternal law of right, is of eternal obligation; and therefore remains in force still, under the Gospel; nor is abrogated by the law of faith, as St. Paul found some ready to infer, Rom. iii. 31, "Do we then make void the law, through faith? God forbid; yea, we establish the law." Nor can it be otherwise: for, were there no law of works, there could be no law of faith. For there could be no need of faith, which should be counted to men for righteousness; if there were no law, to be the rule and measure of righteousness, which men failed in their obedience to. Where there is no law, there is no sin; all are righteous equally, with or without faith.

The rule, therefore, of right, is the same that ever it was; the obligation to observe it is also the same: the difference between the law of works, and the law of faith, is only this: that the law of works makes no allowance for failing on any occasion. Those that obey are righteous; those that in any part disobey, are unrighteous, and must not expect life, the reward of righteousness. But, by the law of faith, faith is allowed to supply the defect of full obedience; and so the believers are admitted to life and immortality, as if they were righteous. Only here we must take notice, that when St. Paul says, that the Gospel establishes the law, he means the moral part of the law of Moses; for that he could not mean the ceremonial, or political part of it, is evident, by what I quoted out of him just now, where he says, That the Gentiles do, by nature, the things contained in the law, their consciences bearing witness. For the Gentiles neither did, nor thought of, the judicial or ceremonial institutions of Moses; it was only the moral part their consciences were concerned in. As for the rest, St. Paul tells the Galatians, chap. iv. they are not under that part of the law, which, ver. 3, he calls elements of the world; and, ver. 9, weak and beggarly elements. And our Saviour himself, in his Gospel sermon on the mount, tells them, Matt. v. 17, That, whatever they might think, he was not come to dissolve the law, but to make it more full and strict: for that that is meant by πληρωσαι is evident from the following part of that chapter, where he gives the precepts in a stricter sense than they were received in before. But they are all precepts of the moral law, which he re-enforces. What should become of the ritual law, he tells the woman of Samaria, in these words, John iv. 21, 23: "The hour cometh, when you shall, neither in this mountain, not yet at Jerusalem, worship the Father. But the true worshippers shall worship the Father in spirit and in truth; for the Father seeketh such to worship him."

Thus then, as to the law, in short: the civil and ritual part of the law, delivered by Moses, obliges not Christians, though, to the Jews, it were a part of the law of works; it being a part of the law of nature, that man ought to obey every positive law of God, whenever he shall please to make any such addition to the law of his nature. But the moral part of Moses's law, or the moral law, (which is everywhere the same, the eternal rule of right) obliges Christians, and all men, everywhere, and is to all men the standing law of works. But Christian believers have the privilege to be under the law of faith too; which is that law, whereby God justifies a man for believing, though by his works he be not just or righteous, i. e. though he come short of perfect obedience to the law of works. God alone does or can justify, or make just, those who by their works are not so: which he doth, by counting their faith for righteousness, i. e. for a complete performance of the law. Rom. iv. 3, "Abraham believed God, and it was counted to him for righteousness." Ver. 5, "To him that believeth on him that justifieth the ungodly, his faith is counted for righteousness." Ver. 6, "Even as David also describeth the blessedness of the man unto whom God imputeth righteousness without works"; i. e. without a full measure of works, which is exact obedience. Ver. 7, saying, "Blessed are they whose iniquities are forgiven, and whose sins are covered." Ver. 8, "Blessed is the man, to whom the Lord will not impute sin."

85. *Reasonableness, Works*, VII, pp. 111–23

Now, that this is the faith for which God of his free grace justifies sinful man, (for "it is God alone that justifieth," Rom. viii. 33. Rom. iii. 26,) we have already showed, by observing through all the history of our Saviour and the apostles, recorded in the evangelists, and in the Acts, what he and his apostles preached, and proposed to be believed. We shall show now, that besides believing him to be the Messiah, their King, it was farther required, that those who would have the privilege, advantage, and deliverance of his kingdom, should enter themselves into it; and by baptism being made denizens, and solemnly incorporated into that kingdom, live as became subjects obedient to the laws of it. For if they believed him to be the Messiah, their King, but would not obey his laws, and would not have him to reign over them; they were but the greater rebels; and God would not justify them for a faith that did but increase their guilt, and oppose diametrically the kingdom and design of the Messiah; "Who gave himself for us, that he might redeem us from all iniquity, and purify unto himself a peculiar people zealous of good works," Titus ii. 14. And therefore

St. Paul tells the Galatians, That that which availeth is faith; but "faith working by love." And that faith without works, i. e. the works of sincere obedience to the law and will of Christ, is not sufficient for our justification, St. James shows at large, chap. ii.

Neither, indeed, could it be otherwise; for life, eternal life, being the reward of justice or righteousness only appointed by the righteous God (who is of purer eyes than to behold iniquity) to those who only had no taint or infection of sin upon them, it is impossible that he should justify those who had no regard to justice at all, whatever they believed. This would have been to encourage iniquity, contrary to the purity of his nature; and to have condemned that eternal law of right, which is holy, just, and good; of which no one precept or rule is abrogated or repealed; nor indeed can be, whilst God is an holy, just, and righteous God, and man a rational creature. The duties of that law, arising from the constitution of his very nature, are of eternal obligation; nor can it be taken away or dispensed with, without changing the nature of things, overturning the measures of right and wrong, and thereby introducing and authorizing irregularity, confusion, and disorder in the world. Christ's coming into the world was not for such an end as that; but, on the contrary, to reform the corrupt state of degenerate man; and out of those who would mend their lives, and bring forth fruit meet for repentance, erect a new kingdom.

This is the law of that kingdom, as well as of all mankind; and that law, by which all men shall be judged at the last day. Only those who have believed Jesus to be the Messiah, and have taken him to be their King, with a sincere endeavour after righteousness, in obeying his law; shall have their past sins not imputed to them; and shall have that faith taken instead of obedience, where frailty and weakness made them transgress, and sin prevailed after conversion; in those who hunger and thirst after righteousness, (or perfect obedience) and do not allow themselves in acts of disobedience and rebellion, against the laws of that kingdom they are entered into.

He did not expect, it is true, a perfect obedience, void of slips and falls: he knew our make, and the weakness of our constitution too well, and was sent with a supply for that defect. Besides, perfect obedience was the righteousness of the law of works; and then the reward would be of debt, and not of grace; and to such there was no need of faith to be imputed to them for righteousness. They stood upon their own legs, were just already, and needed no allowance to be made them for believing Jesus to be the Messiah, taking him for their king, and becoming his subjects. But that Christ does require obedience, sincere obedience, is evident from the law he himself delivers, (unless he can be supposed to give and inculcate laws, only to have them disobeyed) and from the sentence he will pass when he comes to judge.

The faith required was, to believe Jesus to be the Messiah, the Anointed; who had been promised by God to the world. Among the Jews (to whom the promises and prophecies of the Messiah were more immediately delivered) anointing was used to three sorts of persons, at their inauguration; whereby they were set apart to three great offices, viz. of priests, prophets, and kings. Though these three offices be in holy writ attributed to our Saviour, yet I do not remember that he any where assumes to himself the title of a priest, or mentions any thing relating to his priesthood; nor does he speak of his being a prophet but very sparingly, and only once or twice, as it were by the by: but the Gospel, or the good news of the kingdom of the Messiah, is what he preaches every where, and makes it his great business to publish to the world. This he did, not only as most agreeable to the expectation of the Jews, who looked for their Messiah, chiefly as coming in power to be their king and deliverer; but as it best answered the chief end of his coming, which was to be a king, and, as such, to be received by those who would be his subjects in the kingdom which he came to erect. And though he took not directly on himself the title of King, until he was in custody, and in the hands of Pilate; yet it is plain, "King" and "King of Israel" were the familiar and received titles of the Messiah. See John i. 50. Luke xix. 38, compared with Matt. xxi. 9, and Mark xi. 9. John xii. 13. Matt. xxi. 5. Luke xxiii. 2, compared with Matt. xxvii. 11, and John xviii. 33–37. Mark xv. 12, compared with Matt. xxvii. 22, 42.

What those were to do who believed him to be the Messiah, and received him for their king, that they might be admitted to be partakers with him of his kingdom in glory, we shall best know by the laws he gives them, and requires them to obey; and by the sentence which he himself will give, when, sitting on his throne, they shall all appear at his tribunal, to receive every one his doom from the mouth of this righteous Judge of all men.

What he proposed to his followers to be believed, we have already seen, by examining his and his apostles' preaching, step by step, all through the history of the four evangelists, and the Acts of the Apostles. The same method will best and plainest show us whether he required of those who believed him to be the Messiah any thing besides that faith, and what it was. For, he being a king, we shall see by his commands what he expects from his subjects: for, if he did not expect obedience to them, his commands would be but mere mockery; and if there were no punishment for the transgressors of them, his laws would not be the laws of a king, and that authority to command, and power to chastise the disobedient, but empty talk, without force, and without influence.

We shall therefore from his injunctions (if any such there be) see what he has made necessary to be performed, by all those who shall be received into eternal life, in his kingdom prepared in the heavens. And in this we cannot be deceived. What we have from his own mouth, especially if repeated over and over again, in different places and expressions, will be past doubt and controversy. I shall pass by all that is said by St. John Baptist, or any other before our Saviour's entry upon his ministry, and public promulgation of the laws of his kingdom.

He began his preaching with a command to repent, as St. Matthew tells us, iv. 17, "From that time Jesus began to preach, saying, Repent; for the kingdom of heaven is at hand." And Luke v. 32, he tells the Scribes and Pharisees, "I come not to call the righteous," (those who were truly so needed no help, they had a right to the tree of life,) "but sinners to repentance."

In his sermon, as it is called, in the mount, Luke vi. and Matth. v., &c. he commands they should be exemplary in good works: "Let your light so shine amongst men, that they may see your good works, and glorify your Father which is in heaven," Matth. v. 15. And that they might know what he came for, and what he expected of them, he tells them, ver. 17–20, "Think not that I am come to dissolve," or loosen, "the law, or the prophets: I am not come to dissolve," or loosen, "but to make it full," or complete; by giving it you in its true and strict sense. Here we see he confirms, and at once re-enforces all the moral precepts in the Old Testament. "For verily I say to you, Till heaven and earth pass, one jot, or one tittle, shall in nowise pass from the law, till all be done. Whosoever therefore shall break one of these least commandments, and shall teach men so, he shall be called the least (i. e. as it is interpreted, shall not be at all) in the kingdom of heaven." Ver. 21, "I say unto you, That except your righteousness," i. e. your performance of the eternal law of right, "shall exceed the righteousness of the Scribes and Pharisees, ye shall in no case enter into the kingdom of heaven." And then he goes on to make good what he said, ver. 17, viz. "That he was come to complete the law," viz. by giving its full and clear sense, free from the corrupt and loosening glosses of the Scribes and Pharisees, ver. 22–26. He tells them, That not only murder, but causeless anger, and so much as words of contempt, were forbidden. He commands them to be reconciled and kind towards their adversaries; and that upon pain of condemnation. In the following part of his sermon, which is to be read Luke vi. and more at large, Matth. v. vi. vii. he not only forbids actual uncleanness, but all irregular desires, upon pain of hell-fire; causeless divorces; swearing in conversation, as well as forswearing in judgment; revenge; retaliation; ostentation of charity, of devotion, and of fasting; repetitions in prayer, covetousness, worldly care, censoriousness: and on the other side commands loving our enemies, doing good to those that hate us, blessing those that curse us, praying for those that despitefully use us; patience and meekness under injuries, forgiveness, liberality, compassion: and closes all his particular injunctions with this general golden rule, Matt. vii. 12, "All things whatsoever ye would that men should do to you, do you even so to them; for this is the law and the prophets." And to show how much he is in earnest, and expects obedience to these laws, he tells them, Luke vi. 35, That if they obey, "great shall be their *reward*"; they "shall be called, the sons of the Highest." And to all this, in the conclusion, he adds the solemn sanction; "Why call ye me, Lord, Lord, and do not the things that I say?" It is in vain for you to take me for the Messiah your King, unless you obey me. "Not every one who calls me Lord, Lord, shall enter into the kingdom of heaven," or be the sons of God; "but he that doth the will of my Father which is in heaven." To such disobedient subjects, though they have prophesied and done miracles, in my name, I shall say at the day of judgment, "Depart from me, ye workers of iniquity; I know you not."

When, Matt. xii, he was told, that his mother and brethren sought to speak with him, ver. 49, "Stretching out his hands to his disciples," he said, "Behold my mother and my brethren; for whosoever shall do the will of my Father, who is in heaven, he is my brother, and sister, and mother." They could not be children of the adoption, and fellow-heirs with him of eternal life, who did not do the will of his heavenly Father.

Matt. xv. and Mark vi. the Pharisees finding fault, that his disciples eat with unclean hands, he makes this declaration to his apostles: "Do not ye perceive, that whatsoever from without entereth into a man, cannot defile him, because it entereth not into his heart, but his belly? That which cometh out of the man, that defileth the man; for from within, out of the heart of men, proceed evil thoughts, adulteries, fornications, murders, thefts, false witnesses, covetousness, wickedness, deceit, lasciviousness, an evil eye, blasphemy, pride, foolishness. All these ill things come from within, and defile a man."

He commands self-denial, and the exposing ourselves to suffering and danger, rather than to deny or disown him: and this upon pain of losing our souls; which are of more worth than all the world. This we may read, Matt. xvi. 24–27, and the parallel places, Mark viii. and Luke ix.

The apostles disputing among them, who should be greatest in the kingdom of the Messiah, Matt. xviii. 1, he thus determines the controversy, Mark ix. 35, "If any one will be first, let him be last of all, and servant of all": and setting a child before them, adds, Matt. xviii. 3, "Verily, I say unto you, Unless ye turn, and become as children, ye shall not enter into the kingdom of heaven."

Matt. xviii. 15, "If thy brother shall trespass against thee, go and tell him his fault between thee and him alone: if he shall hear thee, thou hast gained thy brother. But if he will not hear thee, then take with thee one or two more, that in the mouth of two or three witnesses every word may be established. And if he shall neglect to hear them, tell it to the church: but if he neglect to hear the church, let him be unto thee as an heathen and publican." Ver. 21, "Peter said, Lord, how often shall my brother sin against me, and I forgive him? Till seven times? Jesus said unto him, I say not unto thee, till seven times; but until seventy times seven." And then ends the parable of the servant, who being himself forgiven, was rigorous to his fellow-servant, with these words, ver. 34: "and his Lord was wroth, and delivered him to the tormentors, till he should pay all that was due to him. So likewise shall my heavenly Father do also unto you, if you from your hearts forgive not every one his brother their trespasses."

Luke x. 25, to the lawyer, asking him, "What shall I do to inherit eternal life? He said, What is written in the law? How readest thou?" He answered, "Thou shalt love the Lord thy God with all thy heart, and with all thy soul, and with all thy strength, and with all thy mind; and thy neighbour as thyself." Jesus said, "This do, and thou shalt live." And when the lawyer, upon our Saviour's parable of the good Samaritan, was forced to confess, that he that showed mercy was his neighbour; Jesus dismissed him with this charge, ver. 37, "Go, and do thou likewise."

Luke xi. 41, "Give alms of such things as ye have: behold, all things are clean unto you."

Luke xii. 15, "Take heed, and beware of covetousness." Ver. 22, "Be not solicitous what ye shall eat, or what ye shall drink, nor what ye shall put on"; be not fearful, or apprehensive of want; "for it is your Father's pleasure to give you a kingdom. Sell that you have, and give alms: and provide yourselves bags that wax not old, a treasure in the heavens, that faileth not: for where your treasure is, there will your heart be also. Let your loins be girded, and your lights burning; and ye yourselves like unto men that wait for the Lord, when he will return. Blessed are those servants, whom the Lord, when he cometh, shall find watching. Blessed is that servant, whom the Lord having made ruler of his household, to give them their portion of meat in due season, the Lord, when he cometh, shall find so doing. Of a truth I say unto you, that he will make him ruler over all that he hath. But if that servant say in his heart, my Lord delayeth his coming; and shall begin to beat the men-servants, and maidens, and to eat and drink, and to be drunken; the Lord of that servant will come in a day when he looketh not for him, and at an hour when he is not aware; and will cut him in sunder, and will appoint him his portion with un-believers. And that servant who knew his Lord's will, and prepared not himself, neither did according to his will, shall be beaten with many stripes. But he that knew not, and did commit things worthy of stripes, shall be beaten with few stripes. For unto whomsoever much is given, of him shall much be required: and to whom men have committed much, of him they will ask the more."

Luke xiv. 11, "Whosoever exalteth himself, shall be abased: and he that humbleth himself, shall be exalted."

Ver. 12, When thou makest a dinner, or supper, call "not thy friends, or thy brethren, neither thy kinsmen, nor thy neighbours; lest they also bid thee again, and a recompense be made thee. But when thou makest a feast, call the poor and maimed, the lame and the blind; and thou shalt be blessed, for they cannot recompense thee; for thou shalt be recompensed at the resurrection of the just."

Ver. 33, "So likewise, whosoever he be of you, that is not ready to forego all that he hath, he cannot be my disciple."

Luke xvi. 9, "I say unto you, make to yourselves friends of the mammon of unrighteousness; that when ye fail, they may receive you into everlasting habitations. If ye have not been faithful in the unrighteous mammon, who will commit to your trust the true riches? And if ye have not been faithful in that which is another man's, who shall give you that which is your own?"

Luke xvii. 3, "If thy brother trespass against thee, rebuke him; and if he repent, forgive him. And if he trespass against thee seven times in a day, and seven times in a day turn again unto thee, saying, I repent; thou shalt forgive him."

Luke xviii. 1, "He spoke a parable to them, to this end, that men ought always to pray, and not to faint."

Ver. 18, "One comes to him, and asks him, saying, Master, what shall I do to inherit eternal life? Jesus said unto him, If thou wilt enter into life, keep the commandments. He says, Which? Jesus said, Thou knowest the commandments. Thou shalt not kill; thou shalt not commit adultery; thou shalt not steal; thou shalt not bear false witness; defraud not; honour thy father and thy mother; and thou shalt love thy neighbour as thyself. He said, All these have I observed from my youth. Jesus hearing this, loved him; and said unto him, Yet lackest thou one thing: sell all that thou hast, and give it to the poor, and thou shalt have treasure in heaven; and come, follow me." To understand this right, we must take notice, that this young man asks our Saviour, what he must do to be admitted effectually into the kingdom of the Messiah? The Jews believed, that when the Messiah came, those of their nation that received him should not die; but that they, with those who, being dead, should then be raised again by him, should enjoy eternal life with him. Our Saviour, in answer to this demand, tells the young man, that to obtain the eternal life of the kingdom of the Messiah, he must keep the commandments. And then enumerating several of the precepts of the law, the young man says, he had observed these from his childhood. For which, the text tells us, Jesus loved him. But our Saviour, to try whether in earnest he believed him to be the Messiah, and resolved to take him to be his King, and to obey him as such, bids him give all that he has to the poor, and come, and follow him; and he should have treasure in heaven. This I look on to be the meaning of the place; this, of selling all he had, and giving it to the poor, not being a standing law of his kingdom; but a probationary command to this young man; to try whether he truly believed him to be the Messiah, and was ready to obey his commands, and relinquish all to follow him, when he, his Prince, required it.

And therefore we see, Luke xix. 14, where our Saviour takes notice of the Jews not receiving him as the Messiah, he expresses it thus: "We will not have this man to reign over us." It is not enough to believe him to be the Messiah, unless we also obey his laws, and take him to be our King, to reign over us.

Matt. xxii. 11–13, he that had not on the wedding-garment, though he accepted of the invitation, and came to the wedding, was cast into utter darkness. By the wedding-garment, it is evident good works are meant here; that wedding-garment of fine linen, clean and white, which we are told, Rev. xix. 8, is the δικαιώματα, "righteous acts of the Saints"; or, as St. Paul calls it, Ephes. iv. 1, "The walking worthy of the vocation wherewith we are called." This appears from the parable itself: "The kingdom of heaven," says our Saviour, ver. 2, "is like unto a king, who made a marriage for his son." And here he distinguishes those who were invited into three sorts: 1. Those who were invited, and came not; i. e. those who had the Gospel, the good news of the kingdom of God proposed to them, but believed not. 2. Those who came, but had not on a wedding-garment; i. e. believed Jesus to be the Messiah, but were not new clad (as I may so say) with a true repentance, and amendment of life: nor adorned with those virtues, which the apostle, Col. iii. requires to be put on. 3. Those who were invited, did come, and had on the wedding-garment; i. e. heard the Gospel, believed Jesus to be the Messiah, and sincerely obeyed his laws. These three sorts are plainly designed here; whereof the last only were the blessed, who were to enjoy the kingdom prepared for them.

Matt. xxiii. "Be not ye called Rabbi; for one is your Master, even the Messiah, and ye are all brethren. And call no man your father upon the earth: for one is your Father which is in heaven. Neither be ye called masters: for one is your Master, even the Messiah. But he that is greatest amongst you shall be your servant. And whosoever shall exalt himself shall be abased; and he that shall humble himself shall be exalted."

Luke xxi. 34, "Take heed to yourselves, lest your hearts be at any time overcharged with surfeiting and drunkenness, and cares of this life."

Luke xxii. 25, "He said unto them, The kings of the Gentiles exercise lordship over them; and they that exercise authority upon them are called benefactors. But ye shall not be so. But he that is greatest among you, let him be as the younger; and he that is chief, as he that doth serve."

John xiii. 34, "A new commandment I give unto you, That ye love one another: as I have loved you, that ye also love one another. By this shall all men know that ye are my disciples, if ye love one another." This command, of loving one another, is repeated again, chap. xv. 12, and 17.

John xiv. 15, "If ye love me, keep my commandments." Ver. 21, "He that hath my commandments, and keepeth them, he it is that loveth me: and he that loveth me, shall be loved of my Father, and I will love him, and manifest myself to him." Ver. 23, "If a man loveth me, he will keep my words." Ver. 24, "He that loveth me not, keepeth not my sayings."

John xv. 8, "In this is my Father glorified, that ye bear much fruit; so shall ye be my disciples." Ver. 14, "Ye are my friends, if ye do whatsoever I command you."

Thus we see our Saviour not only confirmed the moral law, and, clearing it from the corrupt glosses of the Scribes and Pharisees, showed the strictness as well as obligation of its injunctions; but moreover, upon occasion, requires the obedience of his disciples to several of the commands he afresh lays upon them; with the enforcement of unspeakable rewards and punishments in another world, according to their obedience or disobedience. There is not, I think, any of the duties of morality, which he has not, somewhere or other, by himself and his apostles, inculcated over and over again to his followers in express terms. And is it for nothing that he is so instant with them to bring forth fruit? Does he, their King, command, and is it an indifferent thing? Or will their happiness or misery not at all depend upon it, whether they obey or no? They were required to believe him to be the Messiah; which faith is of grace promised to be reckoned to them, for the completing of their righteousness, wherein it was defective: but righteousness, or obedience to the law of God, was their great business, which if they could have attained by their own performances, there would have been no need of this gracious allowance, in reward of their faith: but eternal life, after the resurrection, had been their due by a former covenant, even that of works; the rule whereof was never abolished, though the rigour was abated. The duties enjoined in it were duties still. Their obligations had never ceased, nor a wilful neglect of them was ever dispensed with. But their past transgressions were pardoned, to those who received Jesus, the promised Messiah, for their king; and their future slips covered, if, renouncing their former iniquities, they entered into his kingdom, and continued his subjects with a steady resolution and endeavour to obey his laws. This righteousness, therefore, a complete obedience and freedom from sin, are still sincerely to be endeavoured after. And it is nowhere promised, that those who persist in a willful disobedience to his laws, shall be received into the eternal bliss of his kingdom, how much soever they believe in him.

86. *Reasonableness, Works,* VII, pp. 138–44

Next to the knowledge of one God, Maker of all things, "a clear knowledge of their duty was wanting to mankind." This part of knowledge, though cultivated with some care by some of the heathen philosophers, yet got little footing among the people. All men, indeed, under pain of displeasing the gods, were to frequent the temples: every one went to their sacrifices and services: but the priests made it not their business to teach them virtue. If they were diligent in their observations and ceremonies; punctual in their feasts and solemnities, and the tricks of religion; the holy tribe assured them the gods were pleased, and they looked no farther. Few went to the schools of the philosophers to be instructed in their duties, and to know what was good and evil in their actions. The priests sold the better pennyworths, and therefore had all the custom. Lustrations and processions were much easier than a clean conscience, and a steady course of virtue; and an expiatory sacrifice, that atoned for the want of it, was much more convenient than a strict and holy life. No wonder then, that religion was every where distinguished from, and preferred to virtue; and that it was dangerous heresy and profaneness to think the contrary. So much virtue as was necessary to hold societies together, and to contribute to the quiet of governments, the civil laws of commonwealths taught, and forced upon men that lived under magistrates. But these laws being for the most part made by such, who had no other aims but their own power, reached no farther than those things that would serve to tie men together in subjection; or at most were directly to conduce to the prosperity and temporal happiness of any people. But natural religion, in its full extent, was nowhere, that I know, taken care of, by the force of natural reason. It should seem, by the little that has hitherto been done in it, that it is too hard a task for unassisted reason to establish morality in all its parts, upon its true foundation, with a clear and convincing light. And it is at least a surer and shorter way, to the apprehensions of the vulgar, and mass of mankind, that one manifestly sent from God, and coming with visible authority from him, should, as a king and law-maker, tell them their duties, and require their obedience, than leave it to the long and sometimes intricate deductions of reason, to be made out to them. Such trains of reasoning the greatest part of mankind have neither leisure to weigh, nor, for want of education and use, skill to judge of. We see how unsuccessful in this the attempts of philosophers were before our Saviour's time. How short their several systems came of the perfection of a true and complete morality, is very visible. And if, since that, the Christian philosophers have much outdone them; yet we may observe, that the first knowledge of the truths they have added is owing to revelation: though as soon as they are heard and considered, they are found to be agreeable to reason; and such as can by no means be contradicted. Every one may observe a great many truths, which he receives at first from others, and readily assents to, as consonant to reason, which he would have found it hard, and perhaps beyond his strength, to have discovered himself. Native and original truth is not so easily wrought out of the mine as we, who have it delivered already dug and fashioned into our hands, are apt to imagine. And how often at fifty or three-score years old are thinking men told what they wonder how they could miss thinking of? which yet their own contemplations did not, and possibly never would have helped them to. Experience shows, that the knowledge of morality, by mere natural light, (how agreeable soever it be to it) makes but a slow progress, and little advance in the world. And the reason of it is not hard to be found in men's necessities, passions, vices, and mistaken interests; which turn their thoughts another way: and the designing leaders, as well as following herd, find it not to their purpose to employ much of their meditations this way. Or whatever else was the cause, it is plain, in fact, that human reason unassisted failed men in its great and proper business of morality. It never from unquestionable principles, by clear deductions, made out an entire body of the "law of nature." And he that shall collect all the moral rules of the philosophers, and compare them with those contained in the New Testament, will find them to come short of the morality delivered by our Saviour, and taught by his apostles; a college made up, for the most part, of ignorant, but inspired fishermen.

Though yet, if any one should think, that out of the sayings of the wise heathens before our Saviour's time, there might be a collection made of all those rules of morality, which are to be found in the Christian religion; yet this would not at all hinder, but that the world, nevertheless, stood as much in need of our

Saviour, and the morality delivered by him. Let it be granted (though not true) that all the moral precepts of the Gospel were known by somebody or other, amongst mankind before. But where, or how, or of what use, is not considered. Suppose they may be picked up here and there; some from Solon and Bias in Greece, others from Tully in Italy: and to complete the work, let Confucius, as far as China, be consulted; and Anacharsis, the Scythian, contribute his share. What will all this do, to give the world a complete morality, that may be to mankind the unquestionable rule of life and manners? I will not here urge the impossibility of collecting from men, so far distant from one another, in time and place, and languages. I will suppose there was a Stobeus in those times, who had gathered the moral sayings from all the sages of the world. What would this amount to, towards being a steady rule, a certain transcript of a law that we are under? Did the saying of Aristippus, or Confucius, give it an authority? Was Zeno a lawgiver to mankind? If not, what he or any other philosopher delivered, was but a saying of his. Mankind might hearken to it, or reject it, as they pleased; or as it suited their interest, passions, principles, or humours. They were under no obligation; the opinion of this or that philosopher was of no authority. And if it were, you must take all he said under the same character. All his dictates must go for law, certain and true; or none of them. And then, if you will take any of the moral sayings of Epicurus (many whereof Seneca quotes with esteem and approbation) for precepts of the law of nature, you must take all the rest of his doctrine for such too; or else his authority ceases: and so no more is to be received from him, or any of the sages of old, for parts of the law of nature, as carrying with it an obligation to be obeyed, but what they prove to be so. But such a body of ethics, proved to be the law of nature, from principles of reason, and teaching all the duties of life; I think nobody will say the world had before our Saviour's time. It is not enough, that there were up and down scattered sayings of wise men, conformable to right reason. The law of nature is the law of convenience too: and it is no wonder, that those men of parts, and studious of virtue (who had occasion to think on any particular part of it) should, by meditation, light on the right, even from the observable convenience and beauty of it; without making out its obligation from the true principles of the law of nature, and foundations of morality. But these incoherent apophthegms of philosophers, and wise men, however excellent in themselves, and well intended by them; could never make a moral-

ity, whereof the world could be convinced; could never rise to the
force of a law, that mankind could with certainty depend on.
Whatsoever should thus be universally useful, as a standard to
which men should conform their manners, must have its authority,
either from reason or revelation. It is not every writer of morality,
or compiler of it from others, that can thereby be erected into a
lawgiver to mankind; and a dictator of rules, which are therefore
valid, because they are to be found in his books; under the authority of this or that philosopher. He, that any one will pretend to
set up in this kind, and have his rules pass for authentic directions,
must show, that either he builds his doctrine upon principles of
reason, self-evident in themselves; and that he deduces all the parts
of it from thence, by clear and evident demonstration: or must
show his commission from heaven, that he comes with authority
from God, to deliver his will and commands to the world. In the
former way, nobody that I know, before our Saviour's time, ever
did, or went about to give us a morality. It is true, there is a law
of nature: but who is there that ever did, or undertook to give it us
all entire, as a law; no more, nor no less, than what was contained
in, and had the obligation of that law? Who ever made out all the
parts of it, put them together, and showed the world their obligation? Where was there any such code, that mankind might have
recourse to, as their unerring rule, before our Saviour's time? If
there was not, it is plain there was need of one to give us such a
morality; such a law, which might be the sure guide of those who
had a desire to go right; and, if they had a mind, need not mistake
their duty, but might be certain when they had performed, when
failed in it. Such a law of morality Jesus Christ hath given us in the
New Testament; but by the latter of these ways, by revelation.
We have from him a full and sufficient rule for our direction, and
conformable to that of reason. But the truth and obligation of its
precepts have their force, and are put past doubt to us, by the
evidence of his mission. He was sent by God: his miracles show
it; and the authority of God in his precepts cannot be questioned.
Here morality has a sure standard, that revelation vouches, and
reason cannot gainsay, nor question; but both together witness to
come from God, the great law-maker. And such an one as this, out
of the New Testament, I think the world never had, nor can any
one say, is any where else to be found. Let me ask any one, who
is forward to think that the doctrine of morality was full and clear
in the world, at our Saviour's birth; whither would he have directed
Brutus and Cassius, (both men of parts and virtue, the one whereof

believed, and the other disbelieved a future being) to be satisfied in the rules and obligations of all the parts of their duties; if they should have asked him, Where they might find the law they were to live by, and by which they should be charged, or acquitted, as guilty, or innocent? If to the sayings of the wise, and the declarations of philosophers, he sends them into a wild wood of uncertainty, to an endless maze, from which they should never get out: if to the religions of the world, yet worse: and if to their own reason, he refers them to that which had some light and certainty; but yet had hitherto failed all mankind in a perfect rule; and, we see, resolved not the doubts that had risen amongst the studious and thinking philosophers; nor had yet been able to convince the civilized parts of the world, that they had not given, nor could, without a crime, take away the lives of their children, by exposing them.

If any one shall think to excuse human nature, by laying blame on men's negligence, that they did not carry morality to a higher pitch; and make it out entire in every part, with that clearness of demonstration which some think it capable of; he helps not the matter. Be the cause what it will, our Saviour found mankind under a corruption of manners and principles, which ages after ages had prevailed, and must be confessed, was not in a way or tendency to be mended. The rules of morality were in different countries and sects different. And natural reason nowhere had cured, nor was like to cure the defects and errors in them. Those just measures of right and wrong, which necessity had any where introduced, the civil laws prescribed, or philosophy recommended, stood on their true foundations. They were looked on as bonds of society, and conveniences of common life, and laudable practices. But where was it that their obligation was thoroughly known and allowed, and they received as precepts of a law; of the highest law, the law of nature? That could not be, without a clear knowledge and acknowledgment of the law-maker, and the great rewards and punishments for those that would or would not obey him.

Education as training for virtue
One way to appreciate the force and importance of morality in Locke's concept of the person is to read the passages in *Two Treatises* where Locke explains that a person who rejects the laws of nature and of civil society should be treated as a nonperson (see selection 91). These passages and their location in his work on civil society show us why it was that education for Locke was basically moral train-

ing. The teaching of specific subject matter was subsequent to (or at least contemporaneous with) moral training.

87. *Education*, sections 45, 70, 94, 99–100, 135, 159

He that has not a mastery over his inclinations, he that knows not how to resist the importunity of present pleasure or pain, for the sake of what reason tells him is fit to be done, wants the true principle of virtue and industry, and is in danger never to be good for any thing. This temper, therefore, so contrary to unguided nature, is to be got betimes; and this habit, as the true foundation of future ability and happiness, is to be wrought into the mind, as early as may be, even from the first dawnings of any knowledge or apprehension in children; and so to be confirmed in them, by all the care and ways imaginable, by those who have the oversight of their education.

For you will be ready to say, "What shall I do with my son? If I keep him always at home, he will be in danger to be my young master; and if I send him abroad, how is it possible to keep him from the contagion of rudeness and vice, which is everywhere so in fashion? In my house he will perhaps be more innocent, but more ignorant too of the world: wanting there change of company, and being used constantly to the same faces, he will, when he comes abroad, be a sheepish or conceited creature."

I confess, both sides have their inconveniences. Being abroad, it is true, will make him bolder, and better able to bustle and shift amongst boys of his own age; and the emulation of school-fellows often puts life and industry into young lads. But till you can find a school, wherein it is possible for the master to look after the manners of his scholars, and can show as great effects of his care of forming their minds to virtue, and their carriage to good breeding, as of forming their tongues to the learned languages; you must confess, that you have a strange value for words, when, preferring the languages of the ancient Greeks and Romans to that which made them such brave men, you think it worth while to hazard your son's innocence and virtue, for a little Greek and Latin. For, as for that boldness and spirit, which lads get amongst their playfellows at school, it has ordinarily such a mixture of rudeness, and an ill-turned confidence, that those misbecoming and disingenuous ways of shifting in the world must be unlearned, and all the tincture washed out again, to make way for better principles, and such manners as make a truly worthy man. He that considers how diametrically opposite the skill of living well, and managing, as a man should do, his affairs in the world, is to that malapertness, tricking, or violence, learnt among school-boys, will think the faults of a privater education infinitely to be preferred to such improvements; and will take care to preserve his child's innocence and modesty at home, as being nearer of kin, and more in the way of those qualities, which make an useful and able man. Nor does any one find, or so much as suspect, that the retirement and bashfulness, which their daughters are brought up in, makes them less knowing or less able women. Conversation, when they come into the world, soon gives them a becoming assurance; and whatsoever, beyond that, there is of rough and boisterous, may in men be very well spared too: for courage and steadiness, as I take it, lie not in roughness and ill breeding.

Virtue is harder to be got, than a knowledge of the world; and, if lost in a young man, is seldom recovered. Sheepishness and ignorance of the world, the faults imputed to a private education, are neither the necessary consequences of being bred at home; nor, if they were, are they incurable evils. Vice is the more stubborn, as well as the more dangerous evil of the two; and therefore, in the first place, to be fenced against. If that sheepish softness, which often enervates those, who are bred like fondlings at home, be carefully to be avoided, it is principally so for virtue's sake; for fear lest such a yielding temper should be too susceptible of vicious impressions, and expose the novice too easily to be corrupted. A young man, before he leaves the shelter of his father's house, and the guard of a tutor, should be fortified with resolution, and made acquainted with men, to secure his virtue; lest he should be led into some ruinous course, or fatal precipice, before he is sufficiently acquainted with the dangers of conversation, and has steadiness enough not to yield to every temptation. Were it not for this, a young man's bashfulness, and ignorance of the world, would not so much need an early care. Conversation would cure it in a great measure; or, if that will not do it early enough, it is only a stronger reason for a good tutor at home. For, if pains be to be taken to give him a manly air and assurance betimes, it is chiefly as a fence to his virtue, when he goes into the world, under his own conduct.

It is preposterous, therefore, to sacrifice his innocency to the attaining of confidence, and some little skill of bustling for himself among others, by his conversation with ill-bred and vicious boys; when the chief use of that sturdiness, and standing upon his own legs, is only for the preservation of his virtue. For if confidence or cunning come once to mix with vice, and support his miscarriages, he is only the surer lost; and you must undo again, and strip him of that he has got from his companions, or give him up to ruin. Boys will unavoidably be taught assurance by conversation with men, when they are brought into it; and that is time enough. Modesty and submission, till then, better fits them for instruction: and therefore there needs not any great care to stock them with confidence beforehand. That which requires most time, pains, and assiduity, is to work into them the principles and practice of virtue and good breeding. This is the seasoning they should be prepared with, so as not easily to be got out again: this they had need to be well provided with. For conversation, when they come into the world, will add to their knowledge and assurance, but be too apt to take from their virtue; which therefore they ought to be plentifully stored with, and have that tincture sunk deep into them.

How they should be fitted for conversation, and entered into the world, when they are ripe for it, we shall consider in another place. But how any one's being put into a mixed herd of unruly boys, and there learning to wrangle at trap, or rook at span-farthing, fits him for civil conversation, or business, I do not see. And what qualities are ordinarily to be got from such a troop of play-fellows, as schools usually assemble together, from parents of all kinds, that a father should so much covet it, is hard to divine. I am sure, he who is able to be at the charge of a tutor, at home, may there give his son a more genteel carriage, more manly thoughts, and a sense of what is worthy and becoming, with a greater proficiency in learning into the bargain, and ripen him up sooner into a man; than any at school can do. Not that I blame the school-master in this, or think it to be laid to his charge. The difference is great between two or three pupils in the same house, and three or fourscore boys lodged up and down. For, let the master's industry and skill be ever so great, it is impossible he should have 50 or 100 scholars under his eye, any longer than they are in the school together: nor can it be expected, that he should instruct them successfully in any thing but their books; the forming of their minds and manners requiring a constant attention, and particular application to every single boy; which is impossible in a numerous flock, and would be wholly in vain, (could he have time to study and correct every one's particular defects and wrong inclinations,) when the lad was to be left to himself, or the prevailing infection of his fellows, the greatest part of the four-and-twenty hours.

But fathers, observing that fortune is often most successfully courted by bold and bustling men, are glad to see their sons pert and forward betimes; take it for an happy omen, that they will be thriving men, and look on the tricks they play their school-fellows, or learn from them, as a proficiency in the art of living, and making their way through the world. But I must take the liberty to say, that he that lays the foundation of his son's fortune in virtue and good breeding, takes the only sure and warrantable way. And it is not the waggeries or cheats practised among school-boys, it is not their roughness one to another, nor the well-laid plots of robbing an orchard together, that makes an able man; but the principles of justice, generosity, and sobriety, joined with observation and industry, qualities which I judge school-boys do not learn much of one another. And if a young gentleman, bred at home, be not taught more of them, than he could learn at school, his father has made a very ill choice of a tutor. Take a boy from the top of a grammar-school, and one of the same age, bred as he should be in his father's family, and bring them into good company together; and then see which of the two will have the more manly carriage, and address himself with the more becoming assurance to strangers. Here I imagine the school-boy's confidence will either fail or discredit him; and if it be such as fits him only for the conversation of boys, he had better be without it.

Vice, if we may believe the general complaint, ripens so fast now-a-days, and runs up to seed so early in young people, that it is impossible to keep a lad from the spreading contagion, if you will venture him abroad in the herd, and trust to chance, or his own inclination, for the choice of his company at school. By what fate vice has so thriven amongst us these few years past, and by what hands it has been nursed up into so uncontrolled a dominion, I shall leave to others to inquire. I wish that those who complain of the great decay of christian piety and virtue everywhere, and of learning and acquired improvements in the gentry of this generation, would consider how to retrieve them in the next. This I am sure, that, if the foundation of it be not laid in the education and principling of the youth, all other endeavours will be in vain. And if the innocence, sobriety, and industry of those who are coming up, be not taken care of and preserved, it will be ridiculous to expect, that those who are to succeed next on the stage, should abound in that virtue, ability, and learning, which has hitherto made England considerable in the world. I was going to add courage too, though it has been looked on as the natural inheritance of Englishmen. What has been talked of some late actions at sea, of a kind unknown to our ancestors, gives me occasion to say, that debauchery sinks the courage of men; and when dissoluteness has eaten out the sense of true honour, bravery seldom stays long after it. And I think it impossible to find an instance of any nation, however renowned for their valour, who ever kept their credit in arms, or made themselves redoubtable amongst their neighbours, after corruption had once broke through, and dissolved the restraint of discipline; and vice was grown to such a head, that it durst show itself barefaced, without being out of countenance.

It is virtue then, direct virtue, which is the hard and valuable part to be aimed at in education; and not a forward pertness, or any little arts of shifting. All other considerations and accomplishments should give way, and be postponed, to this. This is the solid and substantial good, which tutors should not only read lectures, and talk of; but the labour and art of education should furnish the mind with, and fasten there, and never cease till the young man had a true relish of it, and placed his strength, his glory, and his pleasure in it.

Besides being well-bred, the tutor should know the world well; the ways, the humours, the follies, the cheats, the faults of the age he is fallen into, and particularly of the country he lives in. These he should be able to show to his pupil, as he finds him capable; teach him skill in men, and their manners; pull off the mask, which their several callings and pretences cover them with; and make his pupil discern what lies at the bottom, under such appearances; that he may not, as unexperienced young men are apt to do, if they are unwarned, take one thing for another, judge by the outside, and give himself up to show, and the insinuation of a fair carriage, or an obliging application. A governor should teach his scholar to guess at, and beware of, the designs of men he hath to do with, neither with too much suspicion, nor too much confidence; but, as the young man is by nature most inclined to either side, rectify him, and bend him the other way. He should accustom him to make, as much as is possible, a true judgment of men by those marks, which serve best to show what they are, and give a prospect into their inside; which often shows itself in little things, especially when they are not in parade, and upon their guard. He should acquaint him with the true state of the world, and dispose him to think no man better or worse, wiser or foolisher, than he really is. Thus, by safe and insensible degrees, he will pass from a boy to a man; which is the most hazardous step in all the whole course of life. This therefore should be carefully watched, and a young man with great diligence handed over it; and not, as now usually is done, be taken from a governor's conduct, and all at once thrown into the world under his own, not without manifest danger of immediate spoiling; there being nothing more frequent, than instances of the great looseness, extravagancy, and debauchery, which young men have run into, as soon as they have been let loose from a severe and strict education: which, I think, may be chiefly imputed to their wrong way of breeding, especially in this part; for, having been bred up in a great ignorance of what the world truly is, and finding it quite another thing, when they come into it, than what they were taught it should be, and so imagined it was; are easily persuaded, by other kind of tutors, which they are sure to meet with, that the discipline they were kept under, and the lectures that were read to them, were but the formalities of education, and the restraints of childhood; that the freedom longing to men, is to take their swing in a full enjoyment of what was before forbidden them. They show the young novice the world, full of fashionable and glittering examples of this every-where, and he is presently dazzled with them. My young master, failing not to be willing to show himself a man, as much as any of the sparks of his years, lets himself loose to all the irregularities he finds in the most debauched; and thus courts credit and manliness, in the casting off the modesty and sobriety he has till then been kept in; and thinks it brave, at his first setting out, to signalize himself in running counter to all the rules of virtue, which have been preached to him by his tutor.

The showing him the world as really it is, before he comes wholly into it, is one of the best means, I think, to prevent this mischief. He should, by degrees, be informed of the vices in fashion, and warned of the applications and designs of those who will make it their business to corrupt him. He should be told the arts they use, and the trains they lay; and now and then have set before him the tragical or ridiculous examples of those who are ruining, or ruined, this way. The age is not like to want instances of this kind, which should be made land-marks to him; that by the disgraces, diseases, beggary, and shame of hopeful young men, thus brought to ruin, he may be precautioned, and be made see, how those join in the contempt and neglect of them that are undone, who, by pretences of friendship and respect, led them into it, and helped to prey upon them whilst they were undoing; that he may see, before he buys it by a too dear experience, that those who persuade him not to follow the sober advices he has received from his governors, and the counsel of his own reason, which they call being governed by others, do it only, that they may have the government of him themselves; and make him believe, he goes like a man of himself, by his own conduct, and for his own pleasure, when, in truth, he is wholly as a child, led by them into those vices, which best serve their purposes. This is a knowledge, which, upon all occasions, a tutor should endeavour to instil, and by all methods try to make him comprehend, and thoroughly relish.

I know it is often said, that to discover to a young man the vices of the age is to teach them him. That, I confess, is a good deal so, according as it is done; and therefore requires a discreet man of parts, who knows the world, and can judge of the temper, inclination, and weak side of his pupil. This farther is to be remembered, that it is not possible now (as perhaps formerly it was) to keep a young gentleman from vice, by a total ignorance of it; unless you will all his life mew him up in a closet, and never let him go into company. The longer he is kept thus hood-winked, the less he will see, when he comes abroad into open day-light, and be the more exposed to be a prey to himself and others. And an old boy, at his first appearance, with all the gravity of his ivy-bush about him, is sure to draw on him the eyes and chirping of the whole town volery; amongst which, there will not be wanting some birds of prey, that will presently be on the wing for him.

The only fence against the world, is a thorough knowledge of it: into which a young gentleman should be entered by degrees, as he can bear it; and the earlier the better, so he be in safe and skillful hands to guide him. The scene should be gently opened, and his entrance made step by step, and the dangers pointed out that attend him, from the several degrees, tempers, designs, and clubs of men. He should be prepared to be shocked by some, and caressed by others; warned who are like to oppose, who to mislead, who to undermine him, and who to serve him. He should be instructed how to know and distinguish men; where he should let them see, and when dissemble the knowledge of them, and their aims and workings. And if he be too forward to venture upon his own strength and skill, the perplexity and trouble of a misadventure now and then, that reaches not his innocence, his health, or reputation, may not be an ill way to teach him more caution.

This, I confess, containing one great part of wisdom, is not the product of some superficial thoughts, or much reading; but the effect of experience and observation in a man, who has lived in the world with his eyes open, and conversed with men of all sorts. And therefore I think it of most value to be instilled into a young man, upon all occasions which offer themselves, that when he comes to launch into the deep himself, he may not be like one at sea without a line, compass, or sea-chart; but may have some notice before-hand of the rocks and shoals, the currents and quick-sands, and know a little how to steer, that he sink not, before he get experience. He that thinks not this of more moment to his son, and for which he more needs a governor, than the languages and learned sciences, forgets of how much more use it is to judge right of men, and manage his affairs wisely with them, than to speak Greek and Latin, or argue in mood and figure; or to have his head filled with the abstruse speculations of natural philosophy and metaphysics; nay, than to be well versed in Greek and Roman writers, though that be much better for a gentleman, than to be a good peripatetic or cartesian: because those ancient authors observed and painted mankind well, and give the best light into that kind of knowledge. He that goes into the eastern parts of Asia, will find able and acceptable men, without any of these: but without virtue, knowledge of the world, and civility, an accomplished and valuable man can be found no-where.

A great part of the learning now in fashion in the schools of Europe, and that goes ordinarily into the round of education, a gentleman may, in a good measure, be unfurnished with, without any great disparagement to himself, or prejudice to his affairs. But prudence and good-breeding are, in all the stations and occurrences of life, necessary; and most young men suffer in the want of them; and come rawer, and more awkward, into the world, than they should, for this very reason; because these qualities, which are, of all other, the most necessary to be taught, and stand most in need of the assistance and help of a teacher, are generally neglected, and thought but a slight, or no part of a tutor's business. Latin and learning make all the noise: and the main stress is laid upon his proficiency in things, a great part whereof belongs not to a gentleman's calling; which is to have the knowledge of a man of business, a carriage suitable to his rank, and to be eminent and useful in his country, according to his station. Whenever either spare hours from that, or an inclination to perfect himself in some parts of knowledge, which his tutor did but just enter him in, set him upon any study; the first rudiments of it, which he learned before, will open the way enough for his own industry to carry him as far as his fancy will prompt, or his parts enable him to go:

or, if he thinks it may save his time and pains, to be helped over
some difficulties by the hands of a master, he may then take
a man that is perfectly well skilled in it, or choose such an one,
as he thinks fittest for his purpose. But to initiate his pupil in any
part of learning, as far as is necessary for a young man in the
ordinary course of his studies, an ordinary skill in the governor is
enough. Nor is it requisite that he should be a thorough scholar,
or possess in perfection all those sciences, which it is convenient
a young gentleman should have a taste of, in some general view,
or short system. A gentleman, that would penetrate deeper, must
do it by his own genius and industry afterwards: for nobody ever
went far in knowledge, or became eminent in any of the sciences,
by the discipline and constraint of a master.

The great work of a governor is to fashion the carriage, and form
the mind; to settle in his pupil good habits, and the principles of
virtue and wisdom; to give him, by little and little, a view of mankind; and work him into a love and imitation of what is excellent
and praise-worthy; and, in the prosecution of it, to give him vigour,
activity, and industry. The studies which he sets him upon, are
but, as it were, the exercises of his faculties, and employment of
his time, to keep him from sauntering and idleness, to teach him
application, and accustom him to take pains, and to give him some
little taste of what his own industry must perfect. For who expects, that under a tutor a young gentleman should be an accomplished critic, orator, or logician; go to the bottom of metaphysics,
natural philosophy, or mathematics, or be a master in history or
chronology? though something of each of these is to be taught
him: but it is only to open the door, that he may look in, and,
as it were, begin an acquaintance, but not to dwell there: and a
governor would be much blamed, that should keep his pupil too
long, and lead him too far in most of them. But of good breeding,
knowledge of the world, virtue, industry, and a love of reputation,
he cannot have too much: and, if he have these, he will not long
want what he needs or desires of the other.

When, by making your son sensible that he depends on you,
and is in your power, you have established your authority; and by
being inflexibly severe in your carriage to him, when obstinately
persisting in any ill-natured trick which you have forbidden, especially lying, you have imprinted on his mind that awe which is
necessary; and on the other side, when (by permitting him the full
liberty due to his age, and laying no restraint in your presence to
those childish actions, and gaiety of carriage, which, whilst he is

very young, are as necessary to him as meat or sleep) you have reconciled him to your company, and made him sensible of your care and love of him by indulgence and tenderness, especially caressing him on all occasions wherein he does any thing well, and being kind to him, after a thousand fashions, suitable to his age, which nature teaches parents better than I can: when, I say, by these ways of tenderness and affection, which parents never want for their children, you have also planted in him a particular affection for you; he is then in the state you could desire, and you have formed in his mind that true reverence, which is always afterwards carefully to be continued and maintained in both parts of it, love and fear, as the great principles whereby you will always have hold upon him to turn his mind to the ways of virtue and honour.

When this foundation is once well laid, and you find this reverence begin to work in him, the next thing to be done is carefully to consider his temper, and the particular constitution of his mind. Stubbornness, lying, and ill-natured actions, are not (as has been said) to be permitted in him from the beginning, whatever his temper be: those seeds of vices are not to be suffered to take any root, but must be carefully weeded out, as soon as ever they begin to show themselves in him; and your authority is to take place, and influence his mind from the very dawning of any knowledge in him, that it may operate as a natural principle, whereof he never perceived the beginning; never knew that it was, or could be otherwise. By this, if the reverence he owes you be established early, it will always be sacred to him; and it will be as hard for him to resist it, as the principles of his nature.

I place virtue as the first and most necessary of those endowments that belong to a man or a gentleman, as absolutely requisite to make him valued and beloved by others, acceptable or tolerable to himself. Without that, I think, he will be happy neither in this, nor the other world.

And now I am by chance fallen on this subject, give me leave to say, that there are some parts of the scripture, which may be proper to be put into the hands of a child to engage him to read; such as are the story of Joseph and his brethren, of David and Goliath, of David and Jonathan, &c. and others, that he should be made to read for his instruction; as that, "What you would have others do unto you, do you the same unto them;" and such other easy and plain moral rules, which, being fitly chosen, might often be made use of both for reading and instruction together; and so often read, till they are thoroughly fixed in his memory; and then afterwards, as he grows ripe for them, may in their turns, on fit occasions, be inculcated as the standing and sacred rules of his life and actions. But the reading of the whole scripture indifferently, is what I think very inconvenient for children, till, after having been made acquainted with the plainest fundamental parts of it, they have got some kind of general view of what they ought principally to believe and practise, which yet, I think, they ought to receive in the very words of the scripture, and not in such as men, prepossessed by systems and analogies, are apt in this case to make use of, and force upon them. Dr. Worthington, to avoid this, has made a catechism, which has all its answers in the precise words of the scripture, a thing of good example, and such a sound form of words as no christian can except against, as not fit for his child to learn. Of this, as soon as he can say the Lord's prayer, creed, and ten commandments by heart, it may be fit for him to learn a question every day, or every week, as his understanding is able to receive, and his memory to retain them. And when he has this catechism perfectly by heart, so as readily and roundly to answer to any question in the whole book, it may be convenient to lodge in his mind the remaining moral rules, scattered up and down in the Bible, as the best exercise of his memory, and that which may be always a rule to him, ready at hand, in the whole conduct of his life.

Locke viewed education as an obligation parents have to their children. Education begins in the family and may (and did in the seventeenth century, when education was for gentlemen) stay in the family context, with the tutor living in or becoming part of that unit. Parental power carried obligations and duties of which education or moral training was one. While presenting his views on civil government, Locke was careful to specify the scope and extent of parental power. The close intermingling of law, duty, freedom, power, and virtue that characterizes Locke's political philosophy finds its origin in his views on the family. Education of the child was one way in which these values were fostered.

88. *Two Treatises*, II, sections 58–61, 63–9

The power, then, that parents have over their children arises from that duty which is incumbent on them, to take care of their offspring during the imperfect state of childhood. To inform the mind, and govern the actions of their yet ignorant nonage, till reason shall take its place, and ease them of that trouble, is what the children want, and the parents are bound to: for God having given man an understanding to direct his actions, has allowed him a freedom of will, and liberty of acting, as properly belonging thereunto, within the bounds of that law he is under. But whilst he is in an estate wherein he has not understanding of his own to direct his will, he is not to have any will of his own to follow: he that understands for him, must will for him too; he must prescribe to his will, and regulate his actions; but when he comes to the estate that made his father a freeman, the son is a freeman too.

This holds in all the laws a man is under, whether natural or civil. Is a man under the law of nature? What made him free of that law? What gave him a free disposing of his property, according to his own will, within the compass of that law? I answer, a state of maturity, wherein he might be supposed capable to know that law, that so he might keep his actions within the bounds of it. When he has acquired that state, he is presumed to know how far that law is to be his guide, and how far he may make use of his freedom, and so comes to have it; till then, somebody else must guide him, who is presumed to know how far the law allows a liberty. If such a state of reason, such an age of discretion made him free, the same shall make his son free too. Is a man under the law of England? What made him free of that law? that is, to have the liberty to dispose of his actions and possessions according to his own will, within the permission of that law? A capacity of knowing that law, which is supposed by that law at the age of one-and-twenty years, and in some cases sooner. If this made the father free, it shall make the son free too. Till then we see the law allows the son to have no will, but he is to be guided by the will of his father or guardian, who is to understand for him. And if the father die, and fail to substitute a deputy in his trust; if he hath not provided a tutor to govern his son during his minority, during his want of understanding, the law takes care to do it; some other must govern him, and be a will to him, till he hath attained to a state of freedom, and his understanding be fit to take the government of his will. But after that, the father and son are equally free as much as tutor and pupil after nonage; equally subjects of the same law together, without any dominion left in the father over the life, liberty, or estate of his son, whether they be only in the state and under the law of nature, or under the positive laws of an established government.

But if, through defects that may happen out of the ordinary course of nature, any one comes not to such a degree of reason wherein he might be supposed capable of knowing the law, and so living within the rules of it, he is never capable of being a free man, he is never let loose to the disposure of his own will, (because he knows no bounds to it, has not understanding, its proper guide) but is continued under the tuition and government of others, all the time his own understanding is incapable of that charge. And so lunatics and idiots are never set free from the government of their parents. "Children, who are not as yet come unto those years whereat they may have; and innocents which are excluded by a natural defect from ever having; thirdly, mad men, which for the present cannot possibly have the use of right reason to guide themselves, have for their guide the reason that guideth other men which are tutors over them, to seek and procure their good for them," says Hooker, Eccl. Pol. lib. i. sect. 7. All which seems no more than that duty which God and nature has laid on man, as well as other creatures, to preserve their offspring till they can be able to shift for themselves, and will scarce amount to an instance or proof of parents' regal authority.

Thus we are born free, as we are born rational; not that we have actually the exercise of either: age, that brings one, brings with it the other too. And thus we see how natural freedom and subjection to parents may consist together, and are both founded on the same principle. A child is free by his father's title, by his father's understanding, which is to govern him till he hath it of his own. The freedom of a man at years of discretion, and the subjection of a child to his parents, whilst yet short of that age, are so consistent, and so distinguishable, that the most blinded contenders for monarchy, by right of fatherhood, cannot miss this difference; the most obstinate cannot but allow their consistency: for were their doctrine all true, were the right heir of Adam now known, and by that title settled a monarch in his throne, invested with all the absolute unlimited power sir Robert Filmer talks of; if he should die as soon as his heir were born, must not the child, notwithstanding he were ever so free, ever so much sovereign, be in subjection to his mother and nurse, to tutors and governors, till age and education brought him reason and ability to govern himself and others? The necessities of his life, the health of his body, and the information of his mind, would require him to be directed by the will of others, and not his own; and yet will any one think that this restraint and subjection were inconsistent with, or spoiled him of that liberty or sovereignty he had a right to, or gave away his empire to those who had the government of his nonage? This government over him only prepared him the better and sooner for it. If any body should ask me, when my son is of age to be free? I shall answer, just when his monarch is of age to govern. "But at what time," says the judicious Hooker, Eccl. Pol. lib. i. sect. 6, "a man may be said to have attained so far forth the use of reason, as sufficeth to make him capable of those laws whereby he is then bound to guide his actions: this is a great deal more easy for sense to discern than for any one by skill and learning to determine."

The freedom then of man, and liberty of acting according to his own will, is grounded on his having reason, which is able to instruct him in that law he is to govern himself by, and make him know how far he is left to the freedom of his own will. To turn him loose to an unrestrained liberty, before he has reason to guide him, is not the allowing him the privilege of his nature to be free; but to thrust him out amongst brutes, and abandon him to a state as wretched, and as much beneath that of a man, as theirs. This is that which puts the authority into the parents' hands to govern the minority of their children. God hath made it their business to employ this care on their offspring, and hath placed in them suitable inclinations of tenderness and concern to temper this power, to apply it, as his wisdom designed it, to the children's good, as long as they should need to be under it.

But what reason can hence advance this care of the parents due to their offspring into an absolute arbitrary dominion of the father, whose power reaches no farther than, by such a discipline as he finds most effectual, to give such strength and health to their bodies, such vigour and rectitude to their minds, as may best fit his children to be most useful to themselves and others; and, if it be necessary to his condition, to make them work when they are able, for their own subsistence. But in this power the mother too has her share with the father.

Nay, this power so little belongs to the father by any peculiar right of nature, but only as he is guardian of his children, that when he quits his care of them, he loses his power over them, which goes along with their nourishment and education, to which it is inseparably annexed; and it belongs as much to the foster-father of an exposed child, as to the natural father of another. So little power does the bare act of begetting give a man over his issue, if all his care ends there, and this be all the title he hath to the name and authority of a father. And what will become of this paternal power in that part of the world where one woman hath more than one husband at a time? or in those parts of America, where, when the husband and wife part, which happens frequently, the children are all left to the mother, follow her, and are wholly under her care and provision? If the father die whilst the children are young, do they not naturally every where owe the same obedience to their mother, during their minority, as to their father were he alive? and will any one say, that the mother hath a legislative power over her children? that she can make standing rules, which shall be of perpetual obligation, by which they ought to regulate all the concerns of their property, and bound their liberty all the course of their lives? or can she enforce the observation of them with capital punishments? for this is the proper power of the magistrate, of which the father hath not so much as the shadow. His command over his children is but temporary, and reaches not their life or property: it is but a help to the weakness and imperfection of their nonage, a discipline necessary to their education: and though a father may dispose of his own possessions as he pleases, when his children are out of danger of perishing for want, yet his power extends not to the lives or goods, which either their own industry or another's bounty has made theirs; nor to their liberty neither, when they are once arrived to the enfranchisement of the years of discretion. The father's empire then ceases, and can from thenceforwards no more dispose of the liberty of his son than that of any other man: and it must be far from an absolute or perpetual jurisdiction, from which a man may withdraw himself, having licence from divine authority to "leave father and mother, and cleave to his wife."

But though there be a time when a child comes to be as free from subjection to the will and command of his father, as the father himself is free from subjection to the will of any body else, and they are each under no other restraint but that which is common to them both, whether it be the law of nature, or municipal law of their country; yet this freedom exempts not a son from that honour which he ought, by the law of God and nature, to pay his parents. God having made the parents instruments in his great design of continuing the race of mankind, and the occasions of life to their children; as he hath laid on them an obligation to nourish, preserve, and bring up their offspring; so he has laid on the children a perpetual obligation of honouring their parents, which containing in it an inward esteem and reverence to be shown by all outward expressions, ties up the child from any thing that may ever injure or affront, disturb or endanger, the happiness or life of those from whom he received his; and engages him in all actions of defence, relief, assistance, and comfort of those by whose means he entered into being, and has been made capable of any enjoyments of life: from this obligation no state, no freedom, can absolve children. But this is very far from giving parents a power of command over their children, or authority to make laws and dispose as they please of their lives and liberties. It is one thing to owe honour, respect, gratitude, and assistance; another to require an absolute obedience and submission. The honour due to parents, a monarch in his throne owes his mother; and yet this lessens not his authority, nor subjects him to her government.

The subjection of a minor, places in the father a temporary government, which terminates with the minority of the child: and the honour due from a child, places in the parents perpetual right to respect, reverence, support, and compliance too, more or less, as the father's care, cost, and kindness in his education, have been more or less. This ends not with minority, but holds in all parts and conditions of a man's life. The want of distinguishing these two powers, viz. that which the father hath in the right of tuition, during minority, and the right of honour all his life, may perhaps have caused a great part of the mistakes about this matter: for, to speak properly of them, the first of these is rather the privilege of children, and duty of parents, than any prerogative of paternal power. The nourishment and education of their children is a charge so incumbent on parents for their children's good, that nothing can absolve them from taking care of it: and though the power of commanding and chastising them go along with it, yet God hath woven into the principles of human nature such a tenderness for their offspring, that there is little fear that parents should use their power with too much rigour; the excess is seldom on the severe side, the strong bias of nature drawing the other way. And therefore God Almighty, when he would express his gentle dealing with the Israelites, he tells them, that though he chastened them, "he chastened them as a man chastens his son," Deut. viii. 5. i. e. with tenderness and affection, and kept them under no severer discipline than what was absolutely best for them, and had been less kindness to have slackened. This is that power to which children are commanded obedience, that the pains and care of their parents may not be increased, or ill rewarded.

On the other side, honour and support, all that which gratitude requires to return for the benefits received by and from them, is the indispensable duty of the child, and the proper privilege of the parents. This is intended for the parents' advantage, as the other is for the child's; though education, the parents' duty, seems to have most power, because the ignorance and infirmities of childhood stand in need of restraint and correction; which is a visible exercise of rule, and a kind of dominion. And that duty which is comprehended in the word honour requires less obedience, though the obligation be stronger on grown than younger children: for who can think the command, "Children obey your parents," requires in a man that has children of his own the same submission to his father, as it does in his yet young children to him; and that by this precept he were bound to obey all his father's commands, if, out of a conceit of authority, he should have the indiscretion to treat him still as a boy?

The first part then of paternal power, or rather duty, which is education, belongs so to the father, that it terminates at a certain season; when the business of education is over, it ceases of itself, and is also alienable before: for a man may put the tuition of his son in other hands; and he that has made his son an apprentice to another, has discharged him, during that time, of a great part of his obedience both to himself and to his mother. But all the duty of honour, the other part, remains nevertheless entire to them; nothing can cancel that: it is so inseparable from them both, that the father's authority cannot dispossess the mother of this right, nor can any man discharge his son from honouring her that bore him. But both these are very far from a power to make laws, and enforcing them with penalties that may reach estate, liberty, limbs, and life. The power of commanding ends with nonage; and though after that, honour and respect, support and defence, and whatsoever gratitude can oblige a man to, for the highest benefits he is naturally capable of, be always due from a son to his parents; yet all this puts no sceptre into the father's hand, no sovereign power of commanding. He has no dominion over his son's property, or actions; nor any right that his will should prescribe to his son's in all things; however it may become his son in many things, not very inconvenient to him and his family, to pay a deference to it.

Social groups and the origin of civil society
In his account of the relation between parents and their children, Locke was describing some of the rights and duties, the functions and purposes of one kind of society. The concept of *society* for Locke was a generic one. Every

instance of that concept has set purposes and activities.
God made man with an inclination toward society. The
first such society is that of man and wife, conjugal society.
It is formed by a voluntary compact, the chief end of which
is procreation. Subsidiary ends of the conjugal society are
mutual support and communion of interests. This society
expands into the family with children and servants, although the master-servant relation is a subsociety with its
own contract.

One interesting feature of Locke's concept of society is
that each society can be dissolved if the purposes for its
formation have been either fulfilled or perverted. Locke
even sees separation of husband and wife as a possibility,
whether the ends of the family have been reached (the
children attaining maturity) or not. Such separation would
occur either by consent or at a certain time as specified in
the compact. Locke also sees the contract between husband and wife as detailing the wife's rights. He is emphatic
about her liberty to separate from her husband, if this has
been part of the contract. The marriage contract would
even specify where the children go upon separation.

The stress upon contracts is a way of indicating the set
purposes and the delimitation of one society's activities
from another's. It can also be an anticipation of the role of
rules and laws in society. Rules and laws are as much a
part of any society as are specific ends and purposes.
Whether the society be that of "philosophers for learning,
of merchants for commerce, or of men of leisure for mutual
conversation and discourse," laws and rules are necessary
to keep that society functioning toward its objectives. In
some societies, the rules would prescribe membership, exclusion, practices, even dissolution.

Societies are formed by voluntary compact, for specific
purposes, with rules and laws about the activities. Another
equally important feature of a society for Locke is the
delimitation of jurisdiction of one society in relation to
others: "nothing being necessary to any society that is not
necessary to the ends for which it is made." The civil magistrate cannot abridge the rights of husband and wife,
but he may help to settle disputes between them. Similarly, and much more importantly for Locke, the civil
magistrate cannot infringe or usurp the ends of religious

societies. The care of souls is the main objective of the latter. The ceremonies and practices of a religious society are specific for that society. Like all societies for Locke, a church is a voluntary society formed for specific purposes: "the public worship of God, and, by means thereof, the acquisition of eternal life." The church or religious society does not deal with "the possession of civil and worldly goods," and the civil society does not concern itself with the form or content of worship.

There were in Locke's day, strong views on the line between matters civil and matters religious. Locke wrote, but never published, some tracts which took up the question of jurisdiction.[24] Part of the issue in 1660–2 was whether religious dress, ceremonies, and practices were outside of civil law. In these early tracts, Locke identified two forms of divine worship: (1) "that inner worship of the heart which God demands, in which the essence and soul of religion consists, and in the absence of which all the other observations of religious worship provoke God rather than propitiate him," and (2) "the outward performances."[25] Under the outward performances, Locke listed "public prayers, acts of thanksgiving, the singing of psalms, participation in the holy sacraments and the hearing of the divine word."[26] The civil magistrate does not have any right "over this worship." However, "Since there are no actions without a host of circumstances which always attend them, such as Time, Place, Appearance, Posture, etc., even divine worship cannot be free from this attendance." Thus, the young Locke concluded, "God in his great wisdom and beneficence has relinquished these rites to the discretion of the magistrate and entrusted them to the care of him who holds power and has the right of governing."[27]

Locke's later *A Letter concerning Toleration* (1689) took a firm stand against the magistrate's having anything to do with those "indifferent" matters of ceremony. "If civil jurisdiction extend thus far, what might not lawfully be introduced into religion?" The bounds and limits of au-

24 These have recently been published, with an introduction and notes, by Philip Abrams, as *Two Tracts on Government* (Cambridge, 1967).
25 *Ibid.*, p. 214. 26 *Ibid.*, p. 215. 27 *Ibid.*, pp. 215–16.

thority between societies became a much firmer feature of Locke's mature view of society. One concern that did not alter – though it was given an extended treatment later – was toleration. In the first of the early *Two Tracts,* Locke saw a need for the civil magistrate to step in and protect one religious society from the zeal of another. Locke gave an extended analysis and defense of toleration between different religious groups and between those groups and civil society in his letters on toleration.

89. *Two Treatises,* II, sections 77–89

God having made man such a creature, that in his own judgment it was not good for him to be alone, put him under strong obligations of necessity, convenience, and inclination, to drive him into society, as well as fitted him with understanding and language to continue and enjoy it. The first society was between man and wife, which gave beginning to that between parents and children; to which, in time, that between master and servant came to be added; and though all these might, and commonly did meet together, and make up but one family, wherein the master or mistress of it had some sort of rule proper to a family; each of these, or all together, came short of political society, as we shall see, if we consider the different ends, ties, and bounds of each of these.

Conjugal society is made by a voluntary compact between man and woman; and though it consist chiefly in such a communion and right in one another's bodies as is necessary to its chief end, procreation; yet it draws with it mutual support and assistance, and a communion of interests too, as necessary not only to unite their care and affection, but also necessary to their common offspring, who have a right to be nourished and maintained by them, till they are able to provide for themselves.

For the end of conjunction between male and female being not barely procreation, but the continuation of the species; this conjunction betwixt male and female ought to last, even after procreation, so long as is necessary to the nourishment and support of the young ones, who are to be sustained by those that got them, till they are able to shift and provide for themselves. This rule, which the infinite wise Maker hath set to the works of his hands, we find the inferior creatures steadily obey. In those viviparous animals which feed on grass, the conjunction between male and female lasts no longer than the very act of copulation; because the teat of the dam being sufficient to nourish the young, till it be able to feed on grass, the male only begets, but concerns not himself for the female or young, to whose sustenance he can contribute nothing. But in beasts of prey the conjunction lasts longer: because the dam not being able well to subsist herself, and nourish her numerous offspring by her own prey alone, a more laborious, as well as more dangerous way of living, than by feeding on grass; the assistance of the male is necessary to the maintenance of their common family, which cannot subsist till they are able to prey for themselves, but by the joint care of male and female. The same is to be observed in all birds, (except some domestic ones, where plenty of food excuses the cock from feeding, and taking care of the young brood) whose young needing food in the nest, the cock and hen continue mates, till the young are able to use their wing, and provide for themselves.

And herein I think lies the chief, if not the only reason, "why the male and female in mankind are tied to a longer conjunction" than other creatures, viz. because the female is capable of conceiving, and *de facto* is commonly with child again, and brings forth too a new birth, long before the former is out of a dependency for support on his parents' help, and able to shift for himself, and has all the assistance that is due to him from his parents: whereby the father, who is bound to take care for those he hath begot, is under an obligation to continue in conjugal society with the same woman longer than other creatures, whose young being able to subsist of themselves before the time of procreation returns again, the conjugal bond dissolves of itself, and they are at liberty, till Hymen at his usual anniversary season summons them again to choose new mates. Wherein one cannot but admire the wisdom of the great Creator, who having given to man foresight, and an ability to lay up for the future, as well as to supply the present necessity, hath made it necessary, that society of man and wife should be more lasting than of male and female amongst other creatures; that so their industry might be encouraged, and their interest better united, to make provision and lay up goods for their common issue, which uncertain mixture, or easy and frequent solutions of conjugal society, would mightily disturb.

But though these are ties upon mankind, which make the conjugal bonds more firm and lasting in man than the other species of animals; yet it would give one reason to inquire, why this compact, where procreation and education are secured, and inheritance taken care for, may not be made determinable, either by consent, or at a certain time, or upon certain conditions, as well as any

other voluntary compacts, there being no necessity in the nature of
the thing, nor to the ends of it, that it should always be for life;
I mean, to such as are under no restraint of any positive law,
which ordains all such contracts to be perpetual.

But the husband and wife, though they have but one common
concern, yet having different understandings, will unavoidably
sometimes have different wills too; it therefore being necessary
that the last determination, i. e. the rule, should be placed somewhere; it naturally falls to the man's share, as the abler and the
stronger. But this reaching but to the things of their common
interest and property, leaves the wife in the full and free possession
of what by contract is her peculiar right, and gives the husband no
more power over her life than she has over his; the power of the
husband being so far from that of an absolute monarch, that the
wife has in many cases a liberty to separate from him, where natural right or their contract allows it; whether that contract be made
by themselves in the state of nature, or by the customs or laws of
the country they live in; and the children upon such separation
fall to the father's or mother's lot, as such contract does determine.

For all the ends of marriage being to be obtained under
politic government, as well as in the state of nature, the civil
magistrate doth not abridge the right or power of either naturally
necessary to those ends, viz. procreation and mutual support and
assistance whilst they are together; but only decides any controversy that may arise between man and wife about them. If it were
otherwise, and that absolute sovereignty and power of life and
death naturally belonged to the husband, and were necessary to the
society between man and wife, there could be no matrimony in any
of those countries where the husband is allowed no such absolute
authority. But the ends of matrimony requiring no such power in
the husband, the condition of conjugal society put it not in him, it
being not at all necessary to that state. Conjugal society could
subsist and attain its ends without it; nay, community of goods,
and the power over them, mutual assistance and maintenance,
and other things belonging to conjugal society, might be varied
and regulated by that contract which unites man and wife in that
society, as far as may consist with procreation and the bringing
up of children till they could shift for themselves; nothing being
necessary to any society, that is not necessary to the ends for which
it is made.

The society betwixt parents and children, and the distinct rights
and powers belonging respectively to them, I have treated of so

largely, in the foregoing chapter, that I shall not here need to say any thing of it. And I think it is plain, that it is far different from a politic society.

Master and servant are names as old as history, but given to those of far different condition; for a freeman makes himself a servant to another, by selling him, for a certain time, the service he undertakes to do, in exchange for wages he is to receive: and though this commonly puts him into the family of his master, and under the ordinary discipline thereof: yet it gives the master but a temporary power over him, and no greater than what is contained in the contract between them. But there is another sort of servants, which by a peculiar name we call slaves, who being captives taken in a just war, are by the right of nature subjected to the absolute dominion and arbitrary power of their masters. These men having, as I say, forfeited their lives, and with it their liberties, and lost their estates; and being in the state of slavery, not capable of any property; cannot in that state be considered as any part of civil society; the chief end whereof is the preservation of property.

Let us therefore consider a master of a family with all these subordinate relations of wife, children, servants, and slaves, united under the domestic rule of a family; which, what resemblance soever it may have in its order, offices, and number too, with a little commonwealth, yet is very far from it, both in its constitution, power, and end: or if it must be thought a monarchy, and the pater-familias the absolute monarch in it, absolute monarchy will have but a very shattered and short power, when it is plain, by what has been said before, that the master of the family has a very distinct and differently limited power, both as to time and extent, over those several persons that are in it: for excepting the slave (and the family is as much a family, and his power as pater-familias as great, whether there be any slaves in his family or no), he has no legislative power of life and death over any of them, and none too but what a mistress of a family may have as well as he. And he certainly can have no absolute power over the whole family, who has but a very limited one over every individual in it. But how a family, or any other society of men, differ from that which is properly political society, we shall best see by considering wherein political society itself consists.

Man being born, as has been proved, with a title to perfect freedom, and uncontrolled enjoyment of all the rights and privileges of the law of nature, equally with any other man, or number of men in the world, hath by nature a power, not only to preserve his property, that is, his life, liberty, and estate, against the injuries and attempts of other men; but to judge of and punish the breaches of that law in others, as he is persuaded the offence deserves, even with death itself, in crimes where the heinousness of the fact, in his opinion, requires it. But because no political society can be, nor subsist, without having in itself the power to preserve the property, and, in order thereunto, punish the offences of all those of that society; there, and there only is political society, where every one of the members hath quitted this natural power, resigned it up into the hands of the community in all cases that exclude him not from appealing for protection to the law established by it. And thus all private judgment of every particular member being excluded, the community comes to be umpire, by settled standing rules, indifferent, and the same to all parties; and by men having authority from the community, for the execution of those rules, decides all the differences that may happen between any members of that society concerning any matter of right; and punishes those offences which any member hath committed against the society, with such penalties as the law has established: whereby it is easy to discern who are, and who are not, in political society together. Those who are united into one body, and have a common established law and judicature to appeal to, with authority to decide controversies between them, and punish offenders, are in civil society one with another: but those who have no such common appeal, I mean on earth, are still in the state of nature, each being, where there is no other, judge for himself, and executioner: which is, as I have before showed it, the perfect state of nature.

And thus the commonwealth comes by a power to set down what punishment shall belong to the several transgressions which they think worthy of it, committed amongst the members of that society, (which is the power of making laws) as well as it has the power to punish any injury done unto any of its members, by any one that is not of it, (which is the power of war and peace:) and all this for the preservation of the property of all the members of that society, as far as is possible. But though every man who has entered into civil society, and is become a member of any commonwealth, has thereby quitted his power to punish offences against the law of nature, in prosecution of his own private judgment; yet with the judgment of offences, which he has given up to the legislative in all cases, where he can appeal to the magistrate, he has given a right to the commonwealth to employ his force, for the execution of the judgments of the commonwealth, whenever he shall be called to it; which indeed are his own judgments, they being made by himself, or his representative. And herein we have the original of the legislative and executive power of civil society, which is to judge by standing laws, how far offences are to be punished when committed within the commonwealth; and also to determine, by occasional judgments founded on the present circumstances of the fact, how far injuries from without are to be vindicated; and in both these to employ all the force of all the members, when there shall be need.

Whenever therefore any number of men are so united into one society, as to quit every one his executive power of the law of nature, and to resign it to the public, there and there only is a political or civil society. And this is done, wherever any number of men, in the state of nature, enter into society to make one people, one body politic, under one supreme government; or else when any one joins himself to, and incorporates with any government already made: for hereby he authorizes the society, or, which is all one, the legislative thereof, to make laws for him, as the public good of the society shall require; to the execution whereof, his own assistance (as to his own degrees) is due. And this puts men out of a state of nature into that of a commonwealth, by setting up a judge on earth, with authority to determine all the controversies, and redress the injuries that may happen to any member of the commonwealth; which judge is the legislative, or magistrate appointed by it. And wherever there are any number of men, however associated, that have no such decisive power to appeal to, there they are still in the state of nature.

90. *Toleration, Works*, VI, pp. 9–45

The commonwealth seems to me to be a society of men constituted only for the procuring, preserving, and advancing their own civil interests.

Civil interest I call life, liberty, health, and indolency of body; and the possession of outward things, such as money, lands, houses, furniture, and the like.

It is the duty of the civil magistrate, by the impartial execution of equal laws, to secure unto all the people in general, and to every one of his subjects in particular, the just possession of these things belonging to this life. If any one presume to violate the laws of public justice and equity, established for the preservation of these things, his presumption is to be checked by the fear of punishment, consisting in the deprivation or diminution of those civil interests, or goods, which otherwise he might and ought to enjoy. But seeing no man does willingly suffer himself to be punished by the deprivation of any part of his goods, and much less of his liberty or life, therefore is the magistrate armed with the force and strength of all his subjects, in order to the punishment of those that violate any other man's rights.

Now that the whole jurisdiction of the magistrate reaches only to these civil concernments; and that all civil power, right, and dominion, is bounded and confined to the only care of promoting these things; and that it neither can nor ought in any manner to be extended to the salvation of souls; these following considerations seem unto me abundantly to demonstrate.

First, Because the care of souls is not committed to the civil magistrate, any more than to other men. It is not committed unto him, I say, by God; because it appears not that God has ever given any such authority to one man over another, as to compel any one to his religion. Nor can any such power be vested in the magistrate by the consent of the people; because no man can so far abandon the care of his own salvation as blindly to leave it to the choice of any other, whether prince or subject, to prescribe to him what faith or worship he shall embrace. For no man can, if he would, conform his faith to the dictates of another. All the life and power of true religion consists in the inward and full persuasion of the mind; and faith is not faith without believing. Whatever profession we make, to whatever outward worship we conform, if we are not fully satisfied in our own mind that the one is true, and the other well-pleasing unto God, such profession and such practice, far from being any furtherance, are indeed great obstacles to our salvation. For in this manner, instead of expiating other sins by the exercise of religion, I say, in offering thus unto God Almighty such a worship as we esteem to be displeasing unto him, we add unto the number of our other sins, those also of hypocrisy, and contempt of his Divine Majesty.

In the second place. The care of souls cannot belong to the civil magistrate, because his power consists only in outward force: but true and saving religion consists in the inward persuasion of the mind, without which nothing can be acceptable to God. And such is the nature of the understanding, that it cannot be compelled to the belief of any thing by outward force. Confiscation of estate, imprisonment, torments, nothing of that nature can have any such efficacy as to make men change the inward judgment that they have framed of things.

It may indeed be alleged that the magistrate may make use of arguments, and thereby draw the heterodox into the way of truth, and procure their salvation. I grant it; but this is common to him with other men. In teaching, instructing, and redressing the erroneous by reason, he may certainly do what becomes any good man to do. Magistracy does not oblige him to put off either humanity or Christianity. But it is one thing to persuade, another to command; one thing to press with arguments, another with penalties. This the civil power alone has a right to do; to the other, good-will is authority enough. Every man has commission to admonish, exhort, convince another of error, and by reasoning to draw him into truth: but to give laws, receive obedience, and compel with the sword, belongs to none but the magistrate. And upon this ground I affirm, that the magistrate's power extends not to the establishing of any articles of faith, or forms of worship, by the force of his laws. For laws are of no force at all without penalties, and penalties in this case are absolutely impertinent; because they are not proper to convince the mind. Neither the profession of any articles of faith, nor the conformity to any outward form of worship, as has been already said, can be available to the salvation of souls, unless the truth of the one, and the acceptableness of the other unto God, be thoroughly believed by those that so profess and practise. But penalties are no ways capable to produce such belief. It is only light and evidence that can work a change in men's opinions; and that light can in no manner proceed from corporal sufferings, or any other outward penalties.

In the third place, The care of the salvation of men's souls cannot belong to the magistrate; because, though the rigour of laws and the force of penalties were capable to convince and change men's minds, yet would not that help at all to the salvation of their souls. For, there being but one truth, one way to heaven; what hopes is there that more men would be led into it, if they had no other rule to follow but the religion of the court, and were put under a necessity to quit the light of their own reason, to oppose the dictates of their own consciences, and blindly to resign up themselves to the will of their governors, and to the religion, which either ignorance, ambition, or supersition had chanced to establish in the countries where they were born? In the variety and contradiction of opinions in religion, wherein the princes of the world are as much divided as in their secular interests, the narrow way would be much straitened; one country alone would be in the right, and all the rest of the world put under an obligation of following their princes in the ways that lead to destruction; and that which heightens the absurdity, and very ill suits the notion of a Deity, men would owe their eternal happiness or misery to the places of their nativity.

These considerations, to omit many others that might have been urged to the same purpose, seem unto me sufficient to conclude, that all the power of civil government relates only to men's civil interests, is confined to the care of the things of this world, and hath nothing to do with the world to come.

Let us now consider what a church is. A church then I take to be a voluntary society of men, joining themselves together of their own accord, in order to the public worshipping of God, in such a manner as they judge acceptable to him, and effectual to the salvation of their souls.

I say, it is a free and voluntary society. Nobody is born a member of any church; otherwise the religion of parents would descend unto children, by the same right of inheritance as their temporal estates, and every one would hold his faith by the same tenure he does his lands; than which nothing can be imagined more absurd. Thus therefore that matter stands. No man by nature is bound unto any particular church or sect, but every one joins himself voluntarily to that society in which he believes he has found that profession and worship which is truly acceptable to God. The hopes of salvation, as it was the only cause of his entrance into that communion, so it can be the only reason of his stay there. For if afterwards he discover any thing either erroneous in the doctrine, or incongruous in the worship of that society to which he has joined himself, why should it not be as free for him to go out as it was to enter? No member of a religious society can be tied with any other bonds but what proceed from the certain expectation of eternal life. A church then is a society of members voluntarily uniting to this end.

It follows now that we consider what is the power of this church, and unto what laws it is subject.

Forasmuch as no society, how free soever, or upon whatsoever slight occasion instituted, (whether of philosophers for learning, of merchants for commerce, or of men of leisure for mutual conversation and discourse) no church or company, I say, can in the least subsist and hold together, but will presently dissolve and break to pieces, unless it be regulated by some laws, and the members all consent to observe some order. Place and time of meeting must be agreed on; rules for admitting and excluding members must be established; distinction of officers, and putting things into a regular course, and such like, cannot be omitted. But since the joining together of several members into this church-society, as has already been demonstrated, is absolutely free and spontaneous, it necessarily follows, that the right of making its laws can belong to none but the society itself, or at least, which is the same thing, to those whom the society by common consent has authorized thereunto.

Some perhaps may object, that no such society can be said to be a true church, unless it have in it a bishop, or presbyter, with ruling authority derived from the very apostles, and continued down unto the present time by an uninterrupted succession.

To these I answer. In the first place, Let them show me the edict by which Christ has imposed that law upon his church. And let not any man think me impertinent, if, in a thing of this consequence, I require that the terms of that edict be very express and positive. – For the promise he has made us, that "wheresoever two or three are gathered together in his name, he will be in the midst of them," Matth. xviii. 20, seems to imply the contrary. Whether such an assembly want any thing necessary to a true church, pray do you consider. Certain I am, that nothing can be there wanting unto the salvation of souls, which is sufficient for our purpose.

Next, pray observe how great have always been the divisions amongst even those who lay so much stress upon the divine institution, and continued succession of a certain order of rulers in the church. Now their very dissension unavoidably puts us upon a necessity of deliberating, and consequently allows a liberty of choosing that, which upon consideration we prefer.

And, in the last place, I consent that these men have a ruler of their church, established by such a long series of succession as they judge necessary, provided I may have liberty at the same time to join myself to that society, in which I am persuaded those things are to be found which are necessary to the salvation of my soul. In this manner ecclesiastical liberty will be preserved on all sides, and no man will have a legislator imposed upon him, but whom himself has chosen.

But since men are so solicitous about the true church, I would only ask them here by the way, if it be not more agreeable to the church of Christ to make the conditions of her communion consist in such things, and such things only, as the Holy Spirit has in the holy Scriptures declared, in express words, to be necessary to salvation? I ask, I say, whether this be not more agreeable to the church of Christ, than for men to impose their own inventions and interpretations upon others, as if they were of divine authority; and to establish by ecclesiastical laws, as absolutely necessary to the profession of Christianity, such things as the holy Scriptures do either not mention, or at least not expressly command? Whosoever requires those things in order to ecclesiastical communion, which Christ does not require in order to life eternal, he may perhaps indeed constitute a society accommodated to his own opinion, and his own advantage; but how that can be called the church of Christ, which is established upon laws that are not his, and which excludes such persons from its communion as he will one day receive into the kingdom of heaven, I understand not. But this being not a proper place to inquire into the marks of the true church, I will only mind those that contend so earnestly for the decrees of their own society, and that cry out continually the CHURCH, the CHURCH, with as much noise, and perhaps upon the same principle, as the Ephesian silversmiths did for their Diana; this, I say, I desire to mind them of, that the Gospel frequently declares, that the true disciples of Christ must suffer persecution; but that the church of Christ should persecute others, and force others by fire and sword to embrace her faith and doctrine, I could never yet find in any of the books of the New Testament.

The end of a religious society, as has already been said, is the public worship of God, and by means thereof the acquisition of eternal life. All discipline ought therefore to tend to that end, and all ecclesiastical laws to be thereunto confined. Nothing ought, nor can be transacted in this society, relating to the possession of civil and worldly goods. No force is here to be made use of, upon any occasion whatsoever: for force belongs wholly to the civil magistrate, and the possession of all outward goods is subject to his jurisdiction.

But it may be asked, by what means then shall ecclesiastical laws be established, if they must be thus destitute of all compulsive power? I answer they must be established by means suitable to the nature of such things, whereof the external profession and observation, if not proceeding from a thorough conviction and approbation of the mind, is altogether useless and unprofitable. The arms by which the members of this society are to be kept within their duty, are exhortations, admonitions, and advice. If by these means the offenders will not be reclaimed, and the erroneous convinced, there remains nothing farther to be done, but that such stubborn and obstinate persons, who give no ground to hope for their reformation, should be cast out and separated from the society. This is the last and utmost force of ecclesiastical authority: no other punishment can thereby be inflicted, than that the relation ceasing between the body and the member which is cut off, the person so condemned ceases to be a part of that church.

These things being thus determined, let us inquire, in the next place, how far the duty of toleration extends, and what is required from every one by it.

And first, I hold, that no church is bound by the duty of toleration to retain any such person in her bosom, as after admonition continues obstinately to offend against the laws of the society. For these being the condition of communion, and the bond of society, if the breach of them were permitted without any animadversion, the society would immediately be thereby dissolved. But nevertheless, in all such cases care is to be taken that the sentence of excommunication, and the execution thereof, carry with it no rough usage, of word or action, whereby the ejected person may any ways be damnified in body or estate. For all force, as has often been said, belongs only to the magistrate, nor ought any private persons, at any time, to use force; unless it be in self-defence against unjust violence. Excommunication neither does nor can deprive the excommunicated person of any of those civil goods that he formerly possessed. All those things belong to the civil government, and are under the magistrate's protection. The whole force of excommunication consists only in this, that the resolution of the society in that respect being declared, the union that was between the body and some member, comes thereby to be dissolved; and that relation ceasing, the participation of some certain things, which the society communicated to its members, and unto which no man has any civil right, comes also to cease. For there is no civil injury done unto the excommunicated person, by the church minister's refusing him that bread and wine, in the celebration of the Lord's supper, which was not bought with his, but other men's money.

Secondly: No private person has any right in any manner to prejudice another person in his civil enjoyments. because he is of another church or religion. All the rights and franchises that belong to him as a man, or as a denison, are inviolably to be preserved to him. These are not the business of religion. No violence nor injury is to be offered him, whether he be Christian or pagan. Nay, we must not content ourselves with the narrow measures of bare justice: charity, bounty, and liberality must be added to it. This the Gospel enjoins, this reason directs, and this that natural fellowship we are born into requires of us. If any man err from the right way, it is his own misfortune, no injury to thee: nor therefore art thou to punish him in the things of this life, because thou supposest he will be miserable in that which is to come.

What I say concerning the mutual toleration of private persons differing from one another in religion, I understand also of particular churches; which stand as it were in the same relation to each other as private persons among themselves; nor has any one of them any manner of jurisdiction over any other, no, not even when the civil magistrate, as it sometimes happens, comes to be of this or the other communion. For the civil government can give no new right to the church, nor the church to the civil government. So that whether the magistrate join himself to any church, or separate from it, the church remains always as it was before, a free and voluntary society. It neither acquires the power of the sword by the magistrate's coming to it, nor does it lose the right of instruction and excommunication by his going from it. This is the fundamental and immutable right of a spontaneous society, that it has to remove any of its members who transgress the rules of its institution: but it cannot, by the accession of any new members, acquire any right of jurisdiction over those that are not joined with it. And therefore peace, equity, and friendship, are always mutually to be observed by particular churches, in the same manner as by private persons, without any pretence of superiority or jurisdiction over one another.

That the thing may be made yet clearer by an example; let us suppose two churches, the one of Arminians, the other of Calvinists, residing in the city of Constantinople. Will any one say, that either of these churches has right to deprive the members of the other of their estates and liberty, as we see practised elsewhere, because of their differing from it in some doctrines or ceremonies; whilst the Turks in the meanwhile silently stand by, and laugh to see with what inhuman cruelty Christians thus rage against Christians? But if one of these churches hath this power of treating the other ill, I ask which of them it is to whom that power belongs, and by what right? It will be answered, undoubtedly, that it is the orthodox church which has the right of authority over the erroneous or heretical. This is, in great and specious words, to say just nothing at all. For every church is orthodox to itself; to others, erroneous or heretical. Whatsoever any church believes, it believes to be true; and the contrary thereunto it pronounces to be error. So that the controversy between these churches about the truth of their doctrines, and the purity of their worship, is on both sides equal; nor is there any judge, either at Constantinople, or elsewhere upon earth, by whose sentence it can be determined. The decision of that question belongs only to the Supreme Judge of all men, to whom also alone belongs the punishment of the erroneous. In the mean while, let those men consider how heinously they sin, who, adding injustice, if not to their error, yet certainly to their pride, do rashly and arrogantly take upon them to misuse the servants of another master, who are not at all accountable to them.

Nay, further: if it could be manifest which of these two dissenting churches were in the right way, there would not accrue thereby unto the orthodox any right of destroying the other. For churches have neither any jurisdiction in worldly matters, nor are fire and sword any proper instruments wherewith to convince men's minds of error, and inform them of the truth. Let us suppose, nevertheless, that the civil magistrate is inclined to favour one of them, and to put his sword into their hands, that, by his consent, they might chastise the dissenters as they pleased. Will any man say, that any right can be derived unto a Christian church, over its brethren, from a Turkish emperor? An infidel, who has himself no authority to punish Christians for the articles of their faith, cannot confer such an authority upon any society of Christians, nor give unto them a right which he has not himself. This would be the case at Constantinople. And the reason of the thing is the same in any Christian kingdom. The civil power is the same in every place: nor can that power, in the hands of a Christian prince, confer any greater authority upon the church, than in the hands of a heathen; which is to say, just none at all.

Nevertheless, it is worthy to be observed, and lamented, that the most violent of these defenders of the truth, the opposers of error, the exclaimers against schism, do hardly ever let loose this their zeal for God, with which they are so warmed and inflamed, unless where they have the civil magistrate on their side. But so soon as ever court favour has given them the better end of the staff, and they begin to feel themselves the stronger; then presently peace and charity are to be laid aside: otherwise they are religiously to be observed. Where they have not the power to carry on persecution, and to become masters, there they desire to live upon

fair terms, and preach up toleration. When they are not strengthened with the civil power, then they can bear most patiently, and
unmovedly, the contagion of idolatry, superstition, and heresy, in
their neighbourhood; of which, on other occasions, the interest of
religion makes them to be extremely apprehensive. They do not
forwardly attack those errors which are in fashion at court, or are
countenanced by the government. Here they can be content to
spare their arguments: which yet, with their leave, is the only right
method of propagating truth; which has no such way of prevailing,
as when strong arguments and good reason are joined with the
softness of civility and good usage.

Nobody therefore, in fine, neither single persons, nor churches,
nay, nor even commonwealths, have any just title to invade the
civil rights and worldly goods of each other, upon pretence of religion. Those that are of another opinion, would do well to consider with themselves how pernicious a seed of discord and war,
how powerful a provocation to endless hatreds, rapines, and slaugh-
ters, they thereby furnish unto mankind. No peace and security,
no, not so much as common friendship, can ever be established
or preserved amongst men, so long as this opinion prevails, "that
dominion is founded in grace, and that religion is to be propagated by force of arms."

In the third place: Let us see what the duty of toleration requires
from those who are distinguished from the rest of mankind, from
the laity, as they please to call us, by some ecclesiastical character
and office; whether they be bishops, priests, presbyters, ministers,
or however else dignified or distinguished. It is not my business to
inquire here into the original of the power or dignity of the clergy.
This only I say, that whencesoever their authority be sprung, since
it is ecclesiastical, it ought to be confined within the bounds of the
church, nor can it in any manner be extended to civil affairs;
because the church itself is a thing absolutely separate and distinct
from the commonwealth. The boundaries on both sides are fixed
and immoveable. He jumbles heaven and earth together, the things
most remote and opposite, who mixes these societies, which are, in
their original, end, business, and in every thing, perfectly distinct,
and infinitely different from each other. No man therefore, with
whatsoever ecclesiastical office he be dignified, can deprive another man, that is not of his church and faith, either of liberty, or
of any part of his worldly goods, upon the account of that difference which is between them in religion. For whatsoever is not law-

ful to the whole church cannot by any ecclesiastical right, become lawful to any of its members.

But this is not all. It is not enough that ecclesiastical men abstain from violence and rapine, and all manner of persecution. He that pretends to be a successor of the apostles, and takes upon him the office of teaching, is obliged also to admonish his hearers of the duties of peace and good-will towards all men; as well towards the erroneous as the orthodox; towards those that differ from them in faith and worship, as well as towards those that agree with them therein: and he ought industriously to exhort all men, whether private persons or magistrates, if any such there be in his church, to charity, meekness, and toleration; and diligently endeavour to allay and temper all that heat, and unreasonable averseness of mind, which either any man's fiery zeal for his own sect, or the craft of others, has kindled against dissenters. I will not undertake to represent how happy and how great would be the fruit, both in church and state, if the pulpits every where sounded with this doctrine of peace and toleration; lest I should seem to reflect too severely upon those men whose dignity I desire not to detract from, nor would have it diminished either by others or themselves. But this I say, that thus it ought to be. And if any one that professes himself to be a minister of the word of God, a preacher of the Gospel of peace, teach otherwise; he either understands not, or neglects the business of his calling, and shall one day give account thereof unto the Prince of Peace. If Christians are to be admonished that they abstain from all manner of revenge, even after repeated provocations and multiplied injuries; how much more ought they who suffer nothing, who have had no harm done them, to forbear violence, and abstain from all manner of ill usage towards those from whom they have received none! This caution and temper they ought certainly to use towards those who mind only their own business, and are solicitous for nothing but that, whatever men think of them, they may worship God in that manner which they are persuaded is acceptable to him, and in which they have the strongest hopes of eternal salvation. In private domestic affairs, in the management of estates, in the conservation of bodily health, every man may consider what suits his own conveniency, and follow what course he likes best. No man complains of the ill management of his neighbour's affairs. No man is angry with another for an error committed in sowing his land, or in marrying his daughter. Nobody corrects a spendthrift for consuming his substance in taverns. Let any man pull down, or build, or make whatsoever expenses he pleases, nobody murmurs, nobody controls him; he has his liberty. But if any man do not frequent the church, if he do not there conform his behaviour exactly to the accustomed ceremonies, or if he brings not his children to be initiated in the sacred mysteries of this or the other congregation; this immediately causes an uproar, and the neighbourhood is filled with noise and clamour. Every one is ready to be the avenger of so great a crime. And the zealots hardly have patience to refrain from violence and rapine, so long till the cause be heard, and the poor man be, according to form, condemned to the loss of liberty, goods, or life. Oh that our ecclesiastical orators, of every sect, would apply themselves, with all the strength of argument that they are able, to the confounding of men's errors! But let them spare their persons. Let them not supply their want of reasons with the instruments of force, which belong to another jurisdiction, and do ill become a churchman's hands. Let them not call in the magistrate's authority to the aid of their eloquence or learning; lest perhaps, whilst they pretend only love for the truth, this their intemperate zeal, breathing nothing but fire and sword, betray their ambition, and show that what they desire is temporal dominion. For it will be very difficult to persuade men of sense, that he, who with dry eyes, and satisfaction of mind, can deliver his brother unto the executioner, to be burnt alive, does sincerely and heartily concern himself to save that brother from the flames of hell in the world to come.

In the last place. Let us now consider what is the magistrate's duty in the business of toleration: which is certainly very considerable.

We have already proved, that the care of souls does not belong to the magistrate: not a magisterial care, I mean, if I may so call it, which consists in prescribing by laws, and compelling by punishments. But a charitable care, which consists in teaching, admonishing, and persuading, cannot be denied unto any man. The care therefore of every man's soul belongs unto himself, and is to be left unto himself. But what if he neglect the care of his soul? I answer, what if he neglect the care of his health, or of his estate; which things are nearlier related to the government of the magistrate than the other? Will the magistrate provide by an express law, that such an one shall not become poor or sick? Laws provide, as much as is possible, that the goods and health of subjects be not injured by the fraud or violence of others; they do not guard them from the negligence or ill husbandry of the possessors themselves. No man can be forced to be rich or healthful, whether he will or no. Nay, God himself will not save men against their wills. Let us suppose, however, that some prince were desirous to force his subjects to accumulate riches, or to preserve the health and strength of their bodies. Shall it be provided by law, that they must consult none but Roman physicians, and shall every one be bound to live according to their prescriptions? What, shall no potion, no broth be taken, but what is prepared either in the Vatican, suppose, or in a Geneva shop? Or to make these subjects rich, shall they all be obliged by law to become merchants, or musicians? Or, shall every one turn victualler, or smith, because there are some that maintain their families plentifully, and grow rich in those professions? But it may be said, there are a thousand ways to wealth, but one only way to heaven. It is well said indeed, especially by those that plead for compelling men into this or the other way; for if there were several ways that lead thither, there would not be so much as a pretence left for compulsion. But now, if I be marching on with my utmost vigour, in that way which, according to the sacred geography, leads straight to Jerusalem; why am I beaten and ill used by others, because, perhaps, I wear not buskins; because my hair is not of the right cut; because, perhaps, I have not been dipt in the right fashion; because I eat flesh upon the road, or some other food which agrees with my stomach; because I avoid certain by-ways, which seem unto me to lead into briars or precipices; because, amongst the several paths that are in the same road, I choose that to walk in which seems to be the straightest and cleanest; because I avoid to keep company with some travellers that are less grave, and others that are more sour than they ought to be; or in fine, because I follow a guide that either is, or is not, clothed in white, and crowned with a mitre? Certainly, if we consider right, we shall find that for the most part they are such frivolous things as these, that, without any prejudice to religion or the salvation of souls, if not accompanied with superstition or hypocrisy, might either be observed or omitted; I say, they are such like things as these, which breed implacable enmities among Christian brethren, who are all agreed in the substantial and truly fundamental part of religion.

But let us grant unto these zealots, who condemn all things that are not of their mode, that from these circumstances arise different ends. What shall we conclude from thence? There is only one of these which is the true way to eternal happiness. But, in this great variety of ways that men follow, it is still doubted which is this right one. Now, neither the care of the commonwealth, nor the right of enacting laws, does discover this way that leads to heaven more certainly to the magistrate, than every private man's search and study discovers it unto himself. I have a weak body, sunk under a languishing disease, for which I suppose there is only one remedy, but that unknown: does it therefore belong unto the magistrate to prescribe me a remedy, because there is but one, and because it is unknown? Because there is but one way for me to escape death, will it therefore be safe for me to do whatsoever the magistrate ordains? Those things that every man ought sincerely to inquire into himself, and by meditation, study, search, and his own endeavours, attain the knowledge of, cannot be looked upon as the peculiar profession of any one sort of men. Princes, indeed, are born superior unto other men in power, but in nature equal. Neither the right, nor the art of ruling, does necessarily carry along with it the certain knowledge of other things; and least of all of the true religion; for if it were so, how could it come to pass that the lords of the earth should differ so vastly as they do in religious matters? But let us grant that it is probable the way to eternal life may be better known by a prince than by his subjects; or, at least, that in this incertitude of things, the safest and most commodious way for private persons is to follow his dictates. You will say, what then? If he should bid you follow merchandize for your livelihood, would you decline that course, for fear it should not succeed? I answer, I would turn merchant upon the prince's command, because in case I should have ill success in trade, he is abundantly able to make up my loss some other way. If it be true, as he pretends, that he desires I should thrive and grow rich, he can set me up again when unsuccessful voyages have broke me. But this is not the case in the things that regard the life to come. If there I take a wrong course, if in that respect I am once undone, it is not in the magistrate's power to repair my loss, to ease my suffering, or to restore me in any measure, much less entirely, to a good estate. What security can be given for the kingdom of heaven?

Perhaps some will say, that they do not suppose this infallible judgment, that all men are bound to follow in the affairs of religion, to be in the civil magistrate, but in the church. What the church has determined, that the civil magistrate orders to be observed; and he provides by his authority, that nobody shall either act or believe, in the business of religion, otherwise than the church teaches; so that the judgment of those things is in the church. The magistrate himself yields obedience thereunto, and requires the like obedience from others. I answer, Who sees not how frequently the name of the church, which was so venerable in the time of the apostles, has been made use of to throw dust in people's eyes, in following ages? But, however, in the present case it helps us not. The one only narrow way which leads to heaven is not better known to the magistrate than to private persons, and therefore I cannot safely take him for my guide, who may probably be as ignorant of the way as myself, and who certainly is less concerned for my salvation than I myself am. Amongst so many kings of the Jews, how many of them were there whom any Israelite, thus blindly following, had not fallen into idolatry, and thereby into destruction? Yet, nevertheless, you bid me be of good courage, and tell me that all is now safe and secure, because the magistrate does not now enjoin the observance of his own decrees in matters of religion, but only the decrees of the church. Of what church, I beseech you? Of that which certainly likes him best. As if he that compels me by laws and penalties to enter into this or the other church, did not interpose his own judgment in the matter. What difference is there whether he lead me himself, or deliver me over to be led by others? I depend both ways upon his will, and it is he that determines both ways of my eternal state. Would an Israelite, that had worshipped Baal upon the command of his king, have been in any better condition, because somebody had told him that the king ordered nothing in religion upon his own head, nor commanded any thing to be done by his subjects in divine worship, but what was approved by the counsel of priests, and declared to be of divine right by the doctors of the church? If the religion of any church become, therefore, true and saving, because the head of that sect, the prelates and priests, and those of that tribe, do all of them, with all their might, extol and praise it; what religion can ever be accounted erroneous, false, and destructive? I am doubtful concerning the doctrine of the Socinians, I am suspicious of the way of worship practised by the Papists or Lutherans; will it be ever a jot the safer for me to join either unto the one or the other of those churches, upon the magistrate's command, because he commands nothing in religion but the authority and counsel of the doctors of that church?

But to speak the truth, we must acknowledge that the church, if a convention of clergymen, making canons, must be called by that name, is for the most part more apt to be influenced by the court, than the court by the church. How the church was under the vicissitude of orthodox and Arian emperors is very well known. Or if those things be too remote, our modern English history affords us fresher examples, in the reigns of Henry VIII, Edward VI, Mary, and Elizabeth, how easily and smoothly the clergy changed their decrees, their articles of faith, their form of worship, every thing, according to the inclination of those kings and queens. Yet were those kings and queens of such different minds, in points of religion, and enjoined thereupon such different things, that no man in his wits, I had almost said none but an atheist, will presume to say that any sincere and upright worshipper of God could, with a safe conscience, obey their several decrees. To conclude, it is the same thing whether a king that prescribes laws to another man's religion pretend to do it by his own judgment, or by the ecclesiastical authority and advice of others. The decisions of churchmen, whose differences and disputes are sufficiently known, cannot be any sounder or safer than his: nor can all their suffrages joined together add any new strength unto the civil power. Though this also must be taken notice of, that princes seldom have any regard to the suffrages of ecclesiastics that are not favourers of their own faith and way of worship.

But after all, the principal consideration, and which absolutely determines this controversy, is this: although the magistrate's opinion in religion be sound, and the way that he appoints be truly evangelical, yet if I be not thoroughly persuaded thereof in my own mind, there will be no safety for me in following it. No way whatsoever that I shall walk in against the dictates of my conscience, will ever bring me to the mansions of the blessed. I may grow rich by an art that I take not delight in; I may be cured of some disease by remedies that I have not faith in; but I cannot be saved by a religion that I distrust, and by a worship that I abhor. It is in vain for an unbeliever to take up the outward show of another man's profession. Faith only, and inward sincerity, are the things that procure acceptance with God. The most likely and most approved remedy can have no effect upon the patient, if his stomach reject it as soon as taken; and you will in vain cram a medicine down a sick man's throat, which his particular constitution will be sure to turn into poison. In a word, whatsoever may be doubtful in religion, yet this at least is certain, that no religion, which I believe not to be true, can be either true or profitable unto me. In vain, therefore, do princes compel their subjects to come into their church-communion, under pretence of saving their souls. If they believe, they will come of their own accord; if they believe not, their coming will nothing avail them. How great, soever, in fine, may be the pretence of good-will and charity, and concern for the salvation of men's souls, men cannot be forced to be saved whether they will or no; and therefore, when all is done, they must be left to their own consciences.

Having thus at length freed men from all dominion over one another in matters of religion, let us now consider what they are to do. All men know and acknowledge that God ought to be publicly worshipped. Why otherwise do they compel one another unto the public assemblies? Men, therefore, constituted in this liberty are to enter into some religious society, that they may meet together, not only for mutual edification, but to own to the world that they worship God, and offer unto his divine majesty such service as they themselves are not ashamed of, and such as they think not unworthy of him, nor unacceptable to him; and finally, that by the purity of doctrine, holiness of life, and decent form of worship, they may draw others unto the love of the true religion, and perform such other things in religion as cannot be done by each private man apart.

These religious societies I call churches: and these I say the magistrate ought to tolerate: for the business of these assemblies of the people is nothing but what is lawful for every man in particular to take care of; I mean the salvation of their souls; nor, in this case, is there any difference between the national church and other separated congregations.

But as in every church there are two things especially to be considered; the outward form and rites of worship, and the doctrines and articles of faith; these things must be handled each distinctly, that so the whole matter of toleration may the more clearly be understood.

Concerning outward worship, I say, in the first place, that the magistrate has no power to enforce by law, either in his own church, or much less in another, the use of any rites or ceremonies whatsoever in the worship of God. And this, not only because these churches are free societies, but because whatsoever is practised in the worship of God is only so far justifiable as it is believed by those that practise it to be acceptable unto him. Whatsoever is not done with that assurance of faith, is neither well in itself, nor can it be acceptable to God. To impose such things, therefore, upon any people, contrary to their own judgment, is, in effect, to command them to offend God; which, considering that the end of all religion is to please him, and that liberty is essentially necessary to that end, appears to be absurd beyond expression.

But perhaps it may be concluded from hence, that I deny unto the magistrate all manner of power about indifferent things; which, if it be not granted, the whole subject matter of law-making is taken away. No, I readily grant that indifferent things, and perhaps none but such, are subjected to the legislative power. But it does not therefore follow, that the magistrate may ordain whatsoever he pleases concerning any thing that is indifferent. The public good is the rule and measure of all law-making. If a thing be not useful to the commonwealth, though it be ever so indifferent, it may not presently be established by law.

But further: Things ever so indifferent in their own nature, when they are brought into the church and worship of God, are removed out of the reach of the magistrate's jurisdiction, because in that use they have no connexion at all with civil affairs. The only business of the church is the salvation of souls: and it no ways concerns the commonwealth, or any member of it, that this or the other ceremony be there made use of. Neither the use, nor the omission, of any ceremonies in those religious assemblies does either advantage or prejudice the life, liberty, or estate, of any man. For example: Let it be granted, that the washing of an infant with water is in itself an indifferent thing: let it be granted also, that if the magistrate understand such washing to be profitable to the curing or preventing of any disease that children are subject unto, and esteem the matter weighty enough to be taken care of by a law, in that case he may order it to be done. But will any one, therefore, say, that the magistrate has the same right to ordain, by law, that all children shall be baptized by priests, in the sacred font, in order to the purification of their souls? The extreme difference of these two cases is visible to every one at first sight. Or let us apply the last case to the child of a Jew, and the thing will speak itself: for what hinders but a Christian magistrate may have subjects that are Jews? Now, if we acknowledge that such an injury may not be done unto a Jew, as to compel him, against his own opinion, to practise in his religion a thing that is in its nature indifferent, how can we maintain that any thing of this kind may be done to a Christian?

Again: Things in their own nature indifferent, cannot, by any human authority, be made any part of the worship of God, for this very reason, because they are indifferent. For since indifferent things are not capable, by any virtue of their own, to propitiate the Deity, no human power or authority can confer on them so much dignity and excellency as to enable them to do it. In the common affairs of life, that use of indifferent things which God has not forbidden is free and lawful; and therefore in those things human authority has place. But it is not so in matters of religion. Things indifferent are not otherwise lawful in the worship of God than as they are instituted by God himself; and as he, by some positive command, has ordained them to be made a part of that worship which he will vouchsafe to accept of at the hands of poor sinful men. Nor when an incensed Deity shall ask us, "Who has required these or such like things at your hands?" will it be enough to answer him, that the magistrate commanded them. If civil jurisdiction extended thus far, what might not lawfully be introduced into religion? What hodge-podge of ceremonies, what superstitious inventions, built upon the magistrate's authority, might not, against conscience, be imposed upon the worshippers of God! For the greatest part of these ceremonies and superstitions consists in the religious use of such things as are in their own nature indifferent: nor are they sinful upon any other account, than because God is not the author of them. The sprinkling of water, and use of bread and wine, are both in their own nature, and in the ordinary occasions of life, altogether indifferent. Will any man, therefore, say that these things could have been introduced into religion, and made a part of divine worship, if not by divine institution? If any human authority or civil power could have done this, why might it not also enjoin the eating of fish, and drinking of ale, in the holy banquet, as a part of divine worship? Why not the sprinkling of the blood of beasts in churches, and expiations by water or fire, and abundance more of this kind? But these things, how indifferent soever they be in common uses, when they come to be annexed unto divine worship, without divine authority, they are as abominable to God as the sacrifice of a dog. And why a dog so abominable? What difference is there between a dog and a goat, in respect of the divine nature, equally and infinitely distant from all affinity with matter; unless it be that God required the use of the one in his worship, and not of the other? We see, therefore, that indifferent things, how much soever they be under the power of the civil magistrate, yet cannot, upon that pretence, be introduced into religion, and imposed upon religious assemblies; because in the worship of God they wholly cease to be indifferent. He that worships God, does it with design to please him, and procure his favour: but that cannot be done by him, who, upon the command of another, offers unto God that which he knows will be displeasing to him, because not commanded by himself. This is not to please God, or appease his wrath, but willingly and knowingly to provoke him, by a manifest contempt; which is a thing absolutely repugnant to the nature and end of worship.

But it will here be asked, If nothing belonging to divine worship be left to human discretion, how is it then that churches themselves have the power of ordering any thing about the time and place of worship, and the like? To this I answer; that in religious worship we must distinguish between what is part of the worship itself, and what is but a circumstance. That is a part of the worship which is believed to be appointed by God, and to be well pleasing to him; and therefore that is necessary. Circumstances are such things which, though in general they cannot be separated from worship, yet the particular instances or modifications of them are not determined; and therefore they are indifferent. Of this sort are the time and place of worship, the habit and posture of him that worships. These are circumstances, and perfectly indifferent, where God has not given any express command about them. For example: amongst the Jews, the time and place of their worship, and the habits of those that officiated in it, were not mere circumstances, but a part of the worship itself; in which, if any thing were defective, or different from the institution, they could not hope that it would be accepted by God. But these, to Christians, under the liberty of the Gospel, are mere circumstances of worship which the prudence of every church may bring into such use as shall be judged most subservient to the end of order, decency, and edification. Though even under the Gospel also, those who believe the first, or the seventh day to be set apart by God, and consecrated still to his worship, to them that portion of time is not a simple circumstance, but a real part of divine worship, which can neither be changed nor neglected.

In the next place: As the magistrate has no power to impose, by his laws, the use of any rites and ceremonies in any church; so neither has he any power to forbid the use of such rites and ceremonies as are already received, approved, and practised by any church: because, if he did so, he would destroy the church itself; the end of whose institution is only to worship God with freedom, after its own manner.

You will say, by this rule, if some congregations should have a mind to sacrifice infants, or, as the primitive Christians were falsely accused, lustfully pollute themselves in promiscuous uncleanness, or practise any other such heinous enormities, is the magistrate obliged to tolerate them, because they are committed in a religious assembly? I answer, No. These things are not lawful in the ordinary course of life, nor in any private house; and, therefore, neither are they so in the worship of God, or in any religious meeting. But, indeed, if any people congregated upon account of religion, should be desirous to sacrifice a calf, I deny that that ought to be prohibited by a law. Meliboeus, whose calf it is, may lawfully kill his calf at home, and burn any part of it that he thinks fit: for no injury is thereby done to any one, no prejudice to another man's goods. And for the same reason he may kill his calf also in a religious meeting. Whether the doing so be well-pleasing to God or no, it is their part to consider that do it. The part of the magistrate is only to take care that the commonwealth receive no prejudice, and that there be no injury done to any man, either in life or estate. And thus what may be spent on a feast may be spent on a sacrifice. But if, peradventure, such were the state of things, that the interest of the commonwealth required all slaughter of beasts should be forborn for some while, in order to the increasing of the stock of cattle, that had been destroyed by some extraordinary murrain; who sees not that the magistrate, in such a case, may forbid all his subjects to kill any calves for any use whatsoever? Only it is to be observed, that in this case the law is not made about a religious, but a political matter: nor is the sacrifice, but the slaughter of calves thereby prohibited.

By this we see what difference there is between the church and the commonwealth. Whatsoever is lawful in the commonwealth, cannot be prohibited by the magistrate in the church. Whatsoever is permitted unto any of his subjects for their ordinary use, neither can nor ought to be forbidden by him to any sect of people for their religious uses. If any man may lawfully take bread or wine, either sitting or kneeling, in his own house, the law ought not to abridge him of the same liberty in his religious worship; though in the church the use of bread and wine be very different, and be there applied to the mysteries of faith, and rites of divine worship. But those things that are prejudicial to the commonweal of a people in their ordinary use, and are therefore forbidden by laws, those things ought not to be permitted to churches in their sacred rites. Only the magistrate ought always to be very careful that he do not misuse his authority, to the oppression of any church, under pretence of public good.

It may be said, What if a church be idolatrous, is that also to be tolerated by the magistrate? In answer, I ask, what power can be given to the magistrate for the suppression of an idolatrous church, which may not, in time and place, be made use of to the ruin of an orthodox one? For it must be remembered, that the civil power is the same every where, and the religion of every prince is orthodox to himself. If, thereore, such a power be granted unto the civil magistrate in spirituals, as that at Geneva, for example; he may extirpate, by violence and blood, the religion which is there reputed idolatrous; by the same rule, another magistrate, in some neighbouring country, may oppress the reformed religion; and, in India, the Christian. The civil power can either change every thing in religion, according to the prince's pleasure, or it can change nothing. If it be once permitted to introduce any thing into religion, by the means of laws and penalties, there can be no bounds put to it; but it will, in the same manner, be lawful to alter every thing, according to that rule of truth which the magistrate has framed unto himself. No man whatsoever ought therefore to be deprived of his terrestrial enjoyments, upon account of his religion. Not even Americans, subjected unto a Christian prince, are to be punished either in body or goods, for not embracing our faith and worship. If they are persuaded that they please God in observing the rites of their own country, and that they shall obtain happiness by that means, they are to be left unto God and themselves. Let us trace this matter to the bottom. Thus it is: an inconsiderable and weak number of Christians, destitute of every thing, arrive in a pagan country; these foreigners beseech the inhabitants, by the bowels of humanity, that they would succour them with the necessaries of life; those necessaries are given them, habitations are granted, and they all join together, and grow up into one body of people. The Christian religion by this means takes root in that country, and spreads itself; but does not suddenly grow the strongest. While things are in this condition, peace, friendship, faith, and equal justice, are preserved amongst them. At length the magistrate becomes a Christian, and by that means their party becomes the most powerful. Then immediately all compacts are to be broken, all civil rights to be violated, that idolatry may be extirpated: and unless these innocent pagans, strict observers of the rules of equity and the law of nature, and no ways offending against the laws of the society, I say unless they will forsake their ancient religion, and embrace a new and strange one, they are to be turned out of the lands and possessions of their forefathers, and perhaps deprived of life itself. Then at last it appears what zeal for the church, joined with the desire of dominion, is capable to produce: and how easily the pretence of religion, and of the care of souls, serves for a cloke to covetousness, rapine, and ambition.

Now, whosoever maintains that idolatry is to be rooted out of any place by laws, punishments, fire, and sword, may apply this story to himself: for the reason of the thing is equal, both in America and Europe. And neither pagans there, nor any dissenting Christians here, can with any right be deprived of their worldly goods by the predominating faction of a court-church; nor are any civil rights to be either changed or violated upon account of religion in one place more than another.

But idolatry, say some, is a sin, and therefore not to be tolerated. If they said it were therefore to be avoided, the inference were good. But it does not follow, that because it is a sin, it ought therefore to be punished by the magistrate. For it does not belong unto the magistrate to make use of his sword in punishing every thing, indifferently, that he takes to be a sin against God. Covetousness, uncharitableness, idleness, and many other things are sins, by the consent of all men, which yet no man ever said were to be punished by the magistrate. The reason is, because they are not prejudicial to other men's rights, nor do they break the public peace of societies. Nay, even the sins of lying and perjury are nowhere punishable by laws; unless in certain cases, in which the real turpitude of the thing, and the offence against God, are not considered, but only the injury done unto men's neighbours, and to the commonwealth. And what if, in another country, to a Mahometan or a pagan prince, the Christian religion seem false and offensive to God; may not the Christians, for the same reason, and after the same manner, be extirpated there?

But it may be urged farther, that by the law of Moses idolaters were to be rooted out. True indeed, by the law of Moses; but that is not obligatory to us Christians. Nobody pretends that every thing, generally, enjoined by the law of Moses, ought to be practised by Christians. But there is nothing more frivolous than that common distinction of moral, judicial, and ceremonial law, which men ordinarily make use of: for no positive law whatsoever can oblige any people but those to whom it is given. "Hear, O Israel," sufficiently restrains the obligation of the law of Moses only to that people. And this consideration alone is answer enough unto those that urge the authority of the law of Moses, for the inflicting of capital punishments upon idolaters. But however I will examine this argument a little more particularly.

The case of idolaters, in respect of the Jewish commonwealth, falls under a double consideration. The first is of those, who, being initiated in the Mosaical rites, and made citizens of that commonwealth, did afterwards apostatize from the worship of the God of Israel. These were proceeded against as traitors and rebels, guilty of no less than high treason; for the commonwealth of the Jews, different in that from all others, was an absolute theocracy: nor was there, or could there be, any difference between that commonwealth and the church. The laws established there concerning the worship of one invisible Deity, were the civil laws of that people, and a part of their political government, in which God himself was the legislator. Now if any one can show me where there is a commonwealth, at this time, constituted upon that foundation, I will acknowledge that the ecclesiastical laws do there unavoidably become a part of the civil; and that the subjects of that government both may, and ought to be, kept in strict conformity with that church, by the civil power. But there is absolutely no such thing, under the Gospel, as a Christian commonwealth. There are, indeed, many cities and kingdoms that have embraced the faith of Christ; but they have retained their ancient forms of government, with which the law of Christ hath not at all meddled. He, indeed, hath taught men how, by faith and good works, they may attain eternal life. But he instituted no commonwealth; he prescribed unto his followers no new and peculiar form of government; nor put he the sword into any magistrate's hand, with commission to make use of it in forcing men to forsake their former religion, and receive his.

Secondly, Foreigners, and such as were strangers to the commonwealth of Israel, were not compelled by force to observe the rites of the Mosaical law: but, on the contrary, in the very same place where it is ordered that an Israelite that was an idolater should be put to death, there it is provided that strangers should not be "vexed nor oppressed," Exod. xxii. 21. I confess that the seven nations that possessed the land which was promised to the Israelites were utterly to be cut off. But this was not singly because they were idolaters; for if that had been the reason, why were the Moabites and other nations to be spared? No; the reason is this: God being in a peculiar manner the King of the Jews, he could not suffer the adoration of any other deity, which was properly an act of high treason against himself, in the land of Canaan, which was his kingdom; for such a manifest revolt could no ways consist with his dominion, which was perfectly political, in that country. All idolatry was therefore to be rooted out of the bounds of his kingdom; because it was an acknowledgment of another God, that is to say, another king, against the laws of empire. The inhabitants were also to be driven out, that the entire possession of the land might be given to the Israelites. And for the like reason the Emims and the Horims were driven out of their countries by the children of Esau and Lot; and their lands, upon the same grounds, given by God to the invaders, Deut. ii. 12. But though all idolatry was thus rooted out of the land of Canaan, yet every idolater was not brought to execution. The whole family of Rahab, the whole nation of the Gibeonites, articled with Joshua, and were allowed by treaty; and there were many captives amongst the Jews, who were idolaters. David and Solomon subdued many countries without the confines of the Land of Promise, and carried their conquests as far as Euphrates. Amongst so many captives taken, of so many nations reduced under their obedience, we find not one man forced into the Jewish religion, and the worship of the true God, and punished for idolatry, though all of them were certainly guilty of it. If any one indeed, becoming a proselyte, desired to be made a denizen of their commonwealth, he was obliged to submit unto their laws; that is, to embrace their religion. But this he did willingly, on his own accord, not by constraint. He did not unwillingly submit, to show his obedience; but he sought and solicited for it, as a privilege; and as soon as he was admitted, he became subject to the laws of the commonwealth, by which all idolatry was forbidden within the borders of the land of Canaan. But that law, as I have said, did not reach to any of those regions, however subjected unto the Jews, that were situated without those bounds.

Thus far concerning outward worship. Let us now consider articles of faith.

The articles of religion are some of them practical, and some speculative. Now, though both sorts consist in the knowledge of truth, yet these terminate simply in the understanding, those influence the will and manners. Speculative opinions, therefore, and articles of faith, as they are called, which are required only to be believed, cannot be imposed on any church by the law of the land; for it is absurd that things should be enjoined by laws which are not in men's power to perform; and to believe this or that to be true does not depend upon our will. But of this enough has been said already. But, will some say, let men at least profess that they believe. A sweet religion, indeed, that obliges men to dissemble, and tell lies both to God and man, for the salvation of their souls! If the magistrate thinks to save men thus, he seems to understand little of the way of salvation; and if he does it not in order to save them, why is he so solicitous about the articles of faith as to enact them by a law?

Further, The magistrate ought not to forbid the preaching or professing of any speculative opinions in any church, because they have no manner of relation to the civil rights of the subjects. If a Roman Catholic believe that to be really the body of Christ, which another man calls bread, he does no injury thereby to his neighbour. If a Jew does not believe the New Testament to be the word of God, he does not thereby alter any thing in men's civil rights. If a heathen doubt of both Testaments, he is not therefore to be punished as a pernicious citizen. The power of the magistrate, and the estates of the people, may be equally secure, whether any man believe these things or no. I readily grant that these opinions are false and absurd; but the business of laws is not to provide for the truth of opinions, but for the safety and security of the commonwealth, and of every particular man's goods and person. And so it ought to be; for truth certainly would do well enough, if she were once left to shift for herself. She seldom has received, and I fear never will receive, much assistance from the power of great men, to whom she is but rarely known, and more rarely welcome. She is not taught by laws, nor has she any need of force to procure her entrance into the minds of men. Errors indeed prevail by the assistance of foreign and borrowed succours. But if truth makes not her way into the understanding by her own light, she will be but the weaker for any borrowed force violence can add to her. Thus much for speculative opinions. Let us now proceed to the practical ones.

A good life, in which consists not the least part of religion and true piety, concerns also the civil government: and in it lies the safety both of men's souls and of the commonwealth. Moral actions belong therefore to the jurisdiction both of the outward and inward court; both of the civil and domestic governor; I mean, both of the magistrate and conscience. Here therefore is great danger, lest one of these jurisdictions intrench upon the other, and discord arise between the keeper of the public peace and the overseers of souls. But if what has been already said concerning the limits of both these governments be rightly considered, it will easily remove all difficulty in this matter.

Every man has an immortal soul, capable of eternal happiness or misery; whose happiness depending upon his believing and doing those things in this life, which are necessary to the obtaining of God's favour, and are prescribed by God to that end: it follows from thence, first, that the observance of these things is the highest obligation that lies upon mankind, and that our utmost care, application, and diligence, ought to be exercised in the search and performance of them; because there is nothing in this world that is of any consideration in comparison with eternity. Secondly, that seeing one man does not violate the right of another, by his erroneous opinions, and undue manner of worship, nor is his perdition any prejudice to another man's affairs; therefore the care of each man's salvation belongs only to himself. But I would not have this understood, as if I meant hereby to condemn all charitable admonitions, and affectionate endeavours to reduce men from errors; which are indeed the greatest duty of a Christian. Any one may employ as many exhortations and arguments as he pleases, towards the promoting of another man's salvation. But all force and compulsion are to be forborn. Nothing is to be done imperiously. Nobody is obliged in that manner to yield obedience unto the admonitions or injunctions of another, farther than he himself is persuaded. Every man, in that, has the supreme and absolute authority of judging for himself; and the reason is, because nobody else is concerned in it, nor can receive any prejudice from his conduct therein.

But besides their souls, which are immortal, men have also their temporal lives here upon earth; the state whereof being frail and fleeting, and the duration uncertain, they have need of several outward conveniences to the support thereof, which are to be procured or preserved by pains and industry; for those things that are necessary to the comfortable support of our lives, are not the spontaneous products of nature, nor do offer themselves fit and prepared for our use. This part, therefore, draws on another care, and necessarily gives another employment. But the pravity of mankind being such, that they had rather injuriously prey upon the fruits of other men's labours than take pains to provide for themselves; the necessity of preserving men in the possession of what honest industry has already acquired, and also of preserving their liberty and strength, whereby they may acquire what they farther want, obliges men to enter into society with one another; that by mutual assistance and joint force, they may secure unto each other their properties, in the things that contribute to the comforts and happiness of this life; leaving in the mean while to every man the care of his own eternal happiness, the attainment whereof can neither be facilitated by another man's industry, nor can the loss of it turn to another man's prejudice, nor the hope of it be forced from him by any external violence. But forasmuch as men thus entering into societies, grounded upon their mutual compacts of assistance, for the defence of their temporal goods, may nevertheless be deprived of them, either by the rapine and fraud of their fellow-citizens, or by the hostile violence of foreigners: the remedy of this evil consists in arms, riches, and multitudes of citizens: the remedy of others in laws: and the care of all things relating both to the one and the other is committed by the society to the civil magistrate. This is the original, this is the use, and these are the bounds of the legislative, which is the supreme power in every commonwealth. I mean, that provision may be made for the security of each man's private possessions; for the peace, riches, and public commodities of the whole people, and, as much as possible, for the increase of their inward strength against foreign invasions.

These things being thus explained, it is easy to understand to what end the legislative power ought to be directed, and by what measures regulated, and that is the temporal good and outward prosperity of the society, which is the sole reason of men's entering into society, and the only thing they seek and aim at in it; and it is also evident what liberty remains to men in reference to their eternal salvation, and that is, that every one should do what he in his conscience is persuaded to be acceptable to the Almighty, on whose good pleasure and acceptance depends his eternal happiness; for obedience is due in the first place to God, and afterwards to the laws.

But some may ask, "What if the magistrate should enjoin any thing by his authority, that appears unlawful to the conscience of a private person?" I answer, that if government be faithfully administered, and the counsels of the magistrate be indeed directed to the public good, this will seldom happen. But if perhaps it do so fall out, I say, that such a private person is to abstain from the actions that he judges unlawful; and he is to undergo the punishment, which is not unlawful for him to bear; for the private judgment of any person concerning a law enacted in political matters, for the public good, does not take away the obligation of that law, nor deserve a dispensation. But if the law indeed be concerning things that lie not within the verge of the magistrate's authority; as, for example, that the people, or any party amongst them, should be compelled to embrace a strange religion, and join in the worship and ceremonies of another church; men are not in these cases obliged by that law, against their consciences; for the political society is instituted for no other end, but only to secure every man's possession of the things of this life. The care of each man's soul, and of the things of heaven, which neither does belong to the commonwealth, nor can be subjected to it, is left entirely to every man's self. Thus the safeguard of men's lives, and of the things that belong unto this life, is the business of the commonwealth; and the preserving of those things unto their owners is the duty of the magistrate; and therefore the magistrate cannot take away these worldly things from this man, or party, and give them to that; nor change property amongst fellow-subjects, no not even by a law, for a cause that has no relation to the end of civil government; I mean for their religion; which, whether it be true or false, does no prejudice to the worldly concerns of their fellow-subjects, which are the things that only belong unto the care of the commonwealth.

"But what if the magistrate believe such a law as this to be for the public good?" I answer: as the private judgment of any particular person, if erroneous, does not exempt him from the obligation of law, so the private judgment, as I may call it, of the magistrate, does not give him any new right of imposing laws upon his subjects, which neither was in the constitution of the government granted him, nor ever was in the power of the people to grant: and least of all, if he make it his business to enrich and advance his followers and fellow-sectaries with the spoils of others. But what if the magistrate believe that he has a right to make such laws, and that they are for the public good; and his subjects believe the contrary? Who shall be judge between them? I answer, God alone; for there is no judge upon earth between the supreme magistrate and the people. God, I say, is the only judge in this case, who will retribute unto every one at the last day according to his deserts; that is, according to his sincerity and uprightness in endeavouring to promote piety, and the public weal and peace of mankind. But what shall be done in the mean while? I answer: the principal and chief care of every one ought to be of his own soul first, and, in the next place, of the public peace: though yet there are few will think it is peace there, where they see all laid waste. There are two sorts of contests amongst men; the one managed by law, the other by force: and they are of that nature, that where the one ends, the other always begins. But it is not my business to inquire into the power of the magistrate in the different constitutions of nations. I only know what usually happens where controversies arise, without a judge to determine them. You will say then the magistrate being the stronger will have his will, and carry his point. Without doubt. But the question is not here concerning the doubtfulness of the event, but the rule of right.

The last phrase in the previous selection, *the rule of right*, indicates a basic feature of Locke's thinking about societies, especially civil society. There are some serious questions about whether the rule of right through laws may in fact run counter to right, if, for example, the laws are unjust, in conflict with the law of nature. Is right articulated by the laws of nature or by the laws of society? There can be no doubt that Locke would answer: "by the laws of nature"; but the previous selection seems to end by defending the laws of society over those of God and nature, should they clash. In this passage, Locke may only be indicating, as he says, what usually happens. Nevertheless, his reference to the rule of right in this context gives some room for doubt and concern.

That same phrase also calls attention to Locke's major disagreement with Filmer, against whom the first of *Two Treatises* was written. Filmer had argued for the right of the magistrate deriving from Adam's right, and Adam's right over his children and family was for Filmer bestowed by God. In Filmer's account of the family, there was no room for a contract between husband and wife. Locke accepted rights defined by God's laws, the laws of nature, but those laws (never very specifically or systematically identified by Locke) did not deal with the formation of civil society, although they were to apply to that and every society.

Had there not been those who, like Filmer, defended some version of the divine right of kings (the right to rule descended from the first man) Locke might have been able to rest his account of the origin of civil societies on the general description of man's inclination toward societies, their formation for specific purposes and activities, via contracts, agreements, and so on. Civil society would

then have been one species of society that met these conditions. That account of the nature of societies defines
rights and duties in the contract. These rights then provided the basis and justification for the rule of right in
civil society. The alternative to Filmer was the claim (perhaps Locke had Hobbes in mind here) that "all government in the world is the product only of force and violence,
and that men live together by no other rules but that of
beasts, where the strongest carries it, and so lays a foundation for perpetual disorder and mischief, tumult, sedition, and rebellion."

It was important for Locke to provide an account of
the origin of civil government other than either that of
Hobbes or Filmer. The whole of his long first treatise is
a meticulous refutation of Filmer (by frequent counter-
references to the Bible and by *reductio ad absurdum*
arguments). There is no such detailed refutation of the
Hobbesian alternative, but the second of *Two Treatises*
constitutes Locke's positive alternative. Like Filmer,
Locke's account derives political power and civil justice
from the prior, nonpolitical state of man. That prior condition of man has rights and laws specified by God, it was
a state of liberty but not a state of license. It was a condition in which men are equal, in which our natural reason
can discover the laws of nature that govern us there.

Locke was not so naive as to think that men in or out
of civil society are always motivated to right, guided by
reason toward mutual assistance. He recognized the "corruption and viciousness of degenerate men" (selection 83),
the "pravity of mankind" that leads men to prey injuriously
"upon the fruits of other men's labours," even "the rapine
and fraud" of members of the same group (selection 90).
Some writers have taken this recognition by Locke of the
nonrational or vicious traits of men as Locke's agreement
with Hobbes on the state of nature.[28] There is in Locke's
philosophy a realistic recognition of what motivates men
to act, not knowledge of the good or right, but fear of pun-

28 For example, Leo Strauss, *Natural Right and History* (Chicago,
1953). For a corrective to Strauss, see my "Locke and the Law of
Nature," *The Philosophical Review* (1958), and Hans Aarsleff,
"The State of Nature and the Nature of Man in Locke," in *John
Locke, Problems and Perspectives*, ed. J. W. Yolton (Cambridge,
1969).

ishment and the desire for happiness. At the same time,
Locke held the firm belief that education and training can
influence and even alter these basic motives. The importance given to education, his distinction between natural
and moral good, between agent and moral agent, his frequent injunction to fit our desires to what is right, and his
urging us to put aside the preferences of the moment for
the sober judgment of careful thought and examination:
these are all indications that Locke took the role of education in society seriously. Degeneracy, pravity, rapine and
fraud are not the norms, or even typical. His account of
the nature of education does not use force or power to turn
the natural inclinations and motives in the way of reason
and virtue. Nor are the announced reasons for men going
from the state of nature to civil society based on these irrational features (see selection 93).

As Locke conceived of the state of nature, it was not a
condition of war, all against all. He certainly thought that
the selfish actions of some individuals would be a factor in
reinforcing the natural inclination toward society; but there
were for him, in the state of nature, laws of nature (given
by God), men did have rights and powers. Filmer was, in
Locke's eyes, wrong on many counts but his basic error lay
in deriving civil power from parental power. Instead, civil
power (and right) comes from the law of nature and our
action in giving up some of our individual rights and powers. Filmer's account denied the important premise, for
Locke, that each individual who enters civil society authorizes the magistrate to act for him.

91. *Two Treatises*, II, sections 1–15

It having been shown in the foregoing discourse, 1. That Adam
had not, either by natural right of fatherhood, or by positive donation from God, any such authority over his children, or dominion
over the world, as is pretended:

2. That if he had, his heirs yet had no right to it:

3. That if his heirs had, there being no law of nature nor positive
law of God that determines which is the right heir in all cases
that may arise, the right of succession, and consequently of bearing
rule, could not have been certainly determined:

4. That if even that had been determined, yet the knowledge
of which is the eldest line of Adam's posterity being so long since

utterly lost, that in the races of mankind and families of the world there remains not to one above another the least pretence to be the eldest house, and to have the right of inheritance:

All these premises having, as I think, been clearly made out, it is impossible that the rulers now on earth should make any benefit, or derive any the least shadow of authority from that, which is held to be the fountain of all power, "Adam's private dominion and paternal jurisdiction"; so that he that will not give just occasion to think that all government in the world is the product only of force and violence, and that men live together by no other rules but that of beasts, where the strongest carries it, and so lay a foundation for perpetual disorder and mischief, tumult, sedition, and rebellion, (things that the followers of that hypothesis so loudly cry out against) must of necessity find out another rise of government, another original of political power, and another way of designing and knowing the persons that have it, than what sir Robert Filmer hath taught us.

To this purpose, I think it may not be amiss to set down what I take to be political power; that the power of a magistrate over a subject may be distinguished from that of a father over his children, a master over his servants, a husband over his wife, and a lord over his slave. All which distinct powers happening sometimes together in the same man, if he be considered under these different relations, it may help us to distinguish these powers one from another, and show the difference betwixt a ruler of a commonwealth, a father of a family, and a captain of a galley.

Political power, then, I take to be a right of making laws with penalties of death, and consequently all less penalties, for the regulating and preserving of property, and of employing the force of the community, in the execution of such laws, and in the defence of the commonwealth from foreign injury; and all this only for the public good.

To understand political power right, and derive it from its original, we must consider what state all men are naturally in, and that is, a state of perfect freedom to order their actions and dispose of their possessions and persons, as they think fit, within the bounds of the law of nature; without asking leave, or depending upon the will of any other man.

A state also of equality, wherein all the power and jurisdiction is reciprocal, no one having more than another; there being nothing more evident than that creatures of the same species and rank, promiscuously born to all the same advantages of nature, and the use of the same faculties, should also be equal one amongst another without subordination or subjection; unless the Lord and Master of them all should, by any manifest declaration of his will, set one above another, and confer on him, by an evident and clear appointment, an undoubted right to dominion and sovereignty.

This equality of men by nature the judicious Hooker looks upon as so evident in itself, and beyond all question, that he makes it the foundation of that obligation to mutual love amongst men, on which he builds the duties we owe one another, and from whence he derives the great maxims of justice and charity. His words are,

"The like natural inducement hath brought men to know that it is no less their duty to love others than themselves; for seeing those things which are equal must needs all have one measure; if I cannot but wish to receive good, even as much at every man's hands as any man can wish unto his own soul, how should I look to have any part of my desire herein satisfied, unless myself be careful to satisfy the like desire, which is undoubtedly in other men, being of one and the same nature? To have any thing offered them repugnant to this desire must needs in all respects grieve them as much as me; so that, if I do harm, I must look to suffer, there being no reason that others should show greater measure of love to me than they have by me showed unto them: my desire therefore to be loved of my equals in nature, as much as possibly may be, imposeth upon me a natural duty of bearing to themward fully the like affection: from which relation of equality between ourselves and them that are as ourselves, what several rules and canons natural reason hath drawn, for direction of life, no man is ignorant."

But though this be a state of liberty, yet it is not a state of licence: though man in that state have an uncontrollable liberty to dispose of his person or possessions, yet he has not liberty to destroy himself, or so much as any creature in his possession, but where some nobler use than its bare preservation calls for it. The state of nature has a law of nature to govern it, which obliges every one: and reason, which is that law, teaches all mankind, who will but consult it, that being all equal and independent, no one ought to harm another in his life, health, liberty, or possessions: for men being all the workmanship of one omnipotent and infinitely wise Maker; all the servants of one sovereign Master, sent into the world by his order, and about his business; they are his property, whose workmanship they are, made to last during his, not another's pleasure: and being furnished with like faculties, sharing all in one community of nature, there cannot be supposed any such subordination among us that may authorize us to destroy another, as if we were made for one another's uses, as the inferior ranks of creatures are for ours. Every one, as he is bound to preserve himself, and not to quit his station wilfully, so by the like reason, when his own preservation comes not in competition, ought he, as much as he can, to preserve the rest of mankind, and may not, unless it be to do justice to an offender, take away or impair the life, or what tends to the preservation of life, the liberty, health, limb, or goods of another.

And that all men may be restrained from invading others' rights, and from doing hurt to one another, and the law of nature be observed, which willeth the peace and preservation of all mankind, the execution of the law of nature is, in that state, put into every man's hands, whereby every one has a right to punish the transgressors of that law to such a degree as may hinder its violation: for the law of nature would, as all other laws that concern men in this world, be in vain, if there were nobody that in the state of nature had a power to execute that law, and thereby preserve the innocent, and restrain offenders. And if any one in the state of nature may punish another for any evil he has done, every one may do so: for in that state of perfect equality, where naturally there is no superiority or jurisdiction of one over another, what any may do in prosecution of that law every one must needs have a right to do.

And thus, in the state of nature, "one man comes by a power over another"; but yet no absolute or arbitrary power to use a criminal, when he has got him in his hands, according to the passionate heats or boundless extravagancy of his own will; but only to retribute to him, so far as calm reason and conscience dictate, what is proportionate to his transgression; which is so much as may serve for reparation and restraint: for these two are the only reasons why one man may lawfully do harm to another, which is that we call punishment. In transgressing the law of nature, the offender declares himself to live by another rule than that of reason and common equity, which is that measure God has set to the actions of men for their mutual security; and so he becomes dangerous to mankind, the tie, which is to secure them from injury and violence, being slighted and broken by him: which being a trespass against the whole species, and the peace and safety of it, provided for by the law of nature; every man upon this score, by the right he hath to preserve mankind in general, may restrain, or, where it is necessary, destroy things noxious to them, and so may bring such evil on any one, who hath transgressed that law, as may make him repent the doing of it, and thereby deter him, and by his example others, from doing the like mischief. And in this case, and upon this ground, "every man hath a right to punish the offender, and be executioner of the law of nature."

I doubt not but this will seem a very strange doctrine to some men: but, before they condemn it, I desire them to resolve me by what right any prince or state can put to death or punish an alien for any crime he commits in their country. It is certain their laws, by virtue of any sanction they receive from the promulgated will of the legislative, reach not a stranger: they speak not to him, nor, if they did, is he bound to hearken to them. The legislative authority, by which they are in force over the subjects of that commonwealth, hath no power over him. Those who have the supreme power of making laws in England, France, or Holland, are to an Indian but like the rest of the world, men without authority: and therefore, if by the law of nature every man hath not a power to punish offences against it, as he soberly judges the case to require, I see not how the magistrates of any community can punish an alien of another country; since, in reference to him, they can have no more power than what every man naturally may have over another.

Besides the crime which consists in violating the law, and varying from the right rule of reason, whereby a man so far becomes degenerate, and declares himself to quit the principles of human nature, and to be a noxious creature, there is commonly injury done to some person or other, and some other man receives damage by his transgression: in which case he who hath received any damage, has, besides the right of punishment common to him with other men, a particular right to seek reparation from him that has done it: and any other person, who finds it just, may also join with him that is injured, and assist him in recovering from the offender so much as may make satisfaction for the harm he has suffered.

From these two distinct rights, the one of punishing the crime for restraint, and preventing the like offence, which right of punishing is in every body; the other of taking reparation, which belongs only to the injured party; comes it to pass that the magistrate, who by being magistrate hath the common right of punishing put into his hands, can often, where the public good demands not the execution of the law, remit the punishment of criminal offences by his own authority, but yet cannot remit the satisfaction due to any private man for the damage he has received. That he who has suffered the damage has a right to demand in his own name, and he alone can remit: the damnified person has this power of appropriating to himself the goods or service of the offender, by right of self-preservation, as every man has a power to punish the crime, to prevent its being committed again, "by the right he has of preserving all mankind," and doing all reasonable things he can in order to that end: and thus it is that every man, in the state of nature, has a power to kill a murderer, both to deter others from doing the like injury, which no reparation can compensate, by the example of the punishment that attends it from every body; and also to secure men from the attempts of a criminal, who having renounced reason, the common rule and measure God hath given to mankind, hath, by the unjust violence and slaughter he hath committed upon one, declared war against all mankind; and therefore may be destroyed as a lion or a tiger, one of those wild savage beasts with whom men can have no society nor security: and upon this is grounded that great law of nature, "Whoso sheddeth man's blood, by man shall his blood be shed." And Cain was so fully convinced that every one had a right to destroy such a criminal, that, after the murder of his brother, he cries out, "Every one that findeth me shall slay me"; so plain was it writ in the hearts of mankind.

By the same reason may a man in the state of nature punish the lesser breaches of that law. It will perhaps be demanded, with death? I answer, each transgression may be punished to that degree, and with so much severity, as will suffice to make it an ill bargain to the offender, give him cause to repent, and terrify others from doing the like. Every offence, that can be committed in the state of nature, may in the state of nature, be also punished equally, and as far forth, as it may in a commonwealth: for though it would be beside my present purpose to enter here into the particulars of the law of nature, or its measures of punishment, yet it is certain there is such a law, and that too as intelligible and plain to a rational creature, and a studier of that law, as the positive laws of commonwealths; nay, possibly plainer, as much as reason is easier to be understood than the fancies and intricate contrivances of men, following contrary and hidden interests put into words; for so truly are a great part of the municipal laws of countries, which are only so far right, as they are founded on the law of nature, by which they are to be regulated and interpreted.

To this strange doctrine, viz. That "in the state of nature every one has the executive power" of the law of nature, I doubt not but it will be objected, that it is unreasonable for men to be judges in their own cases, that self-love will make men partial to themselves and their friends: and, on the other side, that ill-nature, passion, and revenge will carry them too far in punishing others; and hence nothing but confusion and disorder will follow: and that therefore God hath certainly appointed government to restrain the partiality and violence of men. I easily grant, that civil government is the proper remedy for the inconveniences of the state of nature, which must certainly be great, where men may be judges in their own case; since it is easy to be imagined, that he who was so unjust as to do his brother an injury, will scarce be so just as to condemn himself for it: but I shall desire those who make this objection to remember, that absolute monarchs are but men; and if government is to be the remedy of those evils, which necessarily follow from men's being judges in their own cases, and the state of nature is therefore not to be endured; I desire to know what kind of government that is, and how much better it is than the state of nature, where one man, commanding a multitude, has the liberty to be judge in his own case, and may do to all his subjects whatever he pleases, without the least liberty to any one to question or control those who execute his pleasure? and in whatsoever he doth, whether led by reason, mistake, or passion, must be submitted to? Much better it is in the state of nature, wherein men are not bound to submit to the unjust will of another: and if he that judges, judges amiss in his own, or any other case, he is answerable for it to the rest of mankind.

It is often asked, as a mighty objection, "where are or ever were there any men in such a state of nature?" To which it may suffice as an answer at present, that since all princes and rulers of independent governments, all through the world, are in a state of nature, it is plain the world never was, nor ever will be, without numbers of men in that state. I have named all governors of independent communities, whether they are, or are not, in league with others: for it is not every compact that puts an end to the state of nature between men, but only this one of agreeing together mutually to enter into one community, and make one body politic; other promises and compacts men may make one with another, and yet still be in the state of nature. The promises and bargains for truck, &c. between the two men in the desert island, mentioned by Garcilasso de la Vega, in his history of Peru; or between a Swiss and an Indian, in the woods of America; are binding to them, though they are perfectly in a state of nature, in reference to one another: for truth and keeping of faith belongs to men as men, and not as members of society.

To those that say, there were never any men in the state of nature, I will not only oppose the authority of the judicious Hooker, Eccl. Pol. lib. i. sect. 10, where he says, "The laws which have been hitherto mentioned," i. e. the laws of nature, "do bind men absolutely, even as they are men, although they have never any settled fellowship, never any solemn agreement amongst themselves what to do, or not to do: but forasmuch as we are not by ourselves sufficient to furnish ourselves with competent store of things, needful for such a life as our nature doth desire, a life fit for the dignity of man; therefore to supply those defects and imperfections which are in us, as living singly and solely by ourselves, we are naturally induced to seek communion and fellowship with others. This was the cause of men's uniting themselves at first in politic societies," but I moreover affirm that all men are naturally in that state, and remain so, till by their own consents they make themselves members of some politic society; and I doubt not, in the sequel of this discourse, to make it very clear.

92. *Two Treatises*, II, sections 100–4

To this I find two objections made.

First, "That there are no instances to be found in story, of a company of men independent and equal one amongst another, that met together, and in this way began and set up a government."

Secondly, "It is impossible of right, that men should do so, because all men being born under government, they are to submit to that, and are not at liberty to begin a new one."

To the first there is this to answer, that it is not at all to be wondered, that history gives us but a very little account of men that lived together in the state of nature. The inconveniences of that condition, and the love and want of society, no sooner brought any number of them together, but they presently united and incorporated, if they designed to continue together. And if we may not suppose men ever to have been in the state of nature, because we hear not much of them in such a state, we may as well suppose the armies of Salmanasser or Xerxes were never children, because we hear little of them till they were men, and embodied in armies.

Government is every where antecedent to records, and letters seldom come in amongst a people till a long continuation of civil society has, by other more necessary arts, provided for their safety, ease, and plenty: and then they begin to look after the history of their founders, and search into their original, when they have outlived the memory of it: for it is with commonwealths as with particular persons, they are commonly ignorant of their own births and infancies: and if they know any thing of their original, they are beholden for it to the accidental records that others have kept of it. And those that we have of the beginning of any politics in the world, excepting that of the Jews, where God himself immediately interposed, and which favours not at all paternal dominion, are all either plain instances of such a beginning as I have mentioned, or at least have manifest footsteps of it.

He must show a strange inclination to deny evident matter of fact, when it agrees not with his hypothesis, who will not allow, that the beginnings of Rome and Venice were by the uniting together of several men free and independent one of another, amongst whom there was no natural superiority or subjection. And if Josephus Acosta's word may be taken, he tells us, that in many parts of America there was no government at all. "There are great and apparent conjectures," says he, "that these men, speaking of those of Peru, for a long time had neither kings nor commonwealths, but lived in troops, as they do this day in Florida, the Cheriquanas, those of Brasil, and many other nations, which have no certain kings, but as occasion is offered, in peace or war, they choose their captains as they please," l. i. c. 25. If it be said that every man there was born subject to his father, or the head of his family; that the subjection due from a child to a father took not away his freedom of uniting into what political society he thought fit, has been already proved. But be that as it will, these men, it is evident, were actually free; and whatever superiority some politicians now would place in any of them, they themselves claimed it not, but by consent were all equal, till by the same consent they set rulers over themselves. So that their politic societies all began from a voluntary union, and the mutual agreement of men freely acting in the choice of their governors and forms of government.

And I hope those who went away from Sparta with Palantus, mentioned by Justin, l. iii. c. 4, will be allowed to have been freemen, independent one of another, and to have set up a government over themselves, by their own consent. Thus I have given several examples out of history, of people free and in the state of nature, that being met together incorporated and began a commonwealth. And if the want of such instances be an argument to prove that governments were not, nor could not be so begun, I suppose the contenders for paternal empire were better let it alone than urge it against natural liberty: for if they can give so many instances out of history, of governments begun upon paternal right, I think (though at best an argument from what has been, to what should of right be, has no great force) one might, without any great danger, yield them the cause. But if I might advise them in the case, they would do well not to search too much into the original of governments, as they have begun *de facto;* lest they should find, at the foundation of most of them, something very little favourable to the design they promote, and such a power as they contend for.

But to conclude, reason being plain on our side, that men are naturally free, and the examples of history showing, that the governments of the world, that were begun in peace, had their beginning laid on that foundation, and were made by the consent of the people; there can be little room for doubt, either where the right is, or what has been the opinion or practice of mankind about the first erecting of governments.

93. *Two Treatises*, II, sections 124–31

The great and chief end, therefore, of men's uniting into commonwealths, and putting themselves under government, is the preservation of their property. To which in the state of nature there are many things wanting.

First, There wants an established, settled, known law, received and allowed by common consent to be the standard of right and wrong, and the common measure to decide all controversies between them: for though the law of nature be plain and intelligible to all rational creatures; yet men being biassed by their interest, as well as ignorant for want of studying it, are not apt to allow of it as a law binding to them in the application of it to their particular cases.

Secondly, In the state of nature there wants a known and indifferent judge, with authority to determine all differences according to the established law: for every one in that state being both judge and executioner of the law of nature, men being partial to themselves, passion and revenge is very apt to carry them too far, and with too much heat, in their own cases; as well as negligence and unconcernedness, to make them too remiss in other men's.

Thirdly, In the state of nature there often wants power to back and support the sentence when right, and to give it due execution. They who by any injustice offend, will seldom fail, where they are able, by force to make good their injustice; such resistance many times makes the punishment dangerous, and frequently destructive to those who attempt it.

Thus mankind, notwithstanding all the privileges of the state of nature, being but in an ill condition, while they remain in it, are quickly driven into society. Hence it comes to pass, that we seldom find any number of men live any time together in this state. The inconveniences that they are therein exposed to, by the irregular and uncertain exercise of the power every man has of punishing the transgressions of others, make them take sanctuary under the established laws of government, and therein seek the preservation of their property. It is this makes them so willingly give up every one his single power of punishing, to be exercised by such alone as shall be appointed to it amongst them; and by such rules as the community, or those authorized by them to that purpose, shall agree on. And in this we have the original right of both the legislative and executive power, as well as of the governments and societies themselves.

For in the state of nature, to omit the liberty he has of innocent delights, a man has two powers.

The first is to do whatsoever he thinks fit for the preservation of himself and others within the permission of the law of nature: by which law, common to them all, he and all the rest of mankind are one community, make up one society, distinct from all other creatures. And, were it not for the corruption and viciousness of degenerate men, there would be no need of any other; no necessity that men should separate from this great and natural community, and by positive agreements combine into smaller and divided associations.

The other power a man has in the state of nature, is the power to punish the crimes committed against that law. Both these he gives up when he joins in a private, if I may so call it, or particular politic society, and incorporates into any commonwealth, separate from the rest of mankind.

The first power, viz. "of doing whatsoever he thought fit for the preservation of himself" and the rest of mankind, he gives up to be regulated by laws made by the society, so far forth as the preservation of himself and the rest of that society shall require; which laws of the society in many things confine the liberty he had by the law of nature.

Secondly, The power of punishing he wholly gives up, and engages his natural force (which he might before employ in the execution of the law of nature, by his own single authority, as he thought fit), to assist the executive power of the society, as the law thereof shall require: for being now in a new state, wherein he is to enjoy many conveniencies, from the labour, assistance, and society of others in the same community, as well as protection from its whole strength; he is to part also with as much of his natural liberty, in providing for himself, as the good, prosperity, and safety of the society shall require; which is not only necessary, but just, since the other members of the society do the like.

But though men, when they enter into society, give up the equality, liberty, and executive power they had in the state of nature, into the hands of the society, to be so far disposed of by the legislative as the good of the society shall require; yet it being only with an intention in every one the better to preserve himself, his liberty and property (for no rational creature can be supposed to change his condition with an intention to be worse); the power of the society, or legislative constituted by them, can never be supposed to extend farther than the common good; but is obliged to secure every one's property, by providing against those three defects above-mentioned, that made the state of nature so unsafe and uneasy. And so whoever has the legislative or supreme power of any commonwealth, is bound to govern by established standing laws, promulgated and known to the people, and not by extemporary decrees; by indifferent and upright judges, who are to decide controversies by those laws; and to employ the force of the community at home, only in the execution of such laws; or abroad to prevent or redress foreign injuries, and secure the community from inroads and invasion. And all this to be directed to no other end but the peace, safety, and public good of the people.

> Preservation of life, liberty, and property is the main purpose and function of civil society. Locke has given his reasons for saying this purpose can best be achieved within civil society. The move from the state of nature (whether conceived as a historical or only a conceptual move) to civil society is marked by a loss of some individual rights and powers. It is a move from individ-

uality to communality. A problem immediately confronted
Locke concerning his identification of preservation of
property as one of the goals of civil society, for the meat and
drink to be found in nature were not given to individuals.
God has given the earth to mankind in common. This being
supposed, Locke observes, "it seems to some a very great
difficulty how any one should ever come to have a property
in anything." The announced aim of his discussion of property is to 'show how men might come to have a property
in several parts of that which God gave to mankind in
common, and that without any express compact of all the
commoners." There must be some way, some right way, in
which each individual can appropriate the food and drink
needed for his own survival. But how, if all is common, can
we justify appropriation by individuals?

Locke's solution lies in the notion that every "man
has a property in his own person." Thus, we do not start
off with commonness and then seek to justify division. We
begin with private, personal property in our person.
Whether Locke's extended account of the person in the
Essay has prepared the way for such a bold concept, or
whether this notion of my person as my possession is a
clever device to solve the puzzle about property, it does
enable Locke to develop an interesting defense of appropriation of property by the use of my person, by mixing
some of my property (strictly, the labor of my body and the
work of my hands) into that which is common. The account
that follows has been seen as a defense of the landed
gentry, as containing the seeds of individualistic capitalism,
and as a simple labor theory of value. It is easy for us to
see, in Locke's stress on property as the basis for civil
society, some of the anticipations of the later developments
in Western societies; but it is probably wise to keep in mind
that, however we view his account of property, it was
offered against the background of his concept of the person,
and in the context of a strong stress upon education and
training for virtue. The moral person is what education
nurtures; it is also the object of concern in the family, in
the church, and in the political society.

94. *Two Treatises*, II, sections 25–39
Whether we consider natural reason, which tells us that men being
once born have a right to their preservation, and consequently

to meat and drink and such other things as nature affords for their subsistence; or Revelation, which gives us an account of those grants God made of the world to Adam, and to Noah, and his sons; it is very clear, that God, as king David says, Psal. cxv. 16, "has given the earth to the children of men"; given it to mankind in common. But this being supposed, it seems to some a very great difficulty how any one should ever come to have a property in any thing: I will not content myself to answer, that if it be difficult to make out property, upon a supposition that God gave the world to Adam and his posterity in common, it is impossible that any man, but one universal monarch, should have any property, upon a supposition that God gave the world to Adam, and his heirs in succession, exclusive of all the rest of his posterity. But I shall endeavour to show how men might come to have a property in several parts of that which God gave to mankind in common, and that without any express compact of all the commoners.

God, who hath given the world to men in common, hath also given them reason to make use of it to the best advantage of life and convenience. The earth, and all that is therein, is given to men for the support and comfort of their being. And though all the fruits it naturally produces, and beasts it feeds, belong to mankind in common, as they are produced by the spontaneous hand of nature; and nobody has originally a private dominion, exclusive of the rest of mankind, in any of them, as they are thus in their natural state: yet being given for the use of men, there must of necessity be a means to appropriate them some way or other before they can be of any use, or at all beneficial to any particular man. The fruit, or venison, which nourishes the wild Indian, who knows no enclosure, and is still a tenant in common, must be his, and so his, i. e. a part of him, that another can no longer have any right to it, before it can do him any good for the support of his life.

Though the earth, and all inferior creatures, be common to all men, yet every man has a property in his own person: this nobody has any right to but himself. The labour of his body, and the work of his hands, we may say, are properly his. Whatsoever then he removes out of the state that nature hath provided, and left it in, he hath mixed his labour with, and joined to it something that is his own, and thereby makes it his property. It being by him removed from the common state nature hath placed it in, it hath by this labour something annexed to it that excludes the common right of other men. For this labour being the unquestionable property of the labourer, no man but he can have a right to what that is once joined to, at least where there is enough, and as good, left in common for others.

He that is nourished by the acorns he picked up under an oak, or the apples he gathered from the trees in the wood, has certainly appropriated them to himself. Nobody can deny but the nourishment is his. I ask then, when did they begin to be his? when he digested? or when he ate? or when he boiled? or when he brought them home? or when he picked them up? and it is plain, if the first gathering made them not his, nothing else could. That labour put a distinction between them and common: that added something to them more than nature, the common mother of all, had done; and so they became his private right. And will any one say, he had no right to those acorns or apples he thus appropriated, because he had not the consent of all mankind to make them his? was it a robbery thus to assume to himself what belonged to all in common? If such a consent as that was necessary, man had starved, notwithstanding the plenty God had given him. We see in commons, which remain so by compact, that it is the taking any part of what is common, and removing it out of the state nature leaves it in, which begins the property; without which the common is of no use. And the taking of this or that part does not depend on the express consent of all the commoners. Thus the grass my horse has bit; the turfs my servant has cut; and the ore I have digged in any place, where I have a right to them in common with others; become my property, without the assignation or consent of any body. The labour that was mine, removing them out of that common state they were in, hath fixed my property in them.

By making an explicit consent of every commoner necessary to any one's appropriating to himself any part of what is given in common, children or servants could not cut the meat, which their father or master had provided for them in common, without assigning to every one his peculiar part. Though the water running in the fountain be every one's, yet who can doubt but that in the pitcher is his only who drew it out? His labour hath taken it out of the hands of nature, where it was common, and belonged equally to all her children, and hath thereby appropriated it to himself.

Thus this law of reason makes the deer that Indian's who hath killed it; it is allowed to be his goods who hath bestowed his labour upon it, though before it was the common right of every one. And amongst those who are counted the civilized part of mankind, who have made and multiplied positive laws to determine property, this original law of nature, for the beginning of property, in what was before common, still takes place; and by virtue thereof, what fish any one catches in the ocean, that great and still remaining common of mankind; or what ambergris any one takes up here, is by the labour that removes it out of that common state nature left it in made his property who takes that pains about it. And even amongst us, the hare that any one is hunting is thought his who pursues her during the chase: for being a beast that is still looked upon as common, and no man's private possession; whoever has employed so much labour about any of that kind, as to find and pursue her, has thereby removed her from the state of nature, wherein she was common, and hath begun a property.

It will perhaps be objected to this, that "if gathering the acorns, or other fruits of the earth, &c. makes a right to them, then any one may engross as much as he will." To which I answer, Not so. The same law of nature, that does by this means give us property, does also bound that property too. "God has given us all things richly," 1 Tim. vi. 17, is the voice of reason confirmed by inspiration. But how far has he given it us? To enjoy. As much as any one can make use of to any advantage of life before it spoils, so much he may by his labour fix a property in: whatever is beyond this, is more than his share, and belongs to others. Nothing was made by God for man to spoil or destroy. And thus, considering the plenty of natural provisions there was a long time in the world, and the few spenders; and to how small a part of that provision the industry of one man could extend itself, and engross it to the prejudice of others; especially keeping within the bounds, set by reason, of what might serve for his use; there could be then little room for quarrels or contentions about property so established.

But the chief matter of property being now not the fruits of the earth, and the beasts that subsist on it, but the earth itself; as that which takes in, and carries with it all the rest; I think it is plain, that property in that too is acquired as the former. As much land as a man tills, plants, improves, cultivates, and can use the product of, so much is his property. He by his labour does, as it were, enclose it from the common. Nor will it invalidate his right, to say every body else has an equal title to it, and therefore he cannot appropriate, he cannot enclose, without the consent of all his fellow-commoners, all mankind. God, when he gave the world in common to all mankind, commanded man also to labour, and the penury of his condition required it of him. God and his reason commanded him to subdue the earth, i.e. improve it for the benefit of life, and therein lay out something upon it that was his own, his labour. He that, in obedience to this command of God, subdued, tilled, and sowed any part of it, thereby annexed to it something that was his property, which another had no title to, nor could without injury take from him.

Nor was this appropriation of any parcel of land, by improving it, any prejudice to any other man, since there was still enough, and as good left; and more than the yet unprovided could use. So that, in effect, there was never the less left for others because of his enclosure for himself: for he that leaves as much as another can make use of, does as good as take nothing at all. Nobody could think himself injured by the drinking of another man, though he took a good draught, who had a whole river of the same water left him to quench his thirst; and the case of land and water, where there is enough of both, is perfectly the same.

God gave the world to men in common; but since he gave it them for their benefit, and the greatest conveniencies of life they were capable to draw from it, it cannot be supposed he meant it should always remain common and uncultivated. He gave it to the use of the industrious and rational (and labour was to be his title to it), not to the fancy or covetousness of the quarrelsome and contentious. He that had as good left for his improvement as was already taken up, needed not complain, ought not to meddle with what was already improved by another's labour: if he did, it is plain he desired the benefit of another's pains, which he had no right to, and not the ground which God had given him in common with others to labour on, and whereof there was as good left as that already possessed, and more than he knew what to do with, or his industry could reach to.

It is true, in land that is common in England, or any other country, where there is plenty of people under government, who have money and commerce, no one can enclose or appropriate any part without the consent of all his fellow-commoners; because this is left common by compact, i. e. by the law of the land, which is not to be violated. And though it be common, in respect of some men, it is not so to all mankind, but is the joint property of this county, or this parish. Besides, the remainder, after such enclosure, would not be as good to the rest of the commoners as the whole was when they could all make use of the whole; whereas in the beginning and first peopling of the great common of the world it was quite otherwise. The law man was under was rather for appropriating. God commanded, and his wants forced him to labour.

That was his property which could not be taken from him wherever he had fixed it. And hence subduing or cultivating the earth, and having dominion, we see are joined together. The one gave title to the other. So that God, by commanding to subdue, gave authority so far to appropriate: and the condition of human life, which requires labour and materials to work on, necessarily introduces private possessions.

The measure of property nature has well set by the extent of men's labour and the conveniencies of life: no man's labour could subdue, or appropriate all; nor could his enjoyment consume more than a small part; so that it was impossible for any man, this way, to intrench upon the right of another, or acquire to himself a property, to the prejudice of his neighbour, who would still have room for as good and as large a possession (after the other had taken out his) as before it was appropriated. This measure did confine every man's possession to a very moderate proportion, and such as he might appropriate to himself, without injury to any body, in the first ages of the world, when men were more in danger to be lost, by wandering from their company, in the then vast wilderness of the earth, than to be straitened for want of room to plant in. And the same measure may be allowed still without prejudice to any body, as full as the world seems: for supposing a man, or family, in the state they were at first peopling of the world by the children of Adam, or Noah; let him plant in some inland, vacant places of America, we shall find that the possessions he could make himself, upon the measures we have given, would not be very large, nor, even to this day, prejudice the rest of mankind, or give them reason to complain, or think themselves injured by this man's encroachment; though the race of men have now spread themselves to all the corners of the world, and do infinitely exceed the small number was at the beginning. Nay, the extent of ground is of so little value, without labour, that I have heard it affirmed, that in Spain itself a man may be permitted to plough, sow, and reap, without being disturbed, upon land he has no other title to, but only his making use of it. But, on the contrary, the inhabitants think themselves beholden to him, who, by his industry on neglected, and consequently waste land, has increased the stock of corn, which they wanted. But be this as it will, which I lay no stress on; this I dare boldly affirm, that the same rule of propriety, viz. that every man should have as much as he could make use of, would hold still in the world, without straitening any body; since there is land enough in the world to suffice double the inhabitants, had not the invention of money, and the tacit agreement of men to put a value on it, introduced (by consent) larger possessions, and a right to them; which, how it has done, I shall by and by show more at large.

This is certain, that in the beginning, before the desire of having more than man needed had altered the intrinsic value of things, which depends only on their usefulness to the life of man; or had agreed, that a little piece of yellow metal, which would keep without wasting or decay, should be worth a great piece of flesh, or a whole heap of corn; though men had a right to appropriate, by their labour, each one to himself, as much of the things of nature as he could use: yet this could not be much, nor to the prejudice of others, where the same plenty was still left to those who would use the same industry. To which let me add, that he who appropriates land to himself by his labour, does not lessen, but increase the common stock of mankind: for the provisions serving to the support of human life, produced by one acre of enclosed and cultivated land, are (to speak much within compass) ten times more than those which are yielded by an acre of land of an equal richness lying waste in common. And therefore he that encloses land, and has a greater plenty of the conveniencies of life from ten acres, than he could have from an hundred left to nature, may truly be said to give ninety acres to mankind: for his labour now supplies him with provisions out of ten acres, which were by the product of an hundred lying in common. I have here rated the improved land very low, in making its product but as ten to one, when it is much nearer an hundred to one: for I ask, whether in the wild woods and uncultivated waste of America, left to nature, without any improvement, tillage, or husbandry, a thousand acres yield the needy and wretched inhabitants as many conveniencies of life as ten acres equally fertile land do in Devonshire, where they are well cultivated?

Before the appropriation of land, he who gathered as much of the wild fruit, killed, caught, or tamed, as many of the beasts, as he could; he that so employed his pains about any of the spontaneous products of nature, as any way to alter them from the state which nature put them in, by placing any of his labour on them, did thereby acquire a propriety in them: but if they perished, in his possession, without their due use; if the fruits rotted, or the venison putrefied, before he could spend it; he offended against the common law of nature, and was liable to be punished; he invaded his neighbour's share, for he had no right, farther than his use called for any of them, and they might serve to afford him conveniencies of life.

The same measures governed the possession of land too: whatsoever he tilled and reaped, laid up and made use of, before it spoiled, that was his peculiar right; whatsoever he enclosed, and could feed, and make use of, the cattle and product was also his. But if either the grass of his enclosure rotted on the ground, or the fruit of his planting perished without gathering and laying up; this part of the earth, notwithstanding his enclosure, was still to be looked on as waste, and might be the possession of any other. Thus, at the beginning, Cain might take as much ground as he could till, and make it his own land, and yet leave enough to Abel's sheep to feed on; a few acres would serve for both their possessions. But as families increased, and industry enlarged their stocks, their possessions enlarged with the need of them; but yet it was commonly without any fixed property in the ground they made use of, till they incorporated, settled themselves together, and built cities; and then, by consent, they came in time to set out the bounds of their distinct territories, and agree on limits between them and their neighbours; and by laws within themselves settled the properties of those of the same society: for we see that in that part of the world which was first inhabited, and therefore like to be best peopled, even as low down as Abraham's time, they wandered with their flocks, and their herds, which was their substance, freely up and down; and this Abraham did, in a country where he was a stranger. Whence it is plain, that at least a great part of the land lay in common; that the inhabitants valued it not, nor claimed property in any more than they made use of. But when there was not room enough in the same place for their herds to feed together, they by consent, as Abraham and Lot did, Gen. xiii. 5, separated and enlarged their pasture, where it best liked them. And for the same reason Esau went from his father, and his brother, and planted in mount Seir, Gen. xxxvi. 6.

And thus, without supposing any private dominion and property in Adam, over all the world, exclusive of all other men, which can no way be proved, nor any one's property be made out from it; but supposing the world given, as it was, to the children of men in common, we see how labour could make men distinct titles to several parcels of it, for their private uses; wherein there could be no doubt of right, no room for quarrel.

Political obligation and consent

By his actions on the land and the produce of the land, the individual person appropriates for himself some property out of what was common. Such appropriation is not an action that needs to be itemized in a contract. Its justification lies in the fact of my person and my actions. Locke's solution of the puzzle, how privacy can arise out of what is common, is offered more in the spirit of a logical or conceptual resolution than it is as political argument for property. But since one of the main purposes of civil society is the protection of property, property acquires political status. By uniting with others into civil society – into a society whose function is the protection of person and property – I and my possessions become "subject to the government and dominion of that commonwealth as long as it hath a being." Use of the land within the commonwealth puts me under the jurisdiction of the government of that commonwealth. Use of such land involves a *tacit* consent to obey the laws and customs of that society.

Consent for Locke is the origin of obligation in the civil society. The notion of tacit consent may not be entirely clear, but when I consent to enter into such a society, or when I consent with others to form such a society, I am putting myself under an obligation "to every one of that society, to submit to the determination of the majority, and to be concluded by it." Locke uses the metaphor of the body politic, acting as one body under "the will and determination of the majority." The alternative to majority rule is the consent of every individual in the society given singly. This alternative is difficult to achieve, therefore the actions of the majority must be taken as the acts of the whole society.

How are the acts of the whole to be performed? Locke details a governmental structure whose function it is to carry out the acts of the society: a legislative (which contains the supreme power of the community), an executive (which has the prerogative to act for the public good, even in the absence of explicit laws), and so on.

95. *Two Treatises*, II, sections 95–9, 119–23

Men being, as has been said, by nature all free, equal, and independent, no one can be put out of this estate, and subjected to the political power of another, without his own consent. The only way whereby any one divests himself of his natural liberty, and puts on the bonds of civil society, is by agreeing with other men to join and unite into a community, for their comfortable, safe, and peaceable living one amongst another, in a secure enjoyment of their properties, and a greater security against any that are not of it. This any number of men may do, because it injures not the freedom of the rest; they are left as they were in the liberty of the state of nature. When any number of men have so consented to make one community or government, they are thereby presently incorporated, and make one body politic, wherein the majority have a right to act and conclude the rest.

For when any number of men have, by the consent of every individual, made a community, they have thereby made that community one body, with a power to act as one body, which is only by the will and determination of the majority; for that which acts any community being only the consent of the individuals of it, and it being necessary to that which is one body to move one way; it is necessary the body should move that way whither the greater force carries it, which is the consent of the majority: or else it is impossible it should act or continue one body, one community, which the consent of every individual that united into it agreed that it should; and so every one is bound by that consent to be concluded by the majority. And therefore we see that in assemblies, empowered to act by positive laws, where no number is set by that positive law which empowers them, the act of the majority passes for the act of the whole, and of course determines; as having, by the law of nature and reason, the power of the whole.

And thus every man, by consenting with others to make one body politic under one government, puts himself under an obligation to every one of that society to submit to the determination of the majority, and to be concluded by it; or else this original compact, whereby he with others incorporate into one society, would signify nothing, and be no compact, if he be left free, and under no other ties than he was in before in the state of nature. For what appearance would there be of any compact? what new engagement, if he were no farther tied by any decrees of the society than he himself thought fit, and did actually consent to? This would be still as great a liberty as he himself had before his compact, or any one else in the state of nature hath, who may submit himself and consent to any acts of it if he thinks fit.

For if the consent of the majority shall not, in reason, be received as the act of the whole, and conclude every individual, nothing but the consent of every individual can make any thing to be the act of the whole: but such a consent is next to impossible ever to be had, if we consider the infirmities of health, and avocations of business, which in a number, though much less than that of a commonwealth, will necessarily keep many away from the public assembly. To which if we add the variety of opinions, and contrariety of interests which unavoidably happen in all collections of men, the coming into society upon such terms would be only like Cato's coming into the theatre, only to go out again. Such a constitution as this would make the mighty leviathan of a shorter duration than the feeblest creatures, and not let it outlast the day it was born in: which cannot be supposed, till we can think that rational creatures should desire and constitute societies only to be dissolved: for where the majority cannot conclude the rest, there they cannot act as one body, and consequently will be immediately dissolved again.

Whosoever therefore out of a state of nature unite into a community, must be understood to give up all the power necessary to the ends for which they unite into society, to the majority of the community, unless they expressly agreed in any number greater than the majority. And this is done by barely agreeing to unite into one political society, which is all the compact that is, or needs be, between the individuals that enter into, or make up a commonwealth. And thus that which begins and actually constitutes any political society, is nothing but the consent of any number of freemen capable of a majority, to unite and incorporate into such a society. And this is that, and that only, which did or could give beginning to any lawful government in the world.

Every man being, as has been showed, naturally free, and nothing being able to put him into subjection to any earthly power, but only his own consent; it is to be considered, what shall be understood to be a sufficient declaration of a man's consent, to make him subject to the laws of any government. There is a common distinction of an express and a tacit consent, which will concern our present case. Nobody doubts but an express consent of any man entering into any society, makes him a perfect member of that society, a subject of that government. The difficulty is, what ought to be looked upon as a tacit consent, and how far it binds, i. e. how far any one shall be looked on to have consented, and thereby submitted to any government, where he has made no expressions of it at all. And to this I say, that every man, that hath any possessions, or enjoyment of any part of the dominions of any government, doth thereby give his tacit consent, and is as far forth obliged to obedience to the laws of that government, during such enjoyment, as any one under it; whether this his possession be of land, to him and his heirs for ever, or a lodging only for a week; or whether it be barely travelling freely on the highway; and, in effect, it reaches as far as the very being of any one within the territories of that government.

To understand this the better, it is fit to consider, that every man, when he at first incorporates himself into any commonwealth, he, by his uniting himself thereunto, annexes also, and submits to the community those possessions which he has, or shall acquire, that do not already belong to any other government: for it would be a direct contradiction for any one to enter into society with others for the securing and regulating of property, and yet to suppose his land, whose property is to be regulated by the laws of the society, should be exempt from the jurisdiction of that government, to which he himself, the proprietor of the land, is a subject. By the same act therefore, whereby any one unites his person, which was before free, to any commonwealth, by the same he unites his possessions, which were before free, to it also: and they become, both of them, person and possession, subject to the government and dominion of that commonwealth, as long as it hath a being. Whoever, therefore, from thenceforth, by inheritance, purchase, permission, or otherways, enjoys any part of the land so annexed to, and under the government of that commonwealth, must take it with the condition it is under; that is, of submitting to the government of the commonwealth, under whose jurisdiction it is, as far forth as any subject of it.

But since the government has a direct jurisdiction only over the land, and reaches the possessor of it (before he has actually incorporated himself in the society) only as he dwells upon, and enjoys that; the obligation any one is under, by virtue of such enjoyment, to "submit to the government, begins and ends with the enjoyment": so that whenever the owner, who has given nothing but such a tacit consent to the government, will, by donation, sale, or otherwise, quit the said possession, he is at liberty to go and incorporate himself into any other commonwealth; or to agree with others to begin a new one, in *vacuis locis,* in any part of the world they can find free and unpossessed: whereas he that has once, by actual agreement, and any express declaration, given his consent to be of any commonwealth, is perpetually and indispensably obliged to be, and remain unalterably a subject to it, and can never be again in the liberty of the state of nature; unless, by any calamity, the government he was under comes to be dissolved, or else by some public act cuts him off from being any longer a member of it.

But submitting to the laws of any country, living quietly, and enjoying privileges and protection under them, makes not a man a member of that society: this is only a local protection and homage due to and from all those, who, not being in a state of war, come within the territories belonging to any government, to all parts whereof the force of its laws extends. But this no more makes a man a member of that society, a perpetual subject of that commonwealth, than it would make a man a subject to another, in whose family he found it convenient to abide for some time; though, whilst he continued in it, he were obliged to comply with the laws, and submit to the government he found there. And thus we see, that foreigners, by living all their lives under another government, and enjoying the privileges and protection of it, though they are bound, even in conscience, to submit to its administration, as far forth as any denison; yet do not thereby come to be subjects or members of that commonwealth. Nothing can make any man so, but his actually entering into it by positive engagement, and express promise and compact. This is that which I think concerning the beginning of political societies, and that consent which makes any one a member of any commonwealth.

If man in the state of nature be so free as has been said; if he be absolute lord of his own person and possessions, equal to the greatest, and subject to nobody, why will he part with his freedom, why will he give up this empire, and subject himself to the dominion and control of any other power? To which it is obvious to answer, that though in the state of nature he hath such a right, yet the enjoyment of it is very uncertain, and constantly exposed to the invasion of others; for all being kings as much as he, every man his equal, and the greater part no strict observers of equity and justice, the enjoyment of the property he has in this state is very unsafe, very unsecure. This makes him willing to quit a condition, which, however free, is full of fears and continual dangers: and it is not without reason that he seeks out, and is willing to join in society with others, who are already united, or have a mind to unite, for the mutual preservation of their lives, liberties, and estates, which I call by the general name property.

96. *Two Treatises*, II, sections 134–8

The great end of men's entering into society being the enjoyment of their properties in peace and safety, and the great instrument and means of that being the laws established in that society; the first and fundamental positive law of all commonwealths is the establishing of the legislative power; as the first and fundamental natural law, which is to govern even the legislative itself, is the preservation of the society, and (as far as will consist with the public good) of every person in it. This legislative is not only the supreme power of the commonwealth, but sacred and unalterable in the hands where the community have once placed it; nor can any edict of any body else, in what form soever conceived, or by what power soever backed, have the force and obligation of a law, which has not its sanction from that legislative which the public has chosen and appointed: for without this the law could not have that which is absolutely necessary to its being a law, the consent of the society; over whom nobody can have a power to make laws, but by their own consent, and by authority received from them. And therefore all the obedience, which by the most solemn ties any one can be obliged to pay, ultimately terminates in this supreme power, and is directed by those laws which it enacts: nor can any oaths to any foreign power whatsoever, or any domestic subordinate power, discharge any member of the society from his obedience to the legislative, acting pursuant to their trust; nor oblige him to any obedience contrary to the laws so enacted, or farther than they do allow; it being ridiculous to imagine one can be tied ultimately to obey any power in the society which is not supreme.

Though the legislative, whether placed in one or more, whether it be always in being, or only by intervals, though it be the supreme power in every commonwealth; yet,

First, It is not, nor can possibly be absolutely arbitrary over the lives and fortunes of the people: for it being but the joint power of every member of the society given up to that person or assembly which is legislator; it can be no more than those persons had in a state of nature before they entered into society, and gave up to the community: for nobody can transfer to another more power than he has in himself; and nobody has an absolute arbitrary power over himself, or over any other, to destroy his own life, or take away the life or property of another. A man, as has been proved, cannot subject himself to the arbitrary power of another;

and having in the state of nature no arbitrary power over the life, liberty, or possession of another, but only so much as the law of nature gave him for the preservation of himself and the rest of mankind; this is all he doth, or can give up to the commonwealth, and by it to the legislative power, so that the legislative can have no more than this. Their power, in the utmost bounds of it, is limited to the public good of the society. It is a power that hath no other end but preservation, and therefore can never have a right to destroy, enslave, or designedly to impoverish the subjects. The obligations of the law of nature cease not in society, but only in many cases are drawn closer, and have by human laws known penalties annexed to them, to enforce their observation. Thus the law of nature stands as an eternal rule to all men, legislators as well as others. The rules that they make for other men's actions must, as well as their own and other men's actions be comformable to the law of nature, i. e. to the will of God, of which that is a declaration; and the "fundamental law of nature being the preservation of mankind," no human sanction can be good or valid against it.

The legislative or supreme authority cannot assume to itself a power to rule by extemporary, arbitrary decrees; but is bound to dispense justice, and to decide the rights of the subject, by promulgated, standing laws, and known authorized judges. For the law of nature being unwritten, and so nowhere to be found, but in the minds of men, they who, through passion, or interest, shall miscite, or misapply it, cannot so easily be convinced of their mistake, where there is no established judge: and so it serves not, as it ought, to determine the rights, and fence the properties of those that live under it; especially where every one is judge, interpreter, and executioner of it too, and that in his own case: and he that has right on his side, having ordinarily but his own single strength, hath not force enough to defend himself from injuries, or to punish delinquents. To avoid these inconveniencies, which disorder men's properties in the state of nature, men unite into societies, that they may have the united strength of the whole society to secure and defend their properties, and may have standing rules to bound it, by which every one may know what is his. To this end it is that men give up all their natural power to the society which they enter into, and the community put the legislative power into such hands as they think fit; with this trust, that they shall be governed by declared laws, or else their peace, quiet, and property will still be at the same uncertainty as it was in the state of nature.

Absolute arbitrary power, or governing without settled standing laws, can neither of them consist with the ends of society and government, which men would not quit the freedom of the state of nature for, and tie themselves up under, were it not to preserve their lives, liberties, and fortunes, and by stated rules of right and property to secure their peace and quiet. It cannot be supposed that they should intend, had they a power so to do, to give to any one, or more, an absolute arbitrary power over their persons and estates, and put a force into the magistrate's hand to execute his unlimited will arbitrarily upon them. This were to put themselves into a worse condition than the state of nature, wherein they had a liberty to defend their right against the injuries of others, and were upon equal terms of force to maintain it, whether invaded by a single man, or many in combination. Whereas by supposing they have given up themselves to the absolute arbitrary power and will of a legislator, they have disarmed themselves, and armed him, to make a prey of them when he pleases; he being in a much worse condition, who is exposed to the arbitrary power of one man, who has the command of 100,000, than he that is exposed to the arbitrary power of 100,000 single men; nobody being secure that his will, who has such a command, is better than that of other men, though his force be 100,000 times stronger. And therefore, whatever form the commonwealth is under, the ruling power ought to govern by declared and received laws, and not by extemporary dictates and undetermined resolutions; for then mankind will be in a far worse condition than in the state of nature, if they shall have armed one or a few men with the joint power of a multitude, to force them to obey at pleasure the exorbitant and unlimited degrees of their sudden thoughts, or unrestrained, and till that moment unknown wills, without having any measures set down which may guide and justify their actions: for all the power the government has being only for the good of the society, as it ought not to be arbitrary and at pleasure, so it ought to be exercised by established and promulgated laws; that both the people may know their duty, and be safe and secure within the limits of the law; and the rulers too kept within their bounds, and not be tempted, by the power they have in their hands, to employ it to such purposes, and by such measures, as they would not have known, and own not willingly.

Thirdly, The supreme power cannot take from any man part of his property without his own consent: for the preservation of property being the end of government, and that for which men enter into society, it necessarily supposes and requires, that the people should have property, without which they must be supposed to lose that, by entering into society, which was the end for which they entered into it; too gross an absurdity for any man to own. Men therefore in society having property, they have such right to the goods, which by the law of the community are theirs, that nobody hath a right to take their substance or any part of it from them, without their own consent; without this they have no property at all; for I have truly no property in that, which another can by right take from me, when he pleases, against my consent. Hence it is a mistake to think, that the supreme or legislative power of any commonwealth can do what it will, and dispose of the estates of the subject arbitrarily, or take any part of them at pleasure. This is not much to be feared in governments where the legislative consists, wholly or in part, in assemblies which are variable, whose members, upon the dissolution of the assembly, are subjects under the common laws of their country, equally with the rest. But in governments where the legislative is in one lasting assembly always in being, or in one man, as in absolute monarchies, there is danger still that they will think themselves to have a distinct interest from the rest of the community; and so will be apt to increase their own riches and power, by taking what they think fit from the people: for a man's property is not at all secure, though there be good and equitable laws to set the bounds of it between him and his fellow-subjects, if he who commands those subjects have power to take from any private man what part he pleases of his property, and use and dispose of it as he thinks good.

97. *Two Treatises,* II, sections 159–64
Where the legislative and executive power are in distinct hands, (as they are in all moderated monarchies and well-framed governments) there the good of the society requires, that several things should be left to the discretion of him that has the executive power: for the legislators not being able to foresee, and provide by laws, for all that may be useful to the community, the executor of the laws having the power in his hands, has by the common law of nature a right to make use of it for the good of the society, in many cases, where the municipal law has given no direction, till the legislative can conveniently be assembled to provide for it. Many things there are, which the law can by no means provide for; and those must necessarily be left to the discretion of him that has

the executive power in his hands, to be ordered by him as the public good and advantage shall require: nay, it is fit that the laws themselves should in some cases give way to the executive power, or rather to this fundamental law of nature and government, viz. That, as much as may be, all the members of the society are to be preserved: for since many accidents may happen, wherein a strict and rigid observation of the laws may do harm; (as not to pull down an innocent man's house to stop the fire, when the next to it is burning) and a man may come sometimes within the reach of the law, which makes no distinction of persons, by an action that may deserve reward and pardon; it is fit the ruler should have a power, in many cases, to mitigate the severity of the law, and pardon some offenders: for the end of government being the preservation of all, as much as may be, even the guilty are to be spared, where it can prove no prejudice to the innocent.

This power to act according to discretion for the public good, without the prescription of the law, and sometimes even against it, is that which is called prerogative: for since in some governments the lawmaking power is not always in being, and is usually too numerous, and so too slow for the despatch requisite to execution; and because also it is impossible to foresee, and so by laws to provide for all accidents and necessities that may concern the public, or to make such laws as will do no harm, if they are executed with an inflexible rigour on all occasions, and upon all persons that may come in their way; therefore there is a latitude left to the executive power, to do many things of choice which the laws do not prescribe.

This power, whilst employed for the benefit of the community, and suitably to the trust and ends of the government, is undoubted prerogative, and never is questioned; for the people are very seldom or never scrupulous or nice in the point; they are far from examining prerogative, whilst it is in any tolerable degree employed for the use it was meant; that is, for the good of the people, and not manifestly against it: but if there comes to be a question between the executive power and the people, about a thing claimed as a prerogative, the tendency of the exercise of such prerogative to the good or hurt of the people will easily decide that question.

It is easy to conceive, that in the infancy of governments, when commonwealths differed little from families in number of people, they differed from them too but little in number of laws: and the governors being as the fathers of them, watching over them for their good, the government was almost all prerogative. A few established laws served the turn, and the discretion and care of the ruler supplied the rest. But when mistake or flattery prevailed with weak princes to make use of this power for private ends of their own, and not for the public good, the people were fain by express laws to get prerogative determined in those points wherein they found disadvantage from it: and thus declared limitations of prerogative were by the people found necessary in cases which they and their ancestors had left, in the utmost latitude, to the wisdom of those princes who made no other but a right use of it; that is, for the good of their people.

And therefore they have a very wrong notion of government, who say, that the people have encroached upon the prerogative, when they have got any part of it to be defined by positive laws: for in so doing they have not pulled from the prince any thing that of right belonged to him, but only declare, that that power which they indefinitely left in his or his ancestors' hands, to be exercised for their good, was not a thing which they intended him when he used it otherwise: for the end of government being the good of the community, whatsoever alterations are made in it, tending to that end, cannot be an encroachment upon any body, since nobody in government can have a right tending to any other end: and those only are encroachments which prejudice or hinder the public good. Those who say otherwise, speak as if the prince had a distinct and separate interest from the good of the community, and was not made for it; the root and source from which spring almost all those evils and disorders which happen in kingly governments. And indeed, if that be so, the people under his government are not a society of rational creatures, entered into a community for their mutual good; they are not such as have set rulers over themselves, to guard and promote that good; but are to be looked on as an herd of inferior creatures under the dominion of a master, who keeps them and works them for his own pleasure or profit. If men were so void of reason, and brutish, as to enter into society upon such terms, prerogative might indeed be, what some men would have it, an arbitrary power to do things hurtful to the people.

But since a rational creature cannot be supposed, when free, to put himself into subjection to another, for his own harm; (though, where he finds a good and wise ruler, he may not perhaps think it either necessary or useful to set precise bounds to his power in all things) prerogative can be nothing but the people's permitting their rulers to do several things, of their own free choice, where the law was silent, and sometimes too against the direct letter of the law, for the public good; and their acquiescing in it when so done: for as a good prince, who is mindful of the trust put into his hands, and careful of the good of his people, cannot have too much prerogative, that is, power to do good; so a weak and ill prince, who would claim that power which his predecessors exercised without the direction of the law, as a prerogative belonging to him by right of his office, which he may exercise at his pleasure, to make or promote an interest distinct from that of the public; gives the people an occasion to claim their right, and limit that power, which, whilst it was exercised for their good, they were content should be tacitly allowed.

The function of government is circumscribed by the limited ends for which civil society is formed, by the general prescription of the laws of nature, and by the consent of the governed who in relinquishing some of the powers they have in the state of nature, receive in return the protection of the society. Obligation flows both ways, from the governed to the legislative and executive, and vice versa. Implied in many things that Locke says, explicit in others, is the notion that the people keep a watching brief on the workings of government. Selection 97 shows Locke saying that, with respect to the actions of the executive that come under prerogative – those not specified by explicit laws – the people can quite properly interfere if the actions of the executive violate the basic principle of acting for the good of the people.

How can the people intervene? What mechanism is there for protests? While discussing the ways in which governments are dissolved (selection 98), Locke says that, if laws are made in civil society that do not fit the purposes for which that society was established, the authority for those laws has disappeared and the people "may constitute to themselves a new legislative." The power "devolves to the people" when the legislative or executive acts against their interests, in violation of the contract. Locke makes it clear that he is not saying that any time anyone thinks the legislative is acting contrary to the good of the members, dissent is justified, dissolution of the government is in order. He speaks of the special circumstances where those given the authority to rule have badly and on a large scale misused that authority. A person, whether he be a ruler misusing his authority or a member of society dissenting for personal or inadequate reasons, who disrupts the workings of society, is guilty of the highest crime. Such a person is no better than that common criminal who acts against the laws of nature and society: he is "the common enemy and pest of mankind, and is to be treated accordingly."

Does Locke's talk of the right of the people to dissolve the government, of power devolving to the people, amount to nice, theoretical words? Were those words, as it used to be thought, a justification for the 1688 changes in England, or, as Laslett has argued, were they a veiled call for changes prior to 1688?[29] Who is to determine when the misuse of authority by the legislative is sufficient to justify dissolution? How did Locke envisage that dissolution taking place? Locke put some of these questions to himself earlier in *Two Treatises* (selection 89). His answers there are disappointing to those who interpret him as providing for the devolution of powers to the people when the authority given by the people has been violated. If the magistrate believes his laws to be just and good, if he believes he acts within his authority, who, Locke asks, "shall be judge between them? I answer, God alone." True, in that context, Locke was raising the question of an individual's conscience, of what a single individual can or should do if he thinks the government is acting against its trust. There Locke seems to support civil disobedience: "such a private person is to abstain from the action that he judges unlawful, and he is to undergo the punishment which it is not unlawful for him to bear." Thus, God alone can judge the case of private dissent. The right of revolution may still be preserved, if the majority agree that their authority has been misused. There are, however, few details of how the dissolution of government under this condition could or should occur. The answer may be that

29 See Peter Laslett, *Two Treatises of Government. A Critical Edition with an Introduction and Apparatus Criticus* (Cambridge, 1960), Introduction, III.

his *Two Treatises* was not a handbook for political action
but a conceptual analysis of the principles upon which
he thought civil society should be founded and run.

98. *Two Treatises*, II, sections 212–30

Besides this overturning from without, governments are dissolved
from within.

First, When the legislative is altered. Civil society being a state
of peace, amongst those who are of it from whom the state of
war is excluded by the umpirage, which they have provided in
their legislative, for the ending all differences that may arise
amongst any of them; it is in their legislative, that the members
of a commonwealth are united, and combined together into one
coherent living body. This is the soul that gives form, life and unity
to the commonwealth: from hence the several members have their
mutual influence, sympathy, and connexion: and therefore, when
the legislative is broken or dissolved, dissolution and death follows: for, the essence and union of the society consisting in having
one will, the legislative, when once established by the majority,
has the declaring, and as it were keeping of that will. The constitution of the legislative is the first and fundamental act of society,
whereby provision is made for the continuation of their union,
under the direction of persons, and bonds of laws, made by persons
authorized thereunto, by the consent and appointment of the people; without which no one man, or number of men, amongst
them, can have authority of making laws that shall be binding to
the rest. When any one, or more, shall take upon them to make
laws, whom the people have not appointed so to do, they make
laws without authority, which the people are not therefore bound
to obey; by which means they come again to be out of subjection,
and may constitute to themselves a new legislative, as they think
best, being in full liberty to resist the force of those, who without
authority would impose any thing upon them. Every one is at the
disposure of his own will, when those who had, by the delegation of the society, the declaring of the public will, are excluded
from it, and others usurp the place, who have no such authority
or delegation.

This being usually brought about by such in the commonwealth
who misuse the power they have, it is hard to consider it aright,
and know at whose door to lay it, without knowing the form of
government in which it happens. Let us suppose then the legislative
placed in the concurrence of three distinct persons.

1. A single hereditary person, having the constant, supreme, executive power, and with it the power of convoking and dissolving the other two, within certain periods of time.

2. An assembly of hereditary nobility.

3. An assembly of representatives chosen, *pro tempore*, by the people. Such a form of government supposed, it is evident,

First, That when such a single person, or prince, sets up his own arbitrary will in place of the laws, which are the will of the society, declared by the legislative, then the legislative is changed: for that being in effect the legislative, whose rules and laws are put in execution, and required to be obeyed; when other laws are set up, and other rules pretended, and enforced, than what the legislative, constituted by the society, have enacted, it is plain that the legislative is changed. Whoever introduces new laws, not being thereunto authorized by the fundamental appointment of the society, or subverts the old, disowns and overturns the power by which they were made, and so sets up a new legislative.

Secondly, When the prince hinders the legislative from assembling in its due time, or from acting freely, pursuant to those ends for which it was constituted, the legislative is altered: for it is not a certain number of men, no, nor their meeting, unless they have also freedom of debating, and leisure of perfecting, what is for the good of the society, wherein the legislative consists: when these are taken away or altered, so as to deprive the society of the due exercise of their power, the legislative is truly altered: for it is not names that constitute governments, but the use and exercise of those powers that were intended to accompany them; so that he, who takes away the freedom, or hinders the acting of the legislative in its due seasons, in effect takes away the legislative, and puts an end to the government.

Thirdly, When, by the arbitrary power of the prince, the electors, or ways of election, are altered, without the consent, and contrary to the common interest of the people, there also the legislative is altered: for if others than those whom the society hath authorized thereunto, do choose, or in another way than what the society hath prescribed, those chosen are not the legislative appointed by the people.

Fourthly, The delivery also of the people into the subjection of a foreign power, either by the prince or by the legislative, is certainly a change of the legislative, and so a dissolution of the government: for the end why people entered into society being to be preserved one entire, free, independent society, to be governed by its own laws; this is lost, whenever they are given up into the power of another.

Why, in such a constitution as this, the dissolution of the government in these cases is to be imputed to the prince, is evident; because he, having the force, treasure, and offices of the state to employ, and often persuading himself, or being flattered by others, that as supreme magistrate he is uncapable of control; he alone is in a condition to make great advances toward such changes, under pretence of lawful authority, and has it in his hands to terrify or suppress opposers, as factious, seditious, and enemies to the government: whereas no other part of the legislative, or people, is capable by themselves to attempt any alteration of the legislative, without open and visible rebellion, apt enough to be taken notice of; which, when it prevails, produces effects very little different from foreign conquest. Besides, the prince in such a form of government having the power of dissolving the other parts of the legislative, and thereby rendering them private persons, they can never in opposition to him, or without his concurrence, alter the legislative by a law, his consent being necessary to give any of their decrees that sanction. But yet, so far as the other parts of the legislative any way contribute to any attempt upon the government, and do either promote, or not (what lies in them) hinder such designs; they are guilty, and partake in this, which is certainly the greatest crime men can be guilty of one towards another.

There is one way more whereby such a government may be dissolved, and that is, when he who has the supreme executive power, neglects and abandons that charge, so that the laws already made can no longer be put in execution. This is demonstratively to reduce all to anarchy, and so effectually to dissolve the government: for laws not being made for themselves, but to be, by their execution, the bonds of the society, to keep every part of the body politic in its due place and function; when that totally ceases, the government visibly ceases, and the people become a confused multitude, without order or connexion. Where there is no longer the administration of justice, for the securing of men's rights, nor any remaining power within the community to direct the force, or provide for the necessities of the public; there certainly is no government left. Where the laws cannot be executed, it is all one as if there were no laws; and a government without laws is, I suppose, a mystery in politics, inconceivable to human capacity, and inconsistent with human society.

In these and the like cases, when the government is dissolved, the people are at liberty to provide for themselves, by erecting a new legislative, differing from the other, by the change of persons, or form, or both, as they shall find it most for their safety and good: for the society can never, by the fault of another, lose the native and original right it has to preserve itself; which can only be done by a settled legislative, and a fair and impartial execution of the laws made by it. But the state of mankind is not so miserable that they are not capable of using this remedy, till it be too late to look for any. To tell people they may provide for themselves, by erecting a new legislative, when by oppression, artifice, or being delivered over to a foreign power, their old one is gone, is only to tell them, they may expect relief when it is too late, and the evil is past cure. This is in effect no more than to bid them first be slaves, and then to take care of their liberty; and when their chains are on, tell them they may act like freemen. This, if barely so, is rather mockery than relief; and men can never be secure from tyranny, if there be no means to escape it till they are perfectly under it; and therefore it is, that they have not only a right to get out of it, but to prevent it.

There is therefore, secondly, another way whereby governments are dissolved, and that is, when the legislative, or the prince, either of them, act contrary to their trust.

First, the legislative acts against the trust reposed in them, when they endeavour to invade the property of the subject, and to make themselves, or any part of the community, masters, or arbitrary disposers of the lives, liberties, or fortunes of the people.

The reason why men enter into society is the preservation of their property; and the end why they choose and authorize a legislative is, that there may be laws made, and rules set, as guards and fences to the properties of all the members of the society: to limit the power, and moderate the dominion, of every part and member of the society: for since it can never be supposed to be the will of the society that the legislative should have a power to destroy that which every one designs to secure by entering into society, and for which the people submitted themselves to legislators of their own making; whenever the legislators endeavour to take away and destroy the property of the people, or to reduce them to slavery under arbitrary power, they put themselves into a state of war with the people, who are thereupon absolved from any farther obedience, and are left to the common refuge, which God hath provided for all men, against force and violence. Whensoever therefore the legislative shall transgress this fundamental rule of society; and either by ambition, fear, folly, or corruption, endeavour to grasp themselves, or put into the hands of any other, an absolute power over the lives, liberties, and estates of the people; by this breach of trust they forfeit the power the people had put into their hands for quite contrary ends, and it devolves to the people, who have a right to resume their original liberty, and, by the establishment of a new legislative, (such as they shall think fit) provide for their own safety and security, which is the end for which they are in society. What I have said here, concerning the legislative in general, holds true also concerning the supreme executor, who having a double trust put in him, both to have a part in the legislative, and the supreme execution of the law, acts against both, when he goes about to set up his own arbitrary will as the law of the society. He acts also contrary to his trust, when he either employs the force, treasure, and offices of the society to corrupt the representatives, and gain them to his purposes; or openly pre-engages the electors, and prescribes to their choice, such, whom he has, by solicitations, threats, promises, or otherwise, won to his designs; and employs them to bring in such, who have promised beforehand what to vote, and what to enact. Thus to regulate candidates and electors, and new-model the ways of election, what is it but to cut up the government by the roots, and poison the very fountain of public security? for the people having reserved to themselves the choice of their representatives, as the fence to their properties, could do it for no other end, but that they might always be freely chosen, and so chosen, freely act, and advise, as the necessity of the commonwealth and the public good should, upon examination and mature debate, be judged to require. This, those who give their votes before they hear the debate, and have weighed the reasons on all sides, are not capable of doing. To prepare such an assembly as this, and endeavour to set up the declared abettors of his own will, for the true representatives of the people, and the law-makers of the society, is certainly as great a breach of trust, and as perfect a declaration of a design to subvert the government, as is possible to be met with. To which if one shall add rewards and punishments visibly employed to the same end, and all the arts of perverted law made use of, to take off and destroy all that stand in the way of such a design, and will not comply and consent to betray the liberties of their country, it will be past doubt what is doing. What power they ought to have in the society, who thus employ it contrary to the trust that went along with it in its first institution, is easy to determine; and one cannot but see, that he, who has once attempted any such thing as this, cannot any longer be trusted.

To this perhaps it will be said, that the people being ignorant, and always discontented, to lay the foundation of government in the unsteady opinion and uncertain humour of the people, is to expose it to certain ruin; and no government will be able long to subsist, if the people may set up a new legislative, whenever they take offence at the old one. To this I answer, quite the contrary. People are not so easily got out of their old forms, as some are apt to suggest. They are hardly to be prevailed with to amend the acknowledged faults in the frame they have been accustomed to. And if there be any original defects, or adventitious ones intro- duced by time, or corruption; it is not an easy thing to get them changed, even when all the world sees there is an opportunity for it. This slowness and aversion in the people to quit their old con- stitutions, has in the many revolutions, which have been seen in this kingdom, in this and former ages, still kept us to, or, after some interval of fruitless attempts, still brought us back again to, our old legislative of king, lords, and commons: and whatever provocations have made the crown be taken from some of our princes' heads, they never carried the people so far as to place it in another line.

But it will be said, this hypothesis lays a ferment for frequent rebellion. To which I answer,

First, No more than any other hypothesis: for when the people are made miserable, and find themselves exposed to the ill usage of arbitrary power, cry up their governors as much as you will, for sons of Jupiter; let them be sacred and divine, descended, or authorized from heaven; give them out for whom or what you please, the same will happen. The people generally ill-treated, and contrary to right, will be ready upon any occasion to ease them- selves of a burden that sits heavy upon them. They will wish, and seek for the opportunity, which in the change, weakness, and acci- dents of human affairs, seldom delays long to offer itself. He must have lived but a little while in the world, who has not seen exam- ples of this in his time; and he must have read very little, who cannot produce examples of it in all sorts of governments in the world.

Secondly, I answer, such revolutions happen not upon every little mismanagement in public affairs. Great mistakes in the ruling part, many wrong and inconvenient laws, and all the slips of human frailty, will be born by the people without mutiny or murmur. But if a long train of abuses, prevarications, and artifices, all tending the same way, make the design visible to the people, and they cannot but feel what they lie under, and see whither they are going; it is not to be wondered, that they should then rouse themselves, and endeavour to put the rule into such hands which may secure to them the ends for which government was at first erected; and without which, ancient names, and specious forms, are so far from being better, that they are much worse, than the state of nature, or pure anarchy; the inconveniencies, being all as great and as near, but the remedy farther off and more difficult.

Thirdly, I answer, that this doctrine of a power in the people of providing for their safety anew, by a new legislative, when their legislators have acted contrary to their trust, by invading their property, is the best fence against rebellion, and the probablest means to hinder it: for rebellion being an opposition, not to persons, but authority, which is founded only in the constitutions and laws of the government; those, whoever they be, who by force break through, and by force justify their violation of them, are truly and properly rebels: for when men, by entering into society and civil government, have excluded force, and introduced laws for the preservation of property, peace, and unity amongst themselves; those who set up force again in opposition to the laws, do *rebellare*, that is, bring back again the state of war, and are properly rebels: which they who are in power, (by the pretence they have to authority, the temptation of force they have in their hands, and the flattery of those about them) being likeliest to do; the properest way to prevent the evil is to show them the danger and injustice of it, who are under the greatest temptation to run into it.

In both the fore-mentioned cases, when either the legislative is changed, or the legislators act contrary to the end for which they were constituted, those who are guilty are guilty of rebellion: for if any one by force takes away the established legislative of any society, and the laws by them made pursuant to their trust, he thereby takes away the umpirage, which every one had consented to, for a peaceable decision of all their controversies, and a bar to the state of war amongst them. They, who remove, or change the legislative, take away this decisive power, which nobody can have but by the appointment and consent of the people; and so destroying the authority which the people did, and nobody else can set up, and introducing a power which the people hath not authorized, they actually introduce a state of war, which is that of force without authority; and thus, by removing the legislative established by the society (in whose decisions the people acquiesced and united, as to that of their own will) they untie the knot, and expose the people anew to the state of war. And if those, who by force take away the legislative, are rebels, the legislators themselves, as has been shown, can be no less esteemed so; when they, who were set up for the protection and preservation of the people, their liberties and properties, shall by force invade and endeavour to take them away; and so they putting themselves into a state of war with those who made them the protectors and guardians of their peace, are properly, and with the greatest aggravation, *rebellantes*, rebels.

But if they, who say, "it lays a foundation for rebellion," mean that it may occasion civil wars, or intestine broils, to tell the people they are absolved from obedience when illegal attempts are made upon their liberties or properties, and may oppose the unlawful violence of those who were their magistrates, when they invade their properties contrary to the trust put in them; and that therefore this doctrine is not to be allowed, being so destructive to the peace of the world: they may as well say, upon the same ground, that honest men may not oppose robbers or pirates, because this may occasion disorder or bloodshed. If any mischief come in such cases, it is not to be charged upon him who defends his own right, but on him that invades his neighbour's. If the innocent honest man must quietly quit all he has, for peace sake, to him who will lay violent hands upon it, I desire it may be considered, what a kind of peace there will be in the world, which consists only in violence and rapine; and which is to be maintained only for the benefit of robbers and oppressors. Who would not think it an admirable peace betwixt the mighty and the mean, when the lamb, without resistance, yielded his throat to be torn by the imperious wolf? Polyphemus's den gives us a perfect pattern of such a peace, and such a government, wherein Ulysses and his companions had nothing to do, but quietly to suffer themselves to be devoured. And no doubt Ulysses, who was a prudent man, preached up passive obedience, and exhorted them to a quiet submission, by representing to them of what concernment peace was to mankind; and by showing the inconveniences might happen, if they should offer to resist Polyphemus, who had now the power over them.

The end of government is the good of mankind: and which is best for mankind, that the people should be always exposed to the boundless will of tyranny; or that the rulers should be sometimes liable to be opposed, when they grow exorbitant in the use of their power, and employ it for the destruction, and not the preservation of the properties of their people?

Nor let any one say, that mischief can arise from hence, as often as it shall please a busy head, or turbulent spirit, to desire the alteration of the government. It is true, such men may stir, whenever they please; but it will be only to their own just ruin and perdition: for till the mischief be grown general, and the ill designs of the rulers become visible, or their attempts sensible to the greater part, the people, who are more disposed to suffer than right themselves by resistance, are not apt to stir. The examples of particular injustice or oppression, of here and there an unfortunate man, moves them not. But if they universally have a persuasion, grounded upon manifest evidence, that designs are carrying on against their liberties, and the general course and tendency of things cannot but give them strong suspicions of the evil intention of their governors, who is to be blamed for it? Who can help it, if they, who might avoid it, bring themselves into this suspicion? Are the people to be blamed, if they have the sense of rational creatures, and can think of things no otherwise than as they find and feel them? And is it not rather their fault, who put things into such a posture, that they would not have them thought to be as they are? I grant, that the pride, ambition, and turbulency of private men have sometimes caused great disorders in commonwealths, and factions have been fatal to states and kingdoms. But whether the mischief hath oftener begun in the people's wantonness, and a desire to cast off the lawful authority of their rulers, or in the rulers' insolence, and endeavours to get and exercise an arbitrary power over their people; whether oppression, or disobedience, gave the first rise to the disorder; I leave it to impartial history to determine. This I am sure, whoever, either ruler or subject, by force goes about to invade the rights of either prince or people, and lays the foundation for overturning the constitution and frame of any just government, is highly guilty of the greatest crime, I think, a man is capable of; being to answer for all those mischiefs of blood, rapine, and desolation, which the breaking to pieces of governments bring on a country. And he who does it, is justly to be esteemed the common enemy and pest of mankind, and is to be treated accordingly.

99. *Two Treatises*, II, sections 241-3

But farther, this question, ("Who shall be judge?") cannot mean, that there is no judge at all: for where there is no judicature on earth, to decide controversies amongst men, God in heaven is judge. He alone, it is true, is judge of the right. But every man is judge for himself, as in all other cases, so in this, whether another hath put himself into a state of war with him, and whether he should appeal to the supreme Judge, as Jephthah did.

If a controversy arise betwixt a prince and some of the people, in a matter where the law is silent or doubtful, and the thing be of great consequence, I should think the proper umpire, in such a case, should be the body of the people: for in cases where the prince hath a trust reposed in him, and is dispensed from the common ordinary rules of the law; there, if any men find themselves aggrieved, and think the prince acts contrary to, or beyond that trust, who so proper to judge as the body of the people, (who, at first, lodged that trust in him) how far they meant it should extend? But if the prince, or whoever they be in the administration, decline that way of determination, the appeal then lies nowhere but to Heaven; force between either persons, who have no known superior on earth, or which permits no appeal to a judge on earth, being properly a state of war, wherein the appeal lies only to Heaven; and in that state the injured party must judge for himself, when he will think fit to make use of that appeal, and put himself upon it.

To conclude, The power that every individual gave the society, when he entered into it, can never revert to the individuals again, as long as the society lasts, but will always remain in the community; because without this there can be no community, no commonwealth, which is contrary to the original agreement: so also when the society hath placed the legislative in any assembly of men, to continue in them and their successors, with direction and authority for providing such successors, the legislative can never revert to the people whilst that government lasts; because, having provided a legislative with power to continue for ever, they have given up their political power to the legislative, and cannot resume it. But if they have set limits to the duration of their legislative, and made this supreme power in any person, or assembly, only temporary; or else, when by the miscarriages of those in authority it is forfeited; upon the forfeiture, or at the determination of the time set, it reverts to the society, and the people have a right to act as supreme, and continue the legislative in themselves; or erect a new form, or under the old form place it in new hands, as they think good.

Conclusion

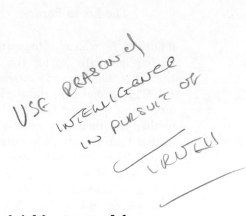

Two sentiments dominated Locke's life, virtue and the love of truth. It was no idle thought or conventional trope that led him to inscribe both sentiments on his gravestone. Whether Locke achieved either truth or virtue is perhaps of less importance than the efforts he made toward both. He was happy to let God judge of his virtue: the testimony of his friends and of those who knew him suggest that that ultimate judgment was favorable. He believed that his books made some progress toward discovering truth, at least toward preparing the way for such discovery. At the same time, he issued warnings against the uncritical acceptance of an author's views and claims. He constantly urged his readers to rely on their own native abilities for arriving at truth, both through living in the world and from cautious but thoughtful reading of diverse authors. Locke's *Conduct of the Understanding* was written as a guide for using our reason and intelligence in the pursuit of truth, in all divisions of the sciences and all areas of human knowledge. Two sections of that work in particular provide a salutary conclusion to this *Locke Reader*.

100. *Conduct*, sections 3, 24

Besides the want of determined ideas, and of sagacity, and exercise in finding out, and laying in order, intermediate ideas; there are three miscarriages that men are guilty of, in reference to their reason, whereby this faculty is hindered in them from that service it might do, and was designed for. And he, that reflects upon the actions and discourses of mankind, will find their defects in this kind very frequent, and very observable.

1. The first is of those who seldom reason at all, but do and think according to the example of others, whether parents, neighbours,

319

ministers, or who else they are pleased to make choice of to have an implicit faith in, for the saving of themselves the pains and trouble of thinking and examining for themselves.

2. The second is of those who put passion in the place of reason, and, being resolved that shall govern their actions and arguments, neither use their own, nor hearken to other people's reason, any farther than it suits their humour, interest, or party; and these one may observe commonly content themselves with words which have no distinct ideas to them, though, in other matters, that they come with an unbiassed indifferency to, they want not abilities to talk and hear reason, where they have no secret inclination that hinders them from being intractable to it.

3. The third sort is of those who readily and sincerely follow reason; but, for want of having that which one may call large, sound, round-about sense, have not a full view of all that relates to the question, and may be of moment to decide it. We are all short-sighted, and very often see but one side of the matter, our views are not extended to all that has a connexion with it. From this defect I think no man is free. We see but in part, and we know but in part, and therefore it is no wonder we conclude not right from our partial views. This might instruct the proudest esteemer of his own parts, how useful it is to talk and consult with others, even such as come short of him in capacity, quickness, and penetration: for, since no one sees all, and we generally have different prospects of the same thing, according to our different, as I may say, positions to it; it is not incongruous to think, nor beneath any man to try, whether another may not have notions of things, which have escaped him, and which his reason would make use of if they came into his mind. The faculty of reasoning seldom or never deceives those who trust to it; its consequences, from what it builds on, are evident and certain; but that which it oftenest, if not only, misleads us in is, that the principles from which we conclude, the grounds upon which we bottom our reasoning, are but a part, something is left out, which should go into the reckoning, to make it just and exact. Here we may imagine a vast and almost infinite advantage the angels and separate spirits may have over us; who, in their several degrees of elevation above us, may be endowed with more comprehensive faculties: and some of them, perhaps, having perfect and exact views of all finite beings that come under their consideration, can, as it were, in the twinkling of an eye, collect together all their scattered and almost boundless relations. A mind so furnished, what reason has it to acquiesce in the certainty of its conclusions!

In this we may see the reason why some men of study and thought, that reason right, and are lovers of truth, do make no great advances in their discoveries of it. Error and truth are uncertainly blended in their minds; their decisions are lame and defective, and they are very often mistaken in their judgments: the reason whereof is, they converse but with one sort of men, they read but one sort of books, they will not come in the hearing but of one sort of notions: the truth is, they canton out to themselves a little Goshen, in the intellectual world, where light shines, and, as they conclude, day blesses them; but the rest of that vast expansum they give up to night and darkness, and so avoid coming near it. They have a pretty traffic with known correspondents, in some little creek; within that they confine themselves, and are dexterous managers enough of the wares and products of that corner, with which they content themselves, but will not venture out into the great ocean of knowledge, to survey the riches that nature hath stored other parts with, no less genuine, no less solid, no less useful, than what has fallen to their lot in the admired plenty and sufficiency of their own little spot, which to them contains whatsoever is good in the universe. Those who live thus mewed up within their own contracted territories, and will not look abroad beyond the boundaries that chance, conceit, or laziness, has set to their inquiries; but live separate from the notions, discourses, and attainments of the rest of mankind; may not amiss be represented by the inhabitants of the Marian islands, who, being separated, by a large tract of sea, from all communion with the habitable parts of the earth, thought themselves the only people of the world. And though the straitness of the conveniencies of life amongst them had never reached so far as to the use of fire till the Spaniards, not many years since, in their voyages from Acapulco to Manilla, brought it amongst them, yet, in the want and ignorance of almost all things, they looked upon themselves, even after that the Spaniards had brought amongst them the notice of variety of nations, abounding in sciences, arts, and conveniencies of life, of which they knew nothing; they looked upon themselves, I say, as the happiest and wisest people of the universe. But, for all that, nobody, I think, will imagine them deep naturalists, or solid metaphysicians; nobody will deem the quick-sighted amongst them to have very enlarged views in ethics, or politics; nor can any one allow the most capable amongst them to be advanced so far in his understanding as to have any other knowledge but of the few little things of his and the neighbouring islands, within his commerce; but far enough from that comprehensive enlargement of mind, which adorns a soul devoted to truth, assisted with letters, and a free generation of the several views and sentiments of thinking men of all sides. Let not men, therefore, that would have a sight of what every one pretends to be desirous to have a sight of, truth in its full extent, narrow and blind their own prospect. Let not men think there is no truth but in the sciences that they study, or books that they read. To prejudge other men's notions, before we have looked into them, is not to show their darkness, but to put out our own eyes. "Try all things, hold fast that which is good," is a divine rule, coming from the Father of light and truth; and it is hard to know what other way men can come at truth, to lay hold of it, if they do not dig and search for it as for gold and hid treasure; but he that does so must have much earth and rubbish, before he gets the pure metal: sand, and pebbles, and dross usually lie blended with it; but the gold is nevertheless gold, and will enrich the man that employs his pains to seek and separate it. Neither is there any danger he should be deceived by the mixture. Every man carries about him a touchstone, if he will make use of it, to distinguish substantial gold from superficial glitterings, truth from appearances. And, indeed, the use and benefit of this touchstone, which is natural reason, is spoiled and lost only by assumed prejudices, overweening presumption, and narrowing our minds. The want of exercising it, in the full extent of things intelligible, is that which weakens and extinguishes this noble faculty in us. Trace it, and see whether it be not so. The day-labourer in a country-village has commonly but a small pittance of knowledge, because his ideas and notions have been confined to the narrow bounds of a poor conversation and employment: the low mechanic of a country town does somewhat out-do him: porters and cobblers of great cities surpass them. A country gentleman who, leaving Latin and learning in the university, removes thence to his mansion-house, and associates with neighbours of the same strain, who relish nothing but hunting and a bottle; with those alone he spends his time, with those alone he converses, and can away with no company whose discourse goes beyond what claret and dissoluteness inspire: – such a patriot, formed in this happy way of improvement, cannot fail, as we see, to give notable decisions upon the bench, at quarter-sessions, and eminent proofs of his skill in politics, when the strength of his purse and party have advanced him to a more conspicuous station. To such a one, truly, an ordinary coffee-house gleaner of the city is an arrant statesman, and as much superior to, as a man conversant about Whitehall and the court is to an ordinary shopkeeper. To carry this a little farther: here is one muffled up in the zeal and infallibility of his own sect, and will not touch a book or enter into debate with a person that will question any of those things which to him are sacred. Another surveys our differences in religion with an equitable and fair indifference, and so finds, probably, that none of them are in every thing unexceptionable. These divisions and systems were made by men, and carry the mark of fallible on them; and in those whom he differs from, and, till he opened his eyes, had a general prejudice against, he meets with more to be said for a great many things than before he was aware of, or could have imagined. Which of these two, now, is most likely to judge right in our religious controversies, and to be most stored with truth, the mark all pretend to aim at? All these men, that I have instanced in, thus unequally furnished with truth, and advanced in knowledge, I suppose of equal natural parts; all the odds between them has been the different scope that has been given to their understandings to range in, for the gathering up of information, and furnishing their heads with ideas and notions and observations, whereon to employ their mind and form their understandings.

It will possibly be objected, "who is sufficient for all this?" I answer, more than can be imagined. Every one knows what his proper business is, and what, according to the character he makes of himself, the world may justly expect of him; and, to answer that, he will find he will have time and opportunity enough to furnish himself, if he will not deprive himself, by a narrowness of spirit, of those helps that are at hand. I do not say, to be a good geographer, that a man should visit every mountain, river, promontory, and creek, upon the face of the earth, view the buildings, and survey the land every where, as if he were going to make a purchase; but yet every one must allow that he shall know a country better, that makes often sallies into it, and traverses up and down, than he that, like a mill-horse, goes still round in the same track, or keeps within the narrow bounds of a field or two that delight him. He that will inquire out the best books in every science, and inform himself of the most material authors of the several sects of philosophy and religion, will not find it an infinite work to acquaint himself with the sentiments of mankind, concerning the most weighty and comprehensive subjects. Let him exercise the freedom of his reason and understanding in such a latitude as this, and his mind will be strengthened, his capacity enlarged, his faculties improved; and the light, which the remote and scattered parts of truth will give to one another, will so assist his judgment, that he will seldom be widely out, or miss giving proof of a clear head and a comprehensive knowledge. At least, this is the only way I know to give the understanding its due improvement to the full extent of its capacity, and to distinguish the two most different things I know in the world, a logical chicaner from a man of reason. Only he, that would thus give the mind its flight, and send abroad his inquiries into all parts after truth, must be sure to settle in his head determined ideas of all that he employs his thoughts about, and never fail to judge himself, and judge unbiassedly, of all that he receives from others, either in their writings or discourses. Reverence or prejudice must not be suffered to give beauty or deformity to any of their opinions.

This partiality, where it is not permitted an authority to render all other studies insignificant or contemptible, is often indulged so far as to be relied upon, and made use of in other parts of knowledge, to which it does not at all belong, and wherewith it has no manner of affinity. Some men have so used their heads to mathematical figures, that, giving a preference to the methods of that science, they introduce lines and diagrams into their study of divinity, or politic inquiries, as if nothing could be known without them; and others, accustomed to retired speculations, run natural philosophy into metaphysical notions, and the abstract generalities of logic; and how often may one meet with religion and morality treated of in the terms of the laboratory, and thought to be improved by the methods and notions of chemistry! But he that will take care of the conduct of his understanding, to direct it right to the knowledge of things, must avoid those undue mixtures, and not, by a fondness for what he has found useful and necessary in one, transfer it to another science, where it serves only to perplex and confound the understanding. It is a certain truth, that *res nolunt malè administrari;* it is no less certain *res nolunt malè intelligi*. Things themselves are to be considered as they are in themselves, and then they will show us in what way they are to be understood. For to have right conceptions about them, we must bring our understandings to the inflexible natures and unalterable relations of things, and not endeavour to bring things to any preconceived notions of our own.

There is another partiality very commonly observable in men of study, no less prejudicial nor ridiculous than the former; and that is a fantastical and wild attributing all knowledge to the ancients alone, or to the moderns. This raving upon antiquity in matter of

poetry, Horace has wittily described and exposed in one
satires. The same sort of madness may be found in refere
all the other sciences. Some will not admit an opinion n
thorised by men of old, who were then all giants in knowl
Nothing is to be put into the treasury of truth or knowledge w
has not the stamp of Greece or Rome upon it; and since their uays
will scarce allow that men have been able to see, think, or write.
Others, with a like extravagancy, condemn all that the ancients
have left us, and, being taken with the modern inventions and
discoveries, lay by all that went before, as if whatever is called old
must have the decay of time upon it, and truth, too, were liable
to mould and rottenness. Men, I think, have been much the same
for natural endowments in all times. Fashion, discipline, and education, have put eminent differences in the ages of several countries, and made one generation much differ from another in arts
and sciences: but truth is always the same; time alters it not, nor
is it the better or worse for being of ancient or modern tradition.
Many were eminent in former ages of the world for their discovery
and delivery of it; but though the knowledge they have left us
be worth our study, yet they exhausted not all its treasure; they
left a great deal for the industry and sagacity of after-ages, and
so shall we. That was once new to them which any one now receives
with veneration for its antiquity, nor was it the worse for appearing
as a novelty; and that which is now embraced for its newness will
to posterity be old, but not thereby be less true or less genuine.
There is no occasion, on this account, to oppose the ancients and
the moderns to one another, or to be squeamish on either side.
He that wisely conducts his mind in the pursuit of knowledge will
gather what lights, and get what helps he can, from either of
them, from whom they are best to be had, without adoring the
errors, or rejecting the truths, which he may find mingled in
them.

Another partiality may be observed, in some to vulgar, in others
to heterodox tenets: some are apt to conclude that what is the
common opinion cannot but be true: so many men's eyes they think
cannot but see right; so many men's understandings of all sorts
cannot be deceived; and, therefore, will not venture to look beyond
the received notions of the place and age, nor have so presumptu-
ous a thought as to be wiser than their neighbours. They are content to go with the crowd, and so go easily, which they think
is going right, or at least serves them as well. But however *vox
populi vox Dei* has prevailed as a maxim, yet I do not remember

where ever God delivered his oracles by the multitude, or nature truths by the herd. On the other side, some fly all common opinions as either false or frivolous. The title of many-headed beast is a sufficient reason to them to conclude that no truths of weight or consequence can be lodged there. Vulgar opinions are suited to vulgar capacities, and adapted to the ends of those that govern. He that will know the truth of things must leave the common and beaten track, which none but weak and servile minds are satisfied to trudge along continually in. Such nice palates relish nothing but strange notions quite out of the way: whatever is commonly received, has the mark of the beast on it; and they think it a lessening to them to hearken to it, or receive it; their mind runs only after paradoxes; these they seek, these they embrace, these alone they vent; and so, as they think, distinguish themselves from the vulgar. But common or uncommon are not the marks to distinguish truth or falsehood, and therefore should not be any bias to us in our inquiries. We should not judge of things by men's opinions, but of opinions by things. The multitude reason but ill, and therefore may be well suspected, and cannot be relied on, nor should be followed as a sure guide; but philosophers, who have quitted the orthodoxy of the community, and the popular doctrines of their countries, have fallen into as extravagant and as absurd opinions as ever common reception countenanced. It would be madness to refuse to breathe the common air, or quench one's thirst with water, because the rabble use them to these purposes; and if there are conveniencies of life which common use reaches not, it is not reason to reject them because they are not grown into the ordinary fashion of the country, and every villager doth not know them.

Truth, whether in or out of fashion, is the measure of knowledge, and the business of the understanding; whatsoever is besides that, however authorised by consent, or recommended by rarity, is nothing but ignorance, or something worse.

Another sort of partiality there is, whereby men impose upon themselves, and by it make their reading little useful to themselves; I mean the making use of the opinions of writers, and laying stress upon their authorities, wherever they find them to favour their own opinions.

There is nothing almost has done more harm to men dedicated to letters than giving the name of study to reading, and making a man of great reading to be the same with a man of great knowledge, or at least to be a title of honour. All that can be recorded in writing are only facts or reasonings. Facts are of three sorts;

1. Merely of natural agents, observable in the ordinary operations of bodies one upon another, whether in the visible course of things left to themselves, or in experiments made by them, applying agents and patients to one another, after a peculiar and artificial manner.

2. Of voluntary agents, more especially the actions of men in society, which makes civil and moral history.

3. Of opinions.

In these three consists, as it seems to me, that which commonly has the name of learning; to which perhaps some may add a distinct head of critical writings, which indeed at bottom is nothing but matter of fact; and resolves itself into this, that such a man, or set of men, use such a word, or phrase, in such a sense; i. e. that they made such sounds the marks of such ideas.

Under reasonings I comprehend all the discoveries of general truths made by human reason, whether found by intuition, demonstration, or probable deductions. And this is that which is, if not alone knowledge, (because the truth or probability of particular propositions may be known too) yet is, as may be supposed, most properly the business of those who pretend to improve their understandings, and make themselves knowing by reading.

Books and reading are looked upon to be the great helps of the understanding, and instruments of knowledge, as it must be allowed that they are; and yet I beg leave to question whether these do not prove an hinderance to many, and keep several bookish men from attaining to solid and true knowledge. This, I think, I may be permitted to say, that there is no part wherein the understanding needs a more careful and wary conduct than in the use of books; without which they will prove rather innocent amusements than profitable employments of our time, and bring but small additions to our knowledge.

There is not seldom to be found, even amongst those who aim at knowledge, who with an unwearied industry employ their whole time in books, who scarce allow themselves time to eat or sleep, but read, and read, and read on, yet make no great advances in real knowledge, though there be no defect in their intellectual faculties, to which their little progress can be imputed. The mistake here is, that it is usually supposed that by reading, the author's knowledge is transfused into the reader's understanding; and so it is, but not by bare reading, but by reading and understanding what he writ. Whereby I mean, not barely comprehending what is affirmed or denied in each proposition (though that great readers do not always think themselves concerned precisely to do), but to see and follow the train of his reasonings, observe the strength and clearness of their connexion, and examine upon what they bottom. Without this a man may read the discourses of a very rational author, writ in a language, and in propositions, that he very well understands, and yet acquire not one jot of his knowledge; which consisting only in the perceived, certain, or probable connexion of the ideas made use of in his reasonings, the reader's knowledge is no farther increased than he perceives that; so much as he sees of this connexion, so much he knows of the truth or probability of that author's opinions.

All that he relies on, without this perception, he takes upon trust, upon the author's credit, without any knowledge of it at all. This makes me not at all wonder to see some men so abound in citations, and build so much upon authorities, it being the sole foundation on which they bottom most of their own tenets; so that, in effect, they have but a second-hand, or implicit knowledge; i. e. are in the right, if such an one from whom they borrowed it were in the right in that opinion which they took from him; which indeed is no knowledge at all. Writers of this or former ages may be good witnesses of matters of fact which they deliver, which we may do well to take upon their authority; but their credit can go no farther than this; it cannot at all affect the truth and falsehood of opinions which have no other sort of trial but reason and proof, which they themselves made use of to make themselves knowing, and so must others too, that will partake in their knowledge. Indeed, it is an advantage that they have been at the pains to find out the proofs, and lay them in that order that may show the truth or probability of their conclusions; and for this we owe them great acknowledgments for saving us the pains in searching out those proofs which they have collected for us, and which possibly, after all our pains, we might not have found, nor been able to have set them in so good a light as that which they left them us in. Upon this account we are mightily beholden to judicious writers of all ages, for those discoveries and discourses they have left behind them for our instruction, if we know how to make a right use of them; which is not to run them over in an hasty perusal, and perhaps lodge their opinions or some remarkable passages in our memories; but to enter into their reasonings, examine their proofs, and then judge of the truth or falsehood, probability or improbability of what they advance, not by any opinion we have entertained of the author, but by the evidence he produces, and the conviction he affords us, drawn from things themselves. Knowing is seeing, and if it be so, it is madness to persuade ourselves that we do so by another man's eyes, let him use ever so many words to tell us that what he asserts is very visible. Till we ourselves see it with our own eyes, and perceive it by our own understandings, we are as much in the dark and as void of knowledge as before, let us believe any learned author as much as we will.

BIBLIOGRAPHY

A listing of some of Locke's publications

1689 *Epistola de Tolerantia ad Clarissimum Virum.* Translated in the same year by William Popple as, *A Letter concerning Toleration.* Two further letters on toleration were published by Locke in English in 1690 and 1962.

1690 *Two Treatises of Government.* Second edition in 1694, third in 1698.

1690 *An Essay concerning Human Understanding.* A second edition, "with large Additions," was published in 1694; a third edition in 1695 (a reprint of the second); a fourth edition, "with large Additions," in 1700; and a fifth edition with more additions after his death in 1706.

1692 *Some Considerations of the Consequences of the Lowering of Interest and the Raising of the Value of Money.*

1693 *Some Thoughts concerning Education.*

1695 *The Reasonableness of Christianity, As Delivered in the Scriptures.* This book was attacked by J. Edwards. Locke replied in *A Vindication of the Reasonableness,* 1695. A second *Vindication* appeared in 1697.

1697 *Mr. Locke's Reply to the Right Rev. the Lord Bishop of Worcester, concerning Some Passages Relating to Mr. Locke's Essay of Human Understanding. In a late Discourse of His Lordship's in Vindication of the Trinity.* This began an important exchange between Locke and the bishop, two replies by Locke appearing in 1697 and 1699.

1705–7 *Paraphrases of the Epistles of St. Paul.*

1706 *Of the Conduct of the Understanding* and *An Examination of P. Malebranche's Opinion of Seeing All Things in God,* first appeared in *Posthumous Works.*

The *Two Tracts on Government* were written in 1660–1 and recently published by Philip Abrams under that title, Cambridge, 1967.

Some early *Essays on the Law of Nature*, written around 1663–4, have been published by W. von Leyden, Oxford, 1954.

A selection of useful books on Locke

Aaron, R. I. *John Locke,* third edition, Oxford, 1971.

Cranston, M. *John Locke, A Biography,* London, 1957.

Dewhurst, K. *John Locke (1632–1704). Physician and Philosopher. A Medical Biography,* London, 1963.

Duchesneau, F. *L'Empirisme de Locke,* The Hague, 1973.

Dunn, John. *The Political Thought of John Locke,* Cambridge, 1969.

Gibson, J. *Locke's Theory of Knowledge and Its Historical Relations,* Cambridge, 1931.

James, D. G. *The Life of Reason: Hobbes, Locke and Bolingbroke,* London, 1949.

Lough, J. *Locke's Travels in France, 1675–9,* Cambridge, 1953.

MacLachlan, H. *The Religious Opinions of Milton, Locke, and Newton,* London, 1941.

MacLean, K. *John Locke and English Literature of the Eighteenth Century,* New Haven, 1936.

Woolhouse, R. S. *Locke's Philosophy of Science and Knowledge,* Oxford, 1971.

Yolton, J. W. *John Locke and the Way of Ideas,* Oxford, 1956 (reprinted, 1968).
    ed., *John Locke: Problems and Perspectives,* Cambridge, 1969.
    Locke and the Compass of Human Understanding, Cambridge, 1970.
    John Locke and Education, New York, 1971.

INDEX